D1286558

Le Grand Tango

Le Grand Tango

The Life and Music of Astor Piazzolla

MARÍA SUSANA AZZI

SIMON COLLIER

WITH A FOREWORD BY YO-YO MA

OXFORD
UNIVERSITY PRESS
2000

Oxford   New York
Athens   Auckland   Bangkok   Bogotá   Buenos Aires   Calcutta
Cape Town   Chennai   Dar es Salaam   Delhi   Florence   Hong Kong   Istanbul
Karachi   Kuala Lumpur   Madrid   Melbourne   Mexico City   Mumbai
Nairobi   Paris   São Paulo   Singapore   Taipei   Tokyo   Toronto   Warsaw

and associated companies in
Berlin   Ibadan

Quotation from "Letter to Lord Byron" from *W. H. Auden: Collected Poems,* edited by Edward Mendelson, copyright © 1937 by W. H. Auden, reprinted by permission of Random House, Inc., and Faber and Faber Ltd.

Published by Oxford University Press, Inc.
198 Madison Avenue, New York, New York 10016

Library of Congress Cataloging-in-Publication Data
Azzi, María Susana.
Le grand tango : the life and music of Astor Piazzolla / María Susana Azzi, Simon Collier.
p.   cm.
Includes discography (p.), bibliographical references (p.), and index.
ISBN 0-19-512777-3
1. Piazzolla, Astor. 2. Composers—Argentina—Biography. 3. Bandoneon players—Argentina—Biography.
I. Collier, Simon. II. Title.
ML410.P579A99 2000
780'.92—dc21
[B]   99-31795

Book design by Adam B. Bohannon

9 8 7 6 5 4 3 2 1

Printed in the United States of America
on acid-free paper

CONTENTS

Illustrations follow page 118

Yo-Yo Ma on Astor Piazzolla

When did you first become aware of Piazzolla's music?
I started listening to Piazzolla recordings about fifteen years ago and was immediately captivated by his music. When I learned of a scheduled visit to Boston (his last) with his sextet, I tried to get tickets, but the concert was sold out. I was able to get only one ticket, which I gave to our babysitter as a thank-you for all the hard work she had been doing. She later told us that, during a backstage conversation, she discovered that José Bragato (cellist in the sextet) was her great-uncle!

Is there a Piazzolla sound?
Piazzolla's music is endlessly passionate—full of yearning—and at the same time tremendously contemporary. There's a quote to the effect that Piazzolla is the Ellington of Argentina, and in a way it's true. He actually took the tango to another level by inhabiting his music. The music grew in him, and he adeptly incorporated the influences of his surroundings—whether from New York, Paris, or Buenos Aires.

During the almost forty years he worked on his music, Astor Piazzolla tried many different variations—even tried an electronic ensemble! Because of this experimentation, and also his ingenuity, focus, and hard work, his music has many levels of expression and a tremendous depth. His is a truly successful synthesis of the tango and the contemporary.

Piazzolla was not only a composer but also a performer. How do you sense both in his work?
In an ideal world, composers would also be performers, as Piazzolla was, living through the daily and nightly performances and seeing the evident flow of interaction between those on stage and those in the audience. When the insights from those experiences are paired with compositional instincts, the results are truly

great. I think Piazzolla had an amazing ear for musical style, and he combined chosen styles—jazz, Bartók, Stravinsky—into a seamless fusion, a very personal and passionate voice.

Do you see Astor Piazzolla as an important influence on the music of the twenty-first century?
Piazzolla's tango no longer belongs to Argentina exclusively—it has become international music in a genuine sense. I had the very great fortune of hearing Piazzolla's first rehearsal of "Le Grand Tango" with Slava Rostropovich. There was Slava, speaking with his heavy Russian accent, and Piazzolla with his very urbane American accent. Despite the contrasts in their voices, "Le Grand Tango" provided the medium for their common voice.

   Piazzolla's music and his work will continue to be an inspiration to many different types of musicians and an important influence in the music of the twenty-first century. "Le Grand Tango" is a great piece of music—a great, great piece of music.

Yo-Yo Ma, *in an interview with María Susana Azzi*
August 1999

PREFACE

By nationality, Astor Piazzolla was Argentine. All four of his grandparents were immigrants from Italy—four among the millions of Italians who moved to Argentina in its golden age of prosperity and whose mark on Argentine culture remains so vivid today. Deep down, Piazzolla himself was always something of an uprooted, nostalgic migrant. At one time or other, he lived in Mar del Plata, New York, Buenos Aires, Rome, Paris, and Punta del Este. Yet although he drew inspiration from several different traditions, his music remained essentially Argentine. As composer, arranger, bandleader, and performer, his specialty was the music of Buenos Aires: the tango. He sometimes said that he had three great music teachers: Alberto Ginastera, Nadia Boulanger—and Buenos Aires.

But although he was thoroughly *tanguero* (that is to say, thoroughly imbued with the tango culture), he always played the music of Buenos Aires in his own way. His work brought about something approaching a convergence of the tango, classical music, and jazz. He took tango music (like jazz, a tradition with murky origins) and turned it into a form of contemporary chamber music. He broke with the traditional tango—ossifying in the 1950s after its thirty years of hegemony as Buenos Aires's popular music—and for this he was never forgiven by traditionalists. The absurd war between *piazzollistas* and anti-*piazzollistas* in Argentina lasted for decades. An agent of deep renewal in tango music, Piazzolla himself constantly evolved, his work reflecting Buenos Aires, the hustle and din of contemporary society, and the whole range of human emotions. Loved and vilified, he died in 1992. He is now regarded as one of the glories of Argentine culture.

Piazzolla always tried to combine his thrust to renew tango music with his own pleasure in experimenting, constantly crossing frontiers and exploring diverse musical cultures and genres. He was a living embodiment of both integration and crossover. That does not mean that he ever denied his Argentine roots. But he was also in a real sense a wanderer, always open to new influences. Without ever ceasing to be *tanguero*, he aimed to fashion something more universal. "Paint your village, and you paint the world"—Tolstoy's phrase was one of Piazzolla's favorites. He painted *his* big village with such consummate skill that musicians (and eventually audiences) flocked to him on four continents. He did not live to

xi

see the scale of it, but the world has now discovered Astor Piazzolla—Argentine, *tanguero*, and above all, musician.

We first thought of this book over lunch in the Recoleta district of Buenos Aires in November 1994 and began work on it in mid-1995. This is a biography, the life of a musician whose vital decisions as a man always had a bearing on his music. There is a real sense in which Piazzolla's glorious music can be left to speak for itself. Neither of us knew him. María Susana Azzi heard him perform many times, and Simon Collier met him just once. He himself, however, reminisced extensively about his life in three extended sets of interviews: with Alberto Speratti in 1968, with his daughter, Diana, in 1980, and with Natalio Gorin in 1990. Our debt to these sources will be obvious. Piazzolla was also interviewed countless times by reporters. We are confident that we have seen most of the interviews that appeared in Spanish, English, French, Italian, and Portuguese.

Interviews with those who *did* know Piazzolla are one of the fundamental sources for this book. María Susana Azzi was responsible for 90 percent of the interviews, most of which were taped and transcribed. Where those interviewed had already gone on record in published interviews or statements—such as those in Diana Piazzolla's admirable book *Astor* (1987) or in the special Piazzolla issue of the Buenos Aires magazine *La Maga* (1996)—we avoided, where possible, covering the same ground twice. We supplemented our interviews with an exhaustive scrutiny of published material about Piazzolla, and, especially, the enormous number of press reports covering his career. We have used these very selectively. Were we to include every news story, chronicle every single journey made by Piazzolla, or mention every single concert by his various ensembles, the book would have an unmanageable compass and would almost certainly be unreadable.

Acknowledgments

One of the rewards for working on this book was that it gave us the chance to meet so many pleasant people. It was, first of all, a genuine delight to get to know "the three Ds," as Piazzolla called his first wife, Dedé Wolff, and their two children, Diana and Daniel. All "the three Ds" were unfailingly generous with their time and in the comprehensiveness and candor of their information. We are especially grateful to Dedé for letting us read Astor's many letters to her, and to Daniel, who did likewise. Laura Escalada Piazzolla, Astor's second wife and president of the Fundación Astor Piazzolla (Buenos Aires), was similarly lavish with her time and her willingness to be talked to at great length, not only giving us the benefit of her obviously vital recollections, but also putting us in touch with numerous additional informants in a dozen cities in the Americas and Europe. To "the three Ds" and Laura we express both gratitude and affection. Notwithstanding their full collaboration and the generous decision of the Fundación Astor Piazzolla to extend its auspices to our book, this is in no sense an "authorized" biography. It speaks volumes for the civilized attitudes of all the Piazzollas that at no time was there ever a suggestion that it should become one.

Our sincere gratitude goes to all those who agreed to be interviewed. Even when we have not quoted them extensively in our text, their testimony has been vital. Nobody refused to help us. We are particularly indebted to Víctor Oliveros, who was kind enough to let us delve in his singularly impressive albums of press clippings and other Piazzolla memorabilia. Other members of Piazzolla's circle of friends and followers were also extremely helpful, as were the musicians who had the great privilege of working with him. We owe a special debt to Amelita Baltar, for the frankness of her reminiscences and for first introducing us to Dedé Wolff. To all of them, our heartfelt thanks.

We respectfully extend our appreciation to His Excellency Carlos Saúl Menem, president of the Argentine Republic, for sharing his thoughts about Piazzolla. Horacio Ferrer, president of the Academia Nacional del Tango, allowed us to scan his letters from Piazzolla and went the proverbial extra mile by writing a special reminiscence. José Gobello, president of the Academia Porteña del Lunfardo, gave us copies of his collected press clippings, as did Oscar B. Himschoot. Jorge Göttling allowed us access to the morgue of his newspaper, *Clarín*, to our great benefit.

Our particular thanks also go to the following, who helped us in (or from) the places indicated:

Argentina (1) Buenos Aires   René Aure; Jorge Benvenuto; Saúl Cosentino; Jorge De Luca; Jorge Fama; Almerinda Augusta de Freitas Carvalho (head of the Cultural Section, Brazilian Embassy); Pedro Pablo García Caffi (Camerata Bariloche); Jorge Glikman; Dr. Pedro Herscovici; Jesús Iglesias Noriega (Press Department, Teatro Colón); Kado Kostzer; Peter Landelius (Ambassador of Sweden in Argentina); Silvina Lanús (Editorial Atlántida); Egle Martin (for her unrivaled knowledge of River Plate rhythms); Juan Carlos F. Martinelli; Eduardo Matrajt; Gianni Mesticheli; Ben Molar; Alberto Moramarco; Lidia Pequeño; Laura Pereiro (Galería Palatina); Cristina Piceda; Milena Plebs; Myriam Porta; Sergio Renán; the late Dr. Víctor Sasson; Maestro Guillermo Scarabino; Mario Sejas (administrative director, Academia Nacional del Tango); Liliana Rojas; Nicholas Tozer (former editor,

Buenos Aires Herald); Ambassador Hugo Urtubey; Xavier Verstraeten; Pepe Wolf; Pablo Ziegler; Miguel Angel Zotto.

Argentina (2) Mar Del Plata Omar Bertolami (for family information); arquitecto Roberto O. Cova (for valuable information about Mar del Plata); Rodolfo Di Paolo; María Pía Castellanos de Hardie; Beatriz Morelli; Mabel Palanza; Walter Provenzano; Nino Ramella (Secretario de Cultura, Municipalidad de General Pueyrredón); Jorge Strada (director, Biblioteca Pública de Música "Astor Piazzolla"); Roberto Tedeschi; Ana María Tiribelli.

France Fabiana Basso; Richard and Giselle Galliano; Pierre Philippe; José Pons (for both information and putting us in touch with Georges Moustaki, Martial Solal, and Raúl Barboza); Thierry Sola; Martín Tiempo (cultural attaché, Argentine Embassy, Paris); Helio Torres.

Italy Hugo Aisemberg (Centro Astor Piazzolla, Pesaro); José Carlos Díaz (Argentine Consul, Milan); Ricardo Fuchs and Roberto Melogli (Società Umanitaria, Milan); Dario De Gregorio, Andrea Rubera, and Grazia Tuzi (Rome).

United States Elizabeth Aldrich; Elliott Antokoletz; Jorge Calandrelli; Oscar Castro-Neves; Keyla Ermecheo; Carlos Groppa; Brenda Hummel, Sally Miller and the late Susanne Koellein (Vanderbilt University); Édouard Pécourt; Peter Prestfelder; Sheldon M. Rich; Alicia Schacter; Professor William F. Sater (for advice on American English); Mónica and Enrique Teuscher; Sarah Vardigans.

England Teddy Peiró; Tony Staveacre (for use of his interviews with Piazzolla, Daniel Piazzolla, and Daniel Astor Piazzolla).

Switzerland Peter Keller (Artistic Management, Musiksommer Gstaad); Ana Simon.

Mexico Dr. Rafael Pérez Tamayo and Ing. Jesús Martínez Portilla (president and secretary, Academia del Tango "Gastón Martínez Matiella").

Uruguay Fernando Tesouro (Punta del Este), not least for his hospitality to us at absurdly short notice.

Spain José María Chinchilla.

Germany Sonia Alejandra López.

Japan Yuki Furuhashi.

Russian Federation Marina Panfilovich (Public Relations, Bolshoi Theater).

Turkey Hayri Erenli.

Our warm gratitude goes to Hermenegildo Sábat, the twentieth century's greatest caricaturist in the River Plate countries, for his generosity in giving us the drawings of Piazzolla in this book.

We also thank the Ufficio Anagrafe del Comune di Trani (Puglia Region, Italy) for genealogical information; Stefano Nespolesi (Coordinamento Palinsesti TV) and Antonella Roscilli (Ricercatore, Direzione Coordinamento Palinsesti TV) of Radio Televisione Italiana (RAI). Among the libraries that gave us special help, we acknowledge the Biblioteca Nacional, Argentina (special thanks to all the staff), the Archivo Museo Histórico Municipal in Mar del Plata (special thanks to Andrés Pereira Barreto), the New York Public Library (Performing Arts Research Center), the Bibliothèque Nationale, Paris (Section Musique), the Bibliothèque-Musée of the Comédie Française (special thanks to Mme. Odile Faliu, Conservateur en Chef), the Biblioteca Nazionale, Rome; the Sormani, Milan; and the Jean & Alexander Heard Library (Central Library and Anne Wilson Potter Music Library) at Vanderbilt University (special thanks to Paula Covington and Shirley Marie Watts). We wish to express our gratitude to the two anonymous reviewers for Oxford University Press for the thoroughness of their reviews and for some valuable suggestions. Our friend, the talented musician Pablo Aslan, gave us invaluable comments and suggestions on some of the musical sections of the book, for which we extend our warm gratitude. Finally, we thank the Interlink Network, Argentina. Our long-distance collaboration would have been quite impossible without e-mail, for whose arrival we ought to applaud the statesmen who gave the world the Cold War.

For permission to quote two lines from W. H. Auden's poem "Letter to Lord Byron," first published in W. H. Auden and Louis MacNeice, *Letters from Iceland* (London: Faber and Faber; New York: Random House, 1937), the authors thank Faber and Faber Ltd., London, and Random House Inc., New York.

October 1999

M.S.A.
Buenos Aires
S.C.
Nashville, Tennessee

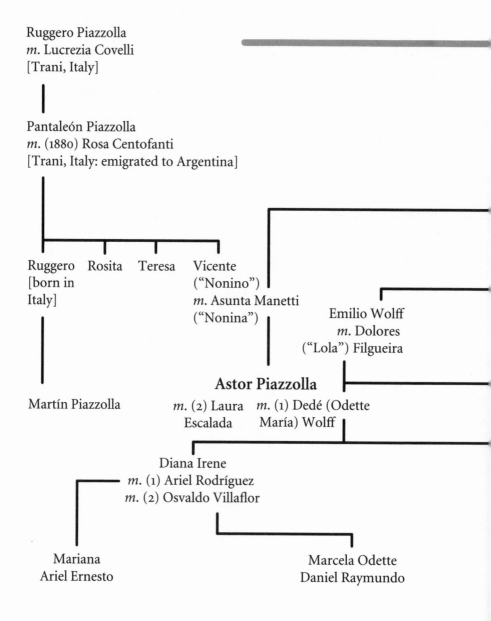

Ruggero Piazzolla
m. Lucrezia Covelli
[Trani, Italy]

Pantaleón Piazzolla
m. (1880) Rosa Centofanti
[Trani, Italy: emigrated to Argentina]

Ruggero   Rosita   Teresa   Vicente
[born in   ("Nonino")
Italy]   *m.* Asunta Manetti
                                ("Nonina")

                                              Emilio Wolff
                                                 m. Dolores
                                              ("Lola") Filgueira

                          Astor Piazzolla

Martín Piazzolla   *m.* (2) Laura   *m.* (1) Dedé (Odette
                    Escalada   María) Wolff

                    Diana Irene
              m. (1) Ariel Rodríguez
            m. (2) Osvaldo Villaflor

        Mariana   Marcela Odette
     Ariel Ernesto   Daniel Raymundo

Family Relationships of Piazzollas, Manettis, Bertolamis, and Wolffs

(not a complete family tree)

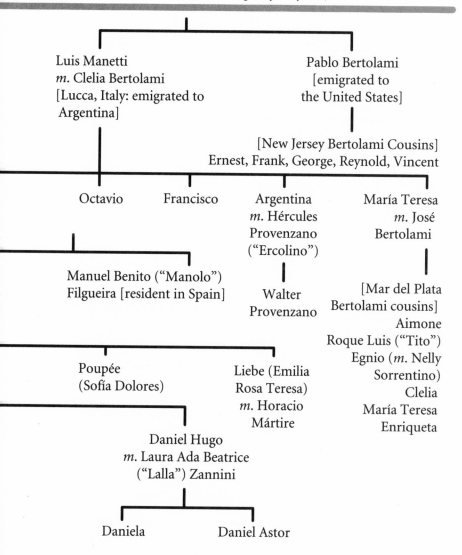

Luis Manetti
m. Clelia Bertolami
[Lucca, Italy: emigrated to
Argentina]

Pablo Bertolami
[emigrated to
the United States]

[New Jersey Bertolami Cousins]
Ernest, Frank, George, Reynold, Vincent

Octavio   Francisco   Argentina
m. Hércules
Provenzano
("Ercolino")

María Teresa
m. José
Bertolami

Manuel Benito ("Manolo")
Filgueira [resident in Spain]

Walter
Provenzano

[Mar del Plata
Bertolami cousins]
Aimone
Roque Luis ("Tito")
Egnio (*m.* Nelly
Sorrentino)
Clelia
María Teresa
Enriqueta

Poupée
(Sofía Dolores)

Liebe (Emilia
Rosa Teresa)
m. Horacio
Mártire

Daniel Hugo
m. Laura Ada Beatrice
("Lalla") Zannini

Daniela   Daniel Astor

➤➤ PART I

Struggle ◂◂

"*I Was Raised in New York*"
1921–1937

> I was raised in New York.
> —Astor Piazzolla, speaking in Central Park (1987)

Mar del Plata

Mar del Plata, located on the Atlantic coast, some 250 miles south of Buenos Aires across the level Argentine pampa, has little claim to antiquity. Formally named a city in 1874, its story really began only ten years later with the arrival of the railroad. Its excellent beaches and invigorating climate then began to attract a growing summertime population, and Argentina's best architects, drawing on a charming potpourri of mostly European styles, transformed Mar del Plata into the most stylish and handsome ocean resort south of the equator. Astor Pantaleón Piazzolla, the only child of Vicente Piazzolla and his wife Asunta Manetti, was born there at around two in the morning on Friday, 11 March 1921, in a rented room behind Angela Bridarolli's confectionery store, "La Marplatense," at Calle Rivadavia 2527, three blocks from the Cathedral. "We all thought," said Asunta later, "that it was a very good omen for a child to be born in that world of sweetness."[1] Asunta's sister Argentina looked after mother and child for a few days after the birth, until Asunta felt well enough to get up.

The Piazzollas came from Trani, in the rather poor Puglia region of southern Italy. Astor's great-grandfather Ruggero was a sailor, his great-grandmother Lucrezia Covelli, a seamstress. Ruggero's son Pantaleo, born 30 October 1855, was also a sailor who, according to family tradition, decided to emigrate after his boat was shipwrecked. He thus become one of hundreds of thousands of Italians who moved to Argentina as its spectacular age of prosperity dawned in the 1880s. (By the 1920s Argentina was the seventh richest country in the world.) Pantaleón, as his name became, settled in Mar del Plata with his wife, Rosa Centofanti, whom he had married in May 1880. He worked as a sailor, fisherman, and lifeguard on the beach during the summer season and as doorman at one of the city's theaters. Tall and fair-haired, he was known as "the Dutchman" by the *marplatenses* he had come to live among. Among his hobbies was woodcarving, at which he became very expert. It was a skill he passed on to his younger son Vicente, born in Mar del Plata on 12 November 1893.[2]

The grown-up Vicente became a small-time businessman. In 1921 he was running a bicycle store, catering to a universal demand in Mar del Plata. However, his real passion was for motorcycles, which he both bought and sold, including one sold to Astor Bolognini. Along with his brothers Ennio and Remo, Bolognini was following a distinguished career as a violinist in orchestras in North America. Ennio joined the first violin section in Toscanini's Philharmonic Symphony Orchestra; Remo was later concertmaster in the same orchestra. Astor Bolognini himself played in the Chicago Symphony. Vicente became good friends with Astor, and so his name was given to Vicente's son. Its recipient was not altogether happy with it: he later complained to his first wife that Astor sounded more like a surname than a first name.

Astor's maternal grandfather, Luis Manetti, "the spitting image of Astor," says Astor's cousin Enriqueta Bertolami, had emigrated with his wife Clelia Bertolami from Lucca in Tuscany. He became a successful farmer on a small scale, still remembered in Mar del Plata for planting the trees in the Plaza Mitre, one of the resort's many fine squares. The Manettis were somewhat better off than the Piazzollas. Luis's daughter Asunta was four years younger than her husband-to-be. Vicente courted her during his military service, and they were married on 11 October 1918.[3] The marriage was a happy one, at least when viewed in retrospect by their son. Their Mar del Plata relatives were also very fond of them. Astor's second cousin Ana María Tiribelli recalls Asunta as "very affectionate, very coquettish." Martín Piazzolla (son of Vicente's Italian-born elder brother Ruggero) thinks of her as "a very good aunt, very helpful." Vicente he saw as "a bit nervous, but very good, very hard-working." According to Asunta's sister Argentina Manetti, members of the Piazzolla family were "very intelligent, all of them. But very good people." Astor probably got his temperament from his father and his physical build from his mother. Vicente was very much taller than his wife. The adult Astor was 5'6" (1.70 meters) tall, and in many ways he was a Manetti in looks, though without the prominent nose of some of the male Manettis.

Years later his mother recounted that, as a baby, "Astor was as good as gold and never cried, though he didn't sleep much."[4] In fact, the boy's first years were horribly complicated. He was born with a defective, badly twisted right leg, for reasons that were never fully clarified. Starting in his second year, Astor underwent repeated operations in the Sanatorio Marítimo, located in the La Perla district, before the problem was at least partially corrected. Almost all his earliest memories were of separations from his mother, of pain, of crying his heart out. It gave him a lifelong aversion to hospitals. Asunta decided to have no further children, although the doctors told her she could. "I would have liked some more," she would say later to her daughter-in-law.

Alberto Rodríguez Egaña, chief surgeon at the Sanatorio, performed the final operation, refusing payment for his services. Astor was left with a thinner but otherwise reasonably normal right leg, two centimeters shorter than the other. Having this condition affected him throughout his life, and it was a point on which he was always touchy. He hated to be described as *rengo*, "lame." One result of the slight deformity was, as Astor remembered, that "papa got it into his head that I had to be something great. He proposed that I should do everything that was forbidden me, so that I would get ahead, not be a solitary person, a person with complexes. If they forbade me to swim, he ordered me to go swimming. If they told me I shouldn't go running, he ordered me to go running."[5] One thinks of an earlier artistic genius, Lord Byron, also born with a bad leg.

> Your mother in a temper cried "Lame brat!"
> Posterity should thank her much for that.[6]

Not being a member of the English upper classes, Asunta would never have dreamed of shouting "Lame brat!" at Astor. In any case, this theory of the childhood roots of creativity is no longer held. But Vicente was right: his son *did* achieve greatness.

A Lower East Side Childhood

Vicente was a restless man, always inclined to believe that the grass was greener elsewhere. Asunta was much less sure that it was. Vicente had heard from friends that a good living could be made in New York. He journeyed there by boat to investigate the prospects, and then decided to emigrate. Astor had just turned four. His first identity card (No. 87979) was issued on 29 March 1925, and the journey, on the SS *Pan America*, must have been made soon afterward. The archival records of arrivals at New York for those weeks have now become illegible, so the precise date eludes us.

The Piazzolla family went first to Port Reading, New Jersey, to stay with Asunta's uncle Pablo Bertolami, who worked on the railroads. A year or two later, when there was a long railroad strike, Vicente and Asunta, defying Prohibition laws, ferried whiskey and vermouth (for the strikers to sell) to New Jersey in the sidecar of their motorcycle. In return, the Bertolamis rewarded them with chicken, eggs, cheese, and vegetables to take back home. As he grew up, Astor enjoyed visiting his cousins in their semirural New Jersey setting. The cousins were five boys: Frank, Ernest, Vincent, Reynold, and George. Astor kept in touch with them for the rest of his life.

The Piazzollas soon found an apartment in Manhattan, at 8 St. Mark's Place, over a billiard saloon run by a Jewish couple, the Wassermans. Asunta scrubbed and polished to make the apartment habitable. St. Mark's Place is nowadays the "main street" of the bohemian and semigentrified East Village, but in the 1920s it was a neighborhood not yet distinguished from the rest of the Lower East Side. The area adjoined two heavily Italian and Jewish districts. The Piazzollas were not far from New York's Little Italy around Mulberry Street, and the family often attended its merry mid-September festival of San Gennaro. To the east of Little Italy stood the overcrowded tenements of what was, in those days, the largest Jewish community in the world. Second Avenue, to the north and south of St Mark's Place, was still the "Jewish Rialto," noted for intellectual talk-fests and Yiddish theater. On one occasion, during Astor's childhood, a wedding party in a nearby synagogue was attacked and several people were killed. "Everything gets under the skin," Astor would say in 1990. "My rhythmic accents, 3-3-2, are similar to those of the Jewish popular music I heard at weddings."[7] As a boy, he became what Yiddish speakers call nonpejoratively a *shabbos goy*, a "sabbath gentile," earning quarters on Saturdays for extinguishing the candles in the synagogue.

Asunta, who had not worked before, took a job in a workshop, gluing hair to animal skins. Vicente, meanwhile, found work as a barber, learning the craft in a shop run by a certain Tony Melli. He soon moved to a barbershop on Lafayette Street owned by a Sicilian immigrant, Nicola Scabuttiello, a man connected with the Mafia, though probably only in a small way. The classic five New York "families" were then consolidating (greatly helped by Prohibition), but most syndicate operations were still very local in scope. Scabuttiello's tiny empire included a number of billiard and gambling saloons. Vicente became something of a trusted friend to Scabutiello, who even allowed Astor to call him "uncle." The relationship had its advantages. When Astor was attacked by some youths in the Wassermans' saloon, Scabuttiello sent a brief note that said, "Never touch Piazzolla's son again." There was no further trouble.[8] Life in his barbershop was also eventful. He once sent Vicente to warn off a rival who had set up shop on nearby Hudson Street, and a day or two later a bomb reinforced the warning.[9] On another occasion, one of Vicente's clients was shot at from the street outside; the bullet grazed Vicente's shoulder, drawing blood. Eventually Vicente moved on, working finally for another Sicilian barber, Vicenzo Baudo, on Seventh Avenue.

In 1926, at the age of five, Astor went to his first school. Asunta equipped him with a medallion of St. Anthony, only to find it missing a few days later: the school was Protestant.[10] The boy quickly adapted to New York life. He soon acquired the fluency in idiomatic English that he was to keep all his life, always with a New York accent. (Joseph Hurley, a New York writer who met him in the late 1980s, found his speech reminiscent of Little Italy, and Kip Hanrahan, his record producer in the same years, remembers it as "a New York English frozen in time.") And he made friends. His earliest bosom companions were two immigrant boys, Nicky Kavalishen, of Polish background, and Willy Lubiansky, a Russian. When Astor was seven, he was allowed to spend several summer weeks in rural Connecticut with Willy and his grandparents. He quickly tired of the Russian borscht they served every day, longing for the salami and cheese his parents brought him on visits, but he did not forget the Connecticut countryside: the flower-strewn hills, the heaps of unthreshed corn, the carts that took the corn away. Years later he was sometimes reminded of the scenes when watching American movies.[11]

Though Astor was very fond of his parents—"parents don't come like that anymore," he would say in 1973[12]—he always recognized that his upbringing was fairly strict. His relationship with his mother was very loving, something that remained true until her death in 1982. His father was a more awesome figure, a man who clearly did not believe in sparing the rod (or at least the strap) to spoil the child. By the same token, he was still eager for his son to succeed in life. When Astor was seven or eight, Vicente bought a notebook and began writing up his progress with fatherly pride. "Astor will go far," he wrote. "He is worth a great deal."[13] Vicente had already been teaching his son how to box, mostly to build up his confidence, and when he was eight or nine, bought him some boxing gloves.

The gloves were probably needed. The boy had a combative, aggressive streak. Well behaved at home, he was mischievous in the street and at school. "I don't think I was a very good schoolboy," he said in 1965. "I never liked being ordered about."[14] He was expelled from one or two of his early schools for fighting and was free with his fists in the streets, where he spent much of his time. His companions nicknamed him "Lefty," because of a stiff left-handed punch, a punch that came in handy when he joined his first gang. Gangs were ubiquitous in New York, ranging from the seriously criminal to the merely rough. They were often ethnically based: Irish, Italian, African-American, Jewish. While not as violent as later urban gangs, they were always prepared for fights with rival groups. Membership in a gang meant that Astor became "streetwise" at an early age, and his youthful attitudes reflected his Lower Manhattan surroundings. He once told his daughter Diana: "I have no friendship for the police. I always had problems with them. I was always getting into fights, was violent, and misbehaved on purpose."[15] Perhaps he exaggerated his wickedness, rather in the way self-made millionaires like to exaggerate their original poverty, but the Lower East Side street world of Astor's childhood was certainly a tough one.

More important from the viewpoint of his life story was that when Astor was eight, his father gave him a bandoneon, bought from either a secondhand clothes dealer in downtown Manhattan or a pawnshop in Brooklyn. Astor was to tell the story in both versions. His uncle Octavio Manetti was visiting New York at the time and he and Vicente saw the squeezebox in the shopwindow, on sale for $18. "What's that?" Astor asked, when shown the instrument. He gazed at it for a very long time before daring to press its buttons. Vicente himself was moderately good on both accordion and guitar. He sometimes played at the New York Italian festivals, and he composed at least one tango. The apartment had phonograph records of the great tango bandleader Julio De Caro, and others by the tango's then recognized superstar, the baritone Carlos Gardel. When Vicente arrived home, usually around eight or nine o'clock, the first thing he did was to play a record, his eyes often moistening as he listened. Nothing would have pleased Vicente more than to see his son become a famous tango musician. He would certainly have seen the bandoneon as the key to that future. The bandoneon, invented in Germany in the 1830s, is a cousin of the accordion, though much more difficult to play. It was used in churches in the Black Forest as a substitute for the harmonium. When it reached Argentina, it was gradually adopted by tango bands. The instrument's rich, plaintive sound somehow became fundamental to the developing tradition of tango music, which was entering its great golden age at the time the Piazzollas migrated to New York and fast becoming Argentina's dominant tradition of popular music.

Astor's attitude toward learning the bandoneon was casual. "To give pleasure to the old man, I clumsily tried to learn," he recalled, "and I was dreadfully bad."[16] Many of his childhood crazes, such as fixing radios, were short-lived, and the bandoneon stayed in the closet much of the time. But Vicente was anxious for his son to play and decided that Astor needed music lessons. Asunta, meanwhile, had been learning hairdressing and had helped an American friend set up a salon called Mary & Susan; its clientele consisted of Italians and Jews, attended to on alternate days. She also began to study cosmetics, inventing an almond-based beauty cream that she continued making for the rest of her life.[17] Its formula, a closely guarded secret, was eventually passed on to a relative. One of her clients was a music teacher, a lady with whom she made a deal: regular manicures in exchange for lessons for Astor. Astor's mischievousness meant that the deal quickly fell through. His second teacher, an Italian friend of Vicente's who taught tonic sol-fa, violin, and mandolin, fared no better. The Italian was always cooking his dinner when Astor arrived for his evening lesson. The odors from the kitchen quickly aroused the boy's curiosity, and he learned several tasty recipes but probably not much else. In the end, the Italian threw him out for lack of progress. He was *not* making progress. Music still seemed far less important to him than his friends, his gang, his street life.

In retrospect, Astor always felt very positive about his lower Manhattan childhood. He was to describe it as "a happy childhood, not a tortured one. I was always coddled . . . , I had everything." (In fact, the care his parents took over his clothing sometimes made him embarrassed when meeting his shabbily attired gang.) And he always recognized that New York left its mark on him. "I have New York very much inside me," he told Peter Watrous in 1987. "I'm sure that New York gave me courage. I learned to make myself tough in life, to take care of myself."[18]

With the Depression, times changed for the Piazzollas, as for millions of others. The heady American prosperity of the 1920s melted away. Vicente decided to beat a retreat back to Argentina. Their friends saw them off at the pier: Scabutiello, the Wassermans, Uncle Pablo and the cousins, Willy Lubiansky and Nicky Kavalishen, even the Italian music teacher. Back in Mar del Plata in early 1930, Vicente used his New York savings to open a barbershop, the Peluquería Nueva York, at the intersection of Boulevard Independencia, where the family took an apartment, and Calle Moreno. Asunta opened a women's salon. Vicente's new barbershop was the most modern in the city—apparently the first to use electric clippers; but business was far from brisk, for the Depression had reached Argentina, too. Before long, Vicente was forced to sell the motorcycle he had brought from New York.

For the nine-year-old Astor, the transition was a tough one. His New York clothes—Scottish raincoat, long trousers, tartan socks—did not go over well with the *marplatense* children. His sturdy American shoes contrasted all too conspicuously with the *alpargatas*, the rough hemp footwear used by his new schoolmates. But if his schoolmates taunted him, or whistled and hissed at him in the street, "Lefty" knew how to handle them. Others were impressed by the smart American pencil case he brought to school. "He hardly knew how to speak Spanish," his teacher, Rosa Carmen Mattalia, would later recall, "and my sister Violeta and I taught him the first words. Our biggest problem was his left-handedness. How brutal we were in those days! We wanted to force him to write with his right hand, but there was no way. We even tied up his arm."[19]

There were a few consolations in the strange town that happened to be his birthplace. He struck up a warm friendship with the daughter of a local physician and told his teacher that he was going to marry her. More exciting, no doubt, were hunting and fishing excursions to the Mar del Plata hinterland with his cousins Egnio, Aimone, and Roque Luis "Tito," the sons of Uncle José Bertolami and Aunt María Teresa Manetti, Asunta's sister. The Bertolamis also had three daughters, Clelia, María Teresa, and Enriqueta. Astor liked them. They took to him; he made their mother laugh. He was "affectionate, a bit of a pest, he liked making jokes," says Enriqueta, "[but] he was restless, very restless." His Piazzolla cousin Martín (six years older than Astor) found him "very playful, very funny." They went bicycling together. Another older *marplatense* boy, Mario Lenceti, played soccer with him and noticed a definite mischievous streak. If Astor did not get his way over something, "there would be blows, that's for sure." Lenceti saw him changing the cards on the presents at wedding receptions—a trick he was not averse to playing in adult life—and altering the prices on articles in shops holding going-out-of-business sales. "He was always thinking up something new."[20]

Music was not neglected back in Mar del Plata. Vicente and Asunta were determined that Astor should build on whatever rudiments he had picked up in New York. So he took bandoneon lessons twice a week with Líbero Pauloni, who turned up at the apartment red-eyed from his stints in *marplatense* nightspots. When Líbero moved to Buenos Aires, his brother Homero took over the lessons. Both were very competent bandoneonists, and their instruction could well have marked a vital moment in Astor's musical development.[21] Asunta's brother Francisco was sometimes enlisted in the educational effort. Since he had a bicycle rental business to attend to, he locked Astor and his bandoneon in the bathroom of his house, sometimes lingering a while outside to listen, finding that "he was studying for real."[22] Cousin Enriqueta Bertolami also thought Astor was seriously applying himself. When cousin Martín Piazzolla, himself a budding musician, called at the apartment one day, Aunt Asunta immediately asked him to test Astor's tonic sol-fa skills.

After nine months or so in Mar del Plata, Vicente decided to cut his losses and return to New York. To Astor it must have seemed like a return to normal. The New York City of the early 1930s was different from the one he had left. The unemployed now lined up at the soup kitchens. There were the "Hoovervilles," the miserable shantytowns in Central Park and Riverside Park. By 1932, nearly half the Italian families in Little Italy were without a grown-up wage earner. But the Depression would never loom large in Astor's memories. Vicente found work as a barber again. The family went back to the old neighborhood, to an apartment at 313 East 9th Street, a block or so from their former home. Astor was sent to Public School No. 92, which soon expelled him for bad behavior. He completed all the formal education he was ever to know at the Maria Aussiliatrice, a school run by the Salesian Order located at East 11th Street and Second Avenue, graduating in mid-1934. He sometimes took his bandoneon to school, to impress the girls, he later claimed. Eventually the Mother Superior gave him a couple of marches to study for a little festival she was organizing. Astor played marches in the schoolyard, surrounded by black-shirted boys. The marches were "Giovinezza" and "Camisa nera," the classic Italian Fascist anthems. One of the school's walls bore the slogan "Win a star. Spit on a Jew." "I think about it today," Astor said in 1983, "and it turns my stomach."[23] The adult Astor Piazzolla was not the slightest bit racist.

At the insistence of his parents, he joined a boys' club and learned swimming and baseball. He became a good pitcher. He took boxing lessons at a nearby gymnasium, whose coach was Tony Canzoneri, the lightweight and junior welterweight world champion in the 1930s. Here Astor also encountered the young Jake La Motta, the future "Raging Bull." He was no older than Astor, but already he commanded the skills that would take him to the world middleweight championship. La Motta once invited Astor into the ring. "He gave me such a blow that I never went back to the gymnasium." Apart from his proficiency as a boxer, Astor learned to roller-skate and to ice-skate, and won several swimming prizes.[24]

Once again he found a place in a gang, a tough crowd of mostly Italian-Americans. One of the gang's friends, though not a member, was Rocky Graziano, a future world middleweight champion. Astor could recite the gang members' names easily more than thirty years later: Nunzio Incataschiatta, Nino Rodosti, John Pomponio, Joseph Campanella, Gaspar Sacco, Peter Renda. One of the gang's habits was to buttonhole film actor (and former assistant to bootleggers) George Raft, who lived on 11th Street, and extract a few coins from him. Another passion was *pase inglés*, a now largely forgotten card game. When a reasonable amount of money had accumulated in a session, Astor sometimes would sneak off and call the police. The sound of approaching sirens scattered his companions, and "Lefty" pocketed the proceeds.[25]

His closest friend in New York after 1930 was outside the gang. He was a young Polish American, Stanley Sommerkovsky (later Sommers). The boys became inseparable. At least twice they ran away from home together, getting only a few miles up Long Island. Astor seems to have been the one who turned for home first. Mostly they simply wandered the streets, played in Central Park, or, disguised as adults with overcoats and hats, made off to Harlem to listen to Cab Calloway or Duke Ellington. Years later, when Astor saw the movie *Cotton Club* (1984), he was moved by its vivid recreation of the sights and sounds he and Stanley had once experienced.[26] His experiences in Harlem gave him one of his lifelong loves, his love for jazz.

Stanley was also his accomplice in an attempted robbery. Astor coveted a large chromatic Hohner harmonica he had seen in Macy's. They stole the harmonica, but a burly policewoman arrested them as they left the store. On their way to the police station, Astor distracted her with a sudden shout. He and Stanley escaped by jumping on to a passing truck.[27] The experience cured them of serious criminal ambition. However, minor misdemeanors were another matter. Astor's New Jersey cousin George Bertolami, who found him "crazy, quite a character, kind of wild," remembers that he usually avoided paying the fare when they rode the trolleys together.

Meanwhile, his parents continued to encourage his musical interest. One night, Vicente took him to a Spanish-owned cabaret, El Gaucho, where Astor played a tango. Soon afterward, Astor joined forces with an Argentine singer and guitarist, Agustín Cornejo, and a Peruvian called Pichardo. On Thursday, 29 December 1932, Astor took part in an entertainment, "An Evening in Argentina," at Roerich Hall on West 103rd Street, announced in the program as the "boy wonder of the bandoneon." The New York Spanish-language papers described him in similarly eulogistic terms. For Astor, who was eleven years old, it was a memorable moment, the first time he felt "the excitement of being on stage, being applauded by people." Three months later he performed again at Roerich Hall, winning praise from the New York newspaper *La Prensa* for his "excellent musical technique."[28]

By this stage Astor was taking lessons from the third of his New York music teachers, Andrés D'Aquila, an Argentine pianist who lived on East 13th Street. D'Aquila had played in tango bands in Buenos Aires during the 1920s, and, in his own words, had gone to New York "as a pure adventurer." He had some ability with the bandoneon and evidently managed to improve Astor's skills. How seriously Astor concentrated is another matter. He often persuaded D'Aquila to take him to the movies, and D'Aquila enjoyed practical jokes, once pretending to be dead in his armchair and laughing loudly when the alarmed Astor called in the neighbors.[29]

When D'Aquila had to give up teaching, after nearly a year, Astor was sent to Terig Tucci, an Argentine musician who worked for the NBC radio network. Tucci lived on 110th Street, well over a hundred blocks from Astor's home, a good walk for Astor and Vicente, who took him to the lesson. What Tucci gave him we cannot be sure. In any case, Astor was, for the moment, more enthusiastic about the harmonica and tap dancing. One of his idols was Bill "Bojangles" Robinson. Vicente was indulgent. He sent Astor to a harmonica "academy" on 42nd Street, and bought him a pair of steel-tipped shoes. Astor and his friend Nunzio Incataschiatta began going over to 14th Street, where they shined shoes, played the harmonica, tap danced, and passed the hat. When Vicente found out, as he did, he once again took the strap to his son.

At the age of thirteen Astor became enamored of Maria Alberti, the daughter of a local baker, only to discover that she preferred his friend Peter Renda, a well-built youth with a striking resemblance to Cary Grant. However, his bitter feelings soon passed, as they usually do at that age. As he would describe in a 1983 interview, his sexual initiation took place around this time, "with a girl they brought to the club to . . . well she served us, more or less. She was horribly fat, and weighed four times more than I did. But anyway, she was a sort of professional who fulfilled her function."[30]

But music was gradually coming to be at least as important as baseball or boxing or *pase inglés*. The Piazzollas' next-door neighbor on East 9th Street was Bela Wilda, a Hungarian pianist and pupil of Sergei Rachmaninoff. Astor was mesmerized by the sound of Wilda's piano as he practiced, and he began staying at home simply to listen. He became obsessed by Wilda's playing of Bach ("I fell in love with Bach, I went crazy,"[31] he would say later) and quickly decided he wanted to study with Wilda. Vicente finally gave in. Wilda had no knowledge of the bandoneon but could arrange piano pieces for the instrument. More important, he introduced Astor to classical music, which soon seemed as alluring as jazz. Wilda was far from well off; he wore patched pants and owned only one suit. Astor frequently took him pasta dishes prepared by Asunta, and Wilda and his wife soon became friends of the Piazzollas, often lunching with them. Astor was to regard him as his "first great master." He later told British interviewer Tony Staveacre that it was only with Wilda that he really learned to read music.[32]

Wilda's example clinched Astor's desire to be a musician. While still in school, and for a year or so afterward, he sometimes performed in theaters or on the radio. Terig Tucci, his former teacher, recruited him from time to time, and on 3 July 1935 he played in a group directed by Tucci in Schenectady, New York.[33] He cannot have had many engagements of this sort, for the Musicians' Union in New York barred minors from working.[34] It *is* faintly possible that he tried to join established dance bands, such as Xavier Cugat's or Pedro Vincent's, but was prevented from doing so by union rules.[35] How long he played his bandoneon in the trio with Pichardo and Cornejo (the latter a popular visitor at East 9th Street) we do not know. They certainly performed folk numbers several times on the radio, and in 1935, Astor played in a radio program transmitted to Argentina, dedicating his pieces to his grandparents.[36]

He was also occasionally "promoted" by Armando Zegrí, a Chilean journalist and novelist who owned the well-known Café Latino on Greenwich Village's Barrow Street.* Zegrí organized bandoneon recitals for Astor in universities, where he played pieces such as Rossini's *William Tell* Overture and Mozart's "Turkish March." Zegrí also secured an engagement for him to play (almost certainly in spring 1933) at the opening of some of the buildings of the new Rockefeller Center, where, as Astor later recounted, "a gentleman did a drawing of me and gave it to me. Afterwards I learned that it was Diego Rivera."[37] Rivera had been painting the famous revolutionary mural that brought his dismissal by the Rockefellers and their destruction of the mural, one of the twentieth century's great acts of artistic vandalism. Rivera noticed Astor playing the bandoneon, and this evidently provoked a friendly feeling. At the time, the boy had no idea of the Mexican artist's fame. He kept the drawing for the rest of his life.

Astor's musical interests were now beginning to take shape. He was eclectic in his enthusiasms. The classical music he studied with Bela Wilda, the jazz he heard in Harlem, the folk numbers he played with Cornejo and Pichardo—all these influenced his adolescent ear. In 1930 he wrote a *ranchera* (a popular South American variant of the mazurka), which he later described as "horrible," and in 1932 a tango he called "Paso a paso por Broadway" ("Step by Step on Broadway").

---

*It was recommended in the classic *W.P.A. Guide to New York City* (1939). After the war, during which he was a correspondent for NBC, Zegrí opened an art gallery/bookstore, the Galería Sudamericana.

Vicente insisted he rechristen it "La Catinga," which sounded more *tanguero.*[38] He still showed no particular enthusiasm for tango music, despite the records in the apartment and his father's insistent urgings. Indeed, Vicente himself by now quite liked hearing Bach played on his son's bandoneon. It was at this point that Astor's young life was briefly touched by the tango's most legendary personality. He was turning thirteen at the time.

Astor and the Creole Thrush

On Thursday, 28 December 1933, Latin America's most famous popular singer arrived in New York from France on board the SS *Champlain.* Carlos Gardel (1890–1935) was modern Argentina's—in fact, modern Latin America's—first genuine superstar. *El zorzal criollo,* "the Creole Thrush," as he was known, had helped create the tango song as a distinct genre. He was the greatest of all tango singers, the idol of Buenos Aires, and a recent star of cabaret and theater in Paris. His first movies, made in France by Paramount, were being shown all over Latin America. He had come to New York for a series of radio programs on NBC. He also hoped to convince Paramount to make more films. The corporation was persuaded. In 1934 and 1935, at the Astoria studios on Long Island, Gardel made four movies, all of them sensational box office hits around Latin America.

Like so many Argentines, Vicente was a devoted Gardel fan. He put his wood-carving talent to good use, cutting the figure of a gaucho playing a guitar. He inscribed it and instructed Astor to deliver the carving to the apartment where Gardel was living with his musical adviser Alberto Castellano, and Alfredo Le Pera, his lyricist and scriptwriter. So it was that on a bright spring morning in 1934 Astor found himself at the entrance to the tall Beaux Arts buildings on East 44th Street. Here he ran into a bald-headed man holding a milk bottle and looking lost. Astor addressed him in English and got a reply in Spanish. It was Alberto Castellano, who had mislaid his key. He asked the nimble boy to climb the fire escape and enter the penthouse apartment through a window. "Gardel is the one in the pajamas with the white spots," he explained.[39] The first person Astor woke up was Alfredo Le Pera, who was bad-tempered about the sudden intrusion. The great man himself, by contrast, proved extremely friendly. He opened the package, contemplated the little figure, offered Astor breakfast, and gave him two signed photographs, one for Vicente.

Astor was to see much of the star over the next year. Gardel found the boy's English particularly useful on shopping expeditions. He was trying to learn English himself, without much success. There were numerous excursions to buy clothes and shoes at Gimbels, Macy's, Florsheim, and Saks. On one occasion recalled by Astor, Gardel was desperate to renew his supply of the striped shirts he wore in his films. "We went around till we found them, one afternoon, I think it was at Saks . . . and he bought twenty or thirty shirts."[40] It did not take long for Astor to reveal that he played the bandoneon. Gardel liked his versions of classical pieces but was unimpressed by his tangos. He put it to him in impeccable *lunfardo*, the street Spanish favored by *porteños*, the inhabitants of Buenos Aires. "*Mirá, pibe, el fueye lo tocás fenómeno, pero el tango lo tocás como un gallego*" ("Look, lad, you're top-notch at playing the squeezebox, but you play the tango like a gringo!").[41] Gardel allowed him—how often we cannot say—to accompany his singing, most likely in private, unless, as the adult Astor occasionally claimed, he was sometimes permitted to join the orchestra that backed Gardel's songs. He certainly accompanied Gardel at a dinner party held at the Astoria studios, and evidently there were parties at Gardel's apartment when Astor played his bandoneon to substitute for the piano, which was usually out of tune.[42] Vicente and Asunta were obviously flattered by the star's interest in their son. They must have relished the one occasion when Astor brought him to eat with them at East 9th Street.

Early in 1935 Gardel gave Astor the tiniest of parts in the third and best of his New York movies, *El día que me quieras*. Astor's pay was $25, and he played a newspaper boy. "The role is just right for a loafer like you," said Gardel. For the rest of his life, Astor was to treasure a still of the fleeting and barely noticeable scene in the movie in which he appears with Gardel and actor Tito Lusiardo. At the end of March, with his fourth and last film completed, Gardel set out on a tour of the countries around the Caribbean. It was the fateful journey that took him to his death on the airfield at Medellín, Colombia, on 24 June. Astor played his bandoneon at one of several farewell parties for the star. Gardel wanted Astor to go with him on the tour, as some kind of factotum or general assistant. Vicente put his foot down; Astor was only fourteen. Another young New York Argentine, José Corpas Moreno, went in Astor's place and so became a victim of the fatal accident in Colombia. Such are the terrible twists of fate. If Astor had gone, as he wrote later, "I would now be playing the harp, not the bandoneon."[43]

There is a slightly eerie postscript to the encounters of Gardel and Astor in the Manhattan of 1934–35. The adult Piazzolla told the story many times, perhaps best in his extended interview with Alberto Speratti in 1968:

> In 1956 or 1957 . . . Andrés D'Aquila came to see me in Buenos Aires, and he said, "Astor, I'm going to tell you something that will stand your hair

on end. Just recently, while walking round Greenwich Village, I saw, in a basement store, a little wooden figure—all scorched and burned—with a label underneath that said FIGURE THAT BELONGED TO AN ARGENTINE SINGER. I go in and ask how much it costs. The assistant says twenty dollars. I only have ten with me, so I tell her I'll come back next day. When I go back next day with the cash, the figure had gone. They'd sold it." It's spine-chilling to think of the travels of that little figure. I'd given it to Gardel, it had been in the crash with him at Medellín and had got partly burned, and someone stole it there. Heaven knows how it got from Colombia to New York, to a business only a block or two away from the house where my father carved it. It's almost as if the figure had wanted to go back for a moment to 9th Street.[44]

Astor always hoped that someone might find the carving and send it to him. Nobody ever did.

Into the Tango World
1937–1944

→→ Mar del Plata Again

Lonesome in Buenos Aires ←←

→→ Dedé

In Aníbal Troilo's Band ←←

> I didn't know whether I played well or badly. . . . But I *had* to get ahead.
> —Astor Piazzolla, reminiscing to his daughter, Diana (1980)

Mar del Plata Again

Carlos Gardel was a memory, albeit an immortal one, when the Piazzollas again returned to Argentina in early 1937. Astor was turning sixteen and did not want to go. Unquestionably Argentine, he felt virtually an American. Years later he would often say that the "Star-Spangled Banner" still excited him more than the Argentine anthem. All his friends were in New York. His English was better than his Spanish. The only attraction held by Mar del Plata was the prospect of hunting and fishing with his Bertolami cousins. The Piazzollas sailed home aboard the SS *Southern Cross*, with Vicente's savings and twelve trunks in the hold. From Buenos Aires Asunta took the train across the pampa; Vicente and Astor went by motorcycle.[1] In Mar del Plata, at the end of March 1937, Vicente bought property at Calle Alberti 1555, selling some land and a house inherited from Pantaleón. The district, close to a new railroad station (now the main bus terminal), was growing fast. The Depression had proved milder in Argentina than in the United States or Great Britain, and the worst was over. Prosperity had returned, and Vicente could make a reasonable living. He opened both a bar and a bicycle store, soon one of the best-known *bicicleterías* in town. Vicente himself became a respected citizen, especially popular among the motorcycling fraternity, where his Harley

Davidson and American clothes attracted attention. He took part in races along Boulevard Independencia and made high-speed dashes to nearby beaches and pampa towns with a group of fellow enthusiasts. Its younger members all called him "papa."[2]

Vicente's bar, the "Nueva York," was not a bar for serious drinkers. Vicente built a small stage so that Astor could perform with a trio consisting of himself and two blind musicians: Rolando, a bass player, and his pianist brother-in-law Pocholo. Astor also did some tap dancing to a jazz accompaniment. Martín Piazzolla, a good pianist, sometimes played with his cousin, mostly "stylized tangos, Julio De Caro's tangos." Rolando and Pocholo spent most of their meager earnings on whiskey. Astor could not resist joking at their expense. When Rolando asked him to signal the arrival of pretty girls so that he could throw out a pleasant compliment, Astor ensured that the compliments all went to men.

But what was he going to *do* now that he was home? "He was a slim boy and good-looking," his mother later recalled, "and he spent his days running after the girls, among whom he had great success."[3] His parents obviously worried about him. They pestered him into taking classes in accounting. Vicente invited him to do the bookkeeping for the bicycle store and bar. An uncle offered to arrange a job at the Casino. None of these options appealed to Astor. "Know something?" he sometimes confessed to his cousin Enriqueta Bertolami, "I don't *like* it here." He was still uncertain about what he wanted. Vicente played records of bandoneonist Pedro Maffia's tango band for him, and he liked them, but found it hard to forget the sounds he had made his own in New York—classical sounds, jazz sounds, Bach, and Cab Calloway. "In my head I had Bach and Schumann and Mozart," he was to say in a New York interview in 1987, "and very little tango."[4]

In Argentina, however, especially urban Argentina, the tango was becoming the overwhelmingly pervasive form of popular music. During his first, listless months back in Mar del Plata, Astor must have heard the music constantly on the radio (the *cadenas de broadcastings*, the national radio networks, were just forming in Argentina) and also in the flesh, when the great tango bands (the *orquestas típicas*, to give them their generic name) visited Mar del Plata as part of their regular circuit, especially during the summer season. A young bandoneonist was bound to be drawn toward the tango world. It was only a matter of time. According to Astor's own account, the real revelation came during his siesta on 14 May 1938, when he turned on the radio and found himself listening to the Elvino Vardaro Sextet. Vardaro led one of the outstanding ensembles of the time. The sextet left no recordings, but Vardaro's own violin playing is still remembered as legendary for its perfect phrasing, its extraordinary expressiveness, and its distinctive rubato touches. Astor was so mesmerized by the broadcast that he immediately typed out a fan letter. Vardaro sent him a polite note in green ink and an autographed photo.[5]

Astor may well have overdramatized his "revelation." Later he claimed that he had been little more than a musical "robot" up to that point.[6] But his musical ambitions were obviously reawakened. He now spent his days with his ear glued to the radio, memorizing the schedules of all the tango broadcasts. He began to take note of the great tango musicians of the time. There was plenty to take note of, for they were a magnificent cluster. The bandleader Julio De Caro, who had done so much in the 1920s to add sophisticated harmony and counterpoint to tango arrangements, was still in his prime, as were notable bandoneonists such as Pedro Laurenz, Pedro Maffia, and Ciriaco Ortiz—musicians who would be joined by the great newcomer of 1937, Aníbal Troilo, otherwise known as "Pichuco." Troilo's band, with its smooth-tongued tenor vocalist Francisco "Fiore" Fiorentino, made its spectacular debut at Buenos Aires's Marabú cabaret in July of that year.

All these musicians were part of the so-called evolutionist tendency in tango music. They were imaginative and innovative, unlike the so-called traditionalists, who stubbornly upheld the strict tempo tradition of earlier generations, not bothering with the evolutionists' attempts to improve musical quality. The outstanding traditionalist in 1938 was pianist and bandleader Juan D'Arienzo, the brisk thump-thump of whose band was bringing about a spectacular renaissance of tango dancing in Argentina, after a period when the music and the tango song, boosted by the genius of Gardel, had threatened to eclipse the dance altogether. Astor found that he loathed the traditionalists. He thought of D'Arienzo as "terrible, barbaric, anti-musical."[7] Years later, however, in conversation with journalist Jorge Göttling, he recognized D'Arienzo's historical role and even had kind words for his "nervous rhythm."

Astor resumed his musical studies, taking piano lessons from Néstor Romano, who later headed the Mar del Plata Symphony. He also formed a very short-lived tango quartet of his own, the Cuarteto Azul, which adopted "an exact imitation of the Vardaro style." He tried to get work with established Mar del Plata bands such as Luis Sebastiano's—Sebastiano auditioned him and thought that he was *too good*, or so the story goes. At some point, he briefly played in Alberto Webb's dance band (tangos, *rancheras*, and Spanish *pasodobles*)—mostly for the experience. When he went for his first pay, Webb retorted: "What pay? You came here to learn!"[8]

His longest working stint in Mar del Plata lasted several months, when he played in a trio and a larger band for LU6 Radio Atlántica, standing in for Marcelo Moro, a bandoneonist who had been attracted into Pedro Laurenz's band. According to Moro, Astor still played with four fingers, but he already had "tremendous mastery." The *marplatense* pianist Pedro Blumetti, who first made Astor's acquaintance at this time, also remembers his bandoneon playing as good. The LU6 studio was the dining room of a house on Calle 20 de Septiembre. Blumetti tells us that the band's tenor was incapable of simulating the offstage voice needed for one particular song. Astor suggested that the tenor sing from the corridor. As soon as he got there, Astor slammed and locked the door.

With his ambition now thoroughly fired, he began to seek out *orquestas típicas* that were visiting Mar del Plata. One such was headed by Alberto Pugliese, brother of the later, more celebrated Osvaldo. Astor buttonholed one of the band's bandoneonists, Juan Sánchez Gorio. "It was like getting to know a god," and he spent hours chatting to him about bandoneon techniques. Vicente was clearly delighted by his son's new enthusiasm and remarked to him, "So the tango has really hooked you after all!"[9]

He made the remark as Astor was setting off to hear the band of Miguel Caló, soon to be one of the star bands of the 1940s, and now, in the summer months of 1939,* drawing the crowds at the Confitería Porta on the ocean front.[10] Astor shyly introduced himself to Caló. Two of Caló's musicians, bandoneonist Julio Ahumada and pianist Héctor "Chupita" Stamponi, took a liking to him. He sought them out at the pension where they were staying, arriving during their siesta. His tactlessness was firmly pointed out. Quite undeterred, he returned day after day to chat with the musicians, quizzing them endlessly, sometimes showing them tango arrangements of his own. "He drove us all crazy," recalled Stamponi. Years later Stamponi would tell Astor that he had seemed like "someone possessed." At the time he was mostly impressed by Astor's "fabulous" bandoneon arrangements.[11] He soon found himself bicycling around Mar del Plata with Astor, and on later trips to the city, Stamponi sometimes stayed with the family.

Two other young bandoneonists staying at the pension, Antonio Ríos and Alberto San Miguel, asked Astor to demonstrate his skills and were impressed. The outcome was that Miguel Caló sent Astor a message, inviting him to join his band in Buenos Aires. Astor did not take up the invitation immediately. He had other things to think about. He had become fond of a girl called Inés Gorgolini.

---

*Readers should note that whenever the narrative is set in Argentina in this book, the Southern Hemisphere seasons apply. The summer months here are December–March.

Many years later he told the story: "It was very sad. She died of typhoid fever, and we took her in a white coffin to the La Loma cemetery, with a long cortege of students. She was fifteen."[12] There was no real future for him, however, as a tango musician in provincial Mar del Plata. Buenos Aires, the tango's birthplace, was still its heart and soul. To anybody aspiring to bright lights and success, Buenos Aires was the most powerful of meccas. And in July 1939, on a cold winter's day, Buenos Aires finally snared the eighteen-year-old Astor Piazzolla.

His cousin Enriqueta Bertolami remembers that Asunta was in floods of tears while he packed his bags. Vicente gave his son 200 pesos (around $50) telling him, "When you spend it all, you come back!"[13] Astor promised to try to come home once every two weeks or so. He traveled to the capital with Mario Sasiain, an acquaintance of Vicente's whose occupations were, at different times, those of a trade unionist, a businessman, the founder (1955) of a Mar del Plata magazine, and a better-than-competent pianist with contacts in the Buenos Aires musical world.[14] Sasiain took nominal charge of Astor, who at eighteen was still legally a minor.

Astor sat on his bandoneon case as the Ford car chugged its way across the pampa. (Most of the highway had recently been paved.) It was an interminable drive, despite Sasiain's merry chatter. Astor's first impressions of Buenos Aires were very unfavorable. The metropolis lay under a cold winter drizzle. The car drew up at the door of the Pensión Alegría, at Calle Sarmiento 1419. Sasiain showed him the neighborhood: the dairy, the cinema, the police station, the post office, the pharmacy, and left him in room number 12, which he would share, at least for the time being, with a fellow bandoneonist. Astor would often recall his feeling of pure dismay. He could not understand "why musicians had to live in such miserable places."[15]

Lonesome in Buenos Aires

Piazzolla (as we mostly shall call him from now on) found leaving home a sad business. Buenos Aires was the largest city south of the equator (with 2,500,000 people in the late 1930s) and by a fair margin the most handsome. But to a newly arrived youngster, the metropolis was unavoidably bewildering. It was a relief that his roommate turned out to be Líbero Pauloni, his former bandoneon teacher. It was comforting that Vicente's sisters, Rosita and Teresa Piazzolla, lived nearby and could help him in various domestic ways. But with almost no *porteño* friends, he felt desperately lonely, something he could never handle well. Nor did he find good work immediately. As planned, he joined Miguel Caló's band, but quickly discovered that Caló had no intention of paying him. He formed a short-lived duo with a fellow bandoneonist, Calixto Sallago, to record pieces by Bach and Rachmaninoff.[16] Sallago recommended Piazzolla to a friend, bandoneonist Gabriel "Chula" Clausi; Clausi was formerly a member of Julio De Caro's band and was now forming a group for Radio Porteña. Piazzolla auditioned at Clausi's house. Piazzolla played Rachmaninoff. Clausi thought his technique needed some polishing. "He plays very well, but he lacks sonority," he told Vicente and Asunta, who were visiting Buenos Aires to see their son.

Piazzolla was always to speak very respectfully of Clausi, but he did not work for him long. Both men found positions in Los Mendocinos, Francisco Lauro's band.[17] At the audition, Piazzolla played music by Mozart and George Gershwin but was asked to perform some tangos. He was duly hired, though Lauro warned him about unconventional playing. Piazzolla stayed with the band while it fulfilled a three-month contract with Radio Belgrano, among other engagements. The pay was minimal. Piazzolla had no illusions about the quality of Lauro's band. Its pianist, Alfredo De Angelis, later an extremely popular bandleader among tango dancers, was the kind of traditionalist he thoroughly despised. Musically he felt frustrated, but he enjoyed himself, as always in his own way. One night he loosened all the screws on Lauro's bandoneon, which came apart in the middle of a tango.[18]

His early months in Buenos Aires revolved round the Novelty, a cabaret, where he worked with Lauro, and his home, the Pensión Alegría, which he soon nicknamed "La Liebre" (the term for "hunger" in *lunfardo*.) Piazzolla's roommate and former teacher Líbero Pauloni would later describe their life there and the way veteran musicians like himself tried to calm Piazzolla's "tremendous drive" by chatting or taking him to the movies. At the pension, Piazzolla spent hours studying, occasionally playing Bach and Chopin on his bandoneon, something that reduced Pauloni to tears. On returning from the Novelty at four in the morning, he often felt depressed, saying how much he wished to be back with his parents, to be fishing with his cousins. And then he and Pauloni and others would go off to a billiard saloon—"At billiards he was God; nobody could get past him on the green velvet."[19]

Piazzolla's circle of acquaintances gradually widened. He began to frequent the Café Germinal on Avenida Corrientes, Buenos Aires's Broadway, sometimes lingering for hours over a single 15-centavo cup of coffee while listening to Aníbal "Pichuco" Troilo's band. He studied the band's repertory, translating everything he heard to his bandoneon back at the pension. He was especially struck by

Troilo's legendary pianist, Orlando Goñi, and by Goñi's amazing ability to translate Troilo's bandoneon phrasing to the piano. Goñi seemed old to him (he was
all of twenty-five), but Piazzolla desperately wanted to imitate his playing. Later
on, when rehearsing alongside Goñi, he jotted down points about his piano technique in a little notebook.[20] The two were never to be really close. Goñi's friends
were mostly drunks in downtown bars. Nor was the pianist much interested in
jazz or classical music. Piazzolla nonetheless revered him, describing him forty
years later as "the real sound of the Aníbal Troilo orchestra."[21]

Piazzolla's admiration for Troilo's band is fully understandable. Troilo had
served his apprenticeship in some of the best ensembles of the 1920s and 1930s,
among them the bands of Alfredo Gobbi, Juan Maglio, and Julio De Caro, and
alongside many of the finest instrumentalists. Troilo's own bandoneon playing,
with its astonishing sensitivity and emotional range, was in a class of its own. His
nocturnal lifestyle and great affability would later give him a unique position
among tango fans, who eventually came to see him as a living legend—"the last
living myth of the tango," as he was sometimes called in the 1960s.

His afternoons and evenings at the Café Germinal gave Piazzolla an overwhelming desire to join Troilo's orchestra. One of the band's violinists, Hugo
Baralis, previously a member of Elvino Vardaro's sextet, noticed Piazzolla drum-
ming his fingers on a café table and engaged him in conversation. Baralis was
astonished to learn and scarcely could believe that Piazzolla knew the band's whole
repertory by heart. The two young men chatted about fishing, bicycles, Baralis's
bass player father, and shoes. Baralis recommended a shoe store on the Calle
Florida. They ended up fishing on the Costanera, Buenos Aires's riverside prom-
enade. Piazzolla had met the man he was to call, half a century later, "perhaps
the best friend I ever had." He and Baralis had endless chats about music and
musicians at the Café Germinal and elsewhere. Piazzolla also began pestering his
new friend to ask Troilo for an audition.[22]

His big chance soon came. Juan Miguel "Toto" Rodríguez, one of Troilo's
bandoneonists, suddenly fell sick. It was a Friday. Troilo urgently needed a replacement for his weekend jobs. Asking Baralis to talk to Troilo, Piazzolla hastened to the pension to pick up his bandoneon. Baralis had disappeared when he
returned to the café, and he simply approached Troilo himself. "So you are the
lad who knows all my repertory?" asked Troilo. "Well, get up there and play."
Piazzolla ran through a respectable tango repertory by ear. Troilo's elliptical way
of telling him that he had got the job was to say that he would now need a blue
suit, his musicians' uniform. Piazzolla was so thrilled that he played Gershwin's

Rhapsody in Blue for the band. "You won't win anybody over with that," the skeptical Orlando Goñi told him. "Leave that stuff for the Americans."[23]

So, in December 1939, Piazzolla got the opportunity for which he had longed. He seized it with both hands. The band was on the point of starting a series of broadcasts on Radio El Mundo.[24] Bandoneonist "Toto" Rodríguez soon returned, and Troilo's bandoneon-playing elder brother Marcos joined the group soon afterward. In early 1940 the orchestra had no less than five bandoneons. Piazzolla suddenly found himself earning 800 pesos (around $200) a month, more than sufficient to live on. (The bandleader Juan D'Arienzo paid 1,000 pesos, but Piazzolla would never have joined him.) Most of all, the band gave him his "little platoon," in Edmund Burke's phrase, the natural unit to which loyalty is given and from which comfort is taken. It also meant his full initiation into the tango world, with its smoke-filled nightclubs, its brilliant music and dancing, and also its seedy underside of alcoholic excess, sex, and drugs.

Hearing of his son's new job, Vicente Piazzolla motorcycled across the pampa, went to see Troilo at his home, and ate a succulent pasta dish cooked by Doña Felisa, Troilo's adored mother. "You're much older than my boy," Vicente told the bandleader. "Look after him for me, please." Troilo, who in fact was only seven years older, interpreted the request in his own peculiar way. The night after Vicente chugged back to Mar del Plata, he took Piazzolla off for a late night session of *pase inglés* in a low-life haunt in Avellaneda, the sprawling working-class suburb to the south of the federal capital. "Like Chicago in the 1930s," was Piazzolla's description. Troilo was astounded by Piazzolla's skill at cards and by his tales of youthful scrapes in New York. "You are the devil in person," said Troilo. "May God save you!"[25]

Troilo's love of nocturnal forays and food and drink was lifelong and passionate. His second nickname, "El Gordo" ("Fat Man"), was well earned. Earlier, in his weeks with Francisco Lauro's band, Piazzolla had taken a strong dislike to this kind of late night roistering. In cabarets such as the Novelty, there were often fights between the cabaret girls who were frustrated by the endless routine of serving drinks and dancing. Piazzolla was well aware, too, of the drugs that circulated in the cabarets. Some of his colleagues told him that cocaine was a useful aid for getting through the long nights. He tried it and found it "a frightful experience." When he attempted to write music under its influence, "all that came out were chords I myself didn't even understand."[26] There is, in fact, circumstantial evidence from family and friends that he occasionally reverted to sniffing cocaine over the ensuing years.

Though a large part of his future career was spent playing in nightspots, Piazzolla was never to lose his inner distaste for them. But the pressure of his peer group was strong. Many of his fellow musicians lived with women (sometimes more than one) they had picked up in the cabarets. As a member of a prestigious band, Piazzolla could easily have followed their example. He was not tempted by cabaret girls and had a horror of venereal disease, instilled by his father. Back in Mar del Plata a year or two earlier (or so he claimed in a 1983 interview), he had taken two friends to a brothel. " 'Well,' I said to myself, 'since I'm here, I might as well take advantage of it.' It was *so* disagreeable, the smell of paraffin, the dirt, that bed. I made the decision never to go back to a place like that."[27] Nonetheless, his solitary life in the pension depressed him. He missed his family. Whenever possible he went back to Mar del Plata to spend time with his parents or to go hunting and fishing with his cousins. Despite his enviable position in the Troilo band, his feelings of loneliness ran deep. He eventually confessed them to his friend Hugo Baralis while they were eating ravioli prepared by Doña Manuela, Baralis's mother. Baralis thought he had an answer.

Dedé

Odette María Wolff, known as "Dedé," was born on 28 November 1923, the youngest of three sisters. Their father, Emilio Wolff, an Argentine of German-French ancestry and a hard-working accountant, was very affectionate to his daughters. Their mother, Dolores "Lola" Filgueira, who came from Galicia, was stricter. As a girl, Dedé became fond of clothes for playing dress-up, of jigsaw puzzles, and of the gas-filled balloons she purchased when having her hair done. Her quickly discovered talent for drawing and painting meant that on completing her primary education, she desperately wanted to enter the Escuela Nacional de Bellas Artes, the national fine arts school (in those days possible after sixth grade). Doña Lola forbade this because her daughter would see nude models. Instead, she studied French for a year at the Alliance Française, and enrolled in a private art school near the Once railroad terminus.

Dedé's sisters, Poupée and Liebe, attended the same night school as Olga and Delia, the sisters of Hugo Baralis, and became their good friends. At their brother's request, Olga and Delia invited the Wolff girls and their parents to a tea party in the family apartment on 21 September 1940. Piazzolla was already there when they arrived. Dedé found him "a rather ugly boy, round faced." She thought that he was paying more attention to her sister Liebe, but in fact he was not. Doña Lola suddenly announced that the Baralises were all invited to Liebe's twenty-first birthday party, on October 19. "Señora," Piazzolla asked her, "Can I come too, since I'm on my own?" Doña Lola had taken to him, so she agreed. Piazzolla followed the Wolffs out of the Baralis apartment, telling them that he was off to Mar del Plata the next day for a weekend of hunting with his cousins.

Piazzolla was so excited by Dedé that he told his parents that he now had a *novia*, a girlfriend. It became true soon enough. On his return to Buenos Aires, he phoned Dedé (who had more or less forgotten him) to confirm the October 19 invitation. At the time, Dedé was infatuated with a young man doing military service. (She learned later that the young man was on the point of declaring his love for her at the birthday party.) October 19 duly came. After the music and dancing, when it was time for the cake, Baralis's sisters insisted that Dedé and Piazzolla share a plate. Dedé felt mildly embarrassed. "Have you ever tried Rochefort cheese chocolates?" asked Piazzolla. "Oh, Astor, what's this about Rochefort cheese chocolates?" replied Dedé, avoiding his eyes. "They're very tasty," he said. "And well," Dedé recalls, "he suddenly seemed friendly. But as for falling in love . . . No way."

He courted Dedé in his own manner. A few days later he met her at her art school and offered to escort her home. Dedé refused to go by taxi, he refused to go by bus, so they walked the fifteen or so blocks to the Wolffs' apartment at Avenida Jujuy 743. They passed a crowd of people waiting to go into a cinema. He took her hand. "You, what do you think?" he asked. "The people who see us holding hands must think we are fiancés." When Dedé arrived home, her mother normally gave her a glass of beaten egg yolk lightly laced with port, an old Argentine custom. Piazzolla asked, "Will you do one for me?" Doña Lola was still favorably struck by him, and he was soon given permission to "visit." The first time he did so, he went straight to the kitchen and prepared strawberries and cream. Later he showed Dedé his right leg, arousing in her the determination to "rid him of that complex." On his next visit, he brought his bandoneon and entranced the household. "I like the boy. A lad with good intentions," declared Doña Lola.

Piazzolla and Dedé started going out. A surviving program shows that on Thursday, 24 October, they were at the Real Cinema on Calle Esmeralda. A week later they had their photos taken in Buenos Aires's splendid Palermo Park, with Doña Lola chaperoning. On his own photo Piazzolla inscribed, "May nobody in the world separate you from my side, for I love you with all my heart." Dedé was still not at all sure she was in love with Piazzolla. A few months later, nevertheless, Piazzolla announced his intention of having a "man-to-man" talk with Dedé's father Don Emilio. It was "like the movies," Dedé recounts.

We closed the door of the little room where my father and Astor were, and we three sisters eavesdropped from the dining room behind the door. Astor said, "Look, Don Emilio, don't form a bad opinion of me just because I work in a cabaret. My intentions are different. I am going to study music, and conduct a symphony orchestra. I hate the atmosphere of the cabaret, and I'm going to leave it very soon." Papa summoned us in, and we went to buy some pizzas. And so I became a fiancée.

She was eighteen. Her husband-to-be was almost twenty.

In Mar del Plata, Vicente and Asunta were mildly worried to learn that Astor was engaged to a painter. Once again Vicente motorcycled across the pampa, accompanied by Uncle Octavio Manetti. Any worries about Dedé vanished immediately; the two were instantly taken with her. However, at the Wolffs, they did not even sit down, merely saying that they approved of the proposed marriage and hoped that it could take place soon. Dedé herself still had rather mixed feelings, but she was eager to set up a household of her own. "I am going to be the best housewife in the world," she told herself.

She soon saw how her fiancé lived at his pension. (He later moved into an apartment at Calle Urquiza 41 that was rented for him by his parents, who sometimes stayed there themselves in the winter.) He had asked her for a photograph. Dedé chose a picture taken at her first communion and delivered it, accompanied by her mother and her sister Poupée. Piazzolla's aunts Rosita and Teresa had cleaned the room from top to bottom. Piazzolla served tea to his guests. He later told Dedé of some of the mischief he got into at the pension: how he and a friend, for instance, had plunged the Paraguayan maid, Argentina, into a full bath and how later she had gone after him with a knife. "One of these days," Argentina told Dedé, "I'll kill him; he's really bad, *señorita*, really bad. You don't know who you're marrying."

Dedé was not deterred. She began to take a greater interest in her fiancé's work. Listening to Troilo's band on the radio, she tried to pick out his bandoneon. They seemed an ideal couple. Dedé, the aspiring painter, could well understand Piazzolla's artistic impulses. He began to seem indispensable to her. Whenever they were separated, he devotedly wrote to her. On a visit to Montevideo with the Troilo orchestra in February 1941, he prefaced a letter, "Tomorrow: one year, five months since I fell in love with you." Visiting Córdoba with the band, he told Dedé how much he longed to honeymoon with her in the nearby mountains. In February 1942, again in Montevideo, he underlined his feelings, "I am madly in love with you, and everyone knows it. God! the only things I think about are you and my music, which are the things I most love."[28]

"You and my music. . . ." About the time he met Dedé, Piazzolla learned that the world famous pianist Arthur Rubinstein was staying in Buenos Aires, in an apartment in the plush Barrio Norte.* Their encounter was to become one of Piazzolla's great standard reminiscences: Rubinstein opening the door with a stained napkin dangling from his collar; his comments when Piazzolla played part of a "piano concerto" (in fact a sonata) he had composed; Rubinstein's question, "Do you seriously want to study?" Piazzolla's spluttered "yes"; Rubinstein's phone call to Juan José Castro, one of Argentina's most eminent musicians. As it happened, Castro could not take Piazzolla as a pupil, but he recommended a younger colleague, the rising composer Alberto Ginastera, then in his middle twenties. Rubinstein gave Piazzolla a signed photo and saw him out the door. The brief encounter was all-important to Piazzolla. Ginastera had no experience of private teaching but agreed to accept him. The lessons lasted for the next five or six years.

Astor and Dedé held their formal engagement party on 10 May 1942. It was attended by several notables from the tango world who were, says Dedé, "crazy . . . that [Astor] was leaving the milieu." Hugo Baralis was now courting Dedé's sister Poupée, and he chose this occasion to detach her from her current boyfriend. However, the romance did not prosper. Soon afterward, when Baralis and Poupée became engaged, Piazzolla told Poupée that he had seen the engagement ring before: on the finger of a certain cabaret girl to whose apartment Baralis had access. He also told Don Emilio, who advised Poupée to break off the engagement. She did. Whatever the truth behind Piazzolla's tale-telling, it was a gratuitous act that made both Poupée and Baralis very miserable. In time, both forgave him, though Poupée was aware from then on that her brother-in-law's personality was more complex than it appeared.

The wedding took place at the end of October 1942, in a civil ceremony on 29 October at the Registro Civil No. 6 in Avenida Belgrano, and two days later at the neoclassical church of Nuestra Señora de Monserrat, farther down the same avenue. Vicente and Asunta and several *marplatense* relatives were in attendance. Piazzolla's youthful appearance deceived the parish priest officiating, Father Emilio Rodríguez. "I entered the church," Dedé later recalled, "and the priest said to

---

*In his autobiography *My Many Years* (New York 1980), pp. 475–76, Rubinstein recounts that he was in Buenos Aires for a few weeks in the second half of 1940, between leaving Europe and settling in the United States. He does not specify months, so the exact date of the Piazzolla-Rubinstein encounter eludes us.

someone: 'Look, the bride is here, and the bridegroom hasn't turned up.' The bridegroom was standing there at the altar with my mother."²⁹ It was a rainy day. Dedé remembered that her first meeting with Astor had also been on a rainy day. She shed a few tears.

Astor and Dedé spent their wedding night in room 1147 at the City Hotel on Calle Bolívar, downtown, and then set off on their honeymoon in the Córdoba sierras. On the train to Córdoba, a fellow passenger looked just a bit too lingeringly at Dedé. Piazzolla stood up and said: "What are you looking at? That's *my* wife!" They began their honeymoon at the Hotel San Martín at La Falda, an agreeable mountain resort. On the second day, Dedé had to throw herself from an out-of-control sulky they had rented, badly spraining her foot. They soon tired of the jokes made about themselves and other honeymooners at the Hotel San Martín and moved to another resort, Capilla del Monte. Dedé was already aware that her husband sometimes walked in his sleep; they had phoned her about it from his pension, on an occasion when he was found talking gibberish and looking at the telephone book. Now she experienced it firsthand. Wakened by blows on her back one night, she found her new husband, wild-eyed, punching in all directions. She shook him awake. "What are you *doing*?" he asked, and immediately went back to sleep. On a later occasion she woke to find him sleeping on the floor. He had taken all the blankets.

Back in Buenos Aires, the couple moved into their first home, a ground floor apartment at Calle Jujuy 895, not far from the Wolffs' home. The tango pianist Horacio Salgán lived in the same building, with the first of his five wives, Carmen Duval, a tango singer Dedé much admired. Vicente Piazzolla gave them a thousand pesos worth of furniture. Dedé found that she liked married life. "I fell crazily in love with Astor," she says. Their daughter Diana Irene was born on 25 July 1943 and their son Daniel Hugo on 28 February 1945. Around the time of Daniel's birth, Piazzolla and the "three Ds," as he took to calling them, moved to a first-floor apartment at Avenida Asamblea 1276 in Parque Chacabuco. It faced the park that gives the neighborhood its name. It was a long bus ride from downtown. The apartment was small and rather dark. Piazzolla had a small room for his work, with an upright piano; there was no room for a grand.

In Aníbal Troilo's Band

It seemed that no force in the world could stop the music in Calle Corrientes in those years. It was the party to end all parties: the night had a whole court of harlequins and columbines, pulcinellas, deceitful princes and decent clowns. . . . On every side, the tango was king.[30]

So the singer Edmundo Rivero (one of the tango's few successful basses) remembered the 1940s. Piazzolla himself remembered the time even more poetically. "God flew over Buenos Aires and touched the city with His hand . . . ," he said in 1986. "Buenos Aires was really miraculous in the 1940s."[31] Far removed from the catastrophes that swept across the northern hemisphere in those years, the lights of the Argentine capital shone as brightly as ever, brighter in fact than ever before. The entertainment scene was never more vigorous. The decade was a spectacular one all round for the tango, the last great flowering of its thirty-year golden age. The dance was danced everywhere: in the open air, in cabarets and dance halls, in the social clubs then springing up on all sides, at trade union festivities, even in the shadow of the great stadiums of the soccer clubs. There were hundreds of *orquestas típicas* to meet the demand, and they were very busy: Troilo's band did an average of more than thirty dances every month. Tangos swamped the airwaves and the record stores. Popular magazines with wide circulations chronicled the doings of the musicians and singers, genuine popular idols of the time, whose fans often organized themselves in passionate *barras* (gangs).

No band of the 1940s was more highly regarded than Troilo's. Piazzolla's membership in the band gave him a superb apprenticeship as a musician and left its permanent mark on him as a *tanguero*. As he would recall:

> When I joined Troilo I tried to imitate many of his things. . . . I learned the tricks of the *tangueros*, those intuitive tricks that helped me later on. I couldn't define them technically; they are forms of playing, forms of feeling; it's something that comes from inside, spontaneously. At the outset I was just one of the bandoneons Troilo had in the orchestra, but I wanted to be the number one, and I got there. El Gordo trusted me.[32]

The status of Troilo's band also meant that Piazzolla had a privileged place in the tango world. It allowed him to mix with some of its leading figures, men like the great Enrique Santos Discépolo (author of some of the most classic tango songs ever written) or the lyricists Homero Manzi and Enrique Cadícamo, who sometimes invited him to their tables at the Café Germinal or the Tibidabo cabaret,[33] Troilo's legendary stronghold from its opening in April 1942. (It is a shame

Piazzolla did not reminisce more about his encounters with such figures.) Many of the tango musicians who first won fame in the 1940s remained in this world for the rest of their lives. But Piazzolla's eclectic musical background and tastes, and his inner urge to move on, were already beginning to drive him in a different direction. Thanks to his meeting with Rubinstein and his introduction to Ginastera, he was studying music again, with dedicated seriousness. This meant a grueling routine where the demands of study, family life, and his work for Troilo were sometimes hard to reconcile.

After his nightly stint with Troilo's band (and the frequent billiards sessions afterward), he often arrived home at the time Dedé's alarm clock sounded, and they would breakfast together. He went for his classes with Alberto Ginastera twice a week, on Tuesdays and Fridays at 8:00 A.M., a long crosstown bus ride to the remote Barracas district. Ginastera was better as a composer than as a teacher, Piazzolla would later say, although he never lost his affection for him. Piazzolla found him withdrawn, introverted, somberly dressed, like "a Protestant pastor."[34] They were only five years apart in age, but they never used the intimate Spanish *tú*. The lessons themselves, however, proved vital for Piazzolla. Ginastera gave him a very thorough grounding in composition, orchestration, and harmony. He also encouraged him to attend the Saturday morning rehearsals of the musicians at the Teatro Colón, Buenos Aires's opera house, the largest and one of the most acoustically perfect in the world. He entered through a discreet side door, let in by a friend. He often listened with his back to the orchestra to familiarize himself with the different instruments. At home, he tested himself by listening to recordings, with Dedé checking the scores. The first time he did this, to Dedé's amusement, he sat with his back to the phonograph. Ginastera also urged Piazzolla to explore the world of culture more widely, telling him that musicians needed to know "everything," since music was "a totalizing art."[35] As a result, Piazzolla began reading seriously more than he had ever done before—writers such as Charles Baudelaire, Paul Verlaine, and Thomas Mann. As for painting, Dedé was already introducing him to impressionism, surrealism, and abstract art.

Piazzolla's new cultural interests heightened his growing disaffection from the world of the cabarets and nightly performances. Reynaldo Nichele, violinist and founding member of the Troilo band, remembers him saying that musicians "were all pimps, that he was the only one who studied." His studying raised the hackles of those band members who had always played by ear. Moreover Ginastera's teaching encouraged him to experiment with his own music, even in his work with the band. Sometimes, after Troilo had gone for the night, Piazzolla stayed behind with colleagues like Baralis, Goñi, the bass player Enrique "Kicho" Díaz, and his violinist brother David. They would "jam" for pleasure, usually imitating the styles of Elvino Vardaro and Julio De Caro, with Piazzolla adding complex and difficult chords to the arrangements. Pichuco caught them at it one night. He was not pleased.

Violinist Hugo Baralis was always aware that his friend was "a rare bird in that environment," that his odd mixture of Spanish and English, not to mention the loud jackets and striped shirts from New York, marked him as different from his fellows. And "worse still, he had played with Gardel but talked about Bach."[36] His musicianship, however, was often noted outside the Troilo band. The Polish-born violinist Simón Bajour, then working in an *orquesta de cambio* (a reserve band that filled in for the main bands when they had a day off or were playing at dances), met Piazzolla around this time and remembers him as someone "who was beginning to stand out, simply because he was a musician who had been well trained." The young lawyer Víctor Sasson, a passionate follower of the Troilo band, recalls that "people had their eye on him; he was very intelligent, and very arrogant."

Troilo himself conceived a strong affection for Piazzolla, and Troilo's wife Zita liked him too. (She bought large quantities of Asunta Piazzolla's beauty cream.) It was Troilo who gave Piazzolla one of his longest lasting nicknames, "Gato" ("Cat"), because, said Troilo, he was always coming and going, but perhaps too because of his piercing, laserlike gaze. (Lasers had not yet been invented; when they were, "Laser" was another nickname given Piazzolla by some of his musicians.) Troilo also sometimes called him *el yoni* (Johnny, i.e., Englishman or American), because of the English vestiges in his speech. When unable to play, he sometimes asked Piazzolla to take the role of lead bandoneon, something resented by the other bandoneonists. Piazzolla also occasionally acted as a pianist when Orlando Goñi was too drunk to appear.

Yet Troilo, despite his growing confidence in *el yoni*, was never really reconciled to Piazzolla's adventurousness. His own much reiterated preference was for "danceable" music. Piazzolla wanted to create music that appealed to the ear rather than the feet. But he was not yet composing it. In 1941 he and Baralis wrote a tango, "Por culpa mía," with words by Enrique Dizeo, and it took them half a year. As Piazzolla recalled, "I had not yet ... been touched with the magic wand of composition."[37] Much of his creative energy in these years went into arrangements of tangos. He pestered Troilo to allow him to make arrangements for the band, and Troilo eventually gave in on an occasion when his main arranger, Argentino Galván, was indisposed. He allowed Piazzolla to make what he could of "Azabache," a *candombe* that the band was to play in a competition organized by Radio El Mundo for its highly popular and now legendary *Ronda de Ases* tango program. Piazzolla's inclusion of rising violin scales and counterpoint raised a few eyebrows, but, as it happened, "Azabache" won first prize in the competition. Troilo, though warning Piazzolla not to be too daring, permitted him to make further arrangements, and he did at least half a dozen more while still with the band.[38] He worked at lightning speed, sometimes dashing his arrangements off over cups of coffee in a *confitería*. He was already showing his astonishing ability to work fast.

The arrangements quickly became more adventurous, though Piazzolla, like arranger Argentino Galván, never altered Orlando Goñi's piano parts; they were already simply too good. Piazzolla's arrangements were marked, as he recalled, by "all the new things: harmony, counterpoint, orchestration, things I was learning from Ginastera."[39] The results were not to everyone's liking. On hearing Piazzolla's version of the vintage tango "Inspiración" with its long cello introduction, his fellow musicians asked him: "Lad, are you crazy or did you just get it wrong?" or "Do you think you're at the Teatro Colón?"[40] When the tango was played at a Carnival dance for the Boca Juniors soccer club, the dancers froze. Some moved closer to the band to listen. Others simply left. Piazzolla's arrangement of another old tango, "Chiqué," had a similar effect, only this time the dancers whistled and threw things at the stage. On yet another occasion, Piazzolla pointed at the people clustered near the orchestra and asked Troilo: "See how people want to *listen* to the music?"[41]

Such incidents brought growing puzzlement from Troilo. "Gato, you're a demon," he would exclaim. He even appealed to Dedé: "Stop Astor, he's turning my band into a symphony orchestra!" He took to editing Piazzolla's drafts, erasing half the notes. Troilo's formidable genius, it must be remembered, was for playing, not arranging. He was peculiarly dependent on his arrangers. But he knew his job, and most of all, he knew his clientèle, the dance-besotted public. Piazzolla's experiments, from his viewpoint, were not "commercial," as he often put it.

Nor did Piazzolla's experiments go down well with the more conventional members of the orchestra. Baralis, Díaz, and Goñi were constantly supportive, but other band members were positively hostile. They began putting garbage in his bandoneon case. Piazzolla was well able to retaliate. He was already well known in the band for his practical jokes. Hugo Baralis remembers picking him up on the way to work and always asking him, " 'Do you have everything, Astor?' the firecrackers, itching powder, stink bombs, snuff, the whole arsenal we took to carry out the devilry we did." According to violinist Reynaldo Nichele, Vicente Piazzolla sometimes phoned his son to order items from the "arsenal" for his own devilry in Mar del Plata. One of Piazzolla's later claims was that he sometimes placed firecrackers in private boxes at cabarets where the curtains were drawn, a recognized sign that the clients inside were having sex. Two visitors to the Tibi-dabo cabaret who went in for this, according to him, were Colonel Juan Domingo Perón and Eva Duarte.[42] We may question whether Colonel Perón got the fire-cracker treatment. He was already seen as the coming man of the nationalist military regime that had taken control in Argentina in June 1943. The music publisher Máximo Perrotti, one of Piazzolla's new friends, met him one night at the Tibidabo. "Sit somewhere away from the orchestra box, and pay attention to the second number," Piazzolla told him. As the second number began, a dramatic explosion shook the glasses off the tables near the stage, causing general panic. Piazzolla looked as if butter would not melt in his mouth. He told Perrotti af-terward that he had devised a time fuse with flypaper, and had lit it in the men's room during the interval between numbers.[43]

Troilo's patience with these pranks was not inexhaustible. When Piazzolla play-fully slapped his cheek with some itching powder one night, he immediately fired both Piazzolla and Baralis from the band. However, he soon took them back again, but the writing clearly was on the wall. Baralis was the first to go, in 1943, dis-missed for failing to turn up one night as well as "for a thousand reasons," as Troilo told Baralis's father. Piazzolla left the following year. It happened simply enough. Francisco Fiorentino, Troilo's main vocalist since 1937 had become one of the most admired voices of the 1940s, largely because of his association with Troilo. Believing, mistakenly as it turned out, he could do better as a soloist, he threw in his lot with a band formed by pianist Orlando Goñi, who had left Troilo in August 1943. Goñi needed a bandoneonist and arranger. Hugo Baralis, already recruited as a violinist, agreed to approach Piazzolla. In a café near the Tibidabo cabaret, he somewhat furtively told him that there might be an opening with a new orchestra. "Yes! But with whom?" asked Piazzolla. Baralis refused to tell him, thinking that Piazzolla might immediately spread the word at the Tibidabo. In-stead, he took his friend to see Fiorentino and Goñi, and Piazzolla agreed to join them. The Fiorentino-Goñi team started work in April 1944.

Troilo's feelings were certainly badly ruffled when the break finally came. His mother, Doña Felisa, phoned Dedé while Piazzolla was standing beside her at the telephone and said to her: "Tell Astor he's an ungrateful wretch. Tell him he'll be sorry for the rest of his life." He was not. Yet he never failed to recognize that the years with Troilo were his apprenticeship, a magnificent one by any standard and in the tango world, unbeatable. Like all apprenticeships, it had to end. It was time for him to leave the chrysalis, time to spread his wings. Looking back on the parting of the ways, Piazzolla was to sum it up very simply: "I left the band because I wanted to be *me*."[44] He soon would be.

The Road to Paris
1944‒1955

→ On His Own

The "Three Ds" ↔

→ Classical Composer?

Paris—and Nadia Boulanger ↔

> I was a sort of Dr. Jekyll and Mr. Hyde. They cut me in two.
> —Astor Piazzolla, talking to Walter Acosta of the BBC (1980)

On His Own

Singer Francisco Fiorentino's partnership with Orlando Goñi did not last long. Goñi was steadily drinking himself to death (he would die in February 1945 in Montevideo), and after a few weeks a desperate Fiorentino told Piazzolla and Hugo Baralis to reorganize the band. "And put whatever name you want on it," "Fiore" added. It was Piazzolla who spoke up: "I'm the arranger; put my name on it."[1] "Francisco Fiorentino with Orchestra conducted by Astor Piazzolla" made its formal debut on 2 September 1944 at the Círculo Almagro in the Villa Urquiza district[2] and started with broadcasts on Radio Belgrano and regular stints at night-spots like Tango Bar, the Piccadilly dance hall, and the Café Ebro. Between May 1945 and May 1946 the band recorded twenty-two songs and two instrumental numbers on twelve 78-rpm discs for the Odeon label. It had a particular success in August 1945 in Montevideo, at the Café Ateneo and Chantecler cabaret, and on Radio El Espectador. The orchestra, Piazzolla reported enthusiastically to Dedé (in the week of Hiroshima and Nagasaki), was "the revelation of the century." People were "crazy" about it, were saying that the musicians "surpassed Troilo, etc."[3]

Fiorentino respected Piazzolla's desire to make innovative arrangements. Piazzolla's fundamental rhythmic preference from then until the end of his career—3-3-2—was used fairly systematically in arrangements he made for the band. (3-3-2 is the subdivision of a 4/4 bar, in uneven groups of eighth notes with emphasis on the first, fourth, and sixth eighth notes: in a 2/4 bar, which Piazzolla used only in his early pieces, it would be sixteenth notes.) Piazzolla sometimes restrained himself for the sake of the partnership. But not always. He did everything possible to make the band sound "*musical*,"[4] as he later said. The dancers did not always like this. The cabaret girls at the Marabú, hearing the very long and complicated cello introduction he had written for the tango "Copas, amigas y besos," mocked him by dancing on the tips of their toes like ballerinas, and with the old taunt, "Do you think you are at the Teatro Colón?" But the new band quickly attracted fans. Rafael Pereyra, then a jazz clarinetist, was enjoying a game of darts in the nightspot where the orchestra was playing, and was astonished: "The darts stayed in my hand. I'd never heard a tango band opening with that kind of chord before." A young violinist, José Carli, sat for hours over a single cup of coffee at the Tango Bar to hear the band over and over again, rather like Piazzolla at the Café Germinal in 1939.

Working with Fiorentino was unlikely to satisfy Piazzolla for very long. His classes with Ginastera, his chats with musicians at the Teatro Colón, the lessons he now began taking with the classical pianist Raúl Spivak, and even his swapping of Stan Kenton records with friends showed his determination to find a new musical path. Meanwhile Fiorentino began to resent the way in which Piazzolla's growing prominence as a bandleader was putting him in the shade. "Astor wanted to form his own orchestra, to have his own band," Dedé remembers, "without instructions from third parties, to play his own pieces, not other people's." The partnership ended, amicably enough, in June 1946.

Piazzolla was now ready to take the decisive step. Dedé encouraged him to take it. The Orquesta Típica de Astor Piazzolla (the "1946 band," as it is now usually called) started work on Radio El Mundo and at the Café Marzotto and Tango Bar on Avenida Corrientes. Within a matter of weeks, on 22 September, it cut its first disc for the Odeon label. Some of the musicians in the former Fiorentino ensemble migrated to the new band, the two most important being violinist Hugo Baralis and the bandoneonist Roberto Di Filippo, one of Piazzolla's stalwart friends and someone he much admired: "a machine gun firing notes," he told his *marplatense* pianist-friend Pedro Blumetti. Pianist Atilio Stampone considers Di Filippo "the fundamental individual" of the orchestra.[5] Di Filippo's influence on Piazzolla's own bandoneon style was significant. In particular, he developed

Piazzolla's use of the right hand. Di Filippo himself would remember his work in the band as a challenge. He found that Piazzolla's "perfectionism, his high demands," meant that some people regarded him as "a despot, haughty, unjust. But they didn't realize that he was giving us something." Piazzolla liked to go to movies and to discuss classical music with Di Filippo. By introducing him to an oboist at the Teatro Colón, he was to change his friend's career. Di Filippo took up the oboe, and in 1951 joined the Colón orchestra. Two years later, when he married, he sold his four bandoneons to help meet his expenses.[6]

Among the newcomers recruited to the band, the twenty-year-old pianist Atilio Stampone was, at the time, doing his military service and sometimes turned up in uniform. Later, he was to have a brilliant career of his own. This was also true of the young bandoneonist Leopoldo Federico. Federico was impressed by Piazzolla's arrangements and persuaded his friend Di Filippo to copy some of them out. However, when asked to join the band, he got scared and avoided the Café Marzotto. Only when Di Filippo left the orchestra in 1948 did Federico finally consent to join it. Initially intimidated by the repertory, he came, like Di Filippo, to find the work tough but rewarding. The atmosphere, he remembers, was far from heavy. Piazzolla "never took things tremendously seriously, always with a longing for jokes. All was merriment."

All tango orchestras in the 1940s included singers as a matter of course. At various periods, Piazzolla employed the vocalists Alfredo Barone, Aldo Campoamor, Héctor Insúa, Fernando Reyes, Alberto Fontán Luna, and Oscar Ferrari for a month or so just before the band dissolved. Fontán Luna remembers that when he was selected, there were scores of other candidates. Another singer, seventeen-year-old Angel "Paya" Díaz, met Piazzolla briefly in 1947 and said to him: "Look, I earn 20 pesos per dance. If you pay me 25, I'll sing with you." The deal fell through. Díaz, on his own admission, had no real idea who Piazzolla was. Angel Fiasché, along with Emilio Vieyra, acted as presenter for the 1946 band at Tango Bar and on the radio, and recalls that Roberto Rufino, one of the most considerable voices of the time, auditioned for Piazzolla, but that nothing came of it. Aldo Campoamor did most of the singing on the band's thirty recordings made between 1946 and 1948. The records themselves did not always win approval. Soon after recording Juan Canaro's tango "Ahí va el dulce" in July 1948, Piazzolla ran into him at the Perrottis' publishing offices and asked him whether he had heard the record. "Yes, you ruined it!" replied Canaro, a traditionalist composer and bandleader. Piazzolla grabbed him by the nose, and Canaro punched him. Máximo Perrotti's father, Alfredo, as Máximo remembers, sternly imposed order.

The 1946 band added a fresh tone to the sounds of the 1940s in Buenos Aires.

Its repertory was conventional, but Piazzolla displayed free rein in his arranging talent, introducing syncopated accents and subtle key changes into the bandoneon parts, with counterpoint effects from violin solos and the piano constantly marking out his 3-3-2 rhythmic arrangement. Piazzolla's semirevolutionary versions of tango classics soon won the interest of the more innovative tango musicians, including bandleader Osvaldo Pugliese and the brilliant pianist Horacio Salgán, to name but two. Aníbal Troilo was another, telling Piazzolla, "Gato, you never get a note wrong!"[7] And he praised the orchestra in the press. "The lad's very good," he declared. The news story where this opinion appeared, in August 1947, indicates that Piazzolla was enjoying something of a burst of popularity.

> Astor Piazzolla is the Benjamin of the tango family. He is also welcome. He is barely 25 and at that age it seems impossible to have a past, other than the past that instant success gives him, a tale told by the public with the applause it showers on him in cafés and at dances. Even so, Astor Piazzolla has an unusual background. He never experienced the stimulating and inevitable Buenos Aires scene of kerosene street lamps, and organ grinders, and everything else. He grew up among the skyscrapers. It is his fate to reconcile opposites, as we can see, which explains how he can offer us the most stubborn tango hits of the old days with chords that seem almost Stravinskian.[8]

Stravinskian or not, Piazzolla himself was still fully involved in the tango world: the late nights, the billiard sessions, the long chats with fellow bandoneonists like the young Roberto Pansera, at whose mother's house in the Constitución district he sometimes ate fried green beans and garlic. This habit got Pansera into trouble with Dedé, who would chide him on the phone for sending her husband home "smelling of garlic." But Piazzolla's attachment to the tango milieu was gradually weakening. The world of the cabaret and dance hall was becoming "a daily nightmare."[9] His urge to study was stronger than ever. He was now seriously analyzing scores composed by Bartók, Prokofiev, and Stravinsky. For several years he had been trying to compose classical music. A suite written for harp and string orchestra, which he labeled Opus 1, was performed in 1945 on Radio Nacional under the baton of Bruno Bandini. Most of his efforts were chamber works, such as cello pieces, piano suites, and a piano sonata, Opus 7 (1945), that was premiered at La Plata in 1948 by Alberto Tauriello. Alberto Ginastera thought the sonata good enough to use at the Conservatory.[10]

Many of these works, in fact, were performed on the radio or in concert halls.

Piazzolla's classical aspirations were no secret, although he also wrote a handful of tangos during these years. One tango, "El Desbande" (1946), he later considered his first true tango; it is certainly the most interesting of the four of his own compositions that he recorded with the 1946 band. At the time he probably considered such pieces less important than his classical efforts. Classical composing merely widened the gap between the tango world and Piazzolla. He became more and more frustrated. He told Roberto Pansera, "I don't want to play the bandoneon any more. I'm ashamed to go through the streets with my bandoneon." He said much the same thing to Roberto Di Filippo, making Di Filippo suspect "he was going to ditch the squeezebox for good." Accompanying Piazzolla to the Teatro Colón rehearsals or to concerts and opera performances, Di Filippo noticed that "listening to classical music rejuvenated Piazzolla."[11]

Meanwhile, the 1946 band picked up what engagements it could, doing specially well on its annual visits to Montevideo. In 1947 it played the soundtrack for and appeared in *El hombre del sábado*, a movie directed by Leopoldo Torres Ríos (father of the more famous Leopoldo Torre Nilsson). And it continued to win admirers, some of them rather unexpected. The American conductor Igor Markevitch applauded the band one evening at Tango Bar. On a night in November 1947, also at Tango Bar, Piazzolla was invited by a lanky, friendly American to sit at his table. The man was Aaron Copland, then on a tour of South America sponsored by the U.S. State Department. "Your tango is music," he told Piazzolla, "and *good* music. I've never heard anything like this."[12] Such encouragement was welcome, but for the moment, not enough. His tango environment seemed far too limited. He needed something more, needed to make a radical departure from tradition. So his studying continued. Radio Porteña bandleader "Chula" Clausi bumped into him one day on Buenos Aires's vast Avenida 9 de Julio, and Piazzolla told him he was waiting for a lesson from a visiting French music teacher. Also at this time, Piazzolla sometimes visited the house of Pablo Sorensen, who owned rare 16-millimeter films of Bartók and Schoenberg. The journalist Armando Rolón was to remember Piazzolla playing the piano in that setting, "partly Ravelian, partly Rubinstein. A byproduct of Bartók and Schoenberg—the tango too, of course."

None of this made working with the orchestra easier. And in any case, despite its initial success, the band was losing ground. The constraint was popular taste. The enthusiastic dance public of Buenos Aires wanted its bands to be dance bands; Piazzolla wanted his orchestra to be *listened to*. "The 1946 band was very modern for its time," he would recall. "For that reason we didn't have much work; the radio stations and the dance [organizers] didn't call on us. I was confronted by a whole lot of *tangueros* who saw my band as an inexplicable danger."[13] However, some, just a few, *were* prepared to listen, and saw the band as a sign of promise rather than a menace. A small, devoted contingent of *piazzollistas* was gradually forming. The teenage Francisco "Kico" Salvo, later a good friend, then growing up in Avellaneda, haunted the record stores in quest of the band's latest 78-rpm records. His friends thought him crazy. "Eh? you can't dance to this stuff," they told him. Such reactions meant that the handwriting was on the wall for Piazzolla's band.

By mid-1949 he was ready to call it quits. Running a tango orchestra at the time was not without its headaches. Argentina was now living through the euphoria of Juan Domingo Perón's first presidency, which, among other things, encouraged the spectacular growth of trade unionism (under Perón's own control). The atmosphere had its effects among musicians. Piazzolla ran his band on principles he was always to maintain: equal rewards for all members, with a double share for himself as bandleader and arranger. He certainly made enough to live on from his work with the band. There were evidently a few union-style demands from the musicians.[14] Much more serious was the pressure exerted on Piazzolla to perform and record suitably patriotic material and to play free for government-sponsored functions. In November 1948 he did record a couple of "suitable" numbers, one the rather harmless patriotic waltz "República Argentina." He never played it again. And in a moment of weakness and at the behest of a poet with Peronist connections, he composed a "Hymn to Perón" that he promptly destroyed. Piazzolla and Dedé were strongly anti-Peronist. Vicente and Asunta Piazzolla, by contrast, favored the Perón government. After July 1952, like many loyal *peronistas*, they kept one of their clocks permanently set at 8:25 P.M., the official time of Evita Perón's death.[15]

Although the band was still performing at a variety of venues in the city and suburbs, Peronist pressure was almost certainly the main reason that Piazzolla dissolved his band in mid-1949.[16] Dedé remembers a phone call from the actress Fanny Novarro, one of the numerous lady-friends of Juan Duarte, brother of the formidable Evita, and President Perón's private secretary. She relayed what amounted to an order for Piazzolla to play at a lavish benefit for Evita's powerful Social Aid Foundation. The show was to be held at Luna Park, Buenos Aires's main indoor sports stadium, on Thursday, 22 September 1949, with several leading *orquestas típicas* on hand.[17] "If there isn't a band, it can't perform," he told Dedé. Over the phone, Piazzolla informed Novarro that he could not attend; he had just dissolved his band.

Piazzolla held a farewell dinner for the musicians. They persuaded him to carry on for just a bit longer. Soon afterward Piazzolla himself had to take ten days off due to illness. The band tried to play without him. The suitcase holding its scores was stolen, and the musicians did their best to play from memory, but it was not good enough. Piazzolla's first band simply melted away—not with a bang but a whimper. A few months later he managed to reassemble some of its members to record four tangos with a string orchestra for the TK label.[18] But that was the end. The 1946 band passed into history.

Piazzolla disappeared from the world of the cabarets and cafés. Roberto Pansera remembers him saying: "I'm going to compose two tangos a year. With four recordings [a year] I can live. I can go on studying." He clearly saw such work, and his arranging, as his bread-and-butter. That was all it would be. As he put it in a 1987 interview with Fernando Gonzalez: "I thought 'the hell with tango, from now on I'll be Stravinsky,' and started writing symphonic trash."[19] He was being too hard on himself. Yet it was true, as he recalled in 1980, "I was a sort of Dr. Jekyll and Mr. Hyde. They cut me in two. When I was Mr. Hyde I wrote tangos, and when I was Dr. Jekyll I did the symphonic works."[20] Piazzolla got it the wrong way round. It was Dr. Jekyll who was the "real Piazzolla," and the homicidal Mr. Hyde who was writing the classical works. Musically, Mr. Hyde had the better of things for the next few years.

The "Three Ds"

At home, Piazzolla was the easygoing Dr. Jekyll. Dedé felt very happy. She had abandoned her art studies, promising herself she would return to them when the children grew up. She found her husband "very obliging, very freehanded with money." His earnings went straight into a closet, from which cash was taken as needed. He often bought her little presents, such as handbags and sweaters. There was plenty of pure fun at the Parque Chacabuco apartment. For example, while collecting washing with Dedé from the clotheslines on the roof of the apartment building, Piazzolla often raced downstairs with the sheets and tablecloths bundled into a tight knot on his head; or there was the nearly nightly ritual in bed, when Dedé would read horrifying thrillers aloud to her enraptured husband. "He was not bad-tempered. Never," she recalls. "Not at all. A family man."

Daughter Diana's first memories of her father were of him eating green apples as soon as he got up, a long enduring habit. She resented his spending so much time talking to her mother. Daniel found his father "super-entertaining, super-playful, loving." He would hoist the children to the top of the wardrobe in the bedroom, waiting for their screams to be let down. He invented mythical creatures for them; one of them was "Melgarejo," a monster with an enormous mouth who was always about to appear through the Córdoba sierras when the family vacationed there. The children learned to identify the distinctive whistle with which he announced his arrival home, "and it was as if God were arriving." His mood was usually sunny. When he was more withdrawn, it was because "he was composing something in his head."

By the time they were old enough to play in the Parque Chacabuco across the street, the children were becoming conscious of their father's central position in the household. "He was the genius, the person talked about. Nobody was allowed to put him in the shade," says Diana. "Everything was programmed for me to do my thing," Piazzolla later recalled.[21] If Daniel's fingers strayed to the piano at times when they should not have done, his father let out shrieks "that shook the house." He was perhaps slightly more attentive to Diana than to Daniel.

Sometimes Piazzolla took his children to work. As a small boy, Daniel watched the bands come and go at Tango Bar from the steps leading up to the stage. Often, Piazzolla allowed the children to sit and watch while he composed, impressing Daniel by the way he simply "sat down and wrote." Jazz and classical music were often played on the phonograph in the apartment, but never tangos.[22] There were many times when all "three Ds" went to listen to Piazzolla's band and to eat with him before or afterward. He was always "freehanded with the cash," Diana recalls.

During the children's school days, there were regular Saturday visits to the movies, either to the local Cine Asamblea or to the downtown theaters along Calle Lavalle, Buenos Aires's classic cinema street. "Today we're going to see three films!" Papa would announce. Sometimes, walking down Calle Lavalle, Piazzolla would let out a huge cry of "Let's gooooooh!"—a sign for the four of them to race to the next corner. A favorite restaurant for lunch was El Palacio de la Papa Frita; Piazzolla particularly liked its "inflated fried potatoes," still popular there today. Late at night, tired and happy, the foursome would ride home to Parque Chacabuco on the 109 bus.

Summer, for the children, meant Mar del Plata and their Piazzolla grandparents, Vicente and Asunta, known to the family as "los Noninos." It was Diana who first called her grandfather "Nonino," in time-honored Italian style.[23] At the end of each school year, Vicente would come to fetch them in his black 1947 Citroën. The Noninos doted on their grandchildren, stuffing their refrigerator with delights, barbecuing juicy steaks, and escorting them to Pepino's pizza parlor across the street. Their parents joined them for part of every summer. They always spent some of their time playing canasta—the new card game from Uruguay—

with Nonina. The family was usually there for Carnival, when Piazzolla was in his element, setting off firecrackers and squirting water pistols. As Diana remembers, "Then Mama put on a disguise, Papa put on a disguise, and off we all went to the carnival procession."

In Mar del Plata there were dozens of second and third cousins for the children to enjoy, and not least, their foul-mouthed great-uncle Hércules Provenzano, known as "Uncle Ercolino." Argentina Manetti's husband made his living by collecting bottles and tins in a cart. "The least cultured, but also the best man in the world," says Daniel. He was devoted to Nonina. Dedé adored him. The children quickly appreciated how much the Noninos loved Dedé. Vicente once told her, within earshot of Daniel, that if he was forced to choose between her and Astor, "I would take you," and on another occasion, he told Astor that if he ever did anything to Dedé, "I'll smash you." Dedé was the only woman Nonino ever allowed on his motorcycle. He liked her, he said, because she was not "stuck up." Dedé proved it by helping him occasionally in his bicycle store, as did Piazzolla.

Piazzolla's brother-in-law, Horacio Mártire, Liebe's husband, remembers the Noninos at this period as "divine. Nonina was picturesque," he says, "and Nonino was a philosopher. When he spoke, you paid attention." Nelly Sorrentino, who had recently married cousin Egnio Bertolami, first got to know the family during these years. She was struck, as were Horacio and Liebe, by the affection Astor and Dedé showed each other, and by their relationship with Nonino and Nonina— "something beautiful." She found Piazzolla "very cheerful, very funny, always joking."

When he was in Mar del Plata, Piazzolla spent part of his time composing with a harmonium in a tranquil *quinta* (small farm) belonging to one of his uncles. He usually sought out local musicians such as bandoneonists Roberto Tedeschi and Manuel de Miguel, or pianist Pedro Blumetti. When Aníbal Troilo vacationed in Mar del Plata, as he did every summer, there were merry gatherings. Blumetti recalls a barbecue at Tedeschi's house, when Piazzolla played a Rachmaninoff prelude and a Bach toccata and fugue, his bandoneon sounding like "an organ, incredible." "Now that this monster has played, I'm going to," said Troilo. Piazzolla turned to him: "Play, Gordo, because there are things you do that I shall *never* be able to do."

In the winter, whenever possible, Piazzolla took the family for a two-week vacation to Río Ceballos, north of Córdoba, where the Noninos owned a house (called "Astor"). Sometimes the Noninos took the children instead, and cousin Enriqueta Bertolami also went fairly often. It was during one of these winter vacations that Nonino stopped giving Dedé motorcycle rides, after a mishap when the machine fell on her.

Piazzolla maintained a strict barrier between his family and his musical life. Sometimes he auditioned musicians at home; they were rarely there otherwise, though Hugo Baralis and the singer Aldo Campoamor occasionally visited. The violinist Simón Bajour remembers family outings—"the women and the children to one side, he and I on the other, talking about music." In general, the Piazzollas did little or no entertaining at home. The children were not encouraged to bring their friends to the apartment and played with them elsewhere. However, Diana and Daniel definitely approved of some of their father's friends—for instance, Aníbal and Zita Troilo, who took them all for car rides. Others were more disconcerting. One day, at Argentine writer Ernesto Sábato's house with Daniel, Piazzolla praised his son's excellent memory. Sábato dealt Daniel a mild whack: "What virtue is there in having a good memory? Virtue lies in creating things." It was not a philosophical point the boy could appreciate.

Among the very few who regularly visited the apartment were the music publisher Máximo Perrotti and his wife Solange; their two children were near the ages of Diana and Daniel. The families often went for excursions in the Perrottis' 1937 Plymouth, with its right-hand steering wheel.* Sometimes they went to the Parque Japonés, a downtown amusement park; sometimes out into the countryside; and often to Escobar to sample the chicken cooked in clay by a semilegendary restaurateur, Señor Spadacchini. There were occasional barbecues at Zárate, up the Paraná River, with the lyricist Homero Expósito and his father. On one famous occasion at Zárate, Piazzolla and Perrotti nearly drowned while swimming in the river, which was running dangerously high at the time. In the late 1940s Piazzolla thought about buying a car, though he did not. Perrotti gave him driving lessons. Piazzolla passed his driving test with ease; the examiner was one of his fans.

Classical Composer?

By the early 1950s, the aspiring classical composer's bandoneon lay at the back of a wardrobe, protected by mothballs and wrapped in chamois leather. Sometime in 1951, Roberto Di Filippo, thinking Piazzolla might need work, proposed the formation of a trio. "Don't even talk about it!" Piazzolla said. "I wish to know

*On Sunday 10 June 1945, Argentina's rule of the road had changed from left to right.

nothing about the bandoneon."²⁴ But he still needed to earn a living. In 1952 he conducted the orchestra for Radio Splendid, for which he remembered making some "horrid" arrangements.* Fortunately he could always fall back on his arranging skills. Roberto Capuano, later his publisher and agent, remembers a strong demand from bandleaders for Piazzolla's help in the 1950s and 1960s. He arranged for several bandleaders, including Miguel Caló, Enrique Mario Francini, Armando Pontier, José Basso, and once again, his old boss, Aníbal "Pichuco" Troilo.

In November 1952, Piazzolla flew to Rio de Janeiro with the Troilo band for appearances at the Night & Day cabaret. This was one of Troilo's very rare trips abroad. As the British airliner took off for the five-hour flight, Piazzolla teased the singer Raúl Berón, who had never flown before, with talk of plane crashes and of an approaching storm, telling him that he was delighted to find someone who was even more scared than he was. Later he translated the captain's announcements in English for the benefit of his fellow passengers, since the captain's Spanish versions were incomprehensible. From Rio's Copacabana Palace Hotel he promised Dedé that the two of them would some day enjoy "this paradise" together.²⁵ He continued to work with Troilo, arranging the music for his highly successful musical comedy *El patio de la morocha*, adding trumpets, saxophones, and percussion to the orchestra. It opened its two-year run in April 1953 at the Teatro Enrique Santos Discépolo (as the Teatro Alvear was then called) with President Perón in attendance. Because of Perón's presence, Piazzolla refused to go on stage at the end of the show.²⁶

He also found work in the film studios, which were, at that time, generously subsidized by the government he despised. In 1949 he had written the music for Leopoldo Torres Ríos's film *Con los mismos colores* (In the Same Colors), which had a soccer theme and made use of real soccer stars such as Mario Boyé and Alfredo di Stefano. Brought up in New York, Piazzolla was largely ignorant of and indifferent to the game. His attitude changed in the 1970s and 1980s, when the rising celebrity of superstar Diego Maradona caused him to affect a greater interest. His allegiance to Buenos Aires teams, first Boca Juniors and later on, River Plate,²⁷ was always rather tenuous.

The movies of the Perón era were mediocre, but *Con los mismos colores* earned Piazzolla 7,000 pesos (around $800), and in 1950 he received the same fee for *Bólidos de acero* (Rockets of Steel), based on automobile racing (one of President

*Alberto Fontán Luna and Nilda Marino were his vocalists; Piazzolla did not play his bandoneon.

Perón's enthusiasms). Later that year he did the sound track for *El cielo en las manos* (Heaven in Our Hands), an undemanding drama. The singer Edmundo Rivero, who appeared in this film, noticed "the anxiety and prejudice" of the musicians, who were mostly drawn from the Teatro Colón, when they learned that a mere bandoneon player was to direct them.[28] In 1953–54 Piazzolla provided the music for two more movies, *Stella Maris* and *Sucedió en Buenos Aires*. The first of these, a drama about a fishing fleet and directed by an old *marplatense* friend, Homero Cárpena, was shot in Mar del Plata. Piazzolla wrote the music while staying there. He asked Atilio Fruttero, a local piano restorer and dealer, to lend him a piano for a few days. It was returned within twenty-four hours. "Last night I was inspired," said Piazzolla. "I've done *all* the music." For the music in the film's dramatic final scene, Cárpena remembers, Piazzolla devised a special instrument from tautly stretched wire.

Film music was to be a constant in his career for the next forty years. His tally eventually came to more than thirty Argentine movies and a solid handful of foreign productions. It was never his favorite kind of work, and sometimes he said that he did it only for the money.[29] From this early period, Dedé attests that he often paid attention to the music when they watched movies, that he always went to the premieres of "his" films, but that he rarely looked at the scripts, asking her to read them to him and to indicate where the music should go.

Film music was a distraction from his real work. Between 1950 and 1952 he wrote several tangos, including "Para Lucirse," "Prepárense," "Fugitiva" (with words by Juan Carlos Lamadrid), "Triunfal," and "Contratiempo." The immensely popular "Contrabajeando," from the same time, was a collaboration with Troilo, although most of the work was Piazzolla's. Here Piazzolla found his vein: these tangos, without ceasing to be tangos, incorporated new and sophisticated harmonic and rhythmic concepts and were the first to bear his true stamp. "Contratiempo" was originally titled "Lo que vendrá" (What will come). Piazzolla sensed that this might be interpreted as a covert allusion to the end of the Perón government and changed it, using the title for another tango composed in 1957. In 1951, Piazzolla presented his publisher friend Máximo Perrotti with "Tanguango," intended to be arranged for either tango orchestra or jazz band. (His interest in jazz had lately revived and he was now buying records by Art Tatum and Oscar Peterson as well as Stan Kenton.) Perrotti duly organized the respective arrangements. "Tanguango" was one of Troilo's successes on his Rio trip, but he stopped playing it after unseemly disturbances broke out between pro- and anti-Piazzolla groups at a dance at the Vélez Sársfield soccer club.

Early in 1952, Piazzolla asked his friend Perrotti for an advance on "Tanguango." Perrotti, already in debt to take a sick daughter to the Córdoba sierras, secured an additional bank loan to meet Piazzolla's request. A few days later, Alfredo Perrotti phoned his son in Córdoba with news that "Tanguango" had just been published by a rival publisher, EMBA (Ediciones Musicales Buenos Aires). EMBA had also given Piazzolla an advance.[30] Shocked by his friend's apparent duplicity, Perrotti hastened to Parque Chacabuco to demand his money back. "You keep the work," he said, "but you're finished in the Perrotti firm. Forever." The two men did not meet again for several years.

Aside from his occasional tangos, Piazzolla's main effort now went into his classical pieces. By 1953 he had assigned opus numbers to nineteen compositions. One that had no opus number, "Epopeya Argentina" (1951) for chorus and orchestra, aroused a certain amount of public attention, and Piazzolla later claimed that it was banned.[31] As he explained in 1980, all his classical works were in different ways "related to Buenos Aires," but "intellectualized."[32] Little of this music has been revived, though a hearing of his 1949 Suite for Oboe and Strings (Opus 9) suggests the work of an intelligent and diligent pupil of Alberto Ginastera but perhaps not much more, although its first movement is mildly Coplandesque. A more ambitious work, the "Rapsodia porteña" for symphony orchestra, Opus 8 (1947), was premiered on the radio by Bruno Bandini and entered in a competition sponsored by the Empire Tractor Company in the United States. The first prize was a six-month scholarship to the University of California at Berkeley and a chance to study with Aaron Copland. Piazzolla set his heart on winning. His letters to Dedé, then with the family in Mar del Plata, show him going frequently to the Instituto Cultural Argentino Norteamericano to find out if there was any news. In February 1948, on what was apparently a weekly visit to Luján, Argentina's chief religious shrine, he prayed that Dedé would enjoy life in the United States.[33] He came in second and was devastated.

Another of his compositions, a Sinfonietta for chamber orchestra (Opus 19), was singled out by the Buenos Aires music critics as the best work of 1953. The conductor Jean Martinon premiered it that year at the Teatro Broadway. Piazzolla was not always happy when he heard his music in the concert hall. Héctor Stamponi, then the pianist in Miguel Caló's band, who was with him on one such occasion, remembers him saying afterward that the work concerned had "too many things" in it, and that he needed to aim at "more synthetic" pieces. It was around this time that Piazzolla took some lessons in orchestration from the distinguished conductor Hermann Scherchen, then visiting Buenos Aires.[34]

He was probably attracted by Scherchen's well-known interest in contemporary music.

Alberto Ginastera once again took a hand in Piazzolla's life. He suggested that Piazzolla show his three-movement symphonic work *Buenos Aires* (Opus 15), written in 1951 and first performed the following year by an orchestra conducted by Igor Markevitch, to the composer Juan José Castro. Castro liked it, made a few deft changes, and urged Piazzolla to enter it in a competition for the 5,000-peso ($250) Fabien Sevitzky Prize. Sevitzky, the conductor of the Indianapolis Symphony Orchestra and nephew of Serge Koussevitzky, would travel to Buenos Aires to conduct the prize-winning work. This time Piazzolla won.

For the performance, Piazzolla invented an instrument that he called a *lija* (sandpaper), a soundbox with three strings, made for him by an instrument maker in the Caballito district. He took it to show Sevitzky, who had just arrived in Buenos Aires. Sevitzky joked that he should at least have made a suitable case. The premiere (16 August 1953) was held in the Buenos Aires University Law School auditorium, which was far from full. Two veterans of the 1946 band, Leopoldo Federico and Abelardo Alfonsín, played the bandoneons that were added to the orchestra, to the disdain of the stuffy Buenos Aires musical establishment. Much of the audience applauded frantically. A minority was scandalized. A chance remark led to a melee of fistfights and shouting. As Piazzolla took his bow, Sevitzky consoled him, reminding him of the rowdy premieres of Stravinsky's *Rite of Spring* and Maurice Ravel's *Bolero*. "*Don't worry,*" he said, "*That's publicity!*" After the concert, an elderly violinist complimented Piazzolla and asked, "You don't have anything to do with the Piazzolla who does tango music, do you?"[35]

Among those who commented favorably on *Buenos Aires* in the city itself was a journalist and national deputy, José Gobello, who was later to be the moving spirit of the Academia Porteña del Lunfardo, founded in 1962, a notable organization that would take the lead in studying *lunfardo* and the tango tradition. Denouncing the "prejudice" of those who looked backward, he commended Piazzolla for taking the tango "to the temple of art." When his article appeared the following year, Gobello sent a copy to Piazzolla. Piazzolla sent him a friendly reply.[36] The letter came not from Buenos Aires but from Paris.

Paris—and Nadia Boulanger
The Fabien Sevitzky Prize won Piazzolla a one-year French government scholarship. Dedé was also given an award, to work under André Lhote, former luminary

of the Cubist movement. Like most Argentines, they were thrilled by the prospect of a visit to Europe. Their friends understood completely. Alberto Ginastera recommended a contact in Paris. Alfredo Perrotti, his son recalls, gave them some francs he had kept from a recent trip. Piazzolla packed his long-neglected bandoneon—just in case. He and Dedé left the children with the Noninos. Diana was now eleven, Daniel nine. Letters and postcards from Paris, not to mention presents, including a Meccano set for Daniel and a splendid doll for Diana, did not compensate for the long separation.

The Piazzollas sailed to Europe on a cargo-passenger boat, the SS *Coracero*. It was a forty-five day voyage, with leisurely calls at numerous ports, and smooth, except for a storm near the Canary Islands. In Liverpool, the stopover was long enough for them to take the train to London and to spend a few days sightseeing. (Thinking of Nonino, Piazzolla noted the copious spare parts for motorcycles available in the stores.)[37] The ship then took them up the English Channel, past the white cliffs of Dover, and called at Dunkirk, still showing signs of its wartime devastation. Piazzolla and some of the *Coracero*'s crew ventured inside a nearby Belgian submarine base. Other Argentines had been there recently. Someone had chalked "Viva D'Arienzo!" on a wall; someone else had added "Viva Piazzolla!" On 24 September 1954 they disembarked in Amsterdam. After a few days of sightseeing, they took the train to Paris.

They settled at the Hôtel Fiat, located at 36 rue de Douai, in a room lent to them by Héctor Grané, a Paris-based Argentine pianist who was away on tour. It was not luxurious. Mice sometimes kept them awake at night. The winter was cold, their budget was tight, and they found Paris expensive. The Noninos sent money, and royalties from the arrangements for *El patio de la morocha* helped, but they had to live modestly. They did not mind very much, however. Being in Paris was enough. "You can't imagine the gorgeous things there are here," Piazzolla wrote to his children in November.[38]

Piazzolla's teacher in Paris was to be Nadia Boulanger. This legendary tutor of composers—including Aaron Copland, Virgil Thomson, Jean Françaix, and Lennox Berkeley—and close friend of Stravinsky was then in her late sixties. Her influence on the younger generation was waning—Pierre Boulez and his contemporaries had no time for her—but her international fame remained considerable, and honors were still being heaped on her. Her fourth-floor apartment at 36 rue Ballu* (where she lived most of her life) was a short walk from the Hôtel Fiat. Before Piazzolla's first lesson, one of Boulanger's American students warned him

*Since 1979, Place Lili Boulanger.

never to mention the name of Rachmaninoff in her presence.* No doubt Piazzolla followed this advice.

Piazzolla was much impressed by Boulanger's old apartment, with its grand piano and organ, with its photos of Stravinsky, André Gide, Paul Valéry, and André Malraux. Every afternoon, her maid Margherita (known as Zita, like Troilo's wife) brought in tea, which Boulanger served herself. "It was like studying with my mother," Piazzolla recalled.[39] (In later years he sometimes described her as his "second mother.")[40] He was intrigued by Boulanger's cat Tascha, who was allowed to claw armchairs and curtains. Boulanger refused to have her declawed. One particular incident during this time always remained in Piazzolla's mind. One day he picked up "a large, carefully wrapped roll" from the postman and took it to her. With a tired expression, she told him, "It's Stravinsky, sending me his latest work. He does this every time he finishes a composition, and I don't have time to look at them all!" Boulanger was skeptical about Stravinsky's later music. "An old man playing with his jewels," she sometimes said.[41]

After his first classes with her, which were in English, a language she spoke fluently, Boulanger came to feel that something was lacking in the scores he showed her. (She must also have listened to the recording he gave her of his prizewinning *Buenos Aires*.) "This music is well written," she told him, "but it lacks *feeling*." It was a verdict Boulanger handed out to most of her pupils. For a while Piazzolla was disheartened, walking the streets and pouring out his woes to his friends. Boulanger soon forced him out of his malaise. She asked him what music he played in Argentina. Piazzolla reluctantly admitted it was the tango. "I love that music!" she exclaimed. "But you don't play the piano to perform tangos. What instrument *do* you play?" Once again Piazzolla could barely bring himself to tell her it was the bandoneon. Boulanger reassured him: she had heard the instrument in music by Kurt Weill, and said that even Stravinsky appreciated its qualities. Finally, Boulanger persuaded Piazzolla to play one of his tangos on the piano. He chose "Triunfal." At the eighth bar she stopped him, took him by his hands, and told him firmly: "*This* is Piazzolla! Don't ever leave it!"[42] In later recollections, he was always to describe the moment as something like an epiphany: "She helped me find myself," he told his daughter Diana.[43]

The individual classes and group sessions with Boulanger went on for almost four months. "I regret that my stay here is so short," Piazzolla wrote to José

---

*Boulanger always blamed Rachmaninoff for not taking the place onstage of her sick mentor and collaborator, the pianist Raoul Pugno, a few days before his death in Moscow in January 1914.

Gobello early in the new year, "I need at least two years to get to know everything I need."[44] What he *did* get to know was all-important: "It felt as if I never studied anything before," he said in 1987, and when once asked what he owed her, he replied, "absolutely everything."[45] Boulanger was a demanding teacher, sometimes giving him forty or fifty exercises at a time, but he liked the discipline. He also noted her opinions, not least those on contemporary music, about which she was skeptical. "This is going to end; they'll go back to Mozart one day," she once told him. On another occasion she recounted a Boulez premiere she had attended: "Luckily they played some Monteverdi in the second half." She took a friendly interest in his personal circumstances, advising him not to smoke or drink excessively and to go to bed early. They attended a few concerts together.[46]

On 14 February 1955, toward the end of his stay, Boulanger inscribed a photograph of herself and Piazzolla: *Que bientôt je vous revoie à la même place, cher Astor Piazzolla* (May I soon see you again in this same place, dear Astor Piazzolla.) Their future contacts would be limited, consisting of very occasional letters and postcards, and only two further meetings: one in New York in April 1958, and one in the summer of 1977, at the American Conservatoire at Fontainebleau, two years before she died at the age of ninety-two. But, as he told her in a postcard in March 1955, "I will never forget my dear Nadia Boulanger."[47] He never did. He was always immensely proud of his time with her. His children noticed that he always spoke of Boulanger with "limitless admiration." Enrique "Zurdo" Roizner, working with Piazzolla in the mid-1970s, observed that he "spoke a lot about her, and marveled at how she played the piano, how she taught." He was never as complimentary about other teachers, including Ginastera.

While Piazzolla studied with Boulanger, Dedé was attending André Lhote's *atelier*. He evidently liked her work, calling her "la petite sudaméricaine." She and Astor went at least once to his house to see his latest paintings. Dedé felt very lonely at the *atelier* until, one day, she encountered two Spanish-speakers, a Spaniard and a Chilean who claimed to know Salvador Dalì. When she arrived home, Astor was usually (against hotel rules) cooking dinner on their portable stove. A favorite menu was "chestnuts and crème Chantilly, salted mushrooms with ham."[48] At night they often went to the movies, partly to improve their French. They avoided nightclubs, spending a good deal of time in museums and at art exhibitions, where Piazzolla tired sooner than Dedé. Traveling on the Metro, they admired French couples' displays of affection. On one occasion, much to Dedé's embarrassment, Piazzolla kissed her in the train, to the delight of the other passengers.

With his confidence fully restored by Boulanger, Piazzolla signed contracts with three French record labels (Barclay, Vogue, and Festival) to compose and record tangos. Within six weeks he had composed sixteen or so. They included "Bando" (French slang for bandoneon), "Chau París," "S'il Vous Plaît," "Imperial," "Río Sena," "Sens Unique," "Marrón y azul," "Tzigane Tango," and "Picasso." "Marrón y azul" (Brown and Blue), according to Piazzolla's official version, was inspired by the artist Georges Braque. Dedé remembers it differently. Noting the contrast between her husband's suit and necktie one morning, she asked: "You're wearing brown and blue?" "It's a title for a tango!" he replied. "Picasso" was a tribute to the painter he so admired. He needed Picasso's permission to use the title and sent him one of his records. To Piazzolla's chagrin, the authorization came from a secretary, not from Picasso.[49] The Parisian tangos are a remarkable sequence, showing Piazzolla shaking himself free from the "historic" tango tradition. Never again would he work within the constraints of a traditional tango orchestra, an *orquesta típica*. He now felt eager (and able) to experiment with different instrumental formats.

Piazzolla's recordings were arranged by the publisher Yves Baquet, who had recently become the proprietor of Éditions Universelles. He signed an exclusive fifteen-year contract with Piazzolla, with whom he became very friendly, negotiating with the Buenos Aires publisher Julio Korn the European rights for some of his compositions. ("A difficult episode," he remembers.) The firm ended up with more than eighty of Piazzolla's works. Baquet was impressed by Piazzolla's music, even though it was largely unknown in France, and found him an office to work in near his own on the rue Faubourg Saint Martin. Piazzolla struck him as "happy. You felt it. He was able to do what he wanted to do."

Piazzolla recorded his new tangos (extended-play discs for Barclay and Festival, a long-playing record for Vogue) with an orchestra drawn largely from the Paris Opera and recruited by Baquet. He roped in fellow Argentine Lalo Schifrin as pianist for the first recordings, telling him that he wanted "a good jazz pianist, someone who knows what swing is. You've got swing."[50] Schifrin soon had to go on tour and recommended Martial Solal, later one of Europe's premier jazz pianists. Solal knew nothing about tango music but needed the work and closely studied the scores he was sent. At the studio he had a sudden sense of "wonder," finding that what he was playing "was a high-powered tango . . . symphonic music." Solal did not socialize with Piazzolla, but he was impressed by his strong feeling for jazz. It was during these 1955 recordings that Piazzolla, in defiance of all convention, adopted the habit of playing his bandoneon standing up, with a leg resting on a chair. "I didn't want to see the other musicians on the same level as me," he said later. "I had to feel I was above them."[51] Standing up, he could observe and command the whole orchestra. Piazzolla had never liked the traditional practice of sitting down while playing his instrument. It reminded him too much, he said, of an old woman doing her knitting. It symbolized the world he was trying to reject, or at least renew. Standing up was his declaration of independence.

Piazzolla was exhilarated by this work. "For the first time in my life," he wrote to Gobello on 24 February, "(though lamentably, in another country) I have had the enormous satisfaction of seeing a triumph for my tangos and my group."[52] He was not exaggerating. His recordings do seem to have made a definite impact. They were played regularly on all the main radio stations. "In less than six months," as Yves Baquet has told Nardo Zalko, noted historian of the tango in Paris, "Piazzolla was known all over France, and elsewhere, in Germany for instance. We succeeded in interesting all the orchestras in the country." On a visit to Argentina in 1958, he told the press that Piazzolla was the best-known Argentine musician in France.[53]

Piazzolla's months in Paris gave him a lifelong affection for the city and for France. Many of his acquaintances in Paris were also from Argentina, musicians such as Lalo Schifrin, Carlos Marcó, and Héctor Grané. Grané was often to meet Piazzolla on his future visits to Paris, always finding him "divine, friendly, intelligent." And there were always Argentine friends passing through Paris who sought out the Piazzollas, including the celebrated lyricist Enrique Cadícamo and his wife, and the erudite tangophile Luis Adolfo Sierra, "every bit a gentleman," Dedé remembers.

Among the French friends Piazzolla made in Paris was Édouard Pécourt. The friendship was to last the rest of his life. Pécourt ran a record store on the rue du Louvre and had learned Spanish to deepen his knowledge of the tango. They first met in a café on the rue du Faubourg Saint Martin, Pécourt impressing Piazzolla with his knowledge of his music. Piazzolla's French was still not particularly good. "He couldn't follow a conversation in French," says Pécourt, who acted as his interpreter on a number of occasions. On their drives round Paris together, Piazzolla frequently joked about the one-way streets, whose number was then growing fast in the French capital. The joke became a tango, "Sens unique." The tango "Chau París" was dedicated to Pécourt and his English wife Valerie.

At the end of February 1955, the Pécourts and the Piazzollas set off on a three-week vacation, traveling in Pécourt's modern car (which greatly impressed Piazzolla) and staying at inexpensive hotels. From Nice they crossed the border and drove down through Italy as far as Naples, with stops at Pisa, Massa,

Lucca, Florence, and Rome, where they went to Mass in St Peter's and received Pope Pius XII's blessing from his Vatican window. On their way home they visited Padua, Venice ("marvelous," they told the children on a postcard),[54] and Milan. The winter stopped them from returning through Switzerland over the Dolomite Mountains. The 3,250-mile excursion went smoothly. Pécourt admired the affectionate relationship between Astor and Dedé—"never the slightest problem."

Well before the Italian trip, Piazzolla had been thinking seriously about his future in Argentina. Nadia Boulanger had firmly pointed him back to the tango. What should he do next? One night his compatriot Luis Adolfo Sierra took him to hear a jazz octet led by the great saxophonist Gerry Mulligan. It was somehow peculiarly memorable. What impressed him was "the happiness on stage. . . . It wasn't like the tango bands . . . which seemed like funeral cortèges, gatherings of the embittered. Here it was like a party: the sax played, the drums played, the whole thing was passed over to the trombone . . . and they were happy. There was a leader, and arrangements, but there was also a wide margin for improvisation; everyone could both enjoy it and shine." Strolling the boulevards with Sierra, and over coffee, he asked: *Why not something similar for the tango, a tango octet perhaps?* Sierra agreed to try to round up suitable musicians in Buenos Aires. Piazzolla told him to prepare them for a revolutionary new experiment, "fit to kill."[55]

He could have stayed in Paris. The Philips label contacted Yves Baquet with a proposal for a major recording deal. But Piazzolla was determined to go home. Baquet pleaded with him. "No, no, no, my children have to go back to school on the first of April. I have to go back," said Piazzolla. On 24 March, a day after his final recording session, he and Dedé took the train to Hamburg and embarked on the SS *Yapeyú,* another Argentine cargo-passenger ship, taking with them some spare parts for Nonino's Citroën and some crochet hooks for Aunt Argentina Manetti.[56]

They reached Montevideo on a night of heavy rain. Piazzolla was buttonholed by a young Uruguayan admirer, Horacio Ferrer. Piazzolla suggested dinner, but first Ferrer dragged him off to the cellar of the Club de la Guardia Nueva at Calle Soriano 1684. This notable club, which lasted until 1973, had been founded the year before by Ferrer and other like-minded fanatics to study and promote new forms of tango music. Piazzolla's reception by "three hundred youngsters, mostly students," was little short of ecstatic. He played his new tangos on his bandoneon and gave the club some of his Paris records. Afterward Ferrer took him off to dine—on a dish they invented that night, "*milanesa de ternera* that was covered with fried onions."[57] It was the start of one of the most important collaborations in Piazzolla's life.

Then it was on to Buenos Aires, across the muddy estuary of the River Plate, to a joyous reunion on Sunday, 17 April 1955 with Diana and Daniel. "You can't imagine how happy I am to be with my children," Piazzolla wrote to Nadia Boulanger a week or two later.[58]

Octet and *Jazz-Tango*
1955–1960

→− The Octet

Return to Manhattan −←

→− "Adiós Nonino"

> I'm going to make tango music as *I* feel it.
> —Astor Piazzolla, *Cantando*, 5 December 1957

The Octet

Piazzolla liked to evoke his return from France in graphic images, as someone descending from the boat "with a stick of dynamite in either hand," ready "to provoke a national scandal, to break with all the musical schemes prevailing in Argentina," throwing his new octet, "eight war-tanks," into battle.[1] From the viewpoint of the history of tango music, the images are fair. The Octeto Buenos Aires (1955) can be seen as marking the real start of the so-called *tango de vanguardia* or "avant-garde tango," of what Piazzolla was to call the "great tango revolution."[2] This first offensive fizzled out within two years, but it paved the way for a larger revolution later on, and its importance in Piazzolla's career is undeniable.

The musicians who joined the revolution were willing accomplices. Atilio Stampone was the pianist, as in 1946. Hugo Baralis and the brilliant Enrique Mario Francini were the violinists. Earlier (1945–55), with bandoneonist Armando Pontier, Francini had led one of the more distinguished bands of the period. This was to be his main collaboration with Piazzolla, who had a high regard for him, nearly always roping him in when recording film music. When Francini got married in November 1957, Piazzolla played for him at the church, rather fearing (as he told his Uruguayan friend Horacio Ferrer) that the church might be closed down for allowing tango music within its walls.

The Octet had three successive bass players—Aldo "Bebe" Nicolini, Hamlet Greco, and Juan Vasallo—none of whom worked with Piazzolla again. José Bragato, the cellist, was one of those recruited before Piazzolla's return from France. He had been working in the orchestra at the Teatro Colón, though he also had experience with both tango music and jazz. He first met Piazzolla at a barbecue soon after the return from France and found him "happy, nervous, his hands moving all the time, without stopping. He wanted to start rehearsing there and then. 'He's crazy,' I thought, and 'I'm staying,' I decided."[3]

Roberto Pansera was Piazzolla's original choice as second bandoneon. However, he was offered the chance of an overseas tour with another band and he took it, with Piazzolla's blessing. His place was taken by Leopoldo Federico, who was once again (as at the time of the 1946 band) dismayed by the complexity of the music. Horacio Malvicino, a well-known jazz musician, played the electric guitar. He was recruited over a chat at the Café Electra on Avenida Callao. He, like Piazzolla, had studied with Ginastera.

Once the team was assembled, the musicians were given a fortnight or so to study the music. Then there were rehearsals at the Rendezvous nightclub on Calle Maipú, bandleader Osvaldo Fresedo's nightspot. The venue was arranged by Pansera, who had worked with him. The musicians were expected to start punctually at 9:00 A.M. Piazzolla was usually in a café across the street, waiting for them to arrive. The rehearsals, Malvicino remembers, were very intense, with Piazzolla demanding the maximum from the musicians, who were initially bemused by the scores he handed out.[4]

The Octet's collective aims were published in October 1955 in a document titled "Decalogue" (presumably written by Piazzolla). It set out the objectives of Piazzolla's revolution in some detail and deserves to be quoted in full.

(1) To join together principally for artistic purposes, leaving the commercial side in second place. (2) To gradually withdraw from participation in other bands, so as to give the ensemble the greatest effectiveness. (3) To perform the tango as it is *felt*, eliminating all kinds of extraneous influences which can impinge on our fixed purposes. (4) Since this is an ensemble consisting of solo instrumentalists, each of whom has an outstanding musical role, there is no director. A musical leadership is recognized: that of Astor Piazzolla. (5) The repertory will consist of contemporary works, works from the *Guardia Vieja*, and new creations as they are produced. (6) In order to take fullest advantage of the musical resources of the tango, works that are sung will not be played, except on rare occasions. (7) Since the ensem-

ble is only to be *listened to* by the public, it will not play at dances. In consequence, its performances will be limited to radio, television, recordings and theater shows. (8) The use of instruments never before included in tango bands (electric guitar) and other effects (percussion), as well as the overall structure of the works with their modern trend, will be explained before each performance so as to facilitate an immediate understanding of them. (9) Since nothing is the fruit of improvisation, the scores will be written with the best musical improvement that can be attained within the genre, which will help it to be evaluated by the most demanding experts. (10) (a) To raise the quality of the tango. (b) To convince those who have moved away from the tango, and its detractors, of the unquestionable value of our music. (c) To attract those who exclusively love foreign music. (d) To conquer the mass public, a task we take for granted as arduous, but certain as soon as they have heard the themes played many times. (e) To take overseas, as an artistic embassy, this musical expression of the land where the tango originated, to demonstrate its evolution and to further justify the appreciation in which it is held.[5]

At one point during rehearsals the musicians asked the bandleader Osvaldo Pugliese to evaluate them. It was a good choice. One of the great innovators of the "evolutionist" school, Pugliese had first made his mark with the rhythmically original tango "Recuerdo" (1924), and the even more original "La Yumba," which had been the talk of Buenos Aires in 1943. Pugliese's band—with Pugliese's brilliant piano playing evoking the African roots of the tango rhythm—was one of the few that Piazzolla's musicians could respect. Piazzolla, as he told tango expert Oscar Del Priore, considered Pugliese's tango "Malandraca" (1949) more "advanced" than anything he had yet written. The musicians asked him to pronounce whether the Octet's music was tango music or not. "Everyone waited very anxiously," recalls Malvicino. "When Pugliese said that it was, everyone got very excited, we were all very happy."[6]

There is a case for viewing the Octet as the most audacious of Piazzolla's various ensembles. For the first time, Piazzolla treated all his musicians as solo instrumentalists. He allowed the electric guitar a high degree of improvisation, something totally unknown in previous tango music. The piano's free-flowing role, the counterpoint achieved with the strings, the percussive effects created by the strings and electric guitar, and the neatly calculated dissonances, gave the ensemble a revolutionary sound. Piazzolla later admitted that it was not easy to get the balance exactly right. The weight of the two bandoneons needed to be countered by careful scoring for the violins and cello. Yet, when all is said, the Octet's performances included some real musical gems. The bandoneon and bass passages in Hugo Baralis's tango "Anoné," the complex chordal structure of the bandoneon parts in Piazzolla's arrangement of the old classic "El Marne," the percussion effects in "Marrón y azul," and the violin solo in "Arrabal" are all good examples.

Artists who try to provoke a "national scandal" do not usually become overnight idols. The Octet *was* controversial, though we may doubt whether it was more of a talking point among Argentines than the recent overthrow of President Perón (September 1955) and the start of a new military regime's ultimately vain efforts to "de-Peronize" Argentina. In the more limited tango world, the new group quickly aroused a good deal of knee-jerk hostility. Conventional tango fans made no real effort to appreciate the Octet. Most traditional musicians were puzzled by it. The battle lines formed immediately. A particular bone of contention was the Octet's blasphemous inclusion of the electric guitar. This drew "a host of criticisms—terrible, fierce, violent," says Malvicino, who even received death threats.[7]

One of those who sprang to the Octet's defense was Carlos Rodari, a twentysomething radio and TV journalist, whose style was forthright, even aggressive. Rodari began playing Piazzolla records on the radio, and in his fervor, he did not hesitate to call Piazzolla's critics "musical illiterates." Tango traditionalists sometimes gathered at the door of his radio station to insult and menace him as he came out. When Rodari finally met Piazzolla, they quickly became good friends. He found him no less aggressive in defending his own music, very adept at adding fuel to the flames, and never averse to making outrageous statements—describing "La Cumparsita" (the most famous of all tangos) as "dreadful," or demanding five years in prison for all reporters writing about the tango. As Rodari remembered it, "this Tango/Not-Tango polemic reached levels of extreme bellicosity. There were blows, insults, punches. And how Astor punched! With that left hand no one could beat him." Piazzolla himself was to recall "telephone menaces" when he was promised an exemplary beating.[8] "It was like a war," he told British interviewer Tony Staveacre in 1989.

Yet the new group also won support from those who had ears to hear. A teenage biology student and aspiring bandoneonist, Rodolfo Mederos, heard the Octet on the radio in Córdoba and found the music "irreverent, subversive, highly exciting." And, as with the 1946 band, foreign musicians visiting Buenos Aires showed their admiration. Dizzy Gillespie was there in July 1956, a momentous visit for Argentine jazz fans,[9] who always tended to view Piazzolla's efforts with sympathy. "We respected him and were crazy about him," remembers one of them, guitarist Rodolfo Alchourron. Gillespie asked to hear some "real" Argentine music and was taken to listen to the Octet at Radio El Mundo. "Dizzy's face turned to an expression of surprise and emotion," recalls guitarist Oscar López Ruiz, who was present. Embracing Piazzolla after the broadcast, Gillespie told him it was "the most incredible thing" he had ever heard.[10]

At the outset, Piazzolla announced that as soon as the Octet got established, it would go to France to fulfill a contract arranged by Yves Baquet.[11] Unfortunately, it never really got established, and such foreign tours remained a dream. However, the group did win a certain amount of local acclaim. After concerts in Rosario and La Plata in June 1956, Piazzolla spoke enthusiastically about its success to Ferrer. In April 1957, with the prospect of a series of programs on Radio Splendid and Radio Provincia (La Plata), he was similarly upbeat. Apart from its radio work, the Octet made a few appearances on Channel 7 (then the only TV station in Buenos Aires),* the programs arranged by Cecilio Madanes, its artistic director. Madanes vividly remembers "hysterical" phone calls to the station, denouncing Piazzolla's music.

Apart from this, there were sporadic theater appearances and visits to provincial cities like Rosario and Córdoba. The Octet also made a couple of long-playing records—not nearly as many as Piazzolla would have liked; in fact, the musicians had to put up some of the money themselves.[12] They did have one memorable success, a concert held in December 1957 in the auditorium of the School of Law. The dean of the school firmly vetoed the idea, but soon yielded to his protesting students. He even apologized for his earlier attitude and allowed a second concert.[13] In retrospect, Piazzolla saw this as his first great incursion into the student milieu of Buenos Aires, from which he was later to draw much support.

But in the end, despite Piazzolla's hopes, there was never enough work to keep the Octet going; "240 days of inactivity" was how he later summed up its annual calendar.[14] Some of the inactive days in March and April 1957, no doubt, were days Piazzolla spent recovering from a temporary near-paralysis of his hands. He was told that he was smoking excessively and drinking too much coffee. He was dosed with penicillin and vitamin B, and told to cut out coffee and have no more than six cigarettes a day, a regime that soon lapsed. Until the early 1970s, we might note here, Piazzolla enjoyed generally good health, apart from a mysterious kidney ailment that appeared after his return from France. He consulted special-

---

*Television started in Buenos Aires in 1951; by 1960 nearly 40 percent of the population had TV sets.

ists in Argentina and later in New York, but it was not cured until 1962, by a doctor in Córdoba.[15]

Sheer enthusiasm kept the Octet going for a while. "We played for the sake of the music, for the new tango movement," says Malvicino. There were certainly times when the Octet appeared without payment, and Piazzolla often waived his rights to additional remuneration. One day on the way to La Plata, Enrique Mario Francini asked him whether he could not make his music "a bit more commercial."[16] This was the last thing Piazzolla had in mind. But commercially speaking, the Octet could *not* compete with established *orquestas típicas*. By the later 1950s, the great tango bands' former predominance was being challenged by a vibrant and confident folklore movement (and by the beginnings of the rock-and-roll coming from abroad), but many of them were still very much in evidence. There was no room in the tango world for the innovative Piazzolla style. Piazzolla was not yet able to create the critical mass of support he needed.

So he turned to other work, both performing and recording with a string orchestra on Radio El Mundo (1957), at the behest of his friend Armando Rolón. Rolón, a journalist, had been banned from the radio after the overthrow of Perón but found his way back as an organizer of bands. The musicians for the string orchestra came from the Octet (Baralis, Greco, Bragato) or were freshly recruited, most of them from the Buenos Aires Symphony. Its pianist, Jaime Gosis, was to work with Piazzolla again. One of the violinists was José Carli, whose admiration for the 1946 band we have already noted. When Hugo Baralis had to go on tour with another band, he suggested violinist Elvino Vardaro, Piazzolla's old idol and former leader of the famed Elvino Vardaro Sextet, as his stand-in. Vardaro stayed in the orchestra and performed occasionally with the Octet. Baralis did not get his job back, which hurt his feelings. An eighteen-year-old violinist, Fernando Suárez Paz, substituted for Vardaro a few times when he fell sick. He was in no way awed by Piazzolla, for he had no idea who he was.

The orchestra's vocalist, Jorge Sobral, was struck by the way Piazzolla used him

> just like another instrument. He gave us the opportunity to sing the words just as they were, but the entrances and exits were not as clear as they are traditionally. He had some very special introductions, and you came in at unusual places. The instrumental and harmonic design meant you had to be very smart not to lose your way. But oh boy! it was a nice game.

Sobral sums up the work of the string orchestra as "Radio El Mundo, a few recordings, some trips to Uruguay, special shows." Piazzolla also took the orchestra to Rosario and one or two other provincial cities, and in fact it recorded more music than the Octet. Piazzolla later claimed to have paid the musicians out of his own pocket for these recordings.[17] The records have always had their admirers, Leopoldo Federico among them. They included conventional tangos, and, on the notable album *Tango en HI-FI*, recorded at the end of 1957, Piazzolla's newly written "Tres minutos con la realidad," a landmark among his own compositions, which he later described to Oscar Del Priore as "a toccata in tango rhythm." He composed it in about four hours, just after hearing Bartók's Second Violin Concerto for the first time. The piece is marked by distinctly Bartokian effects, as well as rhythmic accents reminiscent of Stravinsky's *Rite of Spring.* Jaime Gosis's extraordinary piano solo is a feature that stands out in the recording.

Piazzolla's work with the string orchestra did nothing to lessen hostility toward him. At one point, the orchestra was leaving a venue where the venerable and staunchly traditionalist bandleader Francisco Canaro was to appear. Canaro was heard to remark that he would "remove the bad impression left by those who were here before me." The rival musicians, as cello player José Bragato recalls, almost came to blows. Canaro's autobiography, published soon afterward, includes a hearty sideswipe at "modern" and "avant-garde" tango musicians, without naming names.[18]

As in earlier days, Piazzolla kept busy with composing and arranging, including material for the Octet and the string orchestra, and with such commissions as came his way. (For his work with the Octet and the string orchestra, Piazzolla accumulated, on his own estimate, a repertory of over 300 pieces in different arrangements.)[19] He was also able to find film work, writing scores for five more movies.* Around this time, drawing on recent experience, he even wrote a short article on film music, published in Mario Sasiain's Mar del Plata magazine in May 1958, perhaps as a favor to his father's friend. It revealed no particular philosophy but did explain the technicalities: the exact measurement of the sequences, the ten days or so given for composition, and the final recording—"the composer with a chronometer in his left hand and a baton in his right."[20]

Los tallos amargos (directed by Fernando Ayala), released in June 1956; *Marta Ferrari* (August 1956); *Una viuda difícil* (July 1957), a colonial-era drama; *Continente blanco* (also July 1957), the first Argentine film to be shot entirely in Antarctica; and *Violencia en la ciudad* (1957), which never reached the theaters. He also contributed music to *Historia de una carta* (1957) and *El crack* (1959), and his tango "Lo que vendrá" was the main theme in *Dos basuras* (1958).

All this activity added up to much less than Piazzolla really wanted. He was later to describe the Octet both as "a beautiful experience" and as "a flop, good for nothing,"[21] but at the time it was simply a flop. His musicians, for all their enthusiasm, were naturally unable to go on playing indefinitely without reward. And the controversy provoked by the Octet was, in the end, very wearing. As Piazzolla recalled in 1980: "I was fairly demoralized, and when I am demoralized, I go somewhere else." In a very dispirited mood, he went to see journalist Carlos Rodari, and told him: "I am going to the United States with my family, and I don't want to come back."[22] Piazzolla had long been gnawed by nostalgia for Manhattan, for the scenes of his boyhood. A return to New York suddenly became a fixed idea. It was reinforced by a certain George Greeley, who worked for M.G.M. He had heard the Octet and told Piazzolla that if he ever moved to the United States, he should get in touch, as there were good prospects for film work in Hollywood. It seemed like a golden opportunity. It was also family history repeating itself—Pantaleo migrating to Mar del Plata, Nonino moving to New York.

His mind was made up by November 1957, when he revealed his plans to Horacio Ferrer and other friends, telling them that he was going to settle in New York in the belief that his prospects would be better there. He also expressed his feeling of imminent expatriation in music, in the tango "Melancólico Buenos Aires" (written just in time to be included on the *Tango en HI-FI* album), with a beautiful violin passage in its second section and a superb bandoneon solo from Piazzolla in the finale. A few weeks later, his French publisher Yves Baquet arrived in Buenos Aires to meet some of his Argentine counterparts, and he also had papers for Piazzolla to sign. Baquet held a reception for the press at his hotel, the Plaza, which Piazzolla attended. He slipped off to Mar del Plata the next day, without telling Baquet, who followed him there. "He signed everything I gave him to sign," Baquet remembers. Piazzolla was never much interested in the small print of contracts.

His plan to move to New York soon became public knowledge. He told a reporter in December, "I'm not abandoning the tango, I'm going to make tango music as *I* feel it. . . . If they understood my music in France, it's probable they'll understand it in the United States."[23] Early in 1958 he told another reporter (with what can only have been a touch of either bravado or fantasy) that he was going to the United States to record with his orchestra and with Dizzy Gillespie, though he intended to return to Argentina soon.[24]

So the die was cast. The Parque Chacabuco apartment went on the market. It was bought eventually by the publisher Rómulo Lagos. Daniel was disturbed to think that his piano lessons would be interrupted. "Don't worry," his father said, "when we're there I'll enroll you at the Juilliard." It was a promise he was not able to keep.

Return to Manhattan

In February 1958, leaving the family behind while he went to investigate the prospects, he flew to New York. It was still a long trek in that pre-jet era, with stops in Rio de Janeiro, Belem, Trinidad, and Havana, where he breakfasted.[25] The captain invited him on to the flight deck to quell his flying nerves. On arrival, he went to stay with his Bertolami cousins in Port Reading, New Jersey—his first meeting with them in twenty-one years. All five brothers had served in World War II: two in Europe, one in the Pacific, the other two in the United States. Piazzolla found them "marvelous, good, affectionate" people, and he was impressed by what seemed to him their affluent way of life; among other things, they had a thirty-two-foot yacht for fishing trips. Thanks to their generous hospitality, he began to put on weight. He was delighted to be back in the United States, although, as he told Dedé, it was far colder than it had ever been during their winter in Paris, and he found New York "very changed. Very dirty. Lots of Puerto Ricans."[26]

However dirty it may have been, he now started commuting to Manhattan by train, from Rahway station. He paid an early visit to the old apartment building on East 9th Street. A few people still remembered him. Willie Lubiansky and his mother gave him "a fixed stare" and cried "Astor!!!" His friend Stanley Sommers (ex-Sommerkovsky) was now an aeronautical engineer in Texas. Some members of his old gang, he reported to Dedé, were doing time in Sing Sing and Alcatraz. He looked up his old teacher Andrés D'Aquila, now living in very modest circumstances.[27] He dined with his compatriot, the choreographer Ana Itelman, for whom he had written a ballet score five years earlier,* at her home on East 79th Street. They immediately started talking about possible collaborations. He saw Dizzy Gillespie (then just off to London) and discussed plans to record. His main hopes of work, however, were quickly dashed. He telephoned George Greeley's office in Hollywood and was told, "He died last month." Piazzolla repeated the call so as to be in no doubt and was told the news again.[28] His dreams of a major Hollywood contract melted away.

New York agents and publishers, meanwhile, liked the music Piazzolla showed

---

*"Tango dramático para 13 instrumentos" (1953).

them, though they suggested he tailor it more closely to American taste. At first he resisted. "I've already quarreled with an impresario who wanted me to do the kind of cheap tangos they like," he reported to Dedé on 19 February. "I told them a few things." He soon realized that he would have to compromise a little. One publisher was sufficiently taken with his tangos to plan a twelve-track long-playing record (LP). The rules of the Musicians Union meant that Piazzolla had to complete six months of residence before recording. The setback irked him, but he quickly regained his confidence, "I think I shall get to where I want to be," he told Dedé.[29]

On 23 February 1958 he went to the Argentine consulate to regularize his status as an expatriate voter. On duty that day was the young César "Pipe" Márquez, who shared an eleventh-floor apartment with some Uruguayan friends on the corner of West 82nd Street and Riverside Drive. A Piazzolla fan of some years standing, he was astonished when his idol suddenly materialized in the flesh. He invited him to meet another diplomat and fan later that day at a café on Fifth Avenue. This was Alberto Salem, who worked at the United Nations. Both Márquez and Salem quickly became good friends. Learning Piazzolla was without his family, Márquez invited him to stay at his apartment, clearing it first with his Uruguayan friends. Piazzolla was tiring both of his commute and his cousins' noisy children. At the start of April he moved to West 82nd Street. As he left Port Reading, the Bertolamis said, "Let's see if it takes you another twenty-one years to come back!"[30]

Márquez found Piazzolla a perfect house guest. When he fell sick, Piazzolla prepared him a plate of spaghetti richly seasoned with garlic. "One of these days I'm going to write a Concerto for Garlic and Orchestra," he joked. Márquez urged him to write a tango in honor of the Hudson River, which was in full view from the apartment. Piazzolla improvised a theme on his bandoneon, his "sarcophagus," as he was nicknaming it at the time. "I watch the ships passing," he told Dedé. "How sad it all is; you see the whole city, and the millions of cars going by."[31] Ten years later, the theme reappeared in the music for his "little opera," *María de Buenos Aires*.

On Monday, 28 April, Márquez went with Piazzolla to watch him appear (for a $150 fee) on Garry Moore's morning TV show on CBS. He accompanied an American singer in "Kiss of Fire" (the old tango "El choclo") and played his own new arrangement of the haunting Johnny Mercer–David Raksin theme from Otto Preminger's 1944 movie *Laura*. The musicians he played with included the pianist Howard Smith, guitarist Carl Kress and bass player Herman "Trigger" Alpert. All of them had worked in top-flight bands with great bandleaders (Ray Noble, Glenn

Miller, Tommy Dorsey, Paul Whiteman); Alpert had recorded with Ella Fitzgerald and Frank Sinatra. There was talk (but only talk) of taking the studio group to the Newport Jazz Festival in June. A few days later Piazzolla was introduced to the distinguished jazz arranger and bandleader Johnny Richards, who proved very friendly and asked to hear his records.[32] He liked one of the Octet's records so much that he offered to take it to the Roulette label.

One television appearance (duly reported in the Argentine press)[33] was hardly a breakthrough. Piazzolla was still casting around for solid work. He was visited by Juan Carlos Barbará, an Argentine businessman living in Mexico. (His brother's partner was buying the Parque Chacabuco apartment.) They talked of a possible deal with a Mexican record company, the recordings to be made in New York.[34] Piazzolla did not follow this up, partly because Johnny Richards's initiative with Roulette got him some arranging work with the label. He was to work on an album of songs by the Di Mara Sisters. And the ballet Ana Itelman was devising with his music also seemed very promising. "Very, just very good," he told Dedé.[35] An agent found him some arranging work for the singer Yolande Tornell, with a $250 advance and a fee of $2,000 for twenty arrangements. The deal fell apart; Tornell claimed to find the arrangements too complicated, though Piazzolla told Dedé that they were simple enough for Daniel to sing. At least there was good news from Yves Baquet in Paris, where $850 was due to him in royalties. He was heartened, too, to find two Argentine restaurants in Manhattan (one of them frequented by Tennessee Williams) that constantly played his music. There were enough straws in the wind to make him feel optimistic. "Rest assured, your little Astor will not fail," he told Dedé. "I feel very good in New York."[36]

He was now eager for the family to join him. He sent a flow of detailed instructions to Dedé. José Bragato was to buy his typewriter and be given his remaining supply of manuscript paper. There was no need to bring furniture or clothes, which could be bought more cheaply in New York. He painted a rosy picture of American life: the supermarkets, the television programs, the interesting people, the art galleries where Dedé might show her paintings. (She did in fact show some, at the Ahda Artzt Gallery on West 57th Street in May–June 1959.) "The language is your biggest disadvantage," he told her, "but in New York you'll be able to attend the crash courses at Columbia University." As for the future, they might perhaps spend three years in the United States and a year in Paris before returning to "our beloved Buenos Aires."[37]

But where would they live? Bernardo Altman, an Argentine cellist in the New York Philharmonic Orchestra, was about to go on tour, and offered his fourth-floor apartment at 202 West 92nd Street, between Broadway and Amsterdam

Avenue. Piazzolla noted approvingly that it had a baby grand piano. Here it was that he welcomed the "three Ds" when they finally arrived in New York on 21 May 1958. "He received us," Daniel remembers, "with a menu which he himself had prepared: toasted garlic bread, with rice and delicious clams."[38] When Altman needed his living quarters again a few weeks later, the family moved to another providentially available apartment in the same building. It was in poor condition. Dedé fumigated the rooms, repainted the shabby furniture, and hauled an abandoned carpet up from the basement, from where there also came the shelves she used to construct a makeshift table. Piazzolla installed an upright piano, on which he placed a photograph of Nonino. Daniel and Diana had their own bedrooms; their parents slept on a sofa bed in the living room.

The rhythms of domestic life resumed. Although he told Ferrer a few weeks later that the Piazzolla family had become thoroughly Americanized, this was not completely true. Dedé never altogether liked New York. She never mastered English, giving up after a few lessons. She spent much of her time in the apartment, or with Argentine friends like the Salems or Ana Itelman and her husband Claudio Campusano. When shopping, she found that most of the people she dealt with were Puerto Ricans. She did, however, manage to acquire a stock English phrase when answering the phone, "*My husband will be back at five,*" even though it was not always the case. When the "three Ds" watched television, Piazzolla gave running translations, even for the weather forecasts. Until their language skills improved, he translated his two teenagers' homework for them.

Daniel loved New York. On their first evening, Piazzolla took the children to a supermarket, not yet a common sight in Argentina, and they were stunned. Daniel greatly enjoyed the school he went to, two blocks away. (*Life en Español* printed a short piece about Daniel and Diana at school, done by Ana Itelman's husband Claudio Campusano.)[39] Daniel sang in the school choir and moved his father to tears on at least one occasion. He won a prize for a device to measure the speed of sound, something he had dreamed up with a classmate. Daniel rapidly identified with everything American. He hung the Stars and Stripes on his bedroom wall. Like his father before him, he was often excited in later years when he heard the "Star-Spangled Banner."

Diana reacted very differently. She longed to be back in Buenos Aires. She found her American schoolmates less fun to talk to than the children of immigrants—Yugoslavs, Italians, Puerto Ricans. After the Cuban Revolution began, her bedroom wall was adorned with photos of Fidel Castro, an early sign of the left-wing enthusiasm that would play an important part in her life. (Her teenage sympathy for Peronism had already pleased Nonino.) However, her incipient literary hopes were boosted by the appearance of her first published poem (in an English translation) in the May 1960 issue of *Chelsea* magazine.

The children sometimes played in Central Park or in the much closer Riverside Park, from where, one winter's day, Daniel took a stray dog home. "Get that dog out of here!" his father ordered. Daniel pleaded and pleaded. Within hours Piazzolla was totally won over. The little "mixture of terrier and I don't know what" as Dedé described him, was christened Terry. "He was the dog my dad most loved in his life," says Daniel, who sometimes got up early just to play with him. Terry bit all of the "three Ds" but never Piazzolla. Piazzolla always said that Terry was "bilingual," since he obeyed both English and Spanish commands.[40]

Life in New York had its consolations for the Piazzollas, as well as its comic moments. Astor and Dedé were out shopping one day when they spotted some small cups in a shop window. "Dedé, these little cups are ideal for eggs," said Piazzolla. (Egg cups, for some mysterious reason, are not part of the American way of life.) No, the Spanish-speaking Chinese shopkeeper told them; they were Japanese saké cups. Nearly forty years later, at Dedé's invitation, the authors of this book drank cognac from them.

Piazzolla naturally took pleasure in showing the "three Ds" the scenes of his childhood, such as St. Mark's Place; East 9th Street; the site of the bakery where Maria Alberti, his first love, had lived, and so on. There were at least half a dozen visits to the Bertolami cousins in New Jersey. "Splendid types," Daniel found them. The cousins disliked Manhattan and hardly ever visited, though George and his wife certainly dropped in at West 92nd Street at least once. The home movies shot by Piazzolla in New York show many delightful scenes of family life: the four of them enjoying the snow in Riverside Park at Christmas 1959; a barbecue with the Bertolamis (Piazzolla in a jesting mood); the family at St. Patrick's Cathedral on Thanksgiving Day; Dedé walking Terry in the street; the "three Ds" on the subway; Piazzolla and Daniel looking at paintings in Greenwich Village.

Those who were close to Piazzolla in his New York years all tend to underline his sheer friendliness. He wrote a "Lullaby for Luis Alberto" ("Dernier Lamento" in Yves Baquet's catalogue) in honor of Alberto Salem's newborn son, and sometimes baby-sat for the Salems, often cooking succulent dishes in their kitchen. Salem remembers laughter-filled excursions to supermarkets. The two friends also sometimes went down to Little Italy to eat "Hero" sandwiches. There were evenings in Greenwich Village, when Piazzolla and Salem formed an impromptu bandoneon-guitar duo at parties for "intellectuals or pseudo-intellectuals," their repertory limited to the simplest pieces.

There were also contacts, inevitably, with fellow musicians. Piazzolla some-times asked Bernardo Altman for advice on points of composition, although they did not see each other again in later years. (The Argentine composer of electronic music Mario Davidovsky also lived at 202 West 92nd Street.) He got to know the trumpeter and bandleader Quincy Jones (another pupil of Nadia Boulanger); Daniel remembers taking scores to his apartment. Dizzy Gillespie, entertaining Piazzolla at home one day, put on a record by (as he put it) "the best musician in the world today—and the best arranger." It was Miles Davis's *Miles Ahead* (1957), with arrangements by Gil Evans. Piazzolla agreed that "it sounded like something celestial," and he hoped that he would someday meet Gil Evans. He did—but not for another twenty-five years.

From his earliest weeks in New York Piazzolla occasionally visited Birdland, on Broadway, a club whose honorable place in history is known to all jazz fans. It gave him an idea—an idea he soon communicated to others. Why should there not be a Buenos Aires equivalent of Birdland, somewhere for the best musicians to play avant-garde tango music, his kind of music? The dream remained with him for the rest of his time in New York.[41]

There was one other experience he was always to treasure, a chance encounter with one of his greatest idols. Albino Gómez, a friend in the Argentine mission to the United Nations, phoned him one night to tell him that he was about to pick up Igor Stravinsky and escort him to a cocktail party. Would Piazzolla like to go with him? Piazzolla assumed it was a joke (of a kind he himself was quite capable of perpetrating). He let out a coarse expression and hung up. He went himself that evening to a reception for the visiting *grande dame* of Argentine letters, Victoria Ocampo, at the Metropolitan Club. He did not realize that Gómez had organized the reception on the instructions of his ambassador, or that Stra-vinsky was one of the many twentieth-century cultural luminaries whose friend-ship Ocampo so assiduously cultivated. Suddenly Gómez entered, a frail-looking Stravinsky leaning on his arm. Piazzolla watched his idol sipping whiskies. "It was like looking at God." When finally introduced, he was dumbstruck, just managing to blurt out a hasty "Maestro, I'm a long distance pupil of yours." Stravinsky gave him a warm handshake. Gómez later gave Stravinsky a Piazzolla score; he thinks it was probably some of the music for Ana Itelman's ballet.[42]

One thing Piazzolla could not disguise from the "three Ds," when they arrived, was that he had not really succeeded in establishing himself in New York. The rent was always paid and the teenagers always properly clothed, but there were times Piazzolla could scarcely afford to give Daniel a quarter for the subway. (It cost a nickel in his own boyhood.) There was to be no Juilliard School for Daniel, after all. The Noninos sent money from Mar del Plata, but this was no long-term solution. Even before the family's arrival, Piazzolla had come close to asking the Argentine consulate for translation work. Through a music publisher, he secured a part-time translator's job in a bank, at $300 a week. He left for his first day's work at eight, and was back in the apartment by nine: "I couldn't," he told the family, "I'm no use for that kind of thing."[43] He had stopped on a street corner and simply turned back. The "three Ds" were delighted, despite the threat of continued privations. "It was a very hard time, [but] we were very united," says Daniel.

Musically, Piazzolla had to turn to what he always later described as rather menial work. This was not exactly how he saw it at the beginning. The Roulette Company finally invited him to record for its Ti-Co label. He got together a quintet (bandoneon, electric guitar, vibraphone, piano, double bass), probably thinking of jazz models like Max Roach or George Shearing. He recruited, among others, Chet Amsterdam as bass player and Al Caiola as guitarist. (Caiola was later to be well known from his music publishing, and his work with popular bands and with singers like Frank Sinatra and Tony Bennett.) Piazzolla thought well of his new team. In fact, his admiration for the competence and profession-alism of American musicians was one of the themes of his correspondence at this period. He was at first enthusiastic about his quintet. He even considered changing his name—it was too close to "pizza," he said—to make himself sound more American. Dedé talked him out of it: "Your father would feel bad. Think of Stravinsky, Bartók. They're odd names, too."

The "J-T" or "Jazz-Tango" music Piazzolla wrote or arranged for his new quintet never held a high place in his memories. In private he was frank about its purpose. To Ferrer and others he explained that it was an attempt to capture the American public, whose ear was unaccustomed to "straight" tango music but which might be won over by familiar tunes touched with the tango rhythm. To his friend César Márquez he quipped that the T of J-T should be pronounced Argentine-style, *te*—*yeite* being Buenos Aires slang for "a trick." He told the newspaper *Clarín* that the Jazz-Tango formula "will permit the American public to enjoy our music."[44] It has to be said here, however, that Piazzolla's bid for American popularity was a complete failure. Jazz-Tango had no impact whatever on American popular tastes, unlike the great Cuban dance bands of the period, which did.[45] In fact, Piazzolla supplemented his income during these months by doing arrangements for one or two popular "Latin" bands, including those of Noro Morales and Machito (Frank Grillo), with whom he got along very well.[46]

He also arranged (and occasionally helped record) music for bandleader Pete Terrace, the Trio Los Bandidos, and singer Fernando Lamas. None of these artists made much of a mark, which may be one reason Piazzolla rarely if ever referred to this work in later reminiscences.

The J-T quintet recorded two LPs for the Ti-Co label.* Piazzolla thus immortalized some truly excruciating versions of tango classics like "El choclo" and "Derecho viejo," as well as jazz classics like Ellington's "Sophisticated Lady," popular hits like "Laura" and "April in Paris," and new pieces by himself like "Oscar Peterson," "Boricua," and "Dedita." The most that can be said for these versions is that they are slightly above the level of "muzak." Argentina remained in happy ignorance of Jazz-Tango, although the newspaper *Clarín* learned enough about the recordings to comment: "J-T = JAZZ minus the TANGO."[47] (They are largely minus jazz, too.) In the United States they were a complete flop. The work certainly did little or nothing to boost Piazzolla's self-esteem: "It still pains me to have done it," he said thirteen years later. Later still he compared Jazz-Tango to "indigestible minestrone."[48]

The Ti-Co albums were recorded in mid-1959. His work prospects had seemed more promising somewhat earlier, when Ana Itelman's ballet found a producer. Piazzolla went with her to Puerto Rico for performances at the Club Flamboyan on Ashford Avenue in San Juan, opening on 9 January 1959 after a grueling eight-hour rehearsal. He stayed, with the rest of Itelman's company, at the Hotel Columbus. His new Caribbean surroundings entranced him: "This is divine, a sea such as I have never seen before. Immense waves, very modern hotels, divine colors and landscapes." The ballet itself roused mixed reactions. As Piazzolla reported, only "a very few" people appreciated it, while "the rest say it's very peculiar."[49] Though he assured Dedé that he was following "the Peronist slogan: 'From home to work, and from work to home,' " it seems probable that he had a brief fling with one of Itelman's dancers. Dedé was unaware of this; Daniel and Diana found out later. In fact, they suspected their father of having a number of minor adventures around this time. If so, it can be seen as the start of a new pattern of behavior that was to have disastrous consequences for the "three Ds" (and Piazzolla) only a few years later.

Take Me Dancing. The Latin Rhythms of Astor Piazola [sic] *and His Quintet* (Ti-Co LP LP/ SLP 1066) and *An Evening in Buenos Aires.* (The second was apparently not released.) The "personnel" for the recordings is hard to reconstruct: apart from Caiola and Amsterdam, Eddie Costa seems to have been the vibraphonist. Puerto Rican bandleader Tito Puente may have helped record the first album.

One of the projects Itelman discussed with Piazzolla was a ballet based on Jorge Luis Borges's highly atmospheric short story "Hombre de la esquina rosada," the account of the death of a noted knife fighter. Piazzolla was enthusiastic and later (in March 1960) wrote an appropriate score, though Itelman's plans for the ballet fell through. There can be no doubt that he was temporarily energized by his collaboration with Itelman. Both of them hoped that the Puerto Rico appearances could be parlayed into a longer tour. "Today we sent photo materials to Cuba," he reported to Dedé on 13 January. The moment was not propitious. Five days earlier Fidel Castro had made his triumphal entry into Havana. No offers came from Cuban impresarios. Piazzolla was back in New York ten days later, now pinning his hopes on Europe. On 26 January, possibly with Itelman's encouragement, he wrote to Yves Baquet:

> Two days ago I returned from Puerto Rico, where we had a fabulous success. Both the music and the dancing were much praised. We were going to make our debut in the Tropicana in Cuba, but the revolution prevented this. We are hoping to take this show to Paris, I'm sure we would have a lot of success. It's a great quality show with lots of character. . . . This would be a big thing for my music and getting it known in Europe.[50]

At the time he wrote this, Piazzolla was still contemplating a long stay in New York, despite the difficulties. Nearly three decades later he described these years as "the worst economic period of my life."[51] Yet he was still mesmerized by the cultural vitality of New York—the most *complete* city of all, as he told Horacio Ferrer—and he was half certain that he could still make his way there. It was true that he had not yet meshed with the big public, but anything was possible. He even sometimes wondered whether he might spend the rest of his life in New York.

"Adiós Nonino"

Later that year he worked with another dance company. Juan Carlos Copes (with María Nieves, to win international stardom in *Tango Argentino*, the hit show of the 1980s) was already, in his twenties, on his way to becoming the most celebrated tango dancer of his time. The singer Jorge Sobral had introduced Copes and Nieves to Piazzolla a few years earlier, and Copes had choreographed a ballet to the music of "Contrabajeando," though Piazzolla had shown no particular interest. Since 1956, the Copes-Nieves dance company had been working its way up the American continent—Brazil, Venezuela, Cuba, Central America, Mexico. During its nine-month stint in Mexico, Copes suddenly received a letter from Piazzolla proposing a collaboration.

In mid-September 1959 Piazzolla flew to Mexico City. Copes met him at the airport, and it was "as if we had known each other for ever," he remembers. Piazzolla impressed him as "a machine-gun of jokes."[52] María Nieves found him "sensational . . . God! with Astor you could never stop laughing." Piazzolla quickly warmed to the couple. "They make you love them for being so modest and sincere," he told Dedé. He was impressed by the quality of the ballet and of the dancers: "They are all 100% *tangueros* and know zilch about ballet, but they do what nobody else can with their feet." His opinions of Mexico City, to judge from his letters to Dedé, verged on outright disgust. The altitude tired him. But he met the head of the Mexican RCA-Victor company to discuss possible recordings, and he did some sightseeing. On Sunday, 26 September he visited the monumental ruins at Teotihuacán and was duly impressed. The following Sunday he spent with businessman Juan Carlos Barbará, on "a beautiful farm with all the amenities"—the amenities including 17,000 chickens.[53]

With Piazzolla as musical director, Copes and Nieves took their "Compañía Argentina Tangolandia" to Puerto Rico, flying there via Miami on 6 October 1959. The performance site was the Club Flamboyan once again, and Piazzolla was delighted to be back. The show attracted full houses day after day. Piazzolla, writing excitedly to Dedé, could not resist scoring a point off a fellow tango musician who had recently won huge success around the Caribbean: "We opened last night, and it was SUCCESS-LIKE-CRAZY. We really put the stopper on Marianito Mores. We sank him without trace."[54]

Enthusiastic about the show's success, Piazzolla dreamed of Hollywood and Las Vegas. After visiting other Puerto Rican cities, the company moved on to New York, opening its "Evening in Buenos Aires" show at the Waldorf-Astoria's Starlight Roof Garden on Friday, 6 November. (Such was the demand for seats that the New York firemen had to close the hotel doors.) They repeated the show at the Jefferson Theater and soon afterwards in Chicago (Zenith Theater) and Washington, D.C. (Lotus Club). Piazzolla was excited by these successes. His music, he told Ferrer, sounded rather like the *Tango en HI-FI* album. There was next a three-month contract at the Chateau Madrid nightspot, near the Plaza Hotel. At the end of April 1960, they appeared (with American dancers) on the Arthur Murray show on CBS television (Channel 4, the only color channel). This seems to have been Piazzolla's last show with Copes-Nieves. "It came out terrific," Dedé reported to her father. "The orchestra sounded as if it was from Buenos Aires."[55]

Piazzolla's other appearances in New York were few and hard to trace. The nomadic tango singer Angel Cárdenas, who had first met him in the mid-1940s, was appearing at the Waldorf-Astoria and the Liborio Restaurant (48th Street), and remembers Piazzolla accompanying him, along with another well-known bandoneonist, Ernesto "Titi" Rossi. Cárdenas even took Piazzolla to the races—never one of his enthusiasms. But professionally, Piazzolla was becoming more and more dissatisfied. He resented having to wear a slouch hat and neckerchief (the uniform of the *compadritos*, the street toughs who were such a stereotype of the traditional tango) for the Copes-Nieves show's publicity photo. An acquaintance of his, the young Argentine engineer Eduardo Matrajt, then working in New York for an oil company, encountered him at the Chateau Madrid (which Matrajt thought "deplorable") and asked him: "Piazzolla, what are you doing here? This isn't for you."[56]

Juan Carlos Copes was later to feel that Piazzolla's retrospective accounts of his New York years (always negative) played down his own role. "It's true that he had to mold himself to the classical archetypes of the tango and the milonga," he comments, "but it was a way out for him in a country that knew nothing about him." Piazzolla never felt any personal resentment. When Copes returned to Buenos Aires a year or two later, he met him at the airport and gave him one of his new records, "on account of the moment we had shared in Puerto Rico."

The "moment" was one of the most important in Piazzolla's life. Here we must backtrack to October 1959 and the Club Flamboyan in San Juan. A telegram suddenly arrived from Mar del Plata. Nonino was in critical condition. Having enjoyed lifelong good health, Vicente Piazzolla had fallen from his bicycle and injured a leg; complications had set in. Between the two shows of the night at the Club Flamboyan, Copes and Nieves urged Piazzolla to phone Mar del Plata to find out if there was more news. There was. Cousin Walter Provenzano (Aunt Argentina Manetti's son) told him Nonino was dead—had died, in fact, of a cerebral embolism at 12:30 P.M. on 13 October, a month short of his sixty-sixth birthday.[57] "We plucked up courage and went on working," recalls Copes. "It was the only time I ever saw him cry."[58] For the first time ever, Piazzolla took his companions' hands as they went onstage for their final bow, and neither Copes nor Nieves would forget the strength of his grip that night.

By coincidence, Dedé had already arranged to fly down to San Juan the next day for a vacation. She left the children with her sister Poupée, who had been staying with them since April, largely to keep Dedé company. During the days she spent in Puerto Rico, she and Astor paid a courtesy call on the island's most famous musical resident, cellist Pablo Casals. They waited for him while he finished a cello lesson. He came out to greet them, and a photograph was taken.[59]

Their return to New York was frightening. On landing, their plane skidded badly on the runway, causing general panic in the cabin. On the journey from the airport to West 92nd Street, Piazzolla saw the familiar New York sights pass by and thought of his childhood. So far he had borne his loss with calmness, but the next day, after lunch, he asked Dedé and Poupée to leave him alone for a while. They went into the kitchen, from where they heard him sighing. Neither of them dared open the door. There was silence at first, then the sound of the bandoneon. Piazzolla was playing "Nonino," a pleasant, chirpy tango from the Paris days written in honor of Vicente. He paused, and then began a new, absolutely haunting elegiac tune. It was the sequel. "The sighs became terrible," Dedé recalls. "I had never seen him cry like that, or indeed cry in any way."[60]

"Adiós Nonino" is Piazzolla's single most famous piece. The authors of this book envy those who have still to hear it for the first time. "Perhaps I was surrounded by angels," he said in 1980. "I was able to write the finest tune I have written. I don't know if I shall ever do better. I doubt it."[61] He was to play "Adiós Nonino" thousands of times, in at least twenty different arrangements. Those he seems to have preferred, eventually, were the ones he devised for his Nonet, his electronic group of the mid-1970s, and for his second Quintet,[62] all of them ensembles that, in 1959, still lay in his future.

Life in New York gradually returned to normal. Early in March 1960 the Piazzollas visited the newly opened Guggenheim Museum, much admiring its impressive collection of Kandinskys. On 11 March, Dedé cooked duck *à l'orange* for Astor's thirty-ninth birthday and gave him a cigar. But the shock of Vicente's death, combined with his professional discontents, recalled Piazzolla to his roots. He could no longer bear his Jazz-Tango, his nighttime appearances, the misery of work he had come to consider low grade. His bid to break through to the great American public had failed. "The box office kings," as Dedé told her parents, were now "the rockers."[63] Dedé was worried about the prospects for work in Argentina, but her husband soon made up his mind. He suddenly felt the need to start all over again, although not from scratch. He had assimilated the lessons of the Octet, and now the lessons of New York, and sensed that some kind of new synthesis was possible. But such a synthesis was not attainable in New York. It had to be more firmly grounded in the tango. That meant Buenos Aires, whatever the difficulties.

He needed to pay for four passages back to Argentina. His in-laws the Wolffs sent some money. Piazzolla thought about asking for help from his Bertolami cousins, but did not. He appealed to Yves Baquet in a transatlantic phone call. Baquet remembers that Piazzolla was weeping. In return for some modifications of their contract, he sent him more than enough to cover the fares. Soon afterward, an express package reached Baquet's office on the rue Faubourg Saint Martin. It was the score of "Adiós Nonino"—the jewel in the crown of the Piazzolla list at Éditions Universelles.

Once again, history repeated itself in the Piazzolla family. Daniel, like his father in 1937, did not want to go home. He was hoping to join the U.S. Air Force. A letter summoning him for an interview at a base in New Jersey arrived on the day Piazzolla announced his decision to leave New York. The routines of departure soon took over. There was a farewell visit to the Bertolami cousins, duly recorded on film. The movie camera was also on hand to capture their schoolmates' farewell to Diana and Daniel.

Piazzolla's first thought was to fly back, but it proved cheaper to go by sea. And so in June 1960 the Piazzollas sailed home to Buenos Aires on the SS *Río Atuel*, a journey of about twenty days. The bilingual dog Terry had to travel in a cage, although he was sometimes allowed on deck to play with the children. The ship reached Buenos Aires on a very cold July day. Emilio and Lola Wolff were at the docks to greet the returning travelers.

Talking to the press after his return, Piazzolla insisted that things had gone well for him in New York and that he still hoped to popularize tango music in the United States, while admitting its impact there was minimal.[64] In private—talking to his brother-in-law Horacio Mártire, for instance—he was quite frank about his disillusionment with Jazz-Tango. He told more than one reporter that he was proposing to visit both France and Japan before returning to New York with "a group of musicians, dancers and singers." This was fantasy. His immediate priorities, as he told reporters, were to concentrate on film scores and music for a musical comedy, *New Faces of 1960*,* to be staged on Broadway—a plan that came to nothing.[65]

Meanwhile, he was home. "Astor Piazzolla's return is a complete one," commented *Radiolandia*, showing a picture of him with Diana and Daniel. As for his "local plans" for performing, he announced firmly, to the newspaper *Democracia*: "This time I shall impose my conception of the tango. I shall not simply make music for enthusiastic minorities. I am sure I can conquer the most diverse sections of the public. You'll see."[66]

---

*Leonard Sillman had staged several revues with this name in the past, but the next "New Faces" (without music from Piazzolla) was not produced until 1962. The show, which included dancing from Copes and Nieves, was panned by the critics.

5

Leader of the Avant-Garde 1960–1967

The Revolution Renewed

The First Quintet

Trials and Tribulations: Personal

Trials and Tribulations: Musical

Piazzolla . . . has dared to defy a traditional Establishment greater than the State, greater than the Gaucho, greater than Soccer. He has dared to challenge the Tango.

—*Marcha*, Montevideo, 15 September 1961

The Revolution Renewed

The Buenos Aires to which Piazzolla returned changed fast in the 1960s. The Argentine political scene remained uncertain: President Arturo Frondizi, elected in 1958, was ousted by the military in March 1962, and Arturo Illia, elected a year later, would undergo the same fate. The country was nevertheless invigorated by an inflow of foreign investment and by new cultural stirrings. The music of Buenos Aires, meanwhile, was altered by both national and international trends, as Argentine folk music and imported rock-and-roll steadily gained ground against the once paramount tango. Yet the cultural ferment of the new decade, a lively one everywhere, implied a potentially larger "space" for unconventional artists like Piazzolla, and he was not slow to exploit it. "The 1960s were the nicest years Buenos Aires ever had," he said in 1984.[1] The short-lived Di Tella Institute on Calle Florida, with its exhibitions and "happenings," was a particularly eloquent symbol of the decade's cultural effervescence. And Piazzolla himself became a recognized contributor to the effervescence. Juan Carlos Copes sees him, for Argentina, as "what the Beatles were to the world."[2] This is an exaggeration, but he certainly captured a respectable following among the middle-class young, who took him up as a symbol of the freeing up of cultural norms many of them wanted at the time.

Television played its part here. Soon after his return, Channel 9 invited him to do a program ("Welcome, Mr. Piazzolla"). The vibraphone in the quintet he used for the show (and for some radio work soon afterward) meant that the New York influence was not quite dead, though a number of *orquestas típicas*, notably Osvaldo Fresedo's, had used the instrument earlier. Piazzolla soon substituted a violin. His television appearances on Channel 11 in December 1961 and on Channel 7 the following month won widespread public attention, and he was to return every so often to the small screen. Television helped to turn Piazzolla into one of the Argentine cultural icons of the 1960s.

Even cultural icons have to earn their living, and nightspots were still his bread-and-butter. Buenos Aires's mid-century social changes meant that the plush cabarets of former years were fading away. The Tibidabo closed in 1955, the Marabú in 1968. The new, smaller nightspots that replaced them in the 1960s were designed less for dancing than for music—whether jazz, folk or tango. Those favoring the tango were soon labeled *tanguerías*. Professional people, intellectuals and university students formed much of their clientèle. They were tailor-made for musicians like Piazzolla. Conventional tango fans did not flock immediately to the *tanguerías*, preferring the great surviving golden age bands of Aníbal Troilo, Osvaldo Pugliese, Juan D'Arienzo, Alfredo De Angelis, and others, which continued to play in the theaters. Troilo, in particular, remained a popular idol in a way Piazzolla would never be. The conservatives adored Troilo. Their attitude to Piazzolla was either ambiguous or virulently hostile.

So once again he could not escape controversy. The war between *piazzollistas* and anti-*piazzollistas* resumed. Piazzolla's own natural combativeness sometimes added fuel to the flames. In April 1962, in the studios of Channel 7, he ran into Jorge Vidal, a tango singer whose "archaic" style he absolutely loathed. The two men came to blows and were only separated with difficulty.[3] Such episodes were inevitably seized on by the press. Piazzolla was excellent copy. *He was talked about.* In May 1965, Argentina's leading news magazine, *Primera Plana*, put him on its front cover. All publicity, as Fabien Sevitzky had implied on that noisy night in 1953, at the premiere of Piazzolla's three-movement symphonic work *Buenos Aires,* is good publicity. There were still, however, many unpublicized acts of hostility toward him, just as there had been at the time of the Octet. His friend Mario Antelo remembers times in the 1960s when taxi drivers refused to take him because he had "destroyed the tango." Daniel Piazzolla also witnessed such scenes, and also occasions when taxi drivers refused payment—"Maestro, please, you're offending me." Piazzolla himself sometimes remonstrated with recalcitrant taxi drivers, his standard line (as he told Brazilian musician Oscar Castro-Neves in 1968) being: "You can say my music isn't the tango, but you can't say it isn't Argentina."

Absolutely undeterred by this hostility, Piazzolla was more determined than ever to promote his own revolution, the path he had tried to mark out with the Octet. In the early 1960s, an impresario proposed that he should reconstitute the 1946 band—its recordings had just been reissued—to play in Rosario during Carnival, offering a fee of 2,500,000 pesos ($25,000). "Thank you," said Piazzolla, "I'm doing something else."[4] And he was far from being a passive agent in the controversies that swirled around him. He was more than happy to try to educate reporters. His work, he told one of them in April 1961, reflected a "Buenos Aires with new problems, more active, more difficult." He described his music to another as "the authentic musical expression of this period."[5]

If attacked by name in the press, he hit back hard. When the *lunfardo* poet Julián Centeya criticized him, he called his poems "lamentable." In a round table with Centeya a few years later, Piazzolla put him down harshly with a "since we are talking about culture, why don't you just shut up?"[6] Whenever given the chance, Piazzolla defended his revolution in public forums. In the first months of 1961 he gave several talks at the invitation of the Círculo de Amigos del Buen Tango, a kind of Buenos Aires clone of Montevideo's Club de la Guardia Nueva. In one of these talks, he criticized his fellow musicians Horacio Salgán and Enrique Mario Francini for allowing their art to stagnate. Piazzolla's Parisian friend Édouard Pécourt, then making his first exciting visit to Buenos Aires, was present and remembers the vigor with which Piazzolla stated his case. But Piazzolla was now very clear about his message. The tango, he said, could not be confined to "the canon of a permanent tradition." It was time to jettison the old tango song stereotypes—"the street lamp, the neckerchief, the dagger, the sterile moanings."[7] At a similar meeting in October 1961, Piazzolla played a recording of his tango "Lo que vendrá" (it was applauded) and chided the conservatives: "Everything evolves except the tango. In Brazil the Bossa Nova broke through all the previous music, and there are lots of them doing it now. Here it's different; nobody dares to break the taboos. It's the old Argentine attitude: 'Don't get involved.' " A fierce argument broke out. Luis Adolfo Sierra sprang to Piazzolla's defense. A young man shouted "Youth is with Piazzolla!"[8] It was. So were a growing number of the less youthful.

The First Quintet

Though Diana remembers him complaining, "there's no work around, no work around," there *was* more work for him in the 1960s than there had been after his return from Paris. He reestablished himself with a series of twice-weekly broadcasts with a quintet and string orchestra on Radio Splendid. Here he showcased some of his new tangos, including "Adiós Nonino." The tango expert Oscar Del Priore, first introduced to Piazzolla at one of these broadcasts, recalls bandleader Julio De Caro attending the premiere of Piazzolla's tango "Decarísimo." (De Caro had written Piazzolla encouraging letters during the New York years, something Piazzolla greatly appreciated.) "Why don't you play again?" Piazzolla asked him. "You should do what jazz musicians do. The veterans get together and form bands and play again." But De Caro never did.

The radio programs were well received, but Piazzolla needed a more stable base. He found it when the owner of the small Jamaica nightclub offered a contract to his New Tango Quintet. The Jamaica, on Calle San Martín, was something of a mecca for fans of good quality music. Among tango groups, the recently formed piano-guitar duo of Horacio Salgán and Ubaldo de Lío often played there. Visiting foreign musicians—Ella Fitzgerald, the guitarists Jim Hall and Wes Montgomery, Marlene Dietrich and her accompanist Burt Bacharach—all made a beeline for the Jamaica.

The Quinteto Nuevo Tango ("New Tango Quintet") was the first of Piazzolla's two classic quintets. Violinist Simón Bajour sees it as the real start of "the revolutionary Piazzolla." "His best period," thinks Atilio Stampone. Though sometimes temporarily disbanded, or fused with larger ensembles, the Quintet remained a recognizable entity until 1974. There were some important early changes in its personnel. The first violinist, Simón Bajour, was a veteran of several tango bands, including Osvaldo Pugliese's. (Back in 1950 he had premiered Piazzolla's Opus 12, a violin-piano piece.) When he left early in 1961 to join the Havana Symphony Orchestra in Cuba, Piazzolla sent an imploring letter to his old idol Elvino Vardaro, then in his late fifties and somewhat ailing. (When his ailments prevented him from playing, the Quintet became a quartet, Piazzolla's bandoneon covering for the violin solos.) Vardaro moved on, after about one year, to the Córdoba Symphony. If symphony orchestras could take, they could also give. Vardaro's successor, Antonio Agri, who inherited much of his style, came from the Rosario Symphony. He was unquestionably *the* violinist of the first Quintet. "It still seems a fable that I'm playing with Piazzolla," he told a reporter soon after joining in April 1962. "It's too much, it makes me nervous."[9] He always overcame his nervousness when playing in his incomparably lyrical way. The bass player, Enrique "Kicho" Díaz, Piazzolla's old companion in the Troilo band, was by now the acknowledged prince of his profession—"the father of all bass players," Piazzolla called him.[10] His inward sense of the tango tempo was unrivaled, and he produced a rich, mature sound from his instrument. He stayed with the Quintet throughout.

Jaime "El Ruso" Gosis was the group's first pianist, experienced in both tango music and jazz. Piazzolla was astonished by his extraordinary ability to play music at first glance, and took advantage of it in the complex parts he wrote for Gosis. He "played the piano with a sound," Piazzolla would say, "I never heard from anyone else."[11] After 1962 Gosis alternated with the thoroughly *tanguero* Osvaldo Manzi, who had previously worked with Troilo and Pugliese. Horacio Malvicino was once again the guitarist. He left the Quintet in 1961 but returned later. His successor, Oscar López Ruiz, a twenty-one-year-old jazz musician, was not sure whether he could really master the music. "You have a lot of swing," Piazzolla told him. "Here, take these parts, study them, then tell me whether you can play them or not." López Ruiz shut himself up at home for two weeks and decided he could.[12] He played with Piazzolla on and off until 1984, and later wrote a frank and gossipy memoir that gives us unforgettable glimpses of him. Piazzolla seems to have had a particular respect for López Ruiz's musical opinions.[13]

The Quintet's first two vocalists were Jorge Sobral and Nelly Vázquez. Piazzolla first heard Vázquez in the studio where Eduardo Rovira's ensemble, which she had just joined, was making its television debut. He immediately asked her to audition for the Quintet. Vázquez did not hesitate: "It was like the sun coming out, like a new path opening up," she says. She stayed with Piazzolla for about eighteen months, always remembering the experience as the highlight of her career. She found him very affable, "always humorous and joking." Héctor De Rosas, who joined the Quintet soon after Vázquez, had previously worked with Osvaldo Fresedo's band. He was later described by Piazzolla as the "most meticulous" of all his singers,[14] a remark that touched him. He took to Piazzolla instantly.

The Quintet rehearsed in a celebrated basement on Calle Montevideo. Soundproofed and fitted out as a studio, it belonged to the grandparents of jazz musician Sergio Mihanovich. Bing Crosby and Maurice Chevalier had been there. (A later visitor was Philip, Duke of Edinburgh, who knew Mihanovich's polo-playing brother Alex.) A more informal rehearsal—with Nelly Vázquez firmly chaperoned by her mother—took place at the suburban home of a doctor and musician, Eduardo Lagos. "Do you mind if I record?" asked Lagos, who had some very up-to-date equipment. He hung his single microphone from the chandelier in the living room. The album later released of this session gives us a precious insight into the high spirits, the sheer merriment of the Quintet in its early days.

Its stint at the Jamaica lasted for most of 1961, Piazzolla reportedly receiving a nightly fee of 800 pesos (about $100), the other musicians getting 500.[15] Here Piazzolla frequently rubbed shoulders with jazz musicians like Gustavo Kerestezachi and Sergio Mihanovich, who also played there regularly. He saw much of Mihanovich over the next year or two; they often drank coffee at the nearby Montecarlo café, and Mihanovich sometimes went to the Piazzollas' apartment to chat about jazz. Piazzolla was in buoyant mood at the Jamaica. Héctor De Rosas, so often the butt of his humor, was once left high and dry by an arrangement of the wistful tango classic "Cafetín de Buenos Aires," which had all the musicians except the guitarist leaving the stage. López Ruiz, who was in on the plot, then plucked a long final note and made a hasty exit.[16] De Rosas took such jokes with good humor.

The Jamaica was very small. The engineer Eduardo Matrajt, meeting Piazzolla again after their New York encounters, conceived the idea of a larger venue to showcase Piazzolla's music. He and his architect-partner Corradino Tenaglia bought, equipped, and soundproofed a new nightspot with a capacity of 150 on the first floor at Calle Tucumán 676. Piazzolla inaugurated the new Club 676 (which rapidly became known simply as 676) in April 1962 and played there for the next year, returning again later. It became one of the more important bases for his revolution. Club 676 alternated Piazzolla with jazz groups—Sergio Mihanovich's quintet (with Gato Barbieri on tenor saxophone and Oscar López Ruiz moonlighting as guitarist) and Jorge Calandrelli's trio. "I like that harmony of yours *a lot*," Piazzolla would tell Calandrelli. "You *must* study!" Calandrelli took his advice.

Watching Piazzolla every night at 676, Eduardo Matrajt noticed the contrast between his tense absorption while playing—"he was in another world"—and his high spirits afterward, when he was relaxing at the café on the corner. Corradino Tenaglia was less smitten and did not find his experience at 676 wholly enjoyable. For Piazzolla, however, his appearances at the club were a kind of defining moment. His audiences seemed to understand. Matrajt recalls the "church-like silence" when he played. One newspaper noted that the Quintet's performances were "surrounded by an almost religious silence and expectation"—this was clearly "not 'music to chat through.' "[17] Not that 676 was always crowded. Attendance was poor on the earlier week nights. On one occasion, remembered by Piazzolla's future agent Atilio Talín, the "public" was one newly married couple.

In general, however, 676 made its mark. It became a lively rendezvous for Argentine musicians and for the usual crowd of foreign visitors, for whom it was *the* place to spend an evening. Piazzolla met a host of distinguished musicians at the club—the Israel Chamber Orchestra, the Philadelphia Symphony, the Vegh Quartet, the Modern Jazz Quartet, Tommy Dorsey and his band, and Brazilian stars like Mayssa Matarazzo, João Gilberto, Os Cariocas. He was delighted to add such people to his growing circle of international admirers. Among them was Stan Getz, whose quartet played at 676 in September 1965. Piazzolla and the Quintet were playing when Getz went to inspect the club. Getz was transfixed. He insisted that he and his group should play first, before the Quintet. Piazzolla dissuaded him. It was a memorable night. Getz so dazzled the audience that Piazzolla refused to go on for a second turn. "These fellows have played *everything!*" he announced. At one point that night Getz asked his young vibraphonist, Gary Burton, to play "My Funny Valentine" as a solo. Piazzolla almost fainted, "marveling at this man."[18] Burton did not forget the occasion, either. Hearing Piazzolla, he says, "was a very amazing experience; his music was so different; we were impressed with the sort of progressive modern style of it." He took some Piazzolla records back to the United States and played them to his friends—"They all went 'wow!' " Twenty years later the two men met again, once more memorably.

If television, radio, and nightspots like the Jamaica and 676 boosted Piazzolla's revolution in the early 1960s, so too did the recording studio. He recorded far more than he had ever done before. On his return from New York, he won RCA-Victor's agreement to make two long-playing records—one mostly of his own music, the other of "conventional" tangos. The first, the "avant-garde" album, was recorded (late at night, so as to avoid interruptions) in January 1961, and the second, "danceable" album, in March. The first album sold far better than the second, which Piazzolla saw as an encouraging sign that his revolution was gaining ground. Recording the second, conventional album also inspired him to see whether his Quintet could play at dances. Its single attempt to do so, at the Confitería Nino in the suburb of Vicente López, was a dreadful flop. The audience wanted to listen, not to dance.[19]

Piazzolla could never refrain for very long from experimenting with instrumental formats. Early in 1963 he expanded the quintet into an octet—something he had done late in 1961 to play the sound track for the film *Prisioneros de una noche*; this was Argentine director David Kohon's debut, a highly atmospheric portrayal of Buenos Aires nightlife. The new Octeto Contemporáneo began performing at La Noche, a nightspot a block or so away from 676—named after a popular Thursday program hosted by the well-known TV personality Nicolás "Pipo" Mancera, one of the sponsors of the new *tanguería*. José Bragato joined the group with his cello, along with León Jacobson (percussion) and Jorge Barone (flute), both of whom came from the Teatro Colón orchestra. Piazzolla selected Jacobson even before meeting him casually in a café on Avenida Córdoba, where he was chatting about the planned octet. "Do you have percussion?" asked Jacobson. "Yes, I have León Jacobson; he's from the Colón," replied Piazzolla, not realizing that he was talking to him. Jacobson and Barone usually turned up at La Noche in tuxedos, coming straight from the opera house. At some point each night Piazzolla asked his three extras to stand down while he reverted to playing with the Quintet.

Though it lasted only a few months, the Octeto Contemporáneo won a definite following. It broadcast on Radio Municipal and recorded several of Piazzolla's film scores. Some of its performances were shown on another of "Pipo" Mancera's popular television programs. This paved the way for it to make an album for CBS, *Tango contemporáneo*, which included a fragment read by the distinguished novelist Ernesto Sábato from his classic *Sobre héroes y tumbas* against a musical background by Piazzolla. (Piazzolla certainly thought about basing a musical drama on Sábato's book—something like *West Side Story*, he told Ferrer—but this scheme got no further.) Piazzolla's versatility on this album is extraordinary. The setting of the Sábato fragment, with a flute added to the bandoneon-violin-cello lineup, subtly evokes the Buenos Aires of a past era, while Piazzolla's plaintive bandoneon underscores the solitude of Sábato's fictional protagonist in the anomic modern city. Also remarkable on this album are the versions of Piazzolla's tango "Lo que vendrá," Emilio Balcarce's "Sideral," and José Bragato's "Noposepe," composed specially for the shortlived "New Octet."

A year after his experiment with the Octet, Piazzolla recorded, also for CBS, an EP (extended play) album of four tangos with Roberto Yanés, a well-known bolero singer. Yanés was very favorably struck by Piazzolla's friendly attitude and by his no-nonsense professionalism: "He sat me down at the piano and said: 'How would *you* accompany this?'" Also in 1964, the Philips label brought out a retrospective album covering Piazzolla's music from 1944 to 1964. It included pieces played by a "reconstructed" 1946 band, with Ernesto Baffa as one of the bandoneonists—the only time this well-known instrumentalist recorded with Piazzolla. The album was "a way of showing my evolution," as Piazzolla put it.[20] It was also a sign of the recognition he was at last winning.

Piazzolla's revolutionary advance in the 1960s would never have been achieved without his own new music. It *was* a peculiarly fertile period. The sheer quantity of new works was remarkable, and the works themselves were often longer than before, expanding beyond the old three-minute standard imposed by radio and the now vanished 78-rpm disc. Much of his effort in the first half of the decade went into pieces conceived or adapted for the Quintet. Among the most notable, perhaps, are his "Ángel" and "Diablo" sequences. The first of the "ángel" pieces was written earlier (1957) and used in Alberto Rodríguez Muñoz's three-act play *El tango del ángel* (1962) as was the "Introducción al ángel." The "ángel" sequence has a particularly inspired melodic vein; the "Diablo" pieces reflect a somewhat harsher mood.

There are many other pieces that stand out, some of which—"Decarísimo" (1961), "Buenos Aires Hora Cero" (1963), "Fracanapa" (1963)—survived in his repertory to the end of his performing career. What is perhaps most striking about this cluster is the sheer verve with which Piazzolla constantly extends his techniques and explores new sounds. The counterpoint in the jaunty tango "Revirado" (1963) reflected a skill he had now thoroughly mastered. The fugal themes he uses for the first time in "Calambre" (1961)—a direct ancestor of his celebrated fugue in the "little opera" *María de Buenos Aires* a few years later—would become common in much of his music from then on. In "Buenos Aires Hora Cero" he eliminates altogether the traditional "sections" into which tangos had always been divided, another important precedent. "Fracanapa" is an example of Piazzolla tapping ingeniously into older traditions: rhythmically reminiscent of Pugliese's celebrated "La Yumba," it carries traces of the *milonga*, the forerunner of the tango. The last thirty-six bars of "Imágenes 676" (1962), to mention one further piece, are written in 3/4 time, giving us the feeling of a tango and a *malambo* tap dance fused into one.

Alongside his work for the Quintet, he still did numerous arrangements. He needed to, according to Diana, to keep his finances in reasonable shape. His royalties were probably now slightly more buoyant than previously, though he still relied heavily on income from France. Jorge Barone saw (in 1963) one of Piazzolla's half-yearly statements from SADAIC,* the main royalty-collecting organization for Argentine musicians. Four-fifths of the total 500,000 pesos (around $4,500) came from Éditions Universelles in Paris. In September-October 1962 he both arranged and recorded music for the American evangelist Billy Graham,

---

*SADAIC—Sociedad Argentina de Autores y Compositores de Música, founded 1936, the equivalent of ASCAP in the USA or SACEM in France.

then visiting South America. In 1966 he turned his hand to a ballet score, *Campeón*, for his former partner Juan Carlos Copes. As always, the cinema was a useful standby—ten new film scores between 1960 and 1967.* And he was continuing to write classical works. In February 1963, the Asociación Amigos de la Música awarded him its Alfredo Hirsch Prize, effectively a commission for an orchestral work. The resulting "Serie de tangos sinfónicos" (now usually titled "Tres movimientos tanguísticos porteños") was premiered at a concert in August 1963 at the Teatro Coliseo under Paul Klecki's baton. "It's the first time I've felt the urge to dance a fugue," quipped the distinguished European conductor. The audience liked it, but critical opinions were more mixed. *La Prensa* found it "naive" and declared that it added nothing to the attempt to "raise the status of popular music." *La Razón*, by contrast, admired its "delicate, at times sparkling, thematic line." *La Nación* noted that the work had a "postromantic tone, enhanced by a very varied instrumentation. It was cordially received in the hall, Klecki sharing the applause with the author."[21]

Though Buenos Aires was the focus of Piazzolla's work in the 1960s, he wanted to pick up what engagements he could in the Argentine provinces. He was already looking beyond Argentina. In 1962 and again in 1964 he announced European and perhaps Asian tours for the Quintet.[22] Nothing came of these hopes. For the time being, his expeditions were limited to his native land and to Uruguay, which most Argentines do not consider "abroad." It was harder in the provinces than in Buenos Aires to attract good audiences. Jorge Strada, who first heard the Quintet during these years, suggests that Piazzolla's provincial followers at this period were mostly jazz fans and intellectuals. Piazzolla's principal aim was to make his music better known outside Buenos Aires, and he found, to his pleasure, that audiences often preferred his innovative style to more conventional fare. His later recollections of these forays were philosophical: "Sometimes they paid me on board the plane, as if we were two-bit farmers; sometimes there were absent-minded impresarios who never paid us. It was ugly but necessary."[23]

Some of the early provincial tours were organized by publisher Roberto Capuano, now Piazzolla's agent. The arrangement worked well for a while, but

Sábado a la noche cine and *Las furias* (both released in 1960); *Quinto año nacional* (1961); *Detrás de la mentira* (1962); *Los que verán a Dios* (1963); *El fin del mundo* (1963); *Paula cautiva* (1963); *Con gusto a rabia* (1965); *Las locas del conventillo* (1966); and *Las Pirañas* (1967). None of the movies was particularly memorable. *Detrás de la mentira* was crass anti-communist propaganda. *Los que verán a Dios* was the first Argentine film to deal with the theme of abortion.

Capuano could not always go on tour, and it was not easy for him to see that the Quintet was properly paid. At Mendoza, in the mid-1960s, a particular incident led to a cutting remark from one of the musicians: "What do agents actually *do*?" Piazzolla reported this to Capuano, and he withdrew as his agent, although he remained a friend. Another friend, Miguel Selinger, a Buenos Aires jeweler and devoted fan (and one of the sponsors of La Noche in 1963), did accompany the Quintet on many of its early tours out of pure devotion. Piazzolla asked him one night to fill in as master of ceremonies "You are now the Quintet's official presenter," he told him. Selinger happily served as such for several years.

The tours of the 1960s were later evoked in very animated fashion by Oscar López Ruiz. He depicts them as full of comedy, Piazzolla always indulging in what devilry he could: trapping and annoying a local farmer into embarrassing confessions of masturbation during a "truth game" at Trelew, furtively sneaking up to hit a mediocre jazz trumpeter at Comodoro Rivadavia, introducing a monkey into Elvino Vardaro's hotel room, firing his hunting rifle in the early hours in the (in those days) tranquil Las Rosas district of Córdoba.[24] These stories could go on and on. But sometimes there was hostility. Certain Buenos Aires prejudices evidently followed him to the provinces. Some audiences even affected to find a lack of patriotism in his challenge to the conventional tango world. At a recital in Córdoba Province, an angry audience stopped the Quintet after half an hour and stormed menacingly toward the stage. Héctor De Rosas calmed the crowd by singing some traditional folk songs, with the help of his guitar and Enrique "Kicho" Díaz's double bass. It worked like a charm. Piazzolla was able to chat with the audience, telling them that his music was not "anti-Argentine, but an up-to-date way of doing the tango."

And the tours had their rewards. In Córdoba at the end of 1961, Piazzolla learned of a young local bandoneonist who had formed a tango octet and asked to meet him. It was the young bandoneonist Rodolfo Mederos who had been so dazzled by the music of Piazzolla's Octet a few years earlier. He almost fainted when introduced. He was studying biology at Córdoba University and was ambivalent about abandoning his courses. "This fellow has all the right qualities, he's phenomenal," Piazzolla told Miguel Selinger. On a second visit to Córdoba a year or two later, Piazzolla invited Mederos's octet to be the backing group at his concerts. In the street afterward, he asked him: "Rodolfo, when are you coming to Buenos Aires?" Mederos moved there two weeks later.

In September 1961 the Quintet made its first visit to Montevideo. According to Héctor De Rosas, the Uruguayan fans "followed Piazzolla through the streets as if he were Gardel."[25] The visit won the attention of the left-wing magazine

Marcha (one of the best in Latin America in that now forgotten age of hope) and the Quintet did a recital in its auditorium.[26] *Marcha* organized a televised round table discussion for Piazzolla and some of his Uruguayan critics. One of them, Alberto Luces, denounced Piazzolla's music for including "counterpoint, fugues and other irreverences." Piazzolla castigated Luces as a "throwback" comparable to a chimpanzee, and condemned the "dinosaurs" who opposed him. He and his musicians then walked out.[27]

Despite their comic side, so richly evoked in López Ruiz's memoir, the provincial tours were very hard work. Conditions left everything to be desired: shabby hotels, low-life venues (including at least one bordello, in Tucumán), buses that broke down, unscrupulous impresarios. López Ruiz recalls a particular cabaret in Comodoro Rivadavia, the Patagonian oil-town: torn tablecloths, worn linoleum on the floor, half the light bulbs out, the playbills reading "Astor Zapiola and his Orchestra." And there were always the hisses and whistles, the notes passed to Piazzolla that read "A lot of noise and not much tango."[28] It was a hard slog. The pickings were meager.

It was worth it. By 1965 Piazzolla was enough of a name for President Arturo Illia's government to invite the Quintet to visit both the United States and Brazil to show the flag of Argentine culture, as part of a delegation including the great tango singer Edmundo Rivero. The musicians flew to the United States on 24 May, appearing first at the Pan-American Union in Washington and then in a televised concert at Mount Vernon. Piazzolla was astonished to discover the extent of his reputation in the United States, at least among musicians. While in Washington, he went with Jaime Gosis and Oscar López Ruiz to hear the saxophonist "Cannonball" Adderley playing with *his* quintet. When Piazzolla introduced himself, Adderley exclaimed: "God! I have all your records!"

The musicians moved on to New York, to the Philharmonic (now Avery Fisher) Hall, where the concert was a great success. *New York Times* critic Robert Shelton praised the Quintet for its "freewheeling imagination" and "unusual instrumental timbres"—it combined "a 1920-ish ballroom dance band, a modern jazz combo, then a classical quintet turning from chamber music to bossa nova." In the end, said Shelton, it "sounded like nothing but itself, and that was quite enough."[29] Piazzolla kept a clipping of this review for the rest of his life, always reading it with a touch of sorrow. How could it be that foreigners understood his efforts better than most Argentine critics? Apparently they could. In New York, the noted jazz guitarist Jim Hall, who had met Oscar López Ruiz in Buenos Aires, invited him to attend a recording session for a long-playing record he was making with alto saxophonist Paul Desmond. Piazzolla went with him. Another studio guest, drummer Connie Kay of the Modern Jazz Quartet, learning who he was, flung open the studio door and shouted, "You've no idea who's here!" to the musicians. As López Ruiz recounts, "It seemed they were face to face with the Messiah. They embraced him, touched him, talked to him all at once."[30] Piazzolla was often to be surprised—before the 1970s and 1980s—by the way foreign musicians acclaimed him. By the 1980s and 1990s *not* to have heard of him was a sign of musical ignorance.

The short visits to Brazil (the Quintet's first) and Uruguay that followed the American excursion confirmed Piazzolla's feeling that he was better appreciated abroad than at home. The musicians were wildly acclaimed in São Paulo and Rio de Janeiro. The Quintet performed at the large SODRE (Servicio Oficial de Difusión Radio Eléctrica) auditorium in Montevideo, one of the Uruguayan capital's best-known concert venues. Their appearance was poorly publicized, but word had somehow got around, the hall overflowed, and the applause was overwhelming.[31]

Before leaving on his travels, Piazzolla had agreed to write some music for Alberto Rodríguez Muñoz's play *Melenita de oro*, to be staged in August 1965. The music was to be recorded, with the Quintet miming its performance onstage. Piazzolla realized, on returning to Buenos Aires from Brazil, that the recording was next day—with the music still unwritten. He wrote it overnight.[32] Of the four pieces he composed, the best known is "Verano porteño," the first of his classic "Buenos Aires Seasons." The critics did not handle the play generously but found the music "original and agreeable."[33] A more serious venture, back in Buenos Aires, was an album of the music played at the Philharmonic Hall concert. It was the first long playing record to consist exclusively of Piazzolla's own music. It is a remarkable album. Piazzolla himself regarded it as a significant milestone on his musical journey.

The year 1965 brought a further milestone: a collaboration with Argentina's greatest modern writer, Jorge Luis Borges, who had broken through to worldwide celebrity since the early 1960s. The idea was an album of some new Borges poems and *milongas* set by Piazzolla and sung by the bass Edmundo Rivero, together with Piazzolla's still unused music for the story "Hombre de la esquina rosada." Borges had apparently been asked for the poems by the classical composer Carlos Guastavino.[34] Borges's friend Félix Della Paolera and Piazzolla's friend Alberto Salem (by then news director at Channel 13) helped to arrange the vital meeting between the two men, over tea at the Confitería St. James on Calle Maipú, one of Borges's favorite places. On the afternoon of 14 March 1965 Borges visited the

Piazzollas (much to their excitement) at their apartment on Avenida Entre Ríos, accompanied by his eighty-eight-year old mother, the formidable Doña Leonor. Borges signed one of his books for Dedé, or rather Doña Leonor signed for him, as he was now almost blind. Borges recited one of his newly written *milongas*. Piazzolla played the piano. Dedé, with her untrained but pleasant voice, sang three of the new songs, seeing tears in Borges's eyes.

The recording of the album took place later in the year. In the EMI-Odeon studios in Avenida Córdoba, Borges listened impassively as Edmundo Rivero recorded the *milonga* "A Don Nicanor Paredes," which Piazzolla described as "composed on a ground of eight bars of Gregorian chant, the melodic part without artificial modernisms, all very simple, deeply felt and sincere." Piazzolla asked him if he liked it. "I liked it better when the girl sang it," replied Borges—the "girl" being Dedé. When the LP appeared, Borges expressed equivocal opinions about it, something that irritated Piazzolla. If Borges had any musical preferences at all (he was always happy to admit his tone deafness), they were for the old *milonga* rather than the tango. For whatever reason, he took a permanent dislike to Piazzolla, often referring to him as "Pianola"[35]—hardly one of his happier inspirations. During a television program in the mid-1980s he even credited the *milongas* to Guastavino. He once walked out of a Piazzolla recital in Córdoba, muttering, "I'm leaving. They aren't playing tangos today."[36] It was an opinion shared in the 1960s by many Argentines who should have known better.

Trials and Tribulations: Personal

Returning from New York in July 1960, Astor and Dedé went to stay with Dedé's sister Liebe and her husband Horacio Mártire. The children went to their Wolff grandparents. It was Horacio's idea. Prices had risen since 1958, and Piazzolla needed to check costs thoroughly before buying property. The family soon moved into a rented apartment (9E) at Calle Libertad 942. In May 1962 Piazzolla bought a tenth-floor apartment at Avenida Entre Ríos 505. Journalist and writer León Benarós, interviewing him there soon afterward, noted its "well-stocked library with beautiful art books to the fore."[37] "I shall never move from here," Piazzolla told José Bragato, showing him round. "Look, it's like a castle in the air." And indeed, the cityscape seen from the windows (the high, pinched dome of the Congress building well in view) was very striking.

The Piazzolla family quickly reestablished the routines of Argentine life. The summer after their return from New York they vacationed at Bahía San Blas, south of Bahía Blanca, where Piazzolla was able to fish once again, sometimes

from the shore, sometimes from a launch. They stayed at the Hotel Jorge New-
bery—"very precarious and rudimentary," Dedé remembers—and were joined
there by some of their Bertolami cousins, and by Nonina, who was still mourning
the death of Vicente. They celebrated her birthday with her on 20 February 1961.
Outwardly, Piazzolla's private life seemed to be running smoothly, although there
were some (Eduardo Matrajt at 676, for instance) who suspected that things were
beginning to go wrong. Diana and Daniel had navigated their way through the
shoals of adolescence. Their schooldays were over: Diana was twenty in 1963,
Daniel eighteen. In April 1962, *La Razón* photographed the "three Ds," Piazzolla,
and the bilingual dog Terry in a scene of delightful family bliss. In the same
paper, two years later, Piazzolla paid a warm public tribute to what Dedé had
"given and continues to give me."[38]

Diana, who had earlier seen her parents' relationship as "very close, marvelous," became aware in the early 1960s of "not arguments exactly, but certainly
whisperings." For his part, Daniel was surprised to observe his father ogling a
woman in the street—"My old man looking at girls—how weird!" Piazzolla,
however, stayed off "difficult" topics with his children. He would not tell Diana
openly of his disagreement with her growing political interest, which was moving
toward the left-wing Peronism soon to become prominent in Argentina. Her
relationship to her father was one of "daughter-idol, daughter-musician." It was
not quite what she needed.

Early in 1964 Piazzolla took Dedé on a four-month trip to Europe. They left
on 8 February, and once again traveled both ways on cargo-passenger ships: the
Lago Traful and the *Río Corrientes*. On the outward voyage, Piazzolla acted King
Neptune in the traditional "crossing the Line" festivities. From Las Palmas he
scrawled a note to Ferrer, announcing his new venture—with his two inseparable
companions, Dedé and the bandoneon. They reached Paris by way of London—
where they did the usual sightseeing (Houses of Parliament, Trafalgar Square,
National Gallery, Piccadilly Circus)—and Rotterdam (more sightseeing), at the
beginning of March. They went to stay with their friends Édouard and Valerie
Pécourt at their house in the rue Brancion in the 15th *arrondissement*. Dedé would
have preferred the privacy of a hotel. She recompensed the Pécourts by shopping
for them and helping in the kitchen. Astor and Dedé were allotted the main
bedroom. It was crammed with records, part of Pécourt's legendary collection,
which enormously impressed Piazzolla, as it does anyone lucky enough to have
seen it.

While in Paris, Piazzolla met Yves Baquet several times, once with a representative of the Vogue record label. Piazzolla had evidently had nibbles; he was think-

ing of the kinds of compositions he would offer European record companies. But no recording deals materialized. He was not impressed by the standing of tango music in Paris: his recordings of 1955 were still well known, he told Ferrer, but tango musicians in France had done little to follow his example. He also visited pianist Martial Solal in his studio near the Porte de Champerret and gave him one of his records, rather to Solal's surprise.

From Paris, he and Dedé made side trips to Germany (the Rhine, Bavaria) and Switzerland. Piazzolla also visited Italy on his own. It was on this trip that he first encountered, in a café in Milan, the agent Aldo Pagani, whose part in Piazzolla's future was to be so important. For the Swiss tour they rented a Volkswagen, and Dedé became very expert at interpreting road maps. The home movies that survive show them eating cherries by a lake, and Astor presenting Dedé a bunch of Alpine violets. Their longest excursion that spring was to Spain, where they visited Madrid, the Escorial, and the Valley of the Fallen, General Franco's pharaonic monument. They went to a bullfight, which neither of them liked. In Barcelona, Dedé, with some difficulty, tracked down her long lost "Uncle Manolo," Manuel Filgueira, to whom the Wolffs had sent chocolates and socks during the Spanish Civil War. At the last of several addresses they checked, they learned that "el señor Manuel" had recently moved but still came back to collect his mail. They left him a note, and in due course he found them at their hotel. The white-haired Don Manuel tearfully embraced his niece, exclaiming (in good Galician) *"filha de mi hermana"* ("my sister's daughter!"), and took them out to dinner. There was a happy sequel to this reunion. Emilio and Lola Wolff and Poupée all later visited Uncle Manolo in Spain.

During the Piazzollas' stay in Paris, Édouard Pécourt became aware of tensions between Astor and Dedé. He did not take them too seriously, believing "that all of us men are fairly unfaithful, and that his position as a musician made it much worse." He talked to them both, as he recalls, "trying to temporize, to prevent a separation. I didn't believe in it very much. I thought that it would get sorted out." It did not. Dedé became mildly alarmed by Astor's behavior. "Look after me at night," he suddenly told her, "because I have a double personality." It was something he began repeating often once they got back to Buenos Aires (as in 1955, by way of Hamburg) in July. He now began to fall silent for hours on end. Whenever she tried to get through to him, he would talk about his "double personality," telling her he was simply no longer the Astor she had known. By this stage he was certainly seeing another woman—"a youngish lass, divine," Oscar López Ruiz remembers. She often turned up at the nightspots where the Quintet was playing. When Dedé was also there, López Ruiz asked: "Astor, aren't you aware of the risk you're running?" "Yes, I *am* aware," Piazzolla told him. An old secret admirer of Dedé's eventually told her what was going on.

The domestic situation quickly worsened. There were rows and arguments. José Bragato, collecting a piece of music from the Avenida Entre Ríos apartment, was met by Piazzolla at the door: " 'Get out! there's trouble in the house.' There were some shouts from inside. Impressive, that was." Although they exchanged the customary gifts on their twenty-third wedding anniversary in October 1965— art books from Astor, music scores and clothes from Dedé[39]—the ground was giving way under their feet.

On the morning of Sunday, 2 February 1966, just over a month before his forty-fifth birthday, Piazzolla packed a suitcase and moved out of the apartment. "I hope you find a man who really deserves you," he told Dedé—a remark that simply confused her.[40] He woke Daniel. "Danny, I'm off." "Well, okay, dad, so long." "No, I'm going." "Do you want me to accompany you?" "No, I'm leaving home. I'm separating from Mama, and I'm off." Daniel wept. Diana was paralyzed by feelings she found hard to analyze, either then or later.

Piazzolla moved to the Hotel Tres Sargentos, near the Plaza San Martín, Daniel taking his clothes there later that day. Someone who caught a glimpse of him at this time was the young bandoneonist Rodolfo Mederos. His instrument had been stolen on a train journey. Oscar López Ruiz suggested that Piazzolla might lend him one of his spares, warning Mederos: "Look, he's just separated from his wife." Piazzolla answered the phone in a "rather sad voice," but invited Mederos round. "I entered the room," Mederos remembers, "in semi-darkness, with some break-fast leftovers, and saw him stretched out on the bed. He was really broken-up." Piazzolla regained his composure. He phoned Daniel, telling him to give Mederos "such-and-such a bandoneon on such-and-such a shelf." A few days later, he told Mederos: "I was thinking of selling it anyway. If you like it, pay me whatever way you can, and whenever you can." Whenever reminded about it, however, Piazzolla always refused to accept payment.

After his days at the Tres Sargentos, Piazzolla rented a sixth-floor apartment at Calle Carlos Pellegrini 979. His Steinway piano (bought in 1963) was shifted there from Avenida Entre Ríos later in February. Soon afterward he bought an apartment at Avenida Libertador 1088 (14 "C"), where he was to live until 1972. He started to pick up the pieces. It was not easy. Dedé had been popular among his friends. Several phoned her to express sympathy; violinist Antonio Agri was in tears, Dedé recalls. In due course, the lawyers disentangled the marriage. A legal separation was decreed by the courts on 31 October 1967—the day that would have been their silver wedding anniversary. The separation could not become a divorce, since this was still not legal in Argentina. When it was, twenty years later, the marriage was finally dissolved (19 February 1988).

How long Piazzolla remained in thrall to the "youngish lass" we do not know. He soon took up with a thirty-something woman married to a prominent Swiss businessman. Oscar López Ruiz, whose first marriage had just ended, was then in dalliance with a new girlfriend; the two of them often went out with Piazzolla and his new lover, at least for a while. Piazzolla told Dedé that the woman practiced black magic, but also that she was "a *señora* like you, so respect her." The affair was evidently fairly turbulent. After one particularly violent quarrel, he went to see Dedé, in tears. "Astor, I'm not your mother," Dedé told him, "I'm your wife." The sheer stress of this affair gave Piazzolla some sort of seizure. His doctor got him to the hospital and gave him appropriate treatment, and afterwards arranged for a visit "to see if he needed therapy or not."[41] Piazzolla was feeling very depressed by this stage and agreed to undergo some psychotherapy. The therapist told him bluntly to ditch the woman and find someone else. "How insensitive!" Piazzolla joked years later. "I'm dying of despair and he gives me *that* sort of advice!"[42] The press learned little of what was happening, though early in 1967 the magazine *Gente* printed a photo of the woman (identifying her as "Norma") under the caption, "the protagonist of something nice."[43] The "something nice" ended fairly abruptly, not too long after the photograph. Piazzolla showed his deepest feelings about Norma by changing the title of "Canto de octubre" (a piece from 1965) to "La Mandrágora" ("The Mandrake"), a poisonous plant—his nickname for her.*

His behavior was now changing fairly drastically. "He began to believe that he was a movie heartthrob," says Hugo Baralis. As Daniel recalls, he started to go "around with an impressive number of women."[44] Old friends like Baralis and Máximo Perrotti remonstrated with him, but to no avail. His emotional upheaval (not forgetting the controversies his music was arousing) placed immense strains on him. Some of his friends believed he was sniffing cocaine again. His in-laws Horacio and Liebe Mártire remember a time when he visited their apartment, sat down, tried to say something, could not, and simply left. To Ferrer and others he did manage to say something, telling them that he was in the worst state he could ever remember and complaining bitterly of his terrible loneliness in the Avenida Libertador apartment. He was very depressed.

After Norma, Piazzolla's next serious attachment was the actress, musician,

---

Mandrake no longer means anything to English-speakers. John Donne's famous line, "Get with child a mandrake root," needs to be explained to most modern readers.

and singer Egle Martin, then in her late twenties and married to Eduardo "Lalo" Palacios, a ranch-manager in Corrientes Province. Long a Piazzolla fan, Egle had first met him four years earlier, during one of "Pipo" Mancera's television programs. Soon afterward, acting in Daniel Tinayre's film *Extraña ternura* (1964), she persuaded Piazzolla one night at La Noche to write a song for the movie, and he agreed to set "Graciela Oscura," a poem by the talented Ulyses Petit de Murat. The song, repeated several times, turned out to be the main attraction of the movie when it ran at the Monumental Cinema for six weeks in spring 1964. Piazzolla's relationship with Egle gave him emotional stability—so Daniel, who got on very well with her, believes. Egle found things more complicated. It was "a salvation, a salvation of the spirit, of the soul," she says, yet she was still "very happy" with her husband. "It was very difficult to understand. It was a passion." Music was certainly a fundamental link between them. As Piazzolla told the press several times, he was making great plans to record with her, and they did eventually record together for Philips, in October 1967.

Despite Norma and Egle, Piazzolla's thoughts still often turned to Dedé. She was sometimes drawn into his new way of life in very unfortunate ways. On 31 October 1967, the day of the legal separation, Daniel took her to lunch in a downtown restaurant. Piazzolla had arranged with him to bump into them at the door. Piazzolla and Dedé went for a stroll. In Calle Florida he bought two silver rings, one for Dedé, one for himself. "Why don't we go to my apartment?" he suggested. They went. Piazzolla played some music. The inevitable happened. They made love and Dedé became pregnant. Dedé was now in her forties, and on the advice of her physician, she had an abortion. When she phoned Piazzolla (who had been out of town) with the news, he simply chuckled: "How amusing! They'd have been uncle and nephew at the same age!" (Diana had recently had a child.) Dedé was hurt by this callously cruel remark. She instantly hung up.

Soon afterward he tried again. "Why don't we see each other once a week?" he asked Dedé over dinner. "I'd cook a chicken, we'd make love, we'd listen to some music, and then you'd leave." Very offended, Dedé retorted: "I'm not just any old girl, I'm your wife." But they did not stop seeing each other altogether. Piazzolla sometimes phoned her, there was a fitful correspondence, and several efforts at reconciliation.

It is hard to see the breakup of the marriage as anything other than catastrophic. Dedé's world collapsed. As Liebe Mártire puts it, "Astor destroyed my sister's life," a verdict emphatically shared by Poupée Wolff. Its effects on the children were scarcely less traumatic. Both of them left home. (Terry, the bilingual dog, was given away.) Diana soon got married. For Daniel, the next few years were a confused time. He worked as a ranch hand, also running a restaurant at Villa Gesell, the brash new ocean resort north of Mar del Plata, where at one point he spent a month in prison on a trumped-up charge from the local police. Piazzolla himself certainly had regrets about his decision. In public, he never spoke ill of Dedé. "She was the one who *made* Piazzolla," he declared in 1974.[45] (Like Julius Caesar or Charles de Gaulle, he often spoke of himself in public statements in the third person.) At his cousin Enriqueta Bertolami's house in Mar del Plata, he would examine her paintings on the wall, explaining how well they had done in exhibitions. The Mar del Plata relatives were shocked by the breakup. Cousin Nelly Sorrentino could scarcely believe that "a marriage like that" could end. Nonina remained fond of Dedé, but she took her son's side: "He's Astor, he's my son," she told Diana.

Trials and Tribulations: Musical

On 28 June 1966 the Argentine army deposed the teddy-bearish President Arturo Illia, installed General Juan Carlos Onganía in the Casa Rosada, the presidential palace, and proclaimed an "Argentine Revolution." They talked of holding power for a generation, and held it for seven years. General Onganía had a strong distaste for "exquisite intellectuals." His persecution of Argentina's universities, especially their science departments, was both gratuitous and disastrous. He also had a minor obsession about the obvious wickedness of nightclubs, long hair, and miniskirts.

Not long after the coup d'état, the Quintet was playing at Sí, a nightspot in the leafy Belgrano district. After the show one night, Piazzolla was chatting with his pianist and guitarist when some policemen entered and demanded their documents. Piazzolla made an acid remark, and was immediately bundled into a car and taken to a police station. Only at eight the following morning, after a phone call to an acquaintance who worked at the Casa Rosada, was he released. Very angry, Piazzolla insisted he should be driven home by the officer who had arrested him (long since asleep in bed). When they were in the police car together—so he told Oscar López Ruiz—he promised him that if he ever came across him out of uniform, he would "break every bone in his body."[46]

Whatever its other effects, General Onganía's "revolution" did not dampen Piazzolla's own musical revolution. Controversy continued to swirl around him. But he felt that his revolution was gaining ground. As he told *La Nación* in 1967, only a few had supported the avant-garde tango at first; now there were "many of us who struggle for the new musical current."[47] During a round table at the

Di Tella Institute in July 1969, he observed that he no longer saw himself simply as "a minority musician." He now realized "that along with the painters, writers and students who enjoy my work, executives are enjoying it too."[48] And not only executives: producers of cinema newsreels and television news programs were increasingly using snatches of his music as background.

The press, however, continued to focus on the newsworthy tension between the avant-garde and the conventional tango world. In this classic conflict between ancients and moderns, the press, true to form, decided to personalize the issues. Piazzolla was the obvious champion of the moderns. Who better than Aníbal Troilo, the great popular idol, to champion the ancients? Both Piazzolla and Troilo hated this kind of idiotic stereotyping. Piazzolla's respect for Troilo was always near to absolute, though he almost certainly felt that Troilo was not renewing his art, describing him later as "a sentimentalist" who had somehow got stuck in "his repertory of 1940."[49] Here he was being rather unfair. Troilo's band was one thing, but in his work with smaller ensembles (the Troilo-Grela Quartet and his own quartet), Troilo actually reached his peak in the 1960s, with some awesome bandoneon playing.

Whatever the newspapers said, Troilo's affection for Piazzolla was never really undermined. "Astor could have been my son," he once declared. He sometimes dropped in at 676, imbibing copious amounts of whiskey, his favorite drink, and sometimes retiring to the men's room to sniff the cocaine he also fancied. But what did he think of the music? Journalist Edmundo Eichelbaum several times saw him weeping with emotion at 676. Yet Troilo was also once indiscreet enough to voice a very different feeling, within earshot of Hugo Baralis: "*No, pibe, eso no es tango*" ("No, my boy, that's not the tango"). The remark won instant notoriety. It hurt Piazzolla. But the relationship still mattered intensely to him. In 1965, when he wrote "Verano porteño," he immediately did an arrangement for Troilo's band. Not long afterward, the two men met in a café in Avenida Corrientes. "Gato," said Troilo, "I would like you to do me an arrangement of 'Verano porteño.'" It was at that moment under Piazzolla's arm.[50]

The two men continued to work together on occasion. In December 1961, "forgetting the little irritations," as one newspaper put it,[51] they appeared on Channel 11. Troilo announced that, in Piazzolla's honor, he would play "Lo que vendrá," and he invited Piazzolla to join him. Both the audience and Piazzolla were moved. In the summer season of 1970, to look ahead a bit, the two of them shared the bill in Mar del Plata. Piazzolla paid public tribute to Troilo as "the man who put the tango into long pants," the greatest figure of the 1940s.[52] As a direct outcome of the Mar del Plata show, they joined forces soon afterward in a televised tribute to Carlos Gardel on 24 June 1970, the thirty-fifth anniversary of the Creole Thrush's death, playing the tangos "El motivo" and "Volver." An RCA-Victor executive was so impressed that he suggested to Troilo that the two men should record the numbers. Piazzolla agreed. In August they met at the RCA-Victor studios on Calle Moreno. Over cups of coffee there were "reminiscences, stories, a few jokes," as the executive recalled. "The atmosphere was ideal. They went into the studio, sat down, and started to play. How it sounded! The excitement in the control room was indescribable. Two colossi!"[53] When the record was released, one newspaper commented that the two "sacred monsters" had demonstrated an unparalleled concentration of pure tango.[54]

Piazzolla's personal upheavals had serious effects on his creativity. For a while he wrote little that was original, after several years of extraordinary output. He managed a couple of film scores in 1966–67, but not much else. He and the Quintet, meanwhile, continued their performances. They had returned to 676—the *tanguería* was later renamed *Nuestro Tiempo*—in October 1964, Piazzolla reporting to Ferrer that his appearances were more successful than ever. They also played in 1965–66 at another nightspot, Gotán, in a basement in Calle Talcahuano. Juan Cedrón and Eduardo Rovira also appeared there, as did a jazz trio led by pianist Juan Carlos Cirigliano. As a young boy Cirigliano, had once sat on Piazzolla's knee while his aunts (they had taken him to a dance at the Huracán football club) chatted with their idol, singer Francisco Fiorentino. Piazzolla often admiringly exhorted Cirigliano: "Go! go! you're doing great!"

On 8 March 1966, Rovira and Piazzolla played on the same bill at Gotán. The press quickly sniffed a story. Rovira, with his austere, intellectual approach to tango music, was seen by some as a contender for leadership of the avant-garde, though he was never able to capitalize on the distinction of his work. (He died in 1980, aged fifty-five.) His group had succeeded Piazzolla's at 676 in early 1964, only to be driven away after one night by noisy Piazzolla fans led by the well-known jazz pianist Enrique "Mono" Villegas. The two ensembles were presented by tango expert Oscar Del Priore. The Quintet played first. As they exchanged places onstage, Piazzolla and Rovira embraced. Rovira declared that the night was "unforgettable" because of Piazzolla's presence. Piazzolla and his musicians left before the end of Rovira's first number.[55]

Around now the Quintet also made further incursions into the provinces. And as always, the musicians played for special functions of various kinds. In April 1966, for instance, they helped celebrate Alberto Ginastera's fiftieth birthday at the Teatro San Martín, in a program of works by his pupils. Piazzolla's contribution was his "Diablo" sequence from 1965. In August 1967, to look ahead a bit, the Quintet was on hand at a gathering to speed the Argentine foreign minister on an international trip. Part of the proceedings consisted of a discussion between Piazzolla and the audience, chaired by the well-known journalist Bernardo Neustadt. None of Piazzolla's enemies had turned up, and the audience was sadly disappointed.[56] Neustadt, a casual acquaintance of some years, had once asked Piazzolla to play "Adiós Nonino" at his funeral.[57] As it turned out, Piazzolla's came first.

His routines that spring were suddenly interrupted. On 17 October 1967, he was with Egle Martin at a recording studio when he suddenly felt a spasm of pain and had to be hospitalized for a hernia operation. He blamed the hernia on an informal karate session with his son three months earlier.[58] Daniel came in from the countryside to visit his convalescent father and found him walking around with a sword-stick, flashing its blade at everyone. His father was in a rage. Antonio De la Torre, Aníbal Troilo's agent, had called him a *rengo mufa*, "a bad-luck cripple." Daniel was duly indignant. "Since I can't do it myself because of this hernia thing," said Piazzolla, "*you*'ll have to smash him up." Troilo was playing at the time at a newly opened nightclub, Relieve, on Diagonal Norte. Father and son drove there in Piazzolla's red Fiat 600, and Daniel went upstairs to confront the adversary. De la Torre was a former wrestler with a considerable weight-and-height advantage over Daniel. He puffed cigarette smoke in his face and knocked him halfway down the stairs. "Why didn't you tell me what he was like?" expostulated Daniel to his father. "You're not telling me that son-of-a-bitch actually *hit* you?" said Piazzolla. He could hardly be restrained from taking on De la Torre himself.

He was soon back at work. At the end of October the Quintet played at a tango festival in the pleasant mid-pampa town of Olavarría. Early in December it was at the Teatro Odeón in Montevideo, in a concert sponsored by the Argentine embassy, and later that month at a "Tango and Folklore" festival at Teodelina (Santa Fe Province).[59] The show went on.

But successful performances merely masked a disturbing creative emptiness. His marital breakdown had taken its toll. It was probably for this reason that he was drawn into projects he might otherwise have avoided. One was the brainchild of the publisher Ben Molar, a tireless tango enthusiast whose idea was to associate poets, musicians, and painters in a common effort focusing on the tango: settings of poems for a long-playing record, *Catorce con el tango* (1966), accompanied by suitable paintings. Piazzolla agreed to set Baldomero Fernández Moreno's poem

"Setenta balcones y ninguna flor." He neither arranged it nor chose the musicians recording it, and he was very unhappy with the result.

Another project of this time also ranks among Piazzolla's more forgettable achievements. He agreed to record four long-playing discs for the Phonogram (Philips) label under the title *La historia del tango*, a musical "history" covering all eras of tango music. Owing to disagreements between Piazzolla and the recording company, only the first two albums were completed—twenty-two classic tangos played by an ad hoc orchestra. One of its members was the violinist José Carli, working for a second time with Piazzolla. (He was now mostly an arranger; he was to see Piazzolla at regular intervals over the next twenty years.) López Ruiz, Agri, and Díaz all took part, as did guitarist Rodolfo Alchourron, a jazz musician who was seized by both nervousness and enthusiasm when he studied the arrangements. Piazzolla made no effort whatever to imitate period styles. Santos Lípesker, Philips's musical director, as Miguel Selinger recalls, interrupted the first recording session. "If this is the *old*," he asked, "what are you going to do with the *modern*?" Piazzolla justified the exercise as "a tribute I owed to all those people who did something for the music of Buenos Aires."[60] He did not remember it with pleasure.

Shattered by his personal tribulations, Piazzolla urgently needed to renew his art. Egle Martin did something to restore his confidence. When renewal came, it was from an unexpected quarter. Piazzolla had nearly always had vocalists with his groups, mostly because it was expected of him. Like Duke Ellington, he was usually at his best with purely instrumental pieces. But for the next few years he was to be linked more closely than ever before with *words*. The words were Horacio Ferrer's.

6

𝒫iazzolla-𝒥errer-𝒷altar
1967–1971

→← Piazzolla-Ferrer

"Balada para un loco" →←

→← Amelita

> The Pope of the Avant-Garde . . . reaches the big public.
> —*Gente* magazine (1969)

Piazzolla-Ferrer

It is time for Horacio Ferrer to come more fully into view. Born in Montevideo in June 1933 (and on his mother's side the great-great-great-nephew of the nineteenth-century Argentine tyrant Juan Manuel de Rosas), he discovered during his university days that poetry and tango music, especially recent tango music, had greater attraction for him than the architecture courses he was taking. When Piazzolla played at Montevideo's Café Ateneo in 1948, the teenage Ferrer complimented him after the recital. Six years later he procured Piazzolla's Paris address from the tangophile Luis Adolfo Sierra and wrote him a fan letter, which Piazzolla duly answered from the Hôtel Fiat. Their meeting in Montevideo in April 1955 (already recounted) was the first of many over all the years that followed.

During the summer of 1955–56, getting over a sentimental reverse, Ferrer went for several weeks to Mar del Plata and chatted endlessly with Piazzolla on the jetties and breakwaters while the older man fished. Ferrer arranged for the Octet to perform at his Club de la Guardia Nueva and introduced it at a stormy appearance at Montevideo's Sala Verdi. By this stage Piazzolla was closely interested in the Club, which was always available in the early 1960s when the Quintet visited Montevideo. Piazzolla liked *Romancero canyengue*, a slim book of poems (one dedicated to him) Ferrer published in 1966 and began to talk with him about collaborating.

During his time of personal upheaval, Piazzolla had regularly been consulting Horangel, Argentina's best-known astrologer. The end of his "bad time," said Horangel, in a reading on television, would come with an unexpected knock on his door. Ferrer was visiting Buenos Aires from Montevideo, where the newspaper he then worked for, *El País*, was undergoing a lockout—and on 1 December 1967 he knocked (the bell was out of order) on the door of Apartment 14C at Avenida Libertador 1088. Piazzolla greeted him with "hallucinated eyes," as if his arrival was somehow providential.[1] Egle Martin was in the apartment, discussing the music Piazzolla was writing for a story she had recently sketched out for him. In the conversation that ensued, he told Ferrer of a short trip he had taken to Rio de Janeiro and a show he had seen at the Zum Zum nightspot. In this show, Vinicius de Moraes and other Brazilian artists mixed music and poetry in a riveting combination. The Zum Zum was justly renowned in the Brazil of the mid-1960s. *"Quem não viu esse show?"* ("Who *didn't* see that show?") asks Vinicius's biographer, rhetorically.[2]

Could not something similar be done for Buenos Aires—with "Buenos Aires themes, River Plate themes"? As Egle Martin remembers, Piazzolla told Ferrer of the story she had sketched for him. "Wouldn't you like me to develop it a bit?" asked Ferrer. "Why not?" said Egle. "Take it, develop it, do what you want with it." Ever since his time with Ana Itelman, Piazzolla had hankered after a ballet or some theatrical work—like *West Side Story*, maybe, which had so impressed him in New York. Here, perhaps, was the opportunity. That night, in his modest hotel room on Calle Florida, Ferrer blocked out a few ideas that he showed next day to Piazzolla. Back in Montevideo again, the lockout at *El País* now over, Ferrer began drafting the text of an *operita* ("little opera"), typing much of it in December and January and reading sections to a group of friends who met on Monday nights. Piazzolla and Egle Martin went to one of these sessions, and that same night Piazzolla composed one of the main themes for the *operita*. Egle Martin was thoroughly involved in the project. Ferrer sometimes phoned her to get her opinion of particular lines.

The project energized Piazzolla. In mid-January 1968 he temporarily dissolved the Quintet, declaring that he felt a "physical need to renew myself."[3] In February, he and his friend Miguel Selinger holed up with Ferrer and his wife in a vacation home owned by Ferrer's parents at the small Uruguayan resort of Parque del Plata. There they worked furiously on the "little opera," now named *María de Buenos Aires*. The title came to them while they swam off Montevideo's Carrasco beach. The house had no piano; Piazzolla composed with a bandoneon. In the evenings they sometimes relaxed in Parque del Plata's modest cinema. One of the movies they saw was Philippe de Broca's *Le Roi de Coeur* (1966), and they were much impressed by its remarkable, surreal atmosphere.

They finished the work in Piazzolla's apartment. Ferrer, who was now to settle permanently in Buenos Aires, moved in there on 1 April and stayed until the piece was done. They worked night and day—with frequent excursions to the La Barra restaurant a block down the avenue. With most of the libretto written, Ferrer made nontechnical musical suggestions to Piazzolla—"here I would like an atmosphere like 'Milonga del ángel,' like 'Verano porteño,' " and so on. It seems certain that Piazzolla wanted Raúl Lavié—perhaps the most talented tango singer of his generation—for the male role in the "little opera." But Lavié was far away, working in Mexico, so Piazzolla turned to his former vocalist Héctor De Rosas. Egle Martin, of course, was to take the María role, something the press soon picked up, but Martin, torn between Piazzolla and her husband Eduardo "Lalo" Palacios, began to have doubts. The crisis came to a head at Christmas 1967. As Egle Martin tells it, in language that reflects her own agony of indecision, Piazzolla

confronted Lalo. We were at his apartment. He had invited us to dine. What happened complicated things, because what he did was say: "Lalo, I ask you for Egle's hand." We were on the terrace [of] that apartment I knew so well. . . . I was afraid, very afraid. Lalo was someone who loved me a lot, and I loved him too, it was very hard, because I respected Astor a lot. . . . He said to Lalo: "she is music, she can't *belong* to anybody, no, she is music, she is music, and that's *me*. You can't give her what I can." It was very hard, terrible. What could Lalo do? Lalo had no idea what to do. And I said to [Lalo], in an outburst as a human being, as a wife, as a housewife, as a woman, as a mother, I said: "I am going with you." So, I went back to the countryside because I didn't know what to do.

The press inflated the story considerably. Some reports have Palacios, revolver in hand, dragging Egle off to his ranch in Corrientes Province and placing grilles on the windows of the ranch house.[4] Radio disk jockeys could not resist repeated playings of "Graciela Oscura" ("their" song). Piazzolla believed some of the news stories. He sent an imploring letter to the estancia. Martin wrote gently back. Palacios was infuriated by the press reports, especially when *Gente* magazine alleged he had found Egle and Astor in bed and had menaced them with a gun. He mounted a successful lawsuit, donating the damages to charity. As for Piazzolla, "he wanted to kill him," says Martin, and the two men had at least one very stormy meeting, though no details have survived.

Piazzolla was badly depressed by the episode. A press photo of Martin hung on the wall of his apartment for several months.[5] On 17 March he and Ferrer scrawled her a note.

An endless hug from one who will always remember you. *Astor*. A kiss for someone who, eternally, is MY MARÍA. *Horacio*.[6]

But a replacement was urgently needed for the female role in *María de Buenos Aires*, and she had already been found. Piazzolla, Héctor De Rosas, and a pianist friend, Osvaldo Tarantino, went one night to Nuestro Tiempo (the former 676) to listen to a young contralto folk singer. "A svelte, attractive girl came out, with a guitar, crossed her legs and started singing," recalls De Rosas. "What do you think?" asked Piazzolla. De Rosas found her ideal. What did Piazzolla think? "What legs she has, what legs!" he exclaimed. Her name was Amelita (María Amelia) Baltar. She was in her middle twenties. She had an electrifying stage presence and was doing very well in the folk music world.

When introduced to Piazzolla, Amelita was not especially excited. He auditioned her at the house of some friends on Avenida Libertador. On his forty-seventh birthday (11 March 1968) he invited her out to dinner. They went to Hoyo 19, on Avenida Callao, where, rather abruptly, Piazzolla told her: "Well, you are 'María.' "[7] Amelita found her dinner companion "on the fat side, a bit bald, very friendly," and felt mildly drawn to him. She took him dancing at a nightspot, Snob, and they ended the night with whiskey and music-making at Piazzolla's apartment. Over the next few weeks she joined Piazzolla, Ferrer, and Héctor De Rosas in the final preparations for *María de Buenos Aires*. She quickly and passionately identified with the role of María: "I'd not had a marvelous youth," she explains, "so, I projected and channeled a lot of things into that character, I got inside it *a lot*."

For the *operita*'s ten-piece orchestra, Piazzolla added five musicians to the Quintet: Néstor Panik (viola), Víctor Pontino (cello), Oscar Emilio "Cacho" Tirao (guitar), Arturo Schneider (flute), José "Pepe" Corriale (percussion), and Tito Bisio (vibraphone, xylophone). Pepe Corriale had earlier recorded film music with Piazzolla. Panik was recruited by a phone call to New York, where he was at the time. Cacho Tirao (then twenty-seven) was an excellent guitarist, experienced in several genres, who was soon to join the Quintet. Phoned by Piazzolla out of the blue on a Monday, he asked when rehearsals would begin. "Our starting date is Friday, and the first rehearsal is Wednesday," he was told.

The framework of *María de Buenos Aires* is the birth and death of a symbolic female figure, María, whose spirit eventually gives birth to a second María. Ferrer crammed the libretto with beguiling *porteño* stereotypes, old and new, of his own devising. Some were distinctly surreal—a *payador* (old-style folksinger), a streetwise young man ("Porteño Gorrión con Sueño"), madams, thieves, drunks, marionettes, pasta makers, magician-masons, and, not least, a chorus of psychoanalysts. (Buenos Aires has the highest number of therapists per capita of any city in the world.) Violist Néstor Panik still confesses that he could never quite make head nor tail of what the story was actually about—a feeling Piazzolla himself sometimes hinted at later on. The *operita* nevertheless includes some of his most evocative music and most delicate scoring: the soft "María" theme itself, the spirit-María's song to the trees and chimneys of her district (which "just broke up" Amelita Baltar whenever she sang it), the psychoanalysts' chorus, the lilting "Milonga de la anunciación" (a big hit with audiences), and the purely instrumental "Fuga y misterio" from Act One, a masterpiece of fugal construction. "Fuga y misterio" enjoyed a long independent life as the signature tune for a celebrated Argentine TV program, Bernardo Neustadt's "Tiempo Nuevo," which started a year later.[8]

The *operita* opened at the Sala Planeta (on Calle Suipacha) on 8 May 1968. Critical reaction was mixed. "An exercise of impeccable presentation," declared *La Nación*, though it disliked the photographic images projected during the work. *La Prensa* suggested that the *operita* was little more than "two hours with an unchanging stage setting where the musicians, the reciter and the singers remain in rigorous stasis." *La Prensa* had a point: in its first staged form the *operita* was really an oratorio rather than an opera, even a little one. *Primera Plana* praised the music—"a richness that at times seems inexhaustible"—but thought that Ferrer, the reciter, rather resembled "a political candidate looking for votes."[9] The magazine *Gente* harvested the opinions of well-known tango musicians and poets. For journalist and poet León Benarós, the work was "an opera with a capital O." Bandleader Armando Pontier took a swipe at his compatriots by suggesting that had the *operita* been labeled "Made in England," the theater would have overflowed. The great tango lyricist Homero Expósito complimented Ferrer (rather backhandedly) on creating a style: "When a poet achieves a style he has almost become a poet." The veteran bandleaders Osvaldo Fresedo and Julio De Caro were, on balance, positive.[10]

"This is really exceptional," the great *lunfardo* poet and tango traditionalist Julián Centeya told Pepe Corriale. "It excited me, excited me." Despite their previous differences, he complimented Piazzolla effusively after the last performance. Leopoldo Federico went to five or six performances and was in tears every time.[11] Santos Lípesker, artistic director of the Philips record label, was also moved to tears. Piazzolla himself proudly remembered a visit from Brazilian artists (in Buenos Aires for a show of their own)—Vinicius de Moraes, Baden Powell, Elis Regina, the Cuarteto em Cy, the pianist Oscar Castro-Neves, and others—who rose to applaud when the rest of the audience remained seated.[12] Vinicius de Moraes gave a shout of *"filho da puta!"* ("son of a bitch!")—his habitual expression of approval, not uncommon among musicians. "That's the nicest thing I've had said to me in my life," Piazzolla told him during the intermission.[13] Afterward Piazzolla, Ferrer, and Amelita went with some of the Brazilians and invaded the apartment of doctor and musician Eduardo Lagos on Calle Paraguay, actually getting Lagos out of bed—to his delight. Everyone played or sang something. Vinicius proclaimed the urgent need to create a special island for sons of bitches. He later agreed to do a Portuguese translation of *María de Buenos Aires*, but as far as we know, he never did.

The *operita* was still sometimes playing to full houses at the end of June,[14] but audiences soon began to fall off alarmingly. Even when they were in single figures Piazzolla usually, though not always, insisted that the show should go on. But he "was never at any moment depressed," recalls Héctor De Rosas. "He was very exhausted, very exhausted. But he had such a tremendous spirit." De Rosas found it awesome.

The *operita* finally closed in August 1968. But it was not forgotten. It was broadcast in December, and Piazzolla hoped that Philips (to whom he was still under contract) might do a recording; however, the label, despite its artistic director's tears, was reluctant. Alfredo Radoszynski, proprietor of the new Trova label instantly agreed to make a recording, for release when Piazzolla's agreement with Philips ended. During the recording, Oscar López Ruiz, musical director for Trova, turned at one point to Radoszynski: "It's Bartók! Only Astor could create something like this!" Radoszynski took Piazzolla and Ferrer on a short promotional tour—Bahía Blanca, Mar del Plata, Rosario—when the double album was finally released.

The doctor and musician Eduardo Lagos was also recording with Trova. "Why don't we record something together?" he asked Piazzolla. The Trova people were enthusiastic. Piazzolla joined Lagos's folk group for a late-night session. "But Astor wasn't on the folk wavelength," recalls Dr. Lagos.

It was a big effort for him to get into it, and we went on till five in the morning, trying to record a *chacarera*. The result was so ugly that Astor himself said to me: "No, I don't have the swing you people have for this. So, well, excuse me, but I. . . ." And I was really depressed.

A later session was more successful, with Piazzolla and Lagos's group managing to record two of Lagos's *zambas*.

The staging of *María de Buenos Aires* almost bankrupted Piazzolla. Friends and admirers like lawyer Raúl Bercovich ("our Maecenas," Piazzolla called him) and businessman Jorge "Fino" Figueredo certainly helped. Figueredo lent an "important" sum when the musicians' union threatened to stop the show because of nonpayment of the musicians. (Amelita Baltar is fairly sure that she received nothing at all during the show's final month.) Hermenegildo Sábat, the nonpareil of River Plate caricaturists, contributed a striking poster. Daniel Piazzolla was roped in to organize the lighting and to distribute flysheets around Buenos Aires. Miguel Selinger and Diana Piazzolla sang in the chorus.[15] Piazzolla himself laid out 4 million pesos (about $11,500), sold his car, and took out a loan from SADAIC. But it was "much more important to be broke with *María de Buenos Aires*," he told journalist Alberto Speratti, "than to have done some garbage and to be flush."[16]

Speratti was then conducting a series of ten "in-depth" interviews with Piazzolla (July–October 1968) for his small format book, *Con Piazzolla* (1969). Piazzolla came to dislike the book,[17] but its usefulness to the biographer is obvious. It valuably "freezes" the musician, almost exactly in mid-career. Speratti had heard that Piazzolla was "not very accessible, not very cordial," but he was agreeably surprised: "Drinking whiskey or gin, smoking, expressing himself with gestures or changes of voice or crossing and uncrossing his legs, and with an expressive, radiant, tense, contagious friendliness, Astor Piazzolla contributed his constant liveliness to the experience." Speratti was intrigued by the Avenida Libertador apartment—a reproduction of "Guernica" and a drawing of Piazzolla by Hermenegildo Sábat hanging on its walls, its furnishings in "Spanish rustic style," and an assortment of interesting objects scattered around: photographs, biographies of musicians, beer mugs, some of Nonino's wooden carvings, and pipes. Piazzolla had started to collect pipes on his visit to London in 1964. His pipes were for use as well as ostentation. Like most pipe smokers, he found cleaning them rather tedious.[18]

The pipe smoker reconstituted the Quintet and went back to his normal round of appearances: Buenos Aires nightspots, the provinces, Montevideo (April 1969). During these months he also ran an alternative ensemble, a sextet—Agri and

"Kicho" Díaz from the Quintet, with guitarist Rodolfo Alchourron, jazz pianist Gustavo Kerestezachi (whose trio had appeared at 676) and percussionist Carlos Alberto "Pocho" Lapouble—for gigs in Buenos Aires and, less often, the provinces. The music from *María de Buenos Aires* was the basic repertory, with Héctor De Rosas and Amelita Baltar as vocalists. (After the *operita*, Amelita had returned to folksinging, appearing regularly at the Poncho Verde nightspot.) Alchourron was mesmerized by the music. He never became close with Piazzolla, but musically he was dazzled by him—"He sensitized me a lot." "Pocho" Lapouble had played in jazz groups at 676, and had a nodding acquaintance with Piazzolla. Piazzolla explained to him that what he wanted above all was *swing:* "Play and enjoy yourself," he told Pocho, who did; it remains the most "powerful" of all his musical experiences. When he once came in too soon, cutting off one of Antonio Agri's solos, Piazzolla gave him a huge smile. "You have to get it wrong sometimes," he said.

Enjoying himself as he was with the sextet, Piazzolla was nonetheless thinking of further collaborations of the kind that had yielded *María de Buenos Aires.* He was strongly attracted by the idea of continuing to work with Ferrer. By any standard, it became the key collaboration of his life. It took up much of his time over the next few years. Between 1968 and 1972 the two of them wrote more than twenty songs, and there were more in the early 1980s. They worked well together: "We're like a good marriage," Piazzolla told Ferrer. As in all marriages, there were tiffs, but these were outweighed by the delight they felt when pieces were finished, when, Ferrer remembers, "happiness and rowdiness pushed us into faun-like dances around the piano."[19]

Some of their songs were immediate hits. The first was the wistful waltz "Chiquilín de Bachín" ("Bachín Lad"). The Bachín was a restaurant patronized by Ferrer, by Piazzolla and Amelita Baltar, by friends like diplomat Albino Gómez and the jazz pianist "Mono" Villegas. "We have a little waltz," Piazzolla told Eduardo Lagos, at the hilarious party with the Brazilians during the run of *María de Buenos Aires*, and that was where Amelita first sang it.

> *Por las noches, cara sucia,*
> *de angelito de blue jeans,*
> *vende rosas en las mesas*
> *del boliche de Bachín . . .*
>
> At night, dirty faced,
> A little angel in blue jeans,

He sells roses at the tables
Down at the Bachín dive. . . .

Piazzolla's creative self-renewal in 1968–69 was strikingly confirmed by his cinema work. In 1968 he wrote the remarkable three-movement "Tangata" (dedicated to Oscar Araiz, a choreographer who had used his music in a recent Ana Itelman ballet in Buenos Aires) for a never-released documentary on the tango.* Its middle movement is one of Piazzolla's finest efforts in elegiac vein. An altogether more interesting movie project now beckoned. The Uruguayan painter Carlos Páez Vilaró, then living in Paris, was making an experimental film, *Une Pulsation*, without dialogue or plot, a pulsating sequence of pure images shot during a round-the-world trip taken by Páez Vilaró and his French millionaire collaborator, Gérard Leclery, on a rented schooner. Páez Vilaró's first idea was to ask Ennio Morricone for the music, but one day, at a film laboratory at Saint Cloud, he happened to mention Piazzolla's name. "That man's a genius!" exclaimed a French *montage* expert. Páez Vilaró telephoned Buenos Aires to see whether the genius was interested.[20] He was.

The resulting suite of "Pulsations" was recorded by an ad hoc ensemble: some of the musicians from the *operita*, together with Dante Amicarelli, the first jazz pianist to appear on Argentine television (in 1953),[21] cellist José Bragato, and violist Simón Zlotnik. Four of the "pulsations" soon appeared on a Trova long-playing record, coupled with an instrumental suite distilled from *María de Buenos Aires*. These were Piazzolla's last recordings for Trova. Piazzolla sent Páez Vilaró a cassette, with a note attached: "Thanks to the freedom you gave me, I feel a new Piazzolla."[22] The two men would see a certain amount of each other over the next year or two. Piazzolla visited Páez Vilaró's magical "house village," Casapueblo, then rising on its rocky promontory near Punta del Este, and wrote a tango there. Páez Vilaró's son Carlos Miguel was one of the Uruguayan rugby players whose plane crashed in the Andes in October 1972—the most talked about tragedy of that year. Piazzolla sent his friend a telegram: "FROM TODAY THE SORROW I FEEL OVER YOUR SON'S DEATH WILL BE IN MY MUSIC." Happily, the message was premature. Carlos Miguel was one of the sixteen survivors, rescued after seventy days, having fed on the flesh of their dead companions.

*He also did a conventional film score for Fernando Ayala's movie *La fiaca* (released March 1969).

Piazzolla was once again looking for a stable "base," somewhere like 676. With his friend "Fino" Figueredo he inspected some possible places, but their plans for a *tanguería* fell through when a vital third partner decamped to the United States. A new opportunity suddenly appeared. In May 1969, the Michelangelo, a night-spot that had opened in 1964, moved into three seventeenth-century vaults in the San Telmo district—once part of a colonial-era customs post. Michelangelo's offerings included the tango, folklore, jazz, and chamber music. The Quintet played there regularly, with Amelita Baltar and Héctor De Rosas singing. De Rosas, however, gradually felt excluded, feeling that Amelita was being showcased at his expense—"it was like competing with the director's wife"—and finally left the team.

Piazzolla recommended José Domingo Ledda, who had been regularly tuning the Steinway at the Avenida Libertador apartment, to the nightspot, and Ledda stayed there ten years. His first task was to bring the piano down a quarter-tone, to attune it to the bandoneon. Pianist Osvaldo Manzi, however, was soon afterward injured in an accident. Piazzolla instantly recruited Juan Carlos Cirigliano, whose trio he had enjoyed so much in 1966 at Gotán, promising him that they would play an "easy repertory" for the first night or two. Dante Amicarelli also sometimes played with the Quintet. Piazzolla arranged for him a superb rhapsodic 150-second introduction to "Adiós Nonino." He asked Miguel Selinger to go with him to Amicarelli's house. "If he plays it OK first time round," he threatened, "I'll cut my veins." Amicarelli placed the score on his piano. "Nice little arrangement," he said, and played it straight through, to Piazzolla's chagrin.[23] Recorded at three o'clock in the morning after a Michelangelo session, it can be heard on the Quintet's 1969 album, *Adiós Nonino*.

Piazzolla wrote a piece, "Michelangelo 70," in honor of the nightspot's new incarnation, though claiming later (to Tony Staveacre in 1989) that it was also a tribute to the great Michelangelo himself. The first major batch of new Piazzolla-Ferrer songs was premiered there by Amelita Baltar. It included a trilogy of "ballads": "Balada para mi muerte" ("Ballad for my Death"), "Balada para él" ("Ballad for Him"), and "Balada para un loco," the most famous of them all.

"Balada para un loco"

"Balada para un loco" ("Ballad for a Madman") was the second Piazzolla-Ferrer hit—and their greatest by far. As author María Susana Azzi has suggested, the song "drew a line forever between the pre-Piazzolla and the post-Piazzolla tango."[24] Singer Raúl Lavié sees it as marking "the beginning of a completely different era for our music." Was it, perhaps, a Latin American response to the Beatles, a sort of Argentine "A Day in the Life"?

> *Ya sé que estoy piantao, piantao, piantao.*
> *No ves que va la luna rodando por Callao;*
> *que un corso de astronautas y niños, con un vals,*
> *me baila alrededor. . . . ¡Bailá! ¡Vení! ¡Volá!*

> I know I'm crazy, crazy, crazy,
> Don't you see the moon rolling along Avenida Callao,
> the file of astronauts and children, with a waltz,
> dancing around me? Dance! Come! Fly!

The idea came to Ferrer when, in a mildly melancholic mood, he was walking the Buenos Aires streets. A key phrase ("I'm crazy, crazy, crazy") established itself; the lyric fell into shape in about a week. Ferrer discarded several possible lines, among them, "Yesterday I saw a Beatle biting a bandoneon."[25] At one point during the composition, Ferrer recalls, Piazzolla "turned round, looked at me with eyes full of tears, and closed the piano." The title was fixed last of all. Piazzolla rejected "Balada para mi locura" ("Ballad for My Madness") since audiences would assume *he* was the madman, "when *you* are," he told Ferrer. A first version of the song was performed at Michelangelo and sparked no interest whatever. Piazzolla and Ferrer suddenly remembered the eerie accelerating waltz in *Le Roi de Coeur*, the movie they had seen over in Parque del Plata, in Uruguay. A few touches in waltz tempo made the difference, creating a classic.

The "Balada" was entered for a competition in the First Latin American Festival of Song and Dance. This was an unprecedented (for Buenos Aires) jamboree staged over a week in November 1969 at Luna Park, the large indoor arena at the foot of Avenida Corrientes. More than 500 artists from fifteen countries attended; 1,300 songs competed for prizes. As they entered Luna Park for the first session, Piazzolla turned to Ferrer and said: "Tomorrow, first thing, you must go to a printer and get yourself some cards that say 'Horacio Ferrer, author of "Balada para un loco." ' It will be useful for the rest of your life."[26]

The occasion would become legendary. The "Balada" was one of ten songs that reached the finals in the Tango Section of the Festival. Shortly after nine o'clock on the Saturday night, Piazzolla and Amelita appeared onstage to a mixture of wild applause and furious whistles and hisses. Coins were lobbed on to the stage. There were shouts of "Go and wash dishes!" The jury* voted 25–9 to give the "Balada" second prize, placing it behind "Hasta el último tren" ("Until the Last Train"), sung by Jorge Sobral, Piazzolla's old collaborator of 1957. (He was never entirely forgiven for winning the first prize with such a traditional tango.) The decision stirred the antagonists in the auditorium to greater fury. Arguments and fist fights continued in the streets outside until well after midnight.[27]

Piazzolla, Ferrer, and Baltar went almost immediately from Luna Park to the studios of Radio Belgrano. Amelita sang the song again. Journalist Santo Biasatti remembers "the large number of people who telephoned Astor: 'We support you!' 'It's terrific!' 'Go, Astor!' " The telephones went on ringing through the night, Piazzolla defending his song with passionate vehemence.

Piazzolla later claimed unconvincingly that the motive of the hostile demonstration had been political and left-wing.[28] Sobral wondered whether his own prominence on TV in recent years had boosted his chances. The merest glance at the press shows that the real cause was simply the old conflict between ancients and moderns. Alberto Ginastera told Piazzolla that the opposition was "for Piazzolla," not the song.[29] Some conservatives *did* object to the song. The author of the tango that won third place protested to the Municipality that the "Balada" had only thirty bars in tango rhythm, compared with eighty or so in waltz tempo, and that it was forty-five seconds longer than the rules allowed.[30] Nothing came of this pompous démarche.

It would not have mattered if something had. The song that won first place, "Hasta el último tren," was soon half-forgotten; the last train "got stuck at the platform," as a contemporary joke put it. Piazzolla had reached the mass public. The song swamped the airwaves. When the records became available, stores reported runaway sales—150,000 by March 1970, according to one newspaper report.[31] (Amelita Baltar remembers the figure as being substantially higher.) A neighbor in the apartment below Ferrer's on Avenida Santa Fe played it so often that Ferrer decided to move out. In due course, it went all round Latin America, indeed the world. In 1980 Piazzolla jested that the only person never to have sung it was the Ayatollah Khomeini.[32]

One of the places, to look ahead a bit, where Amelita Baltar and the Quintet performed the song (June 1970) was the Instituto Neuropsiquiátrico Borda, Buenos Aires's main neuropsychiatric hospital. Piazzolla was understandably

---

*A technical jury (Albino Gómez was a member) voted unanimously for the "Balada" but through some jiggery-pokery it was superseded by a so-called popular jury.

nervous about playing this particular number. The doctors reassured him. And all was well. As Baltar began singing, the 200-strong audience gave vent to an ecstatic "Ah!" Jacobo Flichman, a poet who had spent fifteen years in the hospital, was so moved that he went onstage and handed Piazzolla a rose. The audience was reduced to tears.[33]

Piazzolla's attitude to the "Balada" was always somewhat ambivalent. He once almost lost his temper when a woman asked him: "Apart from the Balada, what else have you written?"[34] Guitarist "Cacho" Tirao thinks that "he forgot about it completely." After the early 1970s, the song took a back place in his repertory, although it was revived during his collaboration with the Italian singer Milva a decade later.

The distinguished tango singer Roberto "El Polaco" Goyeneche—with Edmundo Rivero "the best . . . since Gardel," Piazzolla said in 1990[35]—was so taken with the "Balada" that he instantly asked whether he could record it. He did so in early December. Ferrer, who claims to have had Goyeneche's voice in mind when writing the lyric, gave him some coaching over the recited sections in a bar near the RCA-Victor studios. At the end of the session, Piazzolla embraced Goyeneche, exclaiming "Crazy! Just crazy!"[36] Over the next few days, 75,000 copies of the record were sold. Goyeneche's was the second recording of "Balada para un loco" now regarded as classic. (The bandleader Osvaldo Pugliese—who said that the song was not a tango but "a super tango"—recorded a purely instrumental version soon afterward.) The other vocal version, the first recorded, was, for obvious reasons, by Amelita Baltar. She recorded it for CBS two weeks or so before the Luna Park appearance. By this time, Amelita was also, to use the graceless modern expression, Piazzolla's "significant other." The music of the "Balada," Piazzolla told her, was directly inspired by "a rapture of love" for her.

Amelita

They were together for seven years. "She needed me and I needed her," Piazzolla said in 1983. "She needed me as a musician. Fundamentally it was a musical relationship, which began with a thing called love in quotation marks."[37] This was far too cool a backward glance. "Of course it was a musical relationship," comments Amelita. "He had the singer in the house. It was very convenient for him. [But] Astor adored me . . . , I think I was the love of his life." In January 1970 they sketched each other for the press. "An admirable human being," said Amelita of Astor, adding that when composing "he forgets the world around him." "A funny, vital young woman with a great interior life," said Astor of

Amelita.[38] "She doesn't go in for half measures," he said soon afterward. "She can laugh uproariously or get annoyed to the point of venting all her anger. In fact, it's a passionate temperament, which is what I prefer in people."[39] The relationship was nothing if not passionate.

What stands out in Amelita's recollections of the love affair is the sheer *fun*— exuberant socializing, merriment, laughter. She and her small son Mariano moved into the apartment next to Piazzolla's at Libertador 1088. They talked of connecting the two apartments; in the end it proved easier to buy a new one, which they eventually did. In 1969 Piazzolla, without a car since *María de Buenos Aires*, bought a secondhand Fiat (later replaced by a Peugeot 504) and they began making weekend trips to favorite hotels and restaurants in the countryside. There were also surprise visits to Nonina in Mar del Plata. Nonina's initial reservations— "Now he brings this woman to sleep at the house," she once complained to Dedé—were obviously soon overcome. Diana and Daniel got on well with her. She took Diana's children out for walks.

Whenever possible, they went for a break to Bahía San Blas on the fringes of Patagonia, a twelve-hour trip by road. At Christmas 1972 they went there for a week, taking Nonina, Amelita's mother, and Mariano. It was the kind of solitary place Piazzolla loved, and the fishing gave him special pleasure. As Amelita recalls,

> He saw the sharks, and went out of his mind, I think he wanted to get into the water and take them with his hands, he went super crazy. And he used a corvina's head as bait, and . . . "Give me a hand!" and with the boathook . . . a meter away from the shark; I helped him bring it in. In forty-five minutes he caught two sharks. He hung them up by the tail; next day, when we got up and went to see the sharks, and touched them, they were still alive.

The press paid close attention to the Astor-Amelita story. In April–May 1970 there were persistent reports of a possible rift. "Amelita was a very important part of my life," Piazzolla told a reporter; "she is a great woman." The choice of tense was significant. So, too, were his statements that he was looking for "tranquillity" and that he did not feel fulfilled on "the sentimental level."[40] What lay behind such press reports was his most serious effort at reconciliation with Dedé. He had written to her that summer from Mar del Plata: "I hope to marry you on 31 October. This time there will be no 'buts' or anything to come between us."[41] In May Piazzolla and the "three Ds" were spotted in a "discreet restaurant"[42] in Buenos Aires. Some of the musicians (Bragato, Baralis, and Agri among them) planned a party in celebration. But although Astor and Dedé went on a trip together to Mar del Plata, the reconciliation came to nothing. The party was never held. The Astor-Amelita story went on.

Piazzolla described 1969, as it ended, as "the most important year of my life. I have composed more than ever. I realized just how fundamental it was to reach the big public.... Everyone is whistling Piazzolla."[43] His recent success spurred him to continue his collaboration with Ferrer, with Amelita seen as the ideal singer. Amelita herself believed that she could not do "brilliant things without those two men." She certainly added her two cents' worth while their songs were being written, something they both welcomed.[44] By early 1970 they were working on a trilogy of "preludes": "Preludio para un canillita" (Prelude for a Newspaper Boy), "Preludio para la cruz del sur" (Prelude for the Southern Cross), and "Preludio para el año 3001" (Prelude for the Year 3001). A reporter from *Gente* asked the Piazzolla-Ferrer-Baltar trio whether they were not, perhaps, intellectualizing popular music. The three of them responded indignantly, all talking at once. Ferrer proudly pointed out that even truck drivers were now quoting the "Balada para un loco." Amelita disclosed that she sometimes learned the new songs by singing them "in a low voice in the street. People must think I'm half crazy."[45]

In the closing months of 1969, the Quintet, with Amelita, began regular appearances at the Teatro Regina. Its managers, accompanied by the designer Lino Patalano, had heard the Quintet at Michelangelo and were sure that a theater show would be successful. Piazzolla was much less certain that the larger stage would suit him, but they were persuasive. And they were right: "only a few musicians," one of them remarked to piano tuner José Domingo Ledda, "but they sound like a big orchestra." The season was "a huge success," recalls Lino Patalano, "every night like a genuine party." The Regina shows were usually followed by sessions at Michelangelo. It was a grueling routine for the musicians. Amelita hardly had time to go to the bank, often stuffing her earnings among the sweaters in her closet.

During the 1970 summer season the team transferred to the Re-Fa-Si in Mar del Plata, where they shared the bill with Aníbal Troilo. Every night there were long lines outside the *tanguería*. Looking at the Quintet's informal attire, Pichuco quipped to Piazzolla: "All you need is to let your hair grow long, like a hippie."[46] Among those who came to applaud was the Argentine cement magnate Alfredo Fortabat, a keen Piazzolla fan; and there were invitations (taken up) to play at Fortabat's estancia in Olavarría. But the summer was for play as well as work. Leopoldo Federico, who was there with his quartet, remembers convivial nights with Piazzolla and Amelita in a pizza parlor: "with him there, we didn't realize we were staying there till daybreak, just chatting." Piazzolla strolled on the boardwalk with Pichuco and Zita, reliving old times. There were exuberant gatherings in the bar where Troilo held court. To fend off reporters, Piazzolla and Amelita rented a bungalow in the coastal village of Santa Clara del Mar, a few miles to the north. Here they were able to snatch some peace and quiet, with the beach just outside their living room.

The carefree summer over, the Quintet returned to its normal round of engagements, which included a series of programs on Channel 7. And in May 1970 the team went back to the Regina, where the new trilogy of "Preludios" was premiered. On 19 May (a rainy night, but a full house), a live recording was made of the show for issue as a long-playing record, Piazzolla celebrating the tenth anniversary of the Quintet in his opening remarks. An absolute highlight of the show and the album was his now completed suite "Las Cuatro Estaciones Porteñas" (Four Porteño Seasons). One of his best-known works, it is a respectful nod to Vivaldi. Vivaldian traces *can* be heard in the music, most obviously in the closing bars of "Invierno porteño."

The singer Raúl Lavié, now back in Argentina after a period in Mexico, was asked about this time to fill in for Amelita, who was indisposed, at a performance in La Plata. He noticed that there was still hostility to Piazzolla in the out-of-town audience:

> The people were half worked up against us, the majority, 95% or 98% against us. I went out to sing, completely afraid that they were going to throw things at me, and luckily things calmed down, little by little, so that we were able to get on top of the audience, but afterward, the reaction was one of physical aggression not towards me, but towards Astor. I couldn't understand it.

The Quintet's work for the remainder of 1970 was normal enough: appearances at Michelangelo and other nightspots, radio and television programs, and the usual forays into the provinces. At Córdoba University in July, Piazzolla was moved by the enthusiasm of several thousand enraptured students.[47] At Rosario, in December, he helped inaugurate a new municipal amphitheater, with the local archbishop on hand.[48] In Montevideo, in September, he put his foot in it— badly—by publicly declaring his long-held opinion that "La Cumparsita" was "the worst tango of all."[49] This was a tactless remark to make in Uruguay, the birthplace of this most famous of all tangos. The Uruguayan equivalent of

SADAIC reproved him, as did the press in banner headlines. But Montevideo's Teatro Solís "overflowed with people," as "Cacho" Tirao recalls, "people who wanted to see this man who had denounced La Cumparsita." And Tirao wondered if this had been the reason for the remark in the first place. Perhaps as an olive branch, Piazzolla donated a large sum from his Uruguayan royalties to a Montevideo hospital.[50]

Apart from the new songs in 1970, Piazzolla did a film score for director David Kohon's well-received movie *Con alma y vida*, for which he was awarded the first prize of the Argentine film critics' association. He also contributed music to *La ñata contra el vidrio*, an experimental set of "shorts" never released. And he was still trying his hand at classical music. In September 1969 the Melos Ensemble of Buenos Aires premiered his new "Tango 6" on Channel 13. In February 1970 the Ensemble Musical de Buenos Aires, under Pedro Ignacio Calderón, performed his "Tangazo: Variaciones sobre Buenos Aires" at a concert in Washington, D.C., repeating it in other American cities and later in the year in Buenos Aires. In October that year a young Polish-born conductor, Simón Blech, revived the 1963 work "Serie de tangos sinfónicos" at the Teatro Coliseo, with Dante Amicarelli at the piano. Piazzolla was there to share the applause.[51] "Tangazo" is a remarkable work. Densely scored, without bandoneon, it starts with the double basses playing a slow fugato. The strings, as described by conductor Alicia Farace, gradually open out like a fan. The woodwinds invert and develop the main theme. A horn then introduces a new, wistful melody, reinforced by orchestral *tutti*, and is countered by jaunty flute passages. The music seems to be heading toward a bacchanalian finale, but ends abruptly with a rather startling *pianissimo*. This is one of the best of Piazzolla's attempts to translate the tango into symphonic music.

There was a Michelangelo in Mar del Plata as well as Buenos Aires. It became the Quintet's base for the 1971 summer season. There were the usual games on the beach, the hilarious gatherings in the restaurants. Nonina was on hand, of course. So was Aníbal Troilo, who was vacationing by the ocean, as he did every year, and naturally he was visited.[52] But the old routines were suddenly halted. Piazzolla disbanded the Quintet and went off to Europe.

Astor Piazzolla by Hermenegildo Sábat, the nonpareil of River Plate caricaturists, drawn especially for this book

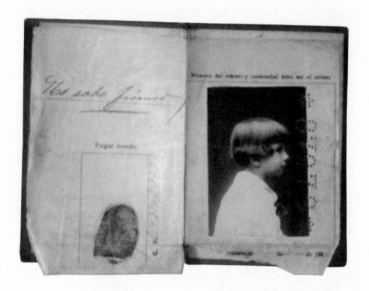

Above: Piazzolla's first identity card, issued 29 March 1925. (DEDÉ WOLFF COLLECTION)

Right: Drawing of the thirteen-year-old Astor Piazzolla by the great Mexican muralist Diego Rivera, Rockefeller Center, New York, 1934. (PIAZZOLLA PRIVATE COLLECTION)

Top: Aníbal Troilo's band, with Piazzolla on the right, seated. (DANIEL PIAZZOLLA COLLEC-
TION)

Middle: Francisco Fiorentino and Band, conducted by Astor Piazzolla. (DANIEL PIAZZOLLA
COLLECTION)

Bottom: The 1946 Band. Pianist Atilio Stampone is on Piazzolla's left, bandoneonist Roberto
Di Filippo on his right. The singers, in white jackets, are Héctor Insúa and Aldo Campoamor.
The photo is inscribed: "To Mama and Papa with great affection, Astor." (DANIEL PIAZZOLLA
COLLECTION)

Top left: The Piazzolla family: Piazzolla, Dedé, Diana, Daniel, Nonino, Nonina, Mar del Plata, December 1947. (DEDÉ WOLFF COLLECTION)

Top right: Nonino and passenger on Nonino's motorcycle. Note its name. (DANIEL PIAZZOLLA COLLECTION)

Bottom left: Astor and Dedé Piazzolla: wedding photo. (DEDÉ WOLFF COLLECTION)

Bottom right: On the boardwalk, Mar del Plata, January 1954. L. to r.: Diana, Dedé, Piazzolla, Daniel. (DEDÉ WOLFF COLLECTION)

Left: Piazzolla and Horacio Ferrer at the Club de la Guardia Nueva, Montevideo, autumn 1955. (HORACIO FERRER COLLECTION)

Below: The Octeto Buenos Aires during a broadcast. L. to r.: Horacio Malvicino, Juan Vasallo, Enrique Mario Francini, Leopoldo Federico, Atilio Stampone, Hugo Baralis, Piazzolla, and José Bragato. (DANIEL PIAZZOLLA COLLECTION)

Top: Piazzolla and Dedé at the piano, New York, July 1958. (DEDÉ WOLFF COLLECTION)

Bottom: Piazzolla and Daniel in New York, July 1958. (DEDÉ WOLFF COLLECTION)

Left: Piazzolla playing at 676, early 1960s.

Below: The first Quintet at 676. L. to r.:
Oscar López Ruiz, Jaime Gosis (piano),
Piazzolla, Kicho Díaz, Antonio Agri.

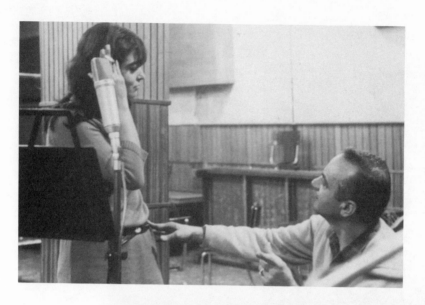

Top: Piazzolla and Egle Martin at the recording of the song "Graciela Oscura," 1967. (EGLE MARTIN COLLECTION)

Bottom: Piazzolla playing in *María de Buenos Aires*, 1968. (GIANNI MESTICHELI)

Top: The party at Dr. Eduardo Lagos's apartment, 1968. L. to r.: Piazzolla, Alfredo Radoszynski, Vinicius de Moraes. (GIANNI MESTICHELI)

Middle: Piazzolla and Dorival Caymmi at the Lagos party, 1968. (GIANNI MESTICHELI)

Bottom: A pause during the recording of *María de Buenos Aires* in the ION studios, Buenos Aires, 1968. L. to r.: Antonio Agri, Piazzolla, Amelita Baltar. (GIANNI MESTICHELI)

Top: Piazzolla rehearsing the first Quintet at the Olympia, Paris, October 1974, with Amelita Baltar (and the dog Georgie). L. to r.: Osvaldo Tarantino, Kicho Díaz (behind piano), Horacio Malvicino, Piazzolla, Antonio Agri.
(AMELITA BALTAR COLLECTION)

Right: Piazzolla and Gerry Mulligan in Italy, 1974. (FRANCA MULLIGAN)

Top left: Portrait of Astor Piazzolla by Carlos Alonso, painted in Rome, 1975. (CARLOS ALONSO COLLECTION)

Top right: Portrait of Piazzolla taken in Rome, 1975. (DEDÉ WOLFF COLLECTION)

Bottom: Piazzolla kept his photo of Béla Bartók over his bed. (DANIEL PIAZZOLLA COLLECTION)

Top: A delightful combination of love and humor. Argentine painter Antonio Berni (center) stages a mock wedding for Astor and Laura, May 1976. (EDUARDO "PEPE" WOLF)

Above: The first electronic octet outside Carnegie Hall, May 1976. L. to r.: José Angel Trelles, Juan Alberto Mateico, Santiago Giacobbe, Daniel Piazzolla, Piazzolla, Horacio Malvicino, Enrique "Zurdo" Roizner, Carlos Farber (record producer), Adalberto Cevasco. (DANIEL PIAZZOLLA COLLECTION)

Left: Piazzolla and Laura in Paris, summer 1976. (LEP COLLECTION)

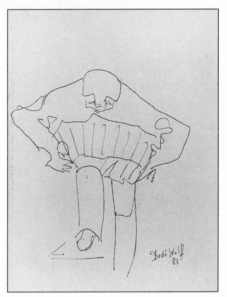

Top: Piazzolla and Laura at Punta del
Este, early 1980s, with their dogs,
Ritchie and Windy. (GIANNI MES-
TICHELI)

Bottom: Drawing of Astor Piazzolla
(ink) by Dedé Wolff, 1983. (MARÍA
SUSANA AZZI COLLECTION)

Top: Piazzolla rehearsing his Bandoneon Concerto with conductor Alicia Farace, Brussels, 1983. (ALICIA FARACE COLLECTION)

Middle: Piazzolla at the Teatro Colón, June 1983, with conductor Pedro Ignacio Calderón. (LA NACIÓN ARCHIVES, BEUNOS AIRES)

Bottom: Piazzolla and Laura, 1984. (LEP COLLECTION).

Top: Piazzolla on the bandoneon, with Milva. (DANIEL PIAZZOLLA COLLECTION)

Middle: Diana and her father at the launch of Diana's book, *Astor*, November 1987. (DEDÉ WOLFF COLLECTION)

Bottom: The second Quintet at Shams in Belgrano. L. to r.: standing: Héctor Console, Piazzolla, Horacio Malvicino; seated: Fernando Suárez Paz, Pablo Ziegler. (PABLO ZIEGLER COLLECTION)

Above: Graffiti of Aníbal Troilo, Roberto Goyeneche, and Piazzolla in the Buenos district of Núñez, 1996. The three never appeared at the same time, although they could have done so. (EDUARDO "PEPE" WOLF)

Right: Piazzolla on the bandoneon, with Nonina. (DANIEL PIAZZOLLA COLLECTION)

Top: The Sextet pretending to be Scotsmen, Glasgow, June 1989. L. to r.: Gerardo Gandini, Piazzolla, Daniel Binelli, Héctor Console, Horacio Malvicino, José Bragato. (SARAH VARDI-GANS)

Bottom: Piazzolla in Istanbul, July 1988. (SARAH VARDIGANS)

Piazzolla and Pablo Ziegler on the boat trip along the Bosphorus, July 1988. (HAYRI ERENLI)

$\mathcal{N}$onet and $\mathcal{B}$reakdown
1971–1974

→→ European Excursion

The Nonet →←

→→ Heart Attack

Last week a genius of jazz was playing to full houses in one of the largest cinemas of Buenos Aires . . . Duke Ellington. Everyone raved about him. Half a mile away, someone arguably as great as Ellington has been playing to half-empty houses in one of the smallest theaters of the capital. Astor Piazzolla.
—*The Buenos Aires Herald*, 28 November 1971

European Excursion

The decision was not unexpected. Piazzolla was beginning to tire of the struggle to make good money in Argentina. "For two years I have been every night at the Michelangelo," he told a reporter late in 1970. "I have done six hundred recitals like the ones in the Teatro Regina. I can't stand it any more!" He needed to "know what's going on in the world" and to try to emulate the international success of the folksinger Atahualpa Yupanqui and the folk composer Ariel Ramírez—whose long-playing record of the *Misa criolla* (1965) had by now gone all around the world. Although annoyed by his decision, Piazzolla's musicians took a fairly stoic view of the disbanding of the Quintet. "He gets tired, he needs to renew himself," said violinist Antonio Agri, "but he always comes back." "If he does it, it's for good reason," commented pianist Osvaldo Manzi.[1]

Piazzolla and Amelita set out on their five-month trip in mid-February 1971. They were followed two weeks later by Horacio Ferrer, to whom Piazzolla remarked: "Know something? I've enjoyed Europe a lot, but this time

I'm going to enjoy watching *you* discover everything." He declared to a reporter: "I feel as if I'm eighteen. Full of illusions, plans, the will to work."[2] At Ezeiza airport, while they were waiting to board their plane, they were introduced to Jacqueline Pons, a Frenchwoman and the daughter of a former governor of Algeria, who was traveling to Paris with two small children. Her husband José, an Argentine architect long resident in France, was well known for his hospitality to Argentine artists passing through Paris. He was on hand at Orly airport to meet his family and was duly introduced. Two days later Piazzolla and Amelita lunched at his apartment on the rue Descartes. "They arrived at midday and left at one in the morning," recalls Pons.

The Argentine Mozarteum, one of Argentina's most distinguished musical organizations, had loaned them a studio it owned at the Cité des Arts–No 113, on the first floor. Along with the fifth floor, this was reserved for musicians. Two or three weeks after his arrival there, Piazzolla was interviewed for French radio by Tomás Barna, a Hungarian-Argentine journalist living in Paris. Barna astonished Piazzolla by telling him that he found traces of Bartók in his music. "There was a moment of silence," says Barna; "I exchanged glances with Ferrer and Amelita. He looked at me and said: 'Well, Barna, it's the first time anyone has said this Bartók thing to me, but you should know that above my bed I have a picture of Béla Bartók. He is my idol.' "

Piazzolla and Amelita found that they enjoyed the Cité des Arts' closeness to the River Seine and to Notre Dame. While Amelita toured the *grands magasins* and saw the sights, Piazzolla and Ferrer settled down to work on an oratorio, *El Pueblo Joven* (The Young People), a successor to *María de Buenos Aires*. German television (Channel 1, Saarbrücken), which had filmed at Michelangelo the previous year, accepted the work. Piazzolla and Ferrer hastened to Saarbrücken to sign the contract. No other major work by Piazzolla has remained in quite such obscurity. No recording of *El Pueblo Joven* has ever been released. Amelita remembers it as "very, very, very, very beautiful." Piazzolla himself described the oratorio as having two parts (fourteen sections), with music for a sixty-piece orchestra, songs, and recitations. The first part was "a sort of musical history" of the River Plate peoples. The second was "an incursion into the terrain of science fiction," focused on "a people of youngsters in grottoes below the Plate estuary."[3]

While work on *El Pueblo Joven* moved ahead, the Piazzolla-Baltar-Ferrer trio sometimes absented itself from Paris—a short trip to Madrid, a couple of excursions into the French provinces: Burgundy, Brittany-Normandy. In Paris itself they savored the theater and the cinema, their evening strolls through the streets, their hippie-watching from the cafés of the Boulevard Saint Germain, and most of all, the restaurants. The three of them sometimes dined together on the Île Saint Louis, where Ferrer lodged at first, though he was later loaned an apartment near the Place Maubert. On 11 March they celebrated Piazzolla's fiftieth birthday with the Pons family in the rue Descartes apartment: Piazzolla played his bandoneon, Amelita sang. They also saw something of Édouard Pécourt, who found Amelita *attirante* (alluring). He now lived in the suburbs at Gretz (Seine-et-Marne), an hour away by train. Piazzolla and Amelita visited him there, and they watched tapes of Carlos Gardel movies, which reduced them all to tears.

In May Piazzolla reported his doings to the Buenos Aires journalist Hugo Guerrero Marthineitz of Radio Belgrano, an old ally of his from the days of the Octet onward. Among other things, he told Marthineitz that the artistic agent Pierre Fastosmes was now representing him in Europe.[4] Fastosmes had met Piazzolla several years earlier on a visit to Buenos Aires with the Swingle Singers (his wife Christiane was one of them) and Piazzolla's music had impressed him: "I promised myself that I would bring him to Europe," he remembers. He and Piazzolla were to remain associated until well into the 1980s.

There were reports in Buenos Aires that the Quintet had been summoned to Paris,[5] but nothing came of this. Instead, Piazzolla and Amelita took a trip to Italy, where on 24 July 1971 they did a television program in Naples with Charles Aznavour.[6] Piazzolla used the trip to stock up on modish shirts and ties, largely at Amelita's urging. "He didn't dress well, he was fairly boring," she says. "I made him buy velvet suits at the time they were beginning to be used, in a shade of beige, and some silk shirts. He changed a lot. He smartened himself up, began to get a taste for nice things." The travelers were back in Buenos Aires at the start of August. A week or two later some of Piazzolla's friends gave him a welcome home dinner in a restaurant on Avenida Córdoba. They noticed that he was now sporting a beard, which "gave him a certain likeness to Ernest Hemingway," and that he was in an exultant mood.[7]

Among his immediate tasks was a new album, *Concierto para quinteto*, whose title number, one of his more substantial pieces, was a conscious tribute to the Quintet. He also recorded six bandoneon solos of classic tangos, and—with Leopoldo Federico, Antonio Ríos, and Rodolfo Mederos—a four-bandoneon version of Enrique Delfino's "Recuerdos de Bohemia." His friend Mario Antelo attended a rehearsal and remembered the awestruck looks the three distinguished bandoneonists gave Piazzolla as he coaxed their best from them.

The Nonet

Piazzolla's biggest decision on returning from Europe was to expand the Quintet into a Nonet, under the name Conjunto 9. "I shall make less money," he said, but "the fundamental thing is to have something new to do."[8] The new group's immediate future was guaranteed by an important contract (October 1971) from the Municipality of Buenos Aires, which agreed to subsidize a regular series of concerts in Buenos Aires, the provinces, and overseas.[9] (The Nonet's first overseas mission, early in December 1971, was a single concert at the Teatro Municipal, in Santiago, Chile.) The contract was supposed to run for two years.

The Quintet—Agri, López Ruiz, Díaz, and Manzi (replaced in 1972 by the experienced and talented Osvaldo Tarantino, who brought to his playing an exceptional sense of swing and improvisation of tango phrases)—was complemented by some familiar figures: Hugo Baralis (violin), Néstor Panik (viola), José Bragato (cello), and José Corriale (percussion). It was one of the most distinguished groups Piazzolla ever formed—for Baralis, "the best Astor ever had"; for Bragato, "his best concept";[10] for Oscar Del Priore, "his highest point." Possibly Piazzolla came closest here to realizing his own quintessential sound. He certainly remembered the Nonet with a sense of excitement. Years later, watching it on film, he was reduced to tears, exclaiming to his wife: "How daring I was!"[11]

The Nonet gave its first major sequence of concerts at the Teatro Regina—not all of them well attended, as this chapter's epigraph indicates. Piazzolla used the concerts to showcase important additions to his repertory: "Vardarito," "Tristezas de un Doble A," "Zum," "En 3×4," "Oda para un hippie," "Homenaje al 40," "Onda 9," "Zurdo," the "9 Series" ("Preludio 9," "Divertimento 9," "Fuga 9"), "Homenaje a Córdoba." These pieces soon appeared on two RCA-Victor albums that were very well received, recorded in January and October 1972. Outstanding among them were "Vardarito" (a tribute to the recently deceased Elvino Vardaro), "Onda 9" (with its long improvised piano passages), "Oda para un hippie" (in which guitar and percussion improvise splendidly), and the long, meditative "Tristezas de un Doble A." The bandoneon solos in "Tristezas," with their shifts of mood from tenderness to something like irritation or impatience, were considered by Hugo Baralis "the most beautiful thing Astor ever did." Piazzolla ranked it among his best compositions.[12] The "double A" of its title ostensibly referred to the classic "Arnold AA" bandoneons he himself used; Horacio Ferrer later divulged that it really meant Astor-Amelita.[13]

In mid-December 1971, Piazzolla and Amelita went to Germany for about two weeks to record the music of *El Pueblo Joven*. Amelita remembers these sessions as unusually intense, with Piazzolla extracting "blood, sweat and tears" from the sixty-piece orchestra—"he was *so* demanding." A final recording stint was fixed for the end of 1972 or the start of 1973. At the end of January, the Nonet undertook its second foreign mission, flying to Caracas, Venezuela, to participate in the Onda Nueva (New Wave) music festival. The invitation apparently came from the Italian agent Aldo Pagani, the festival's artistic director; as we saw, he and Piazzolla had first met in Milan in 1964. "In my own country I have not received popular recognition," Piazzolla told the Venezuelan press.[14] Here he certainly did, winning second prize with "La primera palabra" (a powerful new Piazzolla-Ferrer song, a stirring invocation to Latin America), and a special award for the Nonet. At a post-festival concert by the group in the Central University of Venezuela, the public learned that Amelita was present and made her sing "Balada para un loco." As she recalled, "It was apotheosis-time." She was impressed (as she told reporters) that, far from worrying about Piazzolla's tango credentials, Venezuelans simply accepted his work as "music of our time."[15] Impresario Alejandro Szterenfeld, who had occasionally fixed provincial gigs for the Quintet in the 1960s, flew into Caracas toward the end of the festival and sensed a definite following for Piazzolla in Venezuela.

Back in Buenos Aires, Piazzolla and Amelita moved house to a thirteenth-floor apartment (13A) at Avenida Libertador 4854, overlooking part of the Palermo racecourse. Piazzolla put down 50 percent of the purchase price—the former apartment went for 18 million pesos ($36,000)—and also bought a smart new Alfa Romeo to replace his current Peugeot. The press photographs of the new setting show him in very contented mood. The Alfa Romeo became something of a talking point with reporters. "I'm very fond of zipping along," Piazzolla admitted. "Well, I haven't done more than 112 m.p.h."[16] He did not permit Amelita to drive the Alfa Romeo, which she christened El Mogólico ("The Mongolian"). Before very long it was replaced by another Peugeot.

Because of the municipal contract, the Nonet was kept busy for the whole of 1972. It visited most of the Argentine provinces, playing in hospitals, schools, and prisons as well as clubs and halls. In mid-March, the jazz pianist Enrique "Mono" Villegas turned up at one of its free Monday recitals at the Teatro San Martín, vocally applauding every number and loudly praising Piazzolla for his "courage in not yielding to the 'deaf' we always have among us."[17] At Michelangelo, it was applauded by two great violinists: Isaac Stern (Piazzolla was amazed to see him in the audience)[18] and, later that year, Salvatore Accardo, who had a professional conversation with Antonio Agri. The Nonet was due to record its second album next day. As a mark of esteem Accardo allowed an understandably nervous Agri to keep two of his violins overnight, a Stravidarius and a Guarnerius.

In April and May 1972 the Nonet made its third and fourth overseas trips. The musicians went first to Italy, where Aldo Pagani took them under his wing. Pagani had distribution rights in Italy for Piazzolla's RCA-Victor long-playing records. He publicized them assiduously, sending at least 800 copies to "Italian personalities from the Pope to the prostitute in the Galleria del Corso who saw me pass by every day." Pagani arranged a "Piazzolla special" for Radio Televisione Italiana's (RAI) top-rated "Teatro Dieci" TV show. The popular singer Mina (Ana Maria Mazzini) came in to listen as the Nonet recorded the program. Pagani asked her if she would like to record with Piazzolla. She added "Balada para mi muerte" to a long-playing record she was just finishing, and the Nonet rushed off at a moment's notice to a recording studio and got the job done in fifteen minutes.

While in Rome the musicians lodged at the Istituto Italo-Latinoamericano de Cultura. In gratitude for this hospitality, Piazzolla offered a recital. A day or two before, out for a walk with Oscar López Ruiz, he had chanced on the Argentine embassy but had been rebuffed in his attempt to pay a courtesy call on the ambassador. The incident evidently rankled, rousing Piazzolla's violent side. The ambassador, a portly rear admiral, turned up at the Istituto concert. Piazzolla refused to shake his hand and asked the institute's director to tell him "to go back to the whore who bore him!" "But . . . but . . ." spluttered the ambassador.[19]

Aldo Pagani told the musicians that if they stayed on in Italy he could book them La Scala,[20] but they were due in Brazil. They arrived there at the end of April. In Rio de Janeiro's Teatro Municipal, one Brazilian paper reported, "the big public was excited to the point of tears" by Amelita's singing. On the last day of April the Nonet played on TV-Globo's *Mec-Musica* program, its appearance arranged by impresario Alejandro Szterenfeld. The program also included Piazzolla's "Tangazo." It all added up to what the newspaper *O Día* described as a "great and beautiful success" for Piazzolla in Rio de Janeiro.[21]

And it was not simply because of the applause. In Rio the musicians Dori and Nana Caymmi (children of the great samba composer and singer Dorival Caymmi) bore the Argentines off to hear Milton Nascimento at the Teatro Da Lagoa. Nascimento greeted Piazzolla very shyly but later that night turned up at his hotel and started singing for him. Piazzolla was very touched and offered to do a special concert just for Milton and his friends.[22] The Caymmis found a suitable nightspot and rounded up as many musicians as they could find—their own illustrious father, Chico Buarque, Egberto Gismonti, Luis Carlos Vinhas, Zé Rodrix, Luix Eça, and many more. The impromptu show went on till six in the morning. Oscar López Ruiz describes it as an *"unforgettable"* occasion, and Piazzolla himself could not forget Milton Nascimento's "tears of excitement."[23] A day or two later, Piazzolla and López Ruiz called on Vinicius de Moraes at his house in Rio's Gávea district. They found him in his bath, with papers, a typewriter, and a bottle of whiskey spread out on a plank across the bath-top. "Sons of bitches!" shouted Vinicius in his usual way.[24]

Moving on to São Paulo for some recitals at the University (2–3 May 1972), the musicians were surprised to hear the same shout from the audience. Vinicius had followed them from Rio. At the end of the concert he amiably declared that Piazzolla was *um louco,* "a madman," and then dragged some of the musicians on a tour of the *paulista* nightspots, carrying with him a whiskey glass that was replenished everywhere they went.[25] The local Argentine consul, Federico Erhart del Campo (an acquaintance of Piazzolla's since the early 1960s), was there and remembers that Vinicius installed a chamber pot filled with whiskey in the car.

A Brazilian journalist, Eric Nepomuceno, who had earlier written a long piece about Piazzolla in the *Jornal da Tarde,* introduced him to more musicians; he remembers a particularly animated late-night session at the house of songwriter Edu Lobo. This visit enlarged both Piazzolla's increasingly passionate Brazilian following and his group of Brazilian friends, who were also genuine admirers. Vinicius later told journalist Natalio Gorin that Piazzolla was the best popular musician in the world. Tactfully, Vinicius asked Gorin not to print the opinion without coupling Piazzolla's name with that of his friend and collaborator Antonio Carlos "Tom" Jobim, the great transformer of the Brazilian samba into the bossa nova.[26] Those of Piazzolla's Brazilian friends still alive (Vinicius died in 1980) are quite unable to forget him. The multitalented musician Hermeto Pascoal, for instance, met him only three or four times but roundly declares: "If there existed a musical Pope, to appoint saints on account of music, Piazzolla would be a musical saint." A whole book could be written (perhaps it will be) on his connection with the magnificently vibrant Brazilian musical scene. It was a connection he himself particularly prized. "Why isn't it like this in my own country?" he once asked Brazilian superstar Caetano Veloso. "Brazil treats me so sweetly."[27]

In August 1972 Aldo Pagani phoned Piazzolla from Milan and asked him if he could write music for Bernardo Bertolucci's upcoming movie *Last Tango in Paris.* It was not yet known that Marlon Brando was to be the star. Piazzolla had done no film music since 1970, though the Nonet had appeared in the recently released movie *Argentinísima I,* a showcase of Argentine music (mostly folk). There are contradictory accounts of what happened. Pagani recalls Piazzolla asking for an excessive fee—between $15,000 and $35,000—and Bertolucci turning in consequence to the jazz musician Gato Barbieri for the score. To the press, Piazzolla strongly implied that Bertolucci had asked for *him*. When the movie appeared, an undignified row between Piazzolla and Barbieri broke out in the press. Piazzolla declared that he could have done a much better job. Barbieri riposted that Piazzolla was "nobody" in Europe. Piazzolla was sour about Barbieri's sound track— "a scissors-and-paste job" that reminded him of Glenn Miller.[28] He could not, however, resist second-guessing Barbieri, and he wrote two pieces, "Jeanne et Paul" and "El penúltimo," which show what a Piazzolla sound track for the film might possibly have been like. They were used in Francesco Rosi's 1976 movie *Cadaveri Eccelenti.*

In other works of the time, his creativity was at a peak. In August 1972, his superb "Concierto de Nácar" (for tango nonet and orchestra) was premiered at the Teatro Coliseo, the Nonet playing with the Ensemble Musical de Buenos Aires under Pedro Ignacio Calderón. It deserved the ecstatic response it received from the audience and the critics.[29] It is a marvel of tight construction, the nonet blending perfectly into the orchestral setting, with skillful percussion touches delicately coloring the slow movement and a rhythmic ostinato heightening the powerful thrust of the final Allegro.

September and October 1972 took the Nonet back to Brazil and Venezuela. Controversy marred both trips. Argentine-Brazilian relations were then at a low ebb; a recent visit by the incumbent Argentine military president, General Alejandro Lanusse, had proved very unpopular among Brazilians. At the Maracanazinho Stadium in Rio, where the musicians were taking part in the Sixth International Song Festival, they were greeted with whistles, hisses, and urine-filled condoms lobbed onto the stage. Piazzolla felt like "a Christian in a Roman circus." He vowed never to play at such festivals again—a vow he did not keep. His temper was restored by expressions of solidarity from his Brazilian musician friends and by a highly successful concert (27 September) before university students in São Paulo.[30] There was also a pleasant surprise for him in Rio. The French popular singer Georges Moustaki had earlier visited Argentina and had hoped, without success, to meet Piazzolla. Discovering that Moustaki was in Rio, Piazzolla introduced himself at breakfast one morning at the Copacabana Palace Hotel. After hearing the Nonet and Amelita, Moustaki was "in a really extraordinary state," as he recalls, "and afterwards I said, and he said: 'We'll see each other in Paris.' " They did.

In Venezuela, where the Nonet arrived on 2 October, the controversy was caused not by foolish international squabbles but by Piazzolla's loose tongue. His five concerts in Caracas's Teatro Municipal, arranged by Alejandro Szterenfeld, were a predictable success. But in one of the unconsidered statements he liked throwing at reporters, he described Carlos Gardel as "a mediocrity who only became famous after his death."[31] This fatuous and inaccurate remark provoked instant expressions of outrage from all through Latin America.[32] Piazzolla quickly tried to mend fences and accused the press of misinterpreting him: "Bah! the truth is they understand very little," he said, once safely back in Buenos Aires.[33]

In mid-October he flew to Germany to oversee the progress of *El Pueblo Joven*. He was back home a month later, followed soon after by a TV crew from Saarbrücken which visited Buenos Aires to film urban scenes for the televised version of the oratorio. The Germans also filmed an erotic scene with Amelita and a dancer from Oscar Araiz's company. Amelita chose not to tell Piazzolla of the session, guessing that his reaction would be less than calm.

A November concert at the Rosedal (Rose-Bowl) in Palermo Park was one of the Nonet's more agreeable engagements before this hectic year ended. Sometime in 1972 Piazzolla phoned his third cousin Oscar Cataldi and asked if he could become a partner in his well-known Viejo Pop restaurant, where Piazzolla often ate when he was in Mar del Plata. "Are you a few sheets to the wind?" inquired Cataldi. "No, I'm serious about it," said Piazzolla. He evidently took some dissuading. Did Piazzolla really intend to abandon his musical career? The incident is not unique in musical history. The great English composer Benjamin Britten once seriously considered going to work in a hardware store on Long Island.[34] In both cases the reason was a short fit of the blues rather than a real wish to abandon music.

Heart Attack

At the beginning of March 1973 Piazzolla again flew to Europe. In Italy, he recorded a TV spectacular with Mina, broadcast on 5 April, and announced that he planned a "huge theater tour" with the actress Edmonda Aldini.[35] Nothing more was heard of this, though she would later record with him.

The Municipality of Buenos Aires was unable to underwrite the Nonet for a second year. *Faute de mieux*, Piazzolla fell back on the Quintet, and picked up what engagements he could. Opinions were mixed about its reappearance. In Montevideo in mid-June, several critics compared it unfavorably with the Nonet: "not Piazzolla at his best," one of them asserted. Piazzolla counterattacked immediately, declaring that the Quintet was "much more original" than the Nonet. And there were some who agreed with him. The magazine *El Economista* reported one of his concerts with the comment: "We can tell the admirers of the great Astor that he is better than ever."[36] The few recordings made by the Quintet in

1973 (none released commercially at the time) are certainly riveting in their quality.

In July–August the resurrected Quintet spread its wings and went on tour to Brazil, opening at Porto Alegre's Teatro Leopoldina on 28–29 July and moving north from there. It was the familiar, consoling Brazilian story: packed theaters, impassioned applause. The audiences at São Paulo are remembered as "delirious" by Piazzolla's Uruguayan painter-friend Carlos Páez Vilaró, who accompanied him on this particular tour. The two friends detoured briefly to Guarujá, the ocean resort near Santos, to unveil a new Páez Vilaró mural at the Hotel Delphin. Piazzolla signed it, along with the painter.[37]

While in Brazil, Piazzolla made some very gloomy statements about the de-teriorating political situation in Argentina and its crippling effects on "artistic development."[38] He may well have been depressed by the recent (May 1973) start of the new Peronist government and the ominous groundswell of urban guerrilla violence that had become noticeable over the previous two or three years. But his words almost certainly also reflected a growing personal frustration. With the municipal contract gone, 1973 was proving an altogether more difficult year. "I live from shows," he told a Brazilian reporter, and the shows were thinning out. His royalties, he explained, amounted to about $6,000 a year, and he felt lucky if he sold 3,000 copies of an album in Argentina.[39] Not surprisingly, he began to look toward the outside world. Brazil, where his records sold better than in Ar-gentina, was one promising possibility. One of his composing tasks in 1973 was the sound track for a Brazilian film, directed by Arnaldo Jabor. Released in France under the title *Toute Nudité Sera Chatié*, its explicitness brought trouble from film censors in several countries.

There were bigger prizes to be grasped. His European trip in March was clearly a reconnaissance. He had been encouraged by several European impresarios, and the temptation seemed obvious. Piazzolla felt certain parallels with his experience in 1958: "There are these painful economic moments, when I scarcely have the desire to go on living," he told *Gente*. "Then I escape, I scram, I get out." Rumors had been spreading in the press that he was about to leave Argentina for good, to live in Europe, and Piazzolla admitted that, ideally, he would like to "divide the year in two. Half there, half here."[40]

Amelita was not attracted by the prospect of expatriation. She had returned to folksinging, had been earning good money at the Gallina Embarazada night-spot, and was now starring in the highly successful *Tres Mujeres para el Show* with Susana Rinaldi and Marikena Monti—a mixture of tangos, folk music, and in-ternational fare. Piazzolla envied her success (she was earning more than he was) and did not particularly want her with him in Europe. The relationship had become more than usually stormy over the previous year. While Piazzolla was in Italy, Amelita discovered that she was pregnant. Piazzolla said very harsh things to her, accusing her of simply wanting a child called Piazzolla, and his attitude drove her to an abortion. They were reconciled, but the reconciliation was fragile. Piazzolla became obsessively jealous, often dropping in on her at the theater "to spy," as Amelita remembers, "to see what I was up to, whether I was with someone. It was terrible."

For the first time since the traumas of 1966, Piazzolla was also going through a serious composing block—"a kind of fear, a kind of nullity; I don't know what to call it," he told an interviewer in August.[41] Creative paralysis was if anything more stressful to him than his normal hectic routine. Added to his troubles with Amelita, it was lethal. "I began to smoke and smoke and smoke, and eat and eat and eat, just like that, in desperation," he recalled three years later.[42] He needed to slow down. His doctor issued stern warnings. And on Thursday 25 October,

> I thought that illnesses and death had nothing to do with me, that I was Superman. But when my chest, my arm, my shoulder began to hurt. . . . It was so intolerable I don't even remember it. I only know that I woke up in the intensive care unit of a hospital, full of cables and probes, in pain, exhausted, and feeling very afraid. I had suffered a heart attack.[43]

He left the hospital, where Dedé had been among his visitors, in a wheelchair. As Daniel has memorably recounted, he soon threw it away and started walking. Daniel visited him every night at the apartment. They drank champagne and listened to records of Villa-Lobos and Quincy Jones. Piazzolla told his son that he was going to make a new start, probably in Italy. With Amelita matters went from bad to worse, and on 30 December they separated, Piazzolla telling the press, "I'm afraid of working with her again; the wires might snap."[44]

On doctor's orders, he now cut out smoking completely. Diana, who was always trying to stop, asked him how he did it: "Well, you need to have a big fright," he told her. His own big fright was that he would never be able to play again. In January 1974, by which time he was up and about, the doctors told him that he could perform. He asked Oscar López Ruiz, who lived nearby, to accompany him on the walks the doctors recommended. He was in a reminiscent mood, telling López Ruiz of his regret at not paying more attention to his children: "Look, I really love my children a lot, but I don't have the time." Someone else who often dropped in on him was his Brazilian friend Eric Nepomuceno, then living in Buenos Aires. Nepomuceno noticed him taking tiny sips of whiskey—the "regulatory glass," Piazzolla explained. He played Nepomuceno some music he had written, telling him that he wanted Chico Buarque to set words to it. He recorded a cassette for Nepomuceno to send to Buarque.

He meant what he told Daniel. His recovery from the heart attack merely strengthened his determination to make a new start abroad. As was his habit, he put a bold construction on his decision when talking to the press.

> I am a new Piazzolla. I can assure you that this is the most important stage of my career as a composer. It saddens me that I cannot bring it to fruition in my own country, but Argentines are not yet ready for daring or dangerous creations. Why am I going? It's very clear. I'm going because in Buenos Aires I'm just one of the thousands of unemployed who throng the streets.[45]

In January 1974 he flew to Mar del Plata, where Amelita's show was playing, to persuade her to go to Europe with him. Amelita's first reaction was to say no, but stories of his loneliness (told to her by his friends, almost certainly at his request) eventually swayed her. She agreed to a reconciliation. "Astor had nobody but me," as she would say later.[46] Back in Buenos Aires, she organized a merry fifty-third birthday party for him, and as a surprise, flew Nonina in from Mar del Plata. Piazzolla enjoyed himself hugely and drank too much. His guests pressed him to play his bandoneon, but drink had taken its toll. "It fell from his hand," says Amelita. "He couldn't play anything." A few days later their new adventure began. As one magazine trumpeted, "All roads lead to Rome—music, songs and love."[47]

8

Man

> *Who would you like to have been?*—Bach or Mozart. But they suffered so!
> *What is the main feature of your personality?*—Nervousness. I'm always
> moving my fingers. *Your main defect?*—I never think what I'm going to
> say. That means I do a lot of trashy things and put my foot in it a
> lot. . . .*What would be your biggest misfortune?*—To lose my wife. *What do
> you hate more than anything else?*—To be served bad food. *Your favorite
> name?*—Windy, Sonny, Zum. They're my three dogs. *What does a police-
> man suggest to you?*—Antipathy. I feel revulsion for anyone who carries a
> weapon. . . .*What gift would you like to have from Nature?* . . . To fly, like
> the birds. *How would you like to die?*—Violently . . .*Your ideology?*—My
> only politics is music. I believe in the avant-garde, in freedom, in revolution.
> —Astor Piazzolla in *La Semana*, 21 July 1983

> What a devilish mixture there was inside that man!
> —Máximo Perrotti (1995)

"The Two Sprites That Are Inside Me"

At the time Piazzolla made his decision to move to Europe, he was more than
halfway through his career as an independent musician. He was then in his early
fifties, and as George Orwell once memorably observed, "at fifty everyone has the
face he deserves." Before we follow the story of Piazzolla's life into its new phase,

it is appropriate to pause and examine his "face" a little more closely. What sort of man was he? What were the formative influences on his character? Why did he leave such a strong impression on those who met him? What were some of the characteristics of his behavior as a musician? These are the questions we try to answer in the next two chapters.

It is no coincidence that "Adiós Nonino" is Piazzolla's most celebrated piece of music. Nonino was the biggest single influence on the formation of his character. It was his father who firmly steered him toward the tango when his own boyish enthusiasm was for classical music and jazz. It was his father who gave him his first bandoneon—a cultural message as well as a musical instrument. Nonino, a first-generation Argentine but still highly Italian, was telling his son: "You *must* be Argentine." It is as if Astor received a strong paternal mandate that he could never really escape. As an adolescent, he resisted the tango, and perhaps resisted being Argentine. All his life, in fact, he was something of a rootless migrant. Deep down, however, he became thoroughly *tanguero*—that is to say, thoroughly imbued with the tango culture.

This was not the only legacy from his father. While Nonino was still alive, Piazzolla observed a conventional moral code, becoming a good husband and a good father. Nonino's death in 1959 meant the collapse of a structure, the removal of a strong directing hand of which Piazzolla was aware, and it shook him out of his mold. His personal behavior became erratic. His marriage broke down, his relationship with his children was seriously impaired and never fully reconstructed—a wound Piazzolla took to his grave. It was not until the mid-1970s, with his second wife, Laura Escalada, that his life regained real stability. What is interesting here is that it was precisely the years between Nonino's death and Piazzolla's heart attack—his years of greatest difficulty—that were his most creative period. With the paternal mandate no longer in force, he was able to combine his old love of classical music and jazz with the tango, and to make *his* music at last.

In the mid-1980s Piazzolla's second wife, Laura, did a character sketch of her husband for the press:

> Astor is a very complex man, and at the same time very simple.... I would say he is a synthesis of simplicity and controversy.... He has an inner life that is absolutely his own, and nobody enters there. Not even me. That inner world is something he lives in, enjoys, sorts out, and its nature is something he transmits exclusively by way of music.... He's a tremen-

dously vulnerable man, with a childlike ingenuousness. . . . He has a great shyness . . . which obviously comes from his childhood. . . . Only in intimacy and in very special moments does he open up. . . . It seems to me that this has a lot to do with what Italian and Spanish families were always like in the old days. He's not very demonstrative, he's rather dry. . . . Giving me a spontaneous caress is strange for him. Saying "I love you" and embracing me is not very usual. . . . The odd thing is that Astor is immensely affectionate. . . . In day-to-day life he's simple, not at all pretentious. . . . At first his silences bothered me but then I discovered what it was all about; his silences are the times he takes to think. He's a thinking machine.[1]

Record producer Vera Brandes, who met him toward the end of his life, thinks that "Astor was the same as his music. Totally passionate, vigorous, full of love, tenderness, humor, drama, suffering, joy, intensity, emotion, physical and spiritual at the same time, as unpredictable as life itself."

Nearly everyone who met him noticed his restlessness. His longtime agent Atilio Talín thinks of him as "a volcano" with "tremendous nervous energy." Lidia Pugliese, widow of the bandleader Osvaldo Pugliese, remembers a concert in Amsterdam in 1989 when Piazzolla rushed up and down, frantically checking the sound system and the stage. "Eventually [Osvaldo] called him and said: 'Astor, why are you running around like this? It's not good for you. We're all grown-ups. Come sit down, we're going to have a coffee.' Astor accepted the advice, but not for more than ten minutes."[2]

He could be the best of companions, able to charm and stimulate those he was with. "At bottom he was a very tender type, very much a friend, *when he wanted to be*," says pianist Pablo Ziegler. Eladia Blázquez, the singer and composer, is saddened to think "that people didn't know Astor's real personality, the tender part, which was a bit masked by his mischievous, up-front way of life." This was a side to Piazzolla that was abundantly present during his years with the "three Ds," when he was in every way an admirable family man. Dedé's parents were very fond of him, finding him sensitive, playful, a joker. A friend of later years, Marta Saúl, was always impressed by "his warmth, simplicity and directness. He was the simplest, sanest, most transparent person I ever met," she says.

Pianist Mónica Cosachov, by contrast, senses that he had "a terribly tortured world inside," and certainly he could be both exploitive and aggressive, sometimes indifferent to common conventions of behavior, occasionally cruel. His daughter considers him a man "like all geniuses, with some big weaknesses on the human level." To his Mar del Plata third cousin Oscar Cataldi he was "a good type, but very, very difficult to take, Astor." Oscar López Ruiz, in his highly readable memoir, often nicknames Piazzolla *Luzbelito*, "little Lucifer." "Satan with a bandoneon" was suggested, only half in jest, by one of his Argentine acquaintances as a possible title for our book. Is this going too far? Yes. But there *was* a mildly satanic side to Piazzolla, and it cannot be left completely out of any account.

It stemmed, no doubt, from ambition. He was very ambitious, like all artists with a powerful creative urge. "We are going to be a couple like the Bartóks," he told Dedé. Piazzolla once asked journalist Bernardo Neustadt over lunch: "What will happen after my death? How will they remember me?" Neustadt told him that at first he would be ignored, because he had been a pioneer. Another lunch guest interjected that thousands would attend his funeral. "Very few people will," said Neustadt, at which Piazzolla's face assumed a very gloomy look. Neustadt's first prediction was seriously wrong; he was only partially correct about the funeral.

Piazzolla himself always admitted that he had two sides to his nature. "I think," he told Máximo Perrotti, "that of the two sprites that are inside me, the one that *thinks* is more stupid than the one that *does things* and he always arrives late."[3] One of the things the "sprite that did things" clearly controlled was Piazzolla's notorious verbal frankness. As caricaturist Hermenegildo Sábat says, "He was not a man who pretended." A friend of later years, Ricardo Saúl, found him "very up-front, highly up-front, dangerously up-front," as a man (in the old Spanish expression) *sin pelos en la lengua*, "without hairs on his tongue." Another friend, Ambassador Mario Corcuera Ibáñez, thinks of him in this same context as "profoundly free. He could be influenced by practically nothing."

Verbal frankness sometimes shaded into physical aggression. The "Lefty" Piazzolla of the Lower East Side was sometimes reincarnated in adult life. His brother-in-law Horacio Mártire tells us: "He preferred not to discuss things. He preferred to punch you if you went beyond the limits—his limits." There were several more or less famous instances. During the time of the 1946 band, he knocked a fan of traditionalist bandleader Alfredo De Angelis to the ground for having called him *rengo*, "lame," and had to be pulled off him by his friend Perrotti. There was at least one night at 676 when, coarsely insulted by a drunkard near the rostrum, Piazzolla lifted his left hand from the bandoneon and struck the man a blow that sent him reeling.[4] There is no record, however, of his ever striking a woman.

There were naturally times when his candor or aggressiveness brought trouble. Offended by a magazine report that bracketed his music with Atilio Stampone's, he publicly nicknamed the pianist "Espantone"—meaning, roughly, The Frightful. Stampone sued and won a retraction.[5] Piazzolla almost seems to have courted such episodes deliberately. Jazz critic Peter Watrous, interviewing him in the 1980s, accurately intuited that "if no one had given him a hard time about his music, he probably would have hired someone to do it." And indeed, mentioning the threats made against him at the time of the Octet, Piazzolla told Watrous that they had made him "happy!"[6] The remark was a very revealing one.

Piazzolla himself rationalized his aggressiveness as an inability to suffer fools—especially musical fools—gladly. In part, of course, he found attack to be the best form of defense, and he needed to defend his music against hostile criticism for most of his career. When really angry, he was capable of making major scenes. Playing with him in the mid-1980s, Gary Burton witnessed just such a scene at a concert in Spain

> where things weren't well organized. He got into a whole evening of yelling with the promoter. And later he apologized to me and said: "Oh I'm sorry you had to see all this. I was so angry at this guy, because here I come with my band, and with you as a special guest, and I feel very embarrassed that he didn't have things well organized, and it just made me angry." I have seen musicians have those kinds of blow-ups many times—including myself, sometimes.

In later years he may have mellowed somewhat. At the time of his sixty-seventh birthday in 1988, when asked what his greatest defect was, he replied: "My aggressiveness, although over the years I am changing a bit."[7] Journalist Edmundo Eichelbaum thinks that later on "he controlled his impetuosity to a certain extent." His impatience, however, could still be reflected in other ways. He no longer had much time for children. "If he arrived in a restaurant and there were children there," remembers Daniel, "he turned round and went away."

Piazzolla's aggressiveness and impatience did not stem from an inflated opinion of himself. Author Simon Collier, meeting him in 1985, cannot remember any trace whatever of what the English call "side"—airs of superiority. "He was the least prima-donna-ish man I ever met," says Oscar López Ruiz. He never stood on his dignity. The photographer Gianni Mesticheli once found him waiting patiently in line to buy cheese in Paris, just like any Parisian, and on a later occasion saw him waiting with equal patience to get into a movie theater in Punta del Este. Percussionist Enrique "Zurdo" Roizner's impression is that "he knew he was among the great. But he had an astonishing naturalness about it. It didn't affect him one bit." His second wife, Laura, makes the same point in a somewhat different way: "He did not know who he was. He never had a consciousness of himself. He did his thing, that's all. He wrote, he played, but never had a vision of himself; he did not have a total awareness of his great talent."

There was a downside to this. Incorruptible in anything to do with his music, which he would never alter for mere money, Piazzolla had only a limited business sense. He could certainly *imagine* business opportunities. He once fantasized, with a Mar del Plata acquaintance, Juan Mastropasqua, about setting up a record company in Mar del Plata. It was an ideal place, he said: "In the United States, nobody records in New York; they go to the interior of the United States, to somewhere absolutely quiet, where the musicians gather and where they have a suitable place to work." His reasoning was good. New York and Los Angeles are less important as recording centers than provincial Nashville. But Piazzolla would never have had the patience to organize such a venture. Atilio Talín, who managed his affairs for many years, testifies, "It was a major triumph to get Astor to sit down to talk about the economic side of things. 'I want us to talk.' 'Well, fine, terrific' "—and Piazzolla would immediately lose interest. Record producer Vera Brandes, working with him in 1989, found that "the business aspects were not always as clearly structured as one would expect of an artist of his stature."

As an independent musical entrepreneur—after 1946 he was always his own boss—he was never unaware of the need to make money, but he was bored by the fine print of contracts. This led him into complex tangles with publishers, record companies, and theater managements. Laura agrees that "Astor was a man who always succumbed to frauds," and adds that he "had very bad luck in choosing managers or people to advise him or to contract him. Astor had a sort of lodestone that attracted all kinds of undesirables. It was like a fatal attraction." His innocence in these matters was ultimately due to his reluctance to think about anything other than music. "A man like that," says Laura, "is a man with problems." On this particular score, Piazzolla's character can be contrasted with that of his idol Stravinsky, whose interest in accumulating money once won from his sometime librettist W. H. Auden the suggestion that *millionen* would be the ideal German word for him to set to music. Piazzolla's tangles were to cause endless headaches to his heirs—his two children and his second wife—who in May 1997 formed a new company, Piazzolla Music, to begin sorting them out. In the matter of recordings, in particular, the years immediately after his death saw something approaching anarchy. Emmanuel Chamboredon, the French owner of the Milan label, a good friend of Piazzolla in the last years of his life, and a partner in Piazzolla Music, roundly declares: "There are many people who abused Astor's confidence, and today there are people who have no respect for the rights of artists [and who] happily plunder their property. That means that four out of five Piazzolla records on the market are illegal."

Likes and Dislikes: Serious

Piazzolla was baptized and raised a Catholic, and in 1968 he defined himself as "a Catholic, but not too much."[8] In 1976 he told a reporter: "I believe in a God: we ourselves are both the Devil and God. And, well, I am Christian: when I'm afraid, I pray . . . but I'm only afraid when I travel by plane."[9] The dislike of flying, we might remark here, was genuine enough. Saúl Cosentino, a musician friend who became a pilot for Aerolíneas Argentinas, sometimes arranged to be in charge when Piazzolla was flying on his routes. "I brought him into the cockpit, for take-off or landing," he recalls, "and that took away a bit of the fear." By the 1980s, ironically, he was condemned to more or less constant air travel.

After his separation from Dedé in 1966, Piazzolla claimed to have become "very superstitious."[10] When Horacio Ferrer knocked on his door on that famous December night in 1967, Piazzolla immediately told him about the forecast by the astrologer Horangel. Ferrer's view is that he "was very sensitive to those esoteric things, unlucky stars, things that bring bad luck, destiny, the fates; he lived a prisoner of all that." His friend "El Tuco" Paz remembers an occasion in the late 1960s when he and Piazzolla drove to Avellaneda to consult a well-known seer who lived there. In his middle years at least, Piazzolla sometimes admitted openly to an interest in the occult. In 1968, as he told a reporter, he visited a noted Argentine spiritualist, De Bono, who informed him that there were two "protectors" in his life: Sylphe, the spirit of the air, and Ondine, the spirit of water. It was in their honor that he composed his three-movement "Tangata" (1969), though Amelita Baltar tried to dissuade him from writing it.[11] Daniel confirms that his father carried amulets around at this period, and that on his visits to Brazil he regularly consulted a *pai do santo* of the Brazilian *Candomblé* cult, whose advice he always took. How long this behavior went on we cannot tell, but it was evidently serious while it lasted.

A substantial change in his religious outlook came with his relationship with Laura Escalada, eventually his second wife. He reverted completely to the traditional Catholicism of his upbringing. He himself declared in 1980: "I am Catholic. I believe in God and I pray to him in English. I also like getting inside a church. It's like detoxifying myself. It's like taking a bath of peace."[12] His friend Marta Saúl sees him as "a man of touching faith," essentially very pious, though not a regular attender at Mass. Every year, by this stage, Piazzolla and Laura, along with Atilio Talín and his wife Inés, made an annual pilgrimage to Luján, Argentina's national religious shrine. In his later years he became a particular devotee of the Virgin of the Miraculous Medallion.* From his trips to Europe he now often brought back medallions and stamps of the Virgin, and even small flasks of holy water, as presents for his friends. He offered to donate an image of the Virgin to Maldonado Cathedral in Punta del Este.

Catholicism probably tinged some of Piazzolla's more conservative social attitudes, although his family's old-fashioned Italian antecedents doubtless played a part here too. He had little or no sympathy for feminism, of which there has been more in Argentina than elsewhere in Latin America—though infinitely less than in the United States. Diana was enraged on one occasion when Piazzolla praised her in the press for being a good mother, adding, almost as an afterthought, that she was also a good writer. It was an off-the-cuff remark, and a revealing one. It in no way implied disrespect for his daughter's literary hopes. Indeed, he did what he could to promote her as a writer in the 1960s.

Piazzolla's political opinions were always totally unpredictable, although he was fairly consistent in his antipathy to Peronism. He despised musicians who had compromised with the Perón government. In the elections of September 1973, however, he actually voted for Perón, as did a majority of Argentines in that time of growing national crisis.[13] But he was swiftly disillusioned, and reverted to his standard opinion. "Argentina is rotten because of Juan Domingo Perón," he told a Brazilian journalist in 1986; "He was responsible for dividing people into Peronists and anti-Peronists."[14] His attitude to Evita Perón, however, seems to have softened over the years. In the mid-1970s he even thought of writing an opera about her.

Piazzolla's problem with politics was that he always had to say something when asked. There is no point whatever in attempting to track his ideological variations. In the early 1980s he supported President Raúl Alfonsín, but again he was soon disillusioned. At other times he *could* sound fairly left-wing, and at still others he was prepared to put in a good word for Chilean dictator General Augusto Pinochet. "We Argentines have needed a person like Pinochet," he told Natalio

---

*An extremely popular cult in mid-nineteenth-century France, after the Virgin Mary revealed the design of the medal in 1830 to St. Catherine Labouré (1806–76). The Chapel of the Miraculous Medallion (Chapelle de la Médaille Miraculeuse) in the rue du Bac, Paris, is visited by about two million people every year. Piazzolla went there the day before fate dealt him its severest blow.

Gorin in 1990. "Perhaps Argentina needs a bit of Fascism." Gorin expressed astonishment that a man who had lived so often in democracies like France and Italy could say such things. Piazzolla admitted that he was exaggerating and that he still admired musicians like the lifelong Communist Osvaldo Pugliese, who never found a good reason to change his opinions, opinions he took to his grave.[15] Piazzolla himself was totally incapable of any such ideological consistency.

By his last years, he was at least half aware that he opened his mouth too readily. In a phone conversation with Oscar López Ruiz in late 1989 or early 1990 he admitted: "The truth is I really ought to put my tongue in my ass."[16] And he promised his old guitarist that he would never again make provocative statements on anything other than music. He seems to have kept his word. Piazzolla's political statements, in any case, always need to be taken with a very large grain of salt. He was no more a political animal than his friend and mentor Aníbal Troilo, who always refused to express opinions on politics, on the grounds that such matters were intrinsically less interesting than soccer or horse racing. For Piazzolla, the equivalents were shark fishing or speeding along the highways. As he once said to Antonio Agri: "Presidents come and go. I shall go on playing my bandoneon." What really interested him, inspired him, and moved him was *music.*

Likes and Dislikes: Not So Serious

In August 1964, a reporter asked Piazzolla what most excited him. Apart from music, he replied, it was "the moment when my wife is cooking, or when I make my car go at 90 miles an hour."[17] These tastes are well attested to by all who knew him. Oscar López Ruiz recalls hair-raising car journeys along the Argentine highways. Piazzolla's friend Kico Salvo, accompanying him for weekends at Mar del Plata, would never allow him to drive his smart Datsun coupé. On such occasions, Piazzolla invariably pestered Kico to drive faster. His love of automobiles gave him his Argentine agent for the last twenty years of his career, Atilio Talín, on whom Piazzolla conferred extensive powers of attorney in December 1980. They had first met at the Jamaica nightclub. Talín had just bought an Alfa Romeo. He was surprised one evening, when Piazzolla, descending from the stage, said to him: "Nice, that Alfa." "Don't tell me, maestro, that you like cars?" asked Talín. "After music, they are what I most like," replied Piazzolla. After the show, they went off and roamed Buenos Aires. The friendship soon deepened.[18]

Good eating ranked higher than automobiles among his extracurricular enthusiasms. He became something of a *bon vivant* in his later years. He had a remarkable skill at sniffing out obscure restaurants, in Buenos Aires and in foreign cities. Dedé remembers excursions in the 1940s and 1950s to the modest Spada-vecchia *cantina* in the waterfront La Boca district, but when it was "modernized" and smartened up, Piazzolla lost interest in going there. His preference was for out-of-the way places with a reputation for good cooking. During his years with Amelita he favored the Angiola and Bachín, two traditional *porteño* restaurants—the latter immortalized in song. The Fechoría and the Broccolino were regular stopping points with his second wife Laura. A favorite place, certainly in later years, was the Félix Restaurant in Avellaneda—"the best restaurant in the world," he often called it. Its proprietors, Félix and Irma Estrada, confirm his frequent visits, when he would eat "ham, sucking-pig, maybe a chicken, everyday things, but well done." His taste in wines usually focused on Argentine reds from the López vineyards (Rincón Famoso, Chateau Vieux). Piazzolla sometimes held his birthday dinners at the Félix. If possible, he liked to dine at around 9:00 P.M., rather earlier than most of his compatriots.

He was also a man who enormously enjoyed cooking, which he did "magnif-icently well," says Dedé. And he often cooked for other people. According to Solange Perrotti he had a special way of preparing eggplant, boiling them in white vinegar and then crushing them. Daniel Piazzolla can think of nobody who ever cooked "tastier pasta." His father invented a sauce that, says Daniel, "has been handed down through the family, very simple, but exquisite." Some of Piazzolla's musicians learned how to make it too. After his separation from Dedé, he devel-oped new culinary skills. His "spectacular *milanesas*" are still remembered. In his Punta del Este house in the 1980s, he was always in his element in the kitchen. He installed a baking oven there and made bread. He became expert at cooking fish, though, according to his servants, his favorite dish was steak (done rare) combined with truffles, tomatoes, and a light cheese.[19]

If he liked fish, he liked fishing even more. From boyhood on he had a fond-ness for both hunting, mostly duck and partridge in the Mar del Plata hinterland, and fishing, especially for bigger fish, often in earlier years from the jetties and breakwaters at Mar del Plata. A favorite spot, as we have already noted, was Bahía San Blas, south of Bahía Blanca, whose wild surroundings appealed to him and where he had his first experiences with sharks. Piazzolla himself often alluded to this enthusiasm when talking to reporters. "My psychoanalysis is in the sea," he told one of them.[20] Piazzolla's later shark-fishing trips, however, need a separate look and should be placed in proper context: his move to Punta del Este in the 1980s.

Man cannot live by shark fishing alone. What were his tastes in literature and art? His interest in painting, sparked and cultivated by Dedé, seems to have been lifelong. Alberto Ginastera had advised him to read widely, and for a few years he made a conscientious effort to do so. After that the effort ceased. Diana tells us that "he hated reading." Hermenegildo Sábat's view is that "on the literary side, he wasn't a cultured man." Piazzolla was quite open about this. He told Speratti in 1968 about his reading preferences: "Poetry is what I most like reading. . . . Lorca, Vallejo, the classics of our century. I love poems. Other stuff interests me less and less, except for biographies of musicians, which are, I would say, what I have most read. I am incapable of reading a novel." "I don't have the patience," he said in 1983. "I used to read a lot when I was a snob, and wanted to know what was going on in literature, painting, the cinema, as well as music. . . . Till one fine day, when I said: "No. Why the hell am I reading this if I don't enjoy it?"[21]

For most of his life Piazzolla was a fairly assiduous moviegoer. Here, too, his tastes were simple. Dedé remembers him as fascinated by cartoons; they went to Disney's *Fantasia* together when it reached Buenos Aires in the early 1940s. He was prepared to give a deferential nod to Antonioni, Fellini, or Bergman, but his true allegiance lay elsewhere. "I recognize that I prefer a James Bond movie or a good western," he said in 1968. "Westerns are really good, perfect, little gems."[22]

Humor

Piazzolla's extraordinary sense of humor has left a multitude of stories in its wake. His daughter tells us that "episodes from his travels—he told them in a way that made you laugh, that hurt your stomach from laughing." His Italian agent from 1974, Aldo Pagani, who had his ups and downs with Piazzolla, nonetheless remembers that he made him "die laughing." He often added comic twists to his day-to-day routines. He was fond of pinning nicknames to his friends and collaborators. In the late 1940s, for instance, the bandleader Armando Pontier was "el canguro" ("kangaroo") and journalist Armando Rolón "la liebre" ("the hare") because of his prominent teeth. Horacio Ferrer was "Horacus" for at least a while.[23] His repartee was also fairly quick. When pianist Gustavo Kerestezachi told him he had a *neurosis abandónica* ("a wild abandonic neurosis"), he riposted: "No, I have a *bandoneonic* neurosis!" His friend Lalo Schifrin thinks of his humor as very *porteño*, but also "very Piazzolla."

The humor, though, could be heavy at times—on a few occasions "blacker than the soul of Adolf Hitler," as López Ruiz puts it.[24] Most people leave mischievousness behind with childhood. Piazzolla prolonged it through his adult life, in the form of persistent practical joking. Piazzolla himself, it must be said here, never liked to be on the receiving end. "You had to put up with *his* jokes," says singer Raúl Lavié, "although he never put up with other people's."

This behavior can be documented for every phase of Piazzolla's career. When he was with Francisco Lauro's band in 1939, he once put a very hungry kitten in Lauro's bandoneon-case; the creature naturally scratched the colorful but incompetent bandleader when it was discovered.[25] During the Troilo years, as we saw, itching powder and stink bombs were part of his standard musical equipment. He once dared a fellow musician to race with him "completely nude" through the streets around the Casino in Mendoza, at midnight, when the streets were crowded—and got away with it. In 1943, at Mar del Plata, he lined up some of the musicians for a photograph on the boardwalk, and when the photographer placed himself under the traditional black cloth, Piazzolla dashed over and gave him a fierce kick in the backside before running off with a triumphant shout of "Goal!"[26]

Piazzolla continued his clowning with the Octet—once tying a well-stretched condom round the handle of Elvino Vardaro's violin case, for instance[27]—and with the Quintet in the 1960s, as we noted in an earlier chapter, when the singer Héctor De Rosas was often the victim of his humor. Piazzolla once put a dead iguana in his bed. De Rosas was philosophical: "Nobody could get annoyed with a type like Astor," he says.[28] Percussionist León Jacobson recalls an incident from this same period; late at night, riding in a taxi, he spotted Piazzolla outside a night club, and lowered the window to greet him. Piazzolla threw a lighted cigarette into the car, which landed in a cloud of sparks on the driver's neck. "The man is crazy," said the driver. "It's Maestro Piazzolla," replied Jacobson.

Piazzolla's love of practical joking continued well into his later years. On one of the Brazilian tours in the mid-1970s, as percussionist Enrique "Zurdo" Roizner remembers, he put on a rubber Frankenstein mask, handing a mask of Dr. Jekyll to his son Daniel. Together they burst into the hotel room where electric organist Santiago Giacobbe was sleeping and woke him up. Giacobbe let out a piercing scream. In the 1980s, living at Punta del Este, Piazzolla was not above scaring his neighbors with masks of various kinds, and it was a treatment he applied to his guests too—as singer-composer Eladia Blázquez remembers well. His friend Mario Antelo, turning up for a New Year party, noticed that the house was in complete darkness: "Suddenly something fell on me from above, from a tree, and it was him, dressed up as a witch. He jumped all round me. He said: 'Were you scared? Were you scared?' "

What must have been Piazzolla's most spectacular feat of clowning took place in Paris in the mid-1970s. He and his doctor and friend Marcos Asensio were wandering round the city in the early hours after an excellent dinner. They came to Notre Dame and went inside. As Asensio recalls, Piazzolla seated himself at the organ and began playing—improvising a mix of vaguely religious music and his own. The faithful began arriving for early Mass. "If a cop comes, he'll put you in the clink," suggested Asensio. Piazzolla played on, right through the Mass. As the two friends left the cathedral, one of the officiating priests said to Asensio: "Tell that gentleman that if he can come and play on Saturday nights, or at the Sunday Mass, or at weddings, we'll pay him well. To get people to come to church, you need to give them new sensations, and this man—he played well!"

The "Barra"

Those who were close to Piazzolla doubt whether he ever had really intimate friends, although his circle of acquaintances was enormous. He rarely if ever opened up completely to anyone. Many of his best personal friends were fellow musicians. Talking to journalist Alberto Speratti in 1968, he specifically named Hugo Baralis, José Bragato, Enrique Mario Francini, and Leopoldo Federico (he could certainly have added Roberto Di Filippo), while claiming "some sterling friends" among his current musicians: Antonio Agri, Kicho Díaz, Osvaldo Manzi, Oscar López Ruiz, Jaime Gosis.[29] But there was always a small group of people outside the profession for whom he had a high regard and who constituted his *barra*, his "gang" of followers. "I am very fond of the people who understand me and who have been my followers for years," he said in 1971. "The few friends I have, those thirty or forty people who have followed my progress—that *barra*—are the people I think of when I compose. I write for myself, but also to make them happy."[30] These friends he trusted implicitly, and in return they were fiercely protective of him. We cannot possibly introduce all the members of the *barra*, but half a dozen or so stand out in our story.

The captain of the team was Víctor Oliveros. He was a twelve-year old in the Patagonian oil town, Comodoro Rivadavia, when he first heard Piazzolla's music on the radio. He was transfixed. A few years later, by which time he and his parents had moved to Buenos Aires, he conceived an obsessive desire to meet Piazzolla. He phoned him, and at 4:55 P.M. on Wednesday, 9 June 1955—he would never forget the exact moment—he was greeted by Piazzolla at the Parque Chacabuco apartment. Piazzolla made him listen to an arrangement of the tango "Arrabal" he was doing for the Octet. Oliveros found it "too advanced," but he was soon won over[31]—so much so that he attended virtually all the Octet's rehearsals at the Rendezvous nightclub. Piazzolla warmly appreciated Oliveros's devotion. Oliveros, for his part, began consciously to create a *barra* for his musical idol. It was well in place by the time of the famous night at Luna Park in 1969, when its members proudly displayed a banner reading BALADA PARA UN LOCO. Long before this, Oliveros had started to collect Piazzolla memorabilia, not merely records and press clippings, but also tramcar tickets once used by Piazzolla, the menu offered on his wedding day, one of his fishing hats, countless photos, and his first bandoneon—entrusted to him when Piazzolla went to New York in 1958.

Oliveros's *barra* included well-known journalists like Héctor Ernié (who died in 1991) and Natalio Gorin.[32] Never having dared to approach him in Buenos Aires, Gorin first met Piazzolla in the spring of 1971 while on a visit to Paris, knocking at the door of Apartment 113 in the Cité des Arts. Juan Trigueros, another long-time fan, found himself by chance sitting next to Piazzolla at a concert in 1968. Piazzolla liked him immediately and gave him his phone number. Trigueros was then working in a bank and heard Quito González Azcona, in the next office, whistling a Piazzolla tune. "You like Piazzolla?" Trigueros asked his colleague. They began exchanging records. González Azcona suggested they invite Piazzolla to a discussion of the recently produced *María de Buenos Aires* at his house in the Flores district. Piazzolla, Ferrer, and Amelita not only turned up, but stayed chatting into the early hours. González Azcona's home became one of the more regular meeting places for Piazzolla and members of the *barra*, partly because he had a state-of-the-art audio system. On arrival from his European trips, Piazzolla sometimes phoned him: "Old chum, can we get together at your place? I have a few new things . . ."

In June 1969, González Azcona and Trigueros were helping Piazzolla change a tire after a concert. Víctor Oliveros, who had not yet met González Azcona, suddenly appeared on the scene. "Who are *you*?" he asked González Azcona. Later, in a nearby café, Oliveros administered the exam he sometimes gave would-be members of the *barra*: "How many of his long playing records do you have? Which is the one you like best?" and so on. Quito González Azcona passed the test triumphantly.

Mario Antelo, a lawyer, first met Piazzolla in 1968 at a Sarah Vaughan concert. They took to each other immediately. They were together on New Year's Eve at least eight times, either at Mar del Plata or later at Punta del Este. Once, at Mar del Plata, Antelo's young son put a firecracker under Nonina, exclaiming, "Adiós, Nonina!" Piazzolla was not pleased. He nicknamed Antelo "Milonga," on account of his unrepentant admiration for traditional tango music—hence the title of one of the pieces he wrote in 1986 for his collaboration with Gary Burton: "Milonga Is Coming."

One of the last additions to the *barra*, Francisco "Kico" Salvo, an insurance broker, had adored Piazzolla's music from the days of the Fiorentino band. He could never summon up courage to approach him, though he did once send him a friendly note at a question-and-answer session chaired by journalist Bernardo Neustadt, probably the one in August 1967. In 1980 Piazzolla finally learned of Salvo's faithful record as a fan, and phoned him. "Why didn't you show yourself before?" asked Piazzolla. "The years of being friends we've lost!" They soon made up for them.

Piazzolla derived a great deal of psychological satisfaction from the solidarity of his *barra*, and sometimes practical help as well: in the 1980s Kico Salvo frequently drove him to and from Ezeiza airport. At regular intervals he invited the inner circle of the *barra* to meals in favorite restaurants. These were purely masculine gatherings; the wives stayed at home. During the 1980s, as we shall see, the relationship between Piazzolla and his *barra* changed drastically. What is most remarkable, however, is that it survived Piazzolla's death as a united group, and it still meets regularly. Its members' bitterest regret is that the phone no longer rings and the familiar voice asks, "Old chum, can we get together at your place? I have a few new things . . ."

9

Musician

→→ Composer

Bandoneonist ←←

→→ Director: Piazzolla and His Musicians

The Piazzolla Sound ←←

→→ Piazzolla and the Tango Tradition

> He had a way to make very intricate, very interesting music, very inter-
> esting, but also to make you cry, and that is the highest compliment that
> you can ever give to a musician.
> —Al Di Meola

> Music just flowed into him. It was tremendous.
> —guitarist Cacho Tirao

Music was the absolute focus of Astor Piazzolla's life. His deepest feeling about it
was perhaps expressed to a Chilean interviewer in 1989: "Music is more than a
wife, because you can divorce a wife, but you can't divorce music. When you
marry music, she's your love forever, and you'll go to the grave with her."[1] Piazzolla's sacrifices for music were notable: aspects of his private life; his financial
security; in the end, his health. His marriage to music involved him in a multiple
role: he was composer, arranger, performer, and bandleader all at the same time.
We will leave a technical analysis of his music to the music theorists. Our task is
different. We need to see how his work as a musician interacted with his life—
how Piazzolla operated as composer and performer and bandleader, his relationship with the musicians who worked with him, his role as a revolutionary in the
tango tradition.

148

Composer

"A work machine," his son calls him. He wrote very quickly, with an almost instinctive grasp of the technicalities, something very evident in the speed with which he made arrangements. When Máximo Perrotti asked him for an arrangement of the tango "El Choclo" for the Radio El Mundo orchestra, Piazzolla did it in forty-five minutes, while sipping *mate*, the Paraguayan tea so popular in southern South America.[2] Piazzolla's agent in later years, Atilio Talín, sometimes delayed sending completed film scores to the directors concerned, in case they should be suspicious of work produced so fast. Over the course of his career Piazzolla wrote something in excess of 3,000 different pieces and is recognized by SACEM (Société des Auteurs, Compositeurs et Éditeurs de la Musique), the French equivalent of ASCAP, as belonging to its formal category of unusually prolific composers. No complete catalogue is yet available. Nor will one be easy to complete. Piazzolla sometimes gave away scores or simply forgot about them. At one of his barbecues at Punta del Este in the 1980s, journalist Bernardo Neustadt and cellist José Bragato observed him burning old scores. When Bragato tried to rescue them, Piazzolla simply said: "Don't worry, Pepe, that stuff's no use."[3]

When composing, Piazzolla was capable of total concentration, unbreachable "by earthquakes, wars, states of siege," as he once said.[4] He described the process of composition in greater detail to his daughter Diana. He could sit for hours at the piano, he told her, without writing a note. Then, "in an instant of enlightenment, of magic, of sorrow and pleasure, the main idea appears, and I breathe easily again." The later stages, such as "the logical development of the work, its internal coherence, the orchestration," could give him difficulty, and he was never sure of the quality of his work until he rehearsed it with his musicians.[5] He usually composed at the piano. Alberto Ginastera told him that "the piano is the orchestra," and he took the advice to heart. When he was without the instrument, he found it almost impossible to "imagine a melody in the air,"[6] and he was quite unable to sing or whistle anything he had written. When whistling was needed (in film music, for instance), he sometimes asked Daniel to do it.

Piazzolla often used the "inspiration-perspiration" catchphrase common among creative artists of all kinds. He saw himself as a professional who had to write something every day—"just like a cobbler doing his work."[7] He told his friend Quito González Azcona: "Don't forget that music isn't just a pastime. It's a career, like medicine or engineering." It was a career, however, in which the role of intuition was fundamental. "Bach composed fugues because he was intuitive," he told Speratti in 1968, "not because he was a brilliant egghead."[8] Yet

Piazzolla never underestimated the role of musical training, and certainly not the importance of studying. This was one of his permanent leitmotifs. To Natalio Gorin he quoted with pride a remark by the bandleader Osvaldo Pugliese: "Piazzolla forced all of us *to study*." The rule applied to all musicians, not least rock musicians. Sting, he told Gorin, had the good sense to go to Gil Evans for some of his arrangements.[9]

Piazzolla himself had no *amour propre* about soliciting advice. Oscar López Ruiz recalls a couple of times when he was asked to look over his scores. On the first occasion, in 1972, Piazzolla consulted him about the brass parts in his arrangement of the powerful Piazzolla-Ferrer song "La primera palabra." Twelve years later, in a phone call from Punta del Este, Piazzolla asked him to vet the "Tango Suite" he had written for Brazilian guitarists Sergio and Odair Assad. López Ruiz found the score "difficult and complicated but perfectly playable by virtuosos like the Assads," and he mailed it back immediately to Punta del Este.[10] In fact, Piazzolla's sensitivity to the compositional demands of instruments other than his own was remarkable, though (as the incident just noted shows) he was nervous about brass. León Jacobson noted the excellence of his writing for percussion. He was a quick study. He picked up much of his knowledge of the guitar, for instance, from jazz and tango guitarist Horacio Malvicino at the time of the Octet, in a session at Malvicino's apartment. "I showed him what the instrument was, its form, how the strings were divided, what was difficult, what might be easier," Malvicino recalls. "His capacity was such that just one time was sufficient for him to learn all that was necessary." Piazzolla's use of the guitar in his own ensembles, we might note here, was playful—as a melodic rather than a rhythmic instrument.

It would be wrong to present Piazzolla as a composer in perpetual motion. Sickness or depression sometimes undermined his creativity. There were times when he was completely "blocked": the period after his separation from Dedé, and the months before his heart attack in 1973. In the summer of 1981–82, at Punta del Este, there was a briefer hiatus. "I closed the piano," he told a reporter; "I felt lazy, and lacked motivation."[11] This was not the whole story. The real reason, that summer, was poor health. The summer of 1989–90, when he was eager to work on the last major project of his life, saw a similar composing block.

Outside the tango, the two great traditions on which Piazzolla drew for the creation of his sound-world as a composer were classical music and jazz. He came to have a formidable knowledge of the classical repertory: on road journeys in the 1960s, as Oscar López Ruiz remembers, he would tune the car radio to the classical station and immediately identify the music being played.[12] The scores he closely studied in the 1940s and 1950s, so Dedé tells us, included Vivaldi's *Four Seasons*, Prokofiev's *Love of Three Oranges*, Copland's *Appalachian Spring*, and Rimsky-Korsakoff's *Sheherazade*. Débussy also interested him a lot during that period. In 1964 he singled out Bach, Brahms, Ravel, Stravinsky, and Alban Berg as favorite composers.[13] At other times he added Paul Hindemith to his declared pantheon. Bartók was a firm favorite throughout, especially the Bartók of *Mikrokosmos*.[14] Western Hemisphere "nationalist" composers like Copland, Gershwin, and Villa-Lobos also interested him greatly. He was altogether less positive about twelve-tone music, or the experimental composers appearing after World War II. He respected figures like Pierre Boulez, Stockhausen, Luigi Nono, or Iannis Xenakis, but they did not inspire him. In 1989 he compared contemporary music to the search for an AIDs vaccine: "It's there, but it still isn't there . . . so to speak, it hasn't yet reached the market."[15]

The second prime source of Piazzolla's musical sensibility was jazz, although on at least one occasion he confessed to being quite unable to *write* it.[16] In the 1950s, figures like Stan Getz, Chet Baker, Gil Evans, Gerry Mulligan, Lennie Tristano, and George Shearing, and groups like the Modern Jazz Quartet all made their mark on him and on his work, especially his work with the Octet, perhaps the most jazz-influenced of all his ensembles. Later, at jazz festivals in Europe, North America, and Japan, he regularly rubbed shoulders with most of the greatest jazzmen of the time and was regarded by them as an honorary member of the tribe. As with classical music, however, jazz had its limits. In August 1966 Piazzolla went to hear Steve Lacy's "free jazz" quartet (then in Buenos Aires), and left the concert "disoriented." He went home and listened to Monteverdi and Vivaldi. "I needed to go back to something pure and crystalline," he declared.[17]

In the 1960s and 1970s, Latin American folk music won a good deal of international prominence. It was not something from which Piazzolla drew for the creation of his own sound-world, but he was curious about all forms of music. He several times expressed admiration for the great Chilean *folklorista* Violeta Parra, whose songs he once called "formidable."[18] (He himself set a song in her honor in 1974, "Violetas populares," with words by poet Mario Trejo which some French critics found politically revolutionary, though in fact they are not.) He much admired his world-famous folksinger compatriot Atahualpa Yupanqui. In 1965, after hearing a young accordionist from Corrientes Province, he praised him to the Argentine magazine *Folklore*. The accordionist was Raúl Barboza, a superb exponent and renewer of the *chamamé* music of his native province. Piazzolla first met Barboza briefly a year or two later, and they would see each other from time to time in Paris, where Barboza settled in the 1980s.

During Piazzolla's lifetime, Anglo-American rock music established its global hegemony. He deplored the growing taste for rock among Argentine youngsters. He sometimes told Atilio Talín that Argentina needed a Ministry of Good Taste, and he was unimpressed by the so-called *rock nacional* that swept the country in the 1980s and which roused a certain amount of international comment. "Argentine rock is of very low quality. There is no talent," he told an American interviewer in 1986. "We're imitating the Americans badly," he told another, "and we imitate the English badly."[19] As for the foreign exemplars of *rock nacional*, he admired what he saw as the best of the international bunch. Talking to Natalio Gorin in 1990 he singled out Queen, U-2, Sting, and Emerson Lake and Palmer. "That Keith Emerson is a conservatory type," he told Gorin, "a world-class pianist."[20] By the 1980s, many of the contemporary rock musicians he liked had an equal liking for him. Sting described Piazzolla's music (in typical rock idiom) as "great to make love to if you can't tango." "His sound makes your hair stand on end," declared Mickey Hart of the Grateful Dead.[21] Such opinions remind us of an essential point: the strongest admiration for Piazzolla tended to come from his fellow musicians, whatever their kind of music.

Bandoneonist

The qualities of the bandoneon have often been recognized outside the tango tradition. "Everything can be played on the bandoneon," Pablo Casals once said.[22] It is a formidably difficult instrument to master. The diatonic seventy-one-button variety, favored by all tango bandoneonists, has thirty-eight buttons for the right hand, and thirty-three for the left, with each button producing two notes, depending on whether the instrument is being opened or closed. The button-arrangement appears incomprehensible at first glance. It evolved without much rhyme or reason as more buttons were added to the earlier bandoneons. In Europe a more rational (chromatic) layout was adopted in the mid-1920s. Argentine musicians stuck stubbornly to the diatonic arrangement, which is altogether harder to play.

Piazzolla never left a theoretical treatise on bandoneon playing, though one of his unfulfilled projects was to do for the bandoneon what Bartók had done for the piano with his *Mikrokosmos*. He did sometimes make statements about the essential qualities of the instrument, usually for the benefit of foreign audiences tempted to compare it with the accordion. "The accordion has an acid sound, a sharp sound," he said in New York in 1988. "It's a very happy instrument. The bandoneon has a velvet sound, a religious sound. It was made to play sad music." That made it ideal for the tango, with its strong elements of nostalgia and melancholy. Two years later, in Finland, he made the same point again, declaring that because of its "joyful" timbre, the accordion "would never do justice to the essence of our music."[23] The accordion, in other words, is an extrovert instrument; the bandoneon is an introvert.

Piazzolla's affection for his instrument was passionate. "I would like to die playing the bandoneon," he often said, though the wish was not granted. Playing clearly absorbed him totally. If, as T. E. Lawrence believed, absorption brings happiness, his happiness onstage can only have been extreme. Diana thought he looked "transformed" when playing. His musicians noticed it, too. "When he enjoyed [life] most fully," says bass player Héctor Console, "it was with his bandoneon; then he was at his peak." Piazzolla's Italian promoter Aldo Pagani even thinks that he might have had a preference for playing "thirty times for ten or a hundred dollars rather than just once, in a good place, for 3,000." His own identification with the bandoneon grew over the years. He often included a word or two on its history in the "patter" he developed at concerts abroad. When in Germany, he occasionally dropped in on Konrad Steinhard, a notable collector of bandoneons (he had more than 350) at Dezlinger, near Freiburg.[24] But playing was most important of all. "Some people tell me that when I play . . . I sound like Charlie Parker," he said in New York in 1987. "That comes from the way I feel the music."[25]

The feeling was expressed in a very physical way of playing. The percussionist "Pocho" Lapouble, observing him in the ephemeral sextet of 1968, gives a memorable description:

> He was standing in front of me, with his back to me, of course, and you saw him contort himself and move, he was like an eel; he was really playing with his whole body, and when I realized this, I couldn't take my eyes off him, because he was not a dancer, exactly, but something flowing that played in front of you. It was impressive to see his waist, his back, impressive to see him moving; it was his music.

Another fine word-picture comes from a member of the audience who heard one of Piazzolla's concerts in Vienna nearly twenty years later. It was the onstage Piazzolla so many audiences saw in action.

He has become one with his instrument. . . . And so, he continues to hold on to it in a double-fisted grip, as if grasping the horns of a bull, digs deep into the music, slams on both sides of the bandoneon in spite of its pro-testations, pulls it apart abruptly, pushing, pressing and oppressing it, hangs on to the keys like a race car driver navigating a hairpin bend, then lets single notes glide down his shin—while deftly turning a page with his left hand—then catches them at the bottom and pulls them to the top with him. He sighs, breathes, whispers, cries and thinks with the thing, rests in its melodies, dreams himself into it, makes the bellows tremble by tapping the beat on the black wood, and then looking down at it all of a sudden in surprise, as if he was holding a screaming, roaring, irrepressible life form in his hands. . . . He dances with the instrument, rides it standing still, and finally jumps up high in the air like a kicking pony let loose in the spring-time. Triumphantly, he pulls apart the bandoneon three feet above his head, like a brilliant magician showing off his last card, like a victorious Laocoön pulling off another defeat of the dragon. . . . Piazzolla really has no choice: he must play.[26]

This strenuous playing style meant that Piazzolla often lost weight at perform-ances, sometimes several pounds. When she was with him on the later tours, his second wife, Laura, always made him drink two or three liters of water after an appearance; his shirts were invariably soaked with perspiration. Constant ban-doneon playing also affected Piazzolla's hands, something he first realized in the 1940s, when he still harbored the vague ambition of becoming a concert pianist. He found that his "fingers were already adapted to the bandoneon—were de-formed, twisted, especially the thumbs. They couldn't even reach over an oc-tave."[27] Simón Bajour remembers the amazing flexibility of Piazzolla's hands: "It might seem that instead of bones, he had gristle." And Gerry Mulligan once said: "His fingers move about that instrument as though they were snakes."[28] A doctor who treated his hands in the mid-1980s thought that Piazzolla's ligamentary laxity was congenital rather than acquired.[29]

How much did he practice? In his early years, it was evidently a good deal. By the 1970s, however, he was able to go into a concert without much self-preparation—"Just the day before a concert, to 'get the fingers right,' or to 'soak the asparagus,' as we say in Buenos Aires," as he put it in 1975.[30] Piazzolla usually took two bandoneons on tours, sometimes three. Bandoneons need regular tun-ing, though not every year. His went to the Romualdi and Fabiani workshop in Buenos Aires. Ricardo Romualdi and Fabio Fabiani had migrated from Italy in the late 1940s. He visited them frequently, taking his instruments in for checking and occasional repair. "He would bring it in for the most insignificant thing," they recall, though his energetic manner of playing caused no special problems for his instruments. They found him a friendly and generous client. After one of his stays abroad, he went to see them wearing a French yachting cap. "Nice, Piazzolla, that cap, very nice!" said Fabiani. Piazzolla gave it to him.

Director: Piazzolla and His Musicians

For most of his career Piazzolla ran instrumental groups of his own. It is a matter of common consent that he treated his fellow musicians with consideration and fairness. There was never much of the "boss" about him. Indeed, Pierre Fastosmes, one of his European agents in the 1970s, thought him "very hard, hard on himself." Nor did he claim excessive rewards. "I myself was once a peon in a band," he told a reporter in 1982;[31] he did not want his own musicians to be peons. The arrangements for his Brazilian tour of 1974 show the characteristic division of the proceeds: 27 percent for himself; 13.5 percent for the other four instrumentalists and Amelita Baltar; 5 percent for Daniel, the group's factotum.[32] All Piazzolla's ensembles operated on roughly this basis. "Astor did it as a matter of dignity," says guitarist Cacho Tirao. If the musicians had a complaint, it was that he was far too willing to perform without payment, believing that this was a way of publicizing his music. By the 1970s he was less inclined to behave like this. By the same token, greater fame often meant greater expenses. Laura remembers that he sometimes dug into his own pocket to pay his musicians when concert takings flagged—"it was a rather *sui generis* co-operative, let's say."

Given Piazzolla's temperament, it is not surprising that there were, very occasionally, major quarrels between himself and his musicians. Photographer Gianni Mesticheli recalls a spat in 1969, when Piazzolla was so furious that he withdrew a photo of the first Quintet from the cover of his album *Adiós Nonino*, for which Mesticheli was doing the photographs, and substituted a picture of *María de Buenos Aires*. The musicians themselves were embittered when Piazzolla suddenly disbanded the first Quintet in January 1971. The dissolution of the second Quintet in August 1988, at a time when the musicians were earning very good money, brought similar feelings of recrimination. But such episodes were very rare. On the other hand, Piazzolla always found it hard to pardon musicians who left his ensembles, as both Kicho Díaz and Antonio Agri discovered.

Piazzolla's feelings for the members of his various groups were expressed less in effusive gestures of affection than in insistence on equal treatment. Oscar López

Ruiz remembers an occasion when the musicians and Piazzolla were sent to different hotels in a European city. "Either we all come here or we all go there," he told the tour manager. In Brussels in 1989, Piazzolla was invited to dinner by the Argentine envoy to the European Community, but refused to go without his musicians. They all went.[33] Amusing evidence of his underlying feelings, evidence of a world of affection, comes from an undated note to Daniel—undoubtedly from 1974, since the musicians named (Tarantino, Agri, Díaz, Malvicino) were his instrumentalists that year.

> I'm sending you these four s.o.b.s. I'm fed up with them, but of course they *are* the best musicians in the world. Taranta, an old bore . . . Agri, a hysterical dwarf, Kicho, an old whore, and Malvi, a liar, a cheat and a thief of chords. *Kiss them all!*

For their part, the musicians always recognized Piazzolla's authority as a musician, as an outstanding master of his instrument. "He had the soul of a leader," says León Jacobson. "He marked time, clicking his fingers, with an inner sense of tempo, clicking two fingers of his left hand. . . . It was impressive." The musicians appreciated the opportunities he gave them to shine with their own instruments, as he invariably did. For Hugo Baralis he wrote "some fantastic violin solos," which Baralis "enjoyed just like a dog wagging its tail." He simply demanded that everyone should give of his best, and "everyone did," says percussionist Pepe Corriale, "because it was contagious." Pierre Fastosmes, who accompanied the second Quintet on many of its European tours, observed how demanding Piazzolla was of his musicians. "He wasn't always very fair," he says. "But well, artistically that gave results." Unfair or not, Piazzolla was certainly able to give his musicians fierce tongue-lashings at rehearsals, when his language was not restrained.

The tongue-lashings hardly mattered. There was always fun to be had from Piazzolla's good humor, even his questionable practical jokes. This may have changed a bit by the time the second Quintet was formed in 1978. López Ruiz, returning to work for Piazzolla after a long gap, found him "more distant, more remote from us," perhaps because of the heart attack in 1973.[34] But it is important to note that whatever the tensions, fits of temper, outbursts, and so on, to which they were exposed, especially when on tour, none of the musicians who worked with him will hear a word said against him. Their time with Piazzolla was, quite simply, the time of their lives. And musicians who worked with Piazzolla more sporadically and temporarily than his own instrumentalists were always struck by the quality of the experience. "With Astor I learned a sense of drama," says Gary Burton.

Certainly Piazzolla always set an excellent example of professional behavior to his musicians. Record producer Vera Brandes, working with him toward the end of his career, found him "very sharp and strict and professional." He was absolutely punctilious in fulfilling engagements and almost obsessive about punctuality. When the second Quintet left Córdoba after a performance in 1978, one of its members turned up after the others at the airport, whining that his friends had left him behind. Piazzolla glaringly reproached him: "Look, young man, we do not have *friends* here, we have *professionals*." The musician was never late again.[35]

The Piazzolla Sound

His lifelong friend Lalo Schifrin sees Piazzolla as "a universal musician who needed to focus on the language of Buenos Aires; the more local he was, the more universal he became. He was a fully rounded composer. The content was important, but so too was the structure and form." Piazzolla's music is always immediately identifiable, so strong is his stamp on it. His style has influenced a host of admirers and imitators. Its outstanding characteristic is the way in which he grafted procedures drawn from classical music, especially from his heroes Stravinsky and Bartók, and American jazz onto the tango music he wrote and performed. From these prime influences, and from the training he received from Ginastera and Boulanger, he distilled something uniquely and distinctively his own.

Like all such figures he had his quirks and favorite devices, and the charge that he often repeated them is beside the point; it is one that can be leveled at any composer who finds his own voice. The repetition of motifs and a recurrent recourse to fugal touches are among his more conspicuous hallmarks. His borrowings from other traditions are often well in evidence: harmonic jazz progressions, for instance, or the ground bass technique learned from his idol Bach (used most famously in the "false passacaglia" in the adagio section of "Adiós Nonino," a device often appearing thereafter). Piazzolla's counterpoint skills and the confidence of his arrangement of contrapuntal textures all display his thorough academic grounding. His touch is no less assured in his orchestration, in his rhythmic thrust, in his exploitation of instrumental timbres.

The beginnings of the Piazzolla sound can be traced as far back as the arrangements he made for the Troilo band in the early 1940s and more definitely for the band he formed for singer Francisco Fiorentino. The development of his own compositions—in many ways an outgrowth of his arrangements—led him quickly to appreciate the limitations of the standard *orquesta típica*. Although he retained the basic tango timbres (bandoneon, piano, strings), he constantly experimented with new instrumental lineups: string orchestras with bandoneon solo, quintets, sextets, octets, a nonet, ad hoc ensembles for *María de Buenos Aires*, and larger orchestras. Over the years, in his quest to expand the instrumental range, he included electric guitar, percussion instruments, harp, flute, vibraphone, piccolo, celesta, and synthesizer—not forgetting, on occasion, singers and choruses. But he was certainly happiest and at his best with his smaller ensembles—above all, his two quintets (1960–74 and 1978–88) and his nonet, where "his astonishing ingenuity with the placing of the instruments [in the score] can be most easily appreciated: his use of the electric guitar as an 'inner voice,' " as Pablo Aslan puts it, "and the deployment of bass doubling in the piano's left hand (first introduced by Goñi) are certainly keys to his overall sound."

As his music making matured, Piazzolla deployed a full range of composing skills: canonic writing (or at least imitation), polyrhythms, polytonality, fugues, dissonances, occasional atonal effects, and impressionistic dreamscapes reminiscent of Ravel. Piazzolla also tapped into the "progressive" and "cool" jazz of the 1940s and 1950s that he so admired. He must have had a strong fellow feeling for the musicians renewing the jazz tradition. Like him, they looked to recent classical music for their innovations in rhythm and harmony, and further back to the small-scale works and the polyphony of the Baroque. His feeling was probably heightened by knowing that there were plenty of jazz enthusiasts who insisted that this was not jazz, that the "cool" musicians in particular lacked all feeling and passion. Much the same was said about Piazzolla, throughout his career, by conservative *tangueros*. Yet it could certainly be argued that for all his innovations he preserved more of the true character of the music than did those of his contemporaries who merely tried to "dress up" the tango.

Probably the most fundamental thing Piazzolla got from jazz was the concept of "swing." As he explained to a French jazz magazine in 1974, "Swing is everything; if you don't have swing in music you have nothing. And the tango in itself doesn't have swing. It's a military thing—ran-tan-plan!" Here he was being far too sweeping. Plenty of golden age tango bands have a perfectly identifiable sense of swing. Troilo's versions of tangos are unimaginable without it. In fact, Piazzolla created his own sense of swing, "a 4-beat swing anchored by the bass-piano left hand unit," as Pablo Aslan describes it, and offset by various off-beat figures, many of which he created.

Improvisation, however, was a different matter. He made it clear to the French jazz magazine that the tango had too strict a form to allow improvisation in the manner of jazz. What he did instead—and it was fundamental to his approach— was to encourage considerable freedom of expression in the instrumentalists in his various ensembles. "I give the parts to the violinist," he explained. "It's written down—C, D, E, F, G, A, B, C—but I tell him to play it as he *feels* it."[36] Much of Piazzolla's style of composition derived from his need to write for his own musicians, who were, from the time of the Octet onward, conceived of as *solo instrumentalists* within the framework of the ensemble, soloists in the sense that they were encouraged to improvise tango (not jazz) phrases to ornament Piazzolla's written parts. Pianist Osvaldo Tarantino was a master of tango improvisation, as were violinists Antonio Agri and Fernando Suárez Paz, and percussionist Enrique "Zurdo" Roizner. Piazzolla always needed stimulating musical companions, individual musicians for whom he could write, musicians who could showcase their skills.

The rhythmic arrangement of much of Piazzolla's music has often been commented on. Its characteristic accents, 3-3-2 (his emphasis on the first, fourth, and sixth eighth notes in a 4/4 bar) derive ultimately from the *milonga* and the Cuban *habanera* that fed into the *milonga*. It was easy enough for the *milonga* rhythm to mutate into a 3-3-2 arrangement: the particular ligature that pushed it in that direction was typical of the guitar playing that accompanied *milongas*. The rhythm itself was certainly to be heard in tango orchestras by the 1930s and 1940s. It also appears in the Klezmer music Piazzolla heard at Jewish weddings as a boy in Manhattan, something that registered with him—or so he said more than once. The same rhythm, from Central and Eastern Europe (not least Bulgaria), from where the Klezmer tradition came, was incorporated into the music of Piazzolla's great idol Béla Bartók. He was shown many Bartók scores during his years with Alberto Ginastera. Bartók's influence on Ginastera left a permanent trace on Ginastera's pupil. But wherever Piazzolla got the 3-3-2 rhythm, he made it peculiarly his own. His sensitivity to rhythm was extraordinary. Egle Martin remembers him as a walking encyclopedia of rhythms, with an especially good ear for the African roots of such River Plate dance forms as the *candombe*, the (imported) *habanera*, and the *milonga*—all of which, historically, flowed into the tango itself.

And we must never forget that whatever techniques and influences Piazzolla assimilated from classical music and jazz, they were all placed firmly within the framework of the tango, the music of Buenos Aires, *his* music. His notorious percussion effects, for instance, came from the violinists of the *orquestas típicas* of the so-called *Guardia Vieja* (Old Guard), the formative period of tango music that lasted until the early 1920s. His use of *chicharra* (cicada), *tambor* (drum), and *lija* (sandpaper) effects were all anticipated in the sextets of Julio De Caro and Elvino Vardaro. Piazzolla adapted these typical *yeites* (tricks), so familiar to tango musicians, to his 3-3-2 scheme, and added a few of his own—the imitation of police or ambulance sirens (symbols of the modern city) in some of his music from the early 1970s onward, for instance. Pianist Atilio Stampone remembers Piazzolla's fans going crazy in the 1950s over his rhythmic boldness, but he reminds us that none of this would have mattered one bit had not Piazzolla also possessed "a rich melodic vein which is very Italian, very much in the line of Puccini." Time and again Piazzolla can wrench the heart with his tunes. We need only think of the most famous example, the soaring elegiac melody of "Adiós Nonino."

Piazzolla's works are always well constructed. As guitarist Rodolfo Alchourron tells us, "He had such good ideas about forms, sections, repetitions, orchestration, variety of texture, where to be intense, how to finish a piece off." This excellent sense of structure served him well when he broke with the traditional tango form in the late 1950s and early 1960s with pieces like "Tres Minutos con la Realidad" and "Buenos Aires Hora Cero." A common feature of many of his shorter pieces thereafter is a two-part division: one section, with a heavy rhythmic emphasis or thrust, and another, where a melodic line predominates. While such a scheme had been common enough in tango music from at least the 1910s onward, Piazzolla gave it his own peculiar stamp. In his rhythm-led sections, the melody is often fragmentary, jagged, jerky; in the melody-led sections it is frequently meditative, romantic, or passionate. In a typical piece of his European phase, "Cité Tango" (1977), the division is marked by a very clear line, when the rhythmic opening gives way to one of Piazzolla's strongest elegiac bandoneon passages. We cannot hope to encapsulate all his procedures in a few sentences. Obviously there are pieces when rhythm predominates throughout—for example, the hard-driving "Escualo" (1979)—and there are times when the melody is so powerful, as in "Rain over Santiago" (1975), that there is scarcely room for a countervailing rhythmic section.

"He was not only a composer but also a performer," says Yo-Yo Ma, "so you sense both sides of him, which in today's world is pretty wonderful." An essential aspect of the Piazzolla sound came from his own performances. What dazzled audiences around the world in the 1980s, when they heard him in the flesh, cannot, unfortunately, be fully recaptured in recordings or even videos. Says composer and pianist Gerardo Gandini: "Nobody has ever played the bandoneon like him, with his phrasing, his percussion-like sounds—something strange to the instrument, but very natural in him." Percussionist León Jacobson gives a more precise account of the way in which Piazzolla's performing skills contributed to the Piazzolla sound, emphasizing above all his sheer accuracy as an instrumentalist.

> Astor had a good deal of strength, especially in his left hand, with which he played diabolically well. He was left-handed but had complete mastery in both hands. With his instrument he had *diction*, with emphasis on every note he played . . . staccato when necessary . . . everything properly accented, syncopated—rather like a good percussion player. He played percussively not only in the rhythmic sections but also in the sections with slower cadences, when he played every note as if he were hitting it, or pushing it.

Piazzolla's percussion effects were also achieved, more directly, with the rings he wore on his fingers.

Previous bandoneonists like Eduardo Arolas, Ciriaco Ortiz, Pedro Laurenz, and Pedro Maffia had all developed considerable bandoneon techniques, moving on from the primitive handling of the instruments in the earliest days, when the left hand was used simply to mark the rhythm with repeated fixed chords. Building on this legacy, Piazzolla revealed the bandoneon's full potential as an eminently polyphonic instrument by adding his own rich harmonies—often jazz-derived, and with much of the richness coming from his masterly left hand—and a phrasing that was uniquely his own. He had what his supporters call *polenta tanguera* (tango power). Oscar López Ruiz remembers him making "his instrument sound like four bandoneons." The sheer warmth of his playing energized his fellow musicians. Piazzolla's bandoneon was always the first instrument to provide the "swing" he wanted all his ensembles to display, partly through his own ability to improvise: here he took risks and did not play it safe. His *arrastres* (drags), his anticipatory hints to the rest of the band, were particularly expressive. His bandoneon could touch the heights and depths of drama and romanticism.

And underneath everything there was always the substratum of the tango, and especially the tango's distinctive *canyengue* character, which made its own powerful contribution to Piazzolla's "swing." The term *canyengue* needs some explanation. It refers to the sensual and provocative way of walking and dancing which ill-fitting shoes gave the *compadritos*, the street toughs who invented the tango in the 1880s in the poorer southern districts of Buenos Aires. The modest social background and the knife fights in which *compadritos* were frequently involved are often seen as the bedrock from which the authentic tango springs; the authentic tango spirit must always express the noble qualities of *mugre* (muck) and *roña* or *camorra* (fighting, or the propensity to fight). The tango is defiant and exhibitionistic. The *canyengue* character gives the tango a provocative inflection. Piazzolla often talked with his later pianist Pablo Ziegler about the right way to play his music. "No matter the context," he said, "the tango must express *camorra*, which is how its roots are preserved." Piazzolla's fingers on the buttons always transmitted a *canyengue* spirit, however sophisticated the music he was playing.

Piazzolla grew with his city at a time when the city was itself growing and changing fast. Composer Francisco Kröpfl sees his music as "the logotype of Buenos Aires in the way that Gershwin's is for New York." A Piazzolla score heard through Piazzolla's bandoneon is a musical postcard of Buenos Aires that depicts the sounds and noises of the city by night and day. The sound of the bandoneon is unique and indispensable; it is the sound of Argentina, the sound of Piazzolla. "Astor's work," says pianist Mónica Cosachov, "is tremendously temperamental, very passionate, very changing, with many very sentimental passages, then suddenly an outburst of rhythmic force, all the shattering blasts of his temperament, and then once again the tune that has torn your heart takes you to another place, to the grayness of Buenos Aires, to the river itself. It's all mixed up in his music." For Rodolfo Alchourron, the Piazzolla sound covers "all the range of feeling, merry, histrionic, sarcastic . . . dramatic, sentimental, romantic." Ballet star Maximiliano Guerra says: "His music is celestial and angelic and at the same time sensual, seductive and down to earth. It's rooted in the earth, in fact. It's the knife, the fight, the passion, the sex, the love, the hatred. It has everything. It is magic."

Piazzolla and the Tango Tradition

Although Piazzolla once told a French newspaper that he saw the "classic prewar tango" as belonging, like Art Deco, to "the antique shop,"[37] he was far more intimately connected to the tango tradition than such a remark would imply. He came from the tango world and respected its observances. Alberto Speratti, in 1968, mentioned the bandleader Carlos Di Sarli: "Shut up!" said Piazzolla quickly, crossing his fingers and touching wood.[38] Héctor Olivera, who often worked with Piazzolla in the film studios, remembers times when he was upset on this account. For tango musicians, not mentioning Di Sarli is like the English-speaking actors' taboo on saying "Macbeth" in a theater. And there were other ways in which he showed strong affection for the historic tradition. Guitarist Cacho Tirao remembers informal jam sessions in the dressing room at Michelangelo, with archaic, turn-of-the-century tangos ("El Porteñito," "Unión Cívica," "El Africano") as the repertory—"you just had to see how well he played them!"

Moveover, Piazzolla was certain that the tango tradition had needed revolutionizing. "When the water doesn't run, it rottens," he said, in idiosyncratic English, in 1989. "Tango that doesn't run, it rottens. I have a great respect for the old tango, the primitive tango. But I must do it in my own way."³⁹ That his "New Tango" was linked to the older ways was something he would never have denied. Indeed, in his conversations with Speratti in 1968, he sketched out an essential continuum of growing sophistication in tango music, with his own "avant-garde" an inevitable culmination. Among the pioneers and innovators of the past, Piazzolla assigned a high position to Julio De Caro (Piazzolla's tango "Decarísimo," 1961, was a tribute to the retired bandleader, who reciprocated in 1962 with a piece of his own, "Piazzolla") and to Elvino Vardaro ("Vardarito"), whose place in the continuum was even more decisive, given his constant studying and the care he took with his arrangements.⁴⁰

Piazzolla was always willing to admit that he owed much to De Caro and Vardaro, and a good deal also to Troilo and his brilliant pianist Orlando Goñi. Where he saw genuine innovation he was quick to praise it, as was the case with his contemporary, pianist Horacio Salgán. He regarded violinist and bandleader Alfredo Gobbi—perhaps because of his notable sense of swing—as "the father of all who have done the modern tango," as "the most revolutionary of them all. He was a man who died without realizing the importance that was his due."⁴¹ Gobbi's tango "Redención" was included on Piazzolla's second 1961 album, and he invited Gobbi to the recording. Oscar Del Priore, also there, remembers Gobbi in tears. Piazzolla's romantic and dramatic "Retrato de Alfredo Gobbi" (1970) was a tribute to the bandleader. As for the greatest of all the historical tango figures, Piazzolla had no difficulty in seeing him as an unconscious innovator of the first order. "If Gardel were still alive," he sometimes told journalist Edmundo Eichelbaum, "he would be *piazzollista*."

Among contemporaries or near-contemporaries, the bandleader Osvaldo Pugliese (with whom he had relatively little personal contact) was someone he fairly consistently admired—the only bandleader who "renews himself and has quality," he said in 1968. He several times called him the Count Basie of the tango, and sometimes cracked the joke that *he* (Piazzolla) was Pugliese, since his Piazzolla grandparents were unquestionably *pugliesi*—from Puglia in Italy.⁴²

"We were dining one evening," Lalo Schifrin recalls, "and [Piazzolla] told me he was a bit sad, and indignant too, with *tangueros* who would not recognize him. He went on and on about this. Finally I said, 'Astor, what does it matter what they say? If they say what you are doing is the tango or isn't the tango, that's not your problem. What you are doing is Piazzolla.' " It is not quite as simple as that, of course. Gary Burton sees his relationship to the tango in a more far-reaching context. "We can say that jazz is the national music of America, and samba and bossa nova [of] Brazil," he comments. "Usually a national music remains fairly simple and doesn't progress on to become highly sophisticated and developed, [but] this happened to jazz and it happened to tango. And in the case of tango Astor was the principal figure that helped the transition."

Piazzolla took the tango from the dance hall to the concert hall. He has often been described as the Gershwin of Argentina. He certainly saw Gershwin and himself as musicians who "sought to give class to what we liked and to lift it on to a new level."[43] Yet, as Carlos Kuri has pointed out in his well-known essay on Piazzolla, Gershwin did not change the history of jazz, while Piazzolla *did* change the history of tango music.[44] Indeed, it can now be seen very clearly that, as novelist Ernesto Sábato said more than once, the music of Buenos Aires has to be described in terms of "before or after Piazzolla."[45] His influence on the way tango music was both conceived and played was enormous. "A great revolutionary in the strict sense of the word," President Carlos Menem calls him. "He transformed our popular music and, after many problems, managed to impose it." He was by any standard incomparably the supreme figure in the phase of tango history (1955–70) Horacio Ferrer has labeled "Modernization."[46] At the time of writing, it is far too early to say whether there can ever be a post-Piazzolla tango. All we can say for sure is that there are musicians who are working on it.

PART III

Fame

All Roads Lead to Rome
1974–1975

→ Rome

Piazzolla-Mulligan ←

→ Into the Electronic Phase

> My dream is to impose my music,
> my country's music, all over the world.
> —Astor Piazzolla, *Clarín*, 1 December 1974

Rome

In November 1973, the Italian agent Aldo Pagani, who had heard about the heart attack, called Piazzolla from Venezuela. Amelita answered the phone and told him Astor was now definitely "looking for a contract abroad." Pagani phoned again in March 1974, this time from Brazil, and he and Piazzolla agreed to the essence of a deal: a contract, renewable every three years, whereby Pagani became Piazzolla's European agent. There would be a standard European split (50:50) between them on earnings from compositions offered to Pagani by Piazzolla for each single publication delivered to him, $500 per month for living expenses, and the rental on a small apartment in Rome. Pagani would also take a 15 percent commission on any Piazzolla performances he organized. Piazzolla himself said firmly more than once that the deal with Pagani, which he ended after the second three-year period in 1980, was the key to the international fame he enjoyed in later years. Oscar López Ruiz, who met Pagani in 1982, notes that the two men had "a love-hate relationship . . . that even they found indecipherable. They quarreled and made up three or four thousand times."[1] Piazzolla sometimes refers harshly to Pagani in the copious letters he wrote to his son Daniel in the 1970s. Pagani himself remembers numerous spats. Pagani's wife Angela sometimes pleaded with her husband to break the connection, knowing that it caused him endless frustration. Yet, at the end of the day, Pagani *believed* in Piazzolla. Twenty years later he could roundly assert that Piazzolla's were the "most important records" he had ever produced. "Every time I listen to Piazzolla," he says, "I get goose bumps."

"I'm going to live in Rome for three years," Piazzolla announced, just before leaving Argentina, "and I'm sure that I'm going to write better there than in Buenos Aires."[2] He and Amelita flew first to Geneva, where Piazzolla bought a used 1967 Volkswagen in which they drove on to Milan. Pagani had already arranged a television appearance for them on 25 March 1974 in Rome, in a program with Charles Aznavour. They drove down there immediately and threw themselves into rehearsals, Amelita memorizing Italian versions of a couple of the Piazzolla-Ferrer songs. The program went well. "It was a fabulous beginning," Piazzolla told Daniel.[3] A second television appearance followed a few days later in Milan.

He and Amelita soon found an apartment in Rome, "primo piano, interno cinque" in a sixteenth-century house at Via dei Coronari 222. The street, famous for its antique dealers, is close to the exuberantly baroque Piazza Navona, a favorite gathering place for Romans. They moved in on 2 April, Amelita immediately going out to buy sheets, towels, and kitchen gadgets. Piazzolla rented a piano; they rounded up some furniture. Their television table had built-in shelves where they stored records and bottles of their favorite Queen Anne brand of whiskey. They slept in a balconied upstairs space, reached by a little wooden staircase from the living room.

Encouraged by Amelita, Piazzolla went for vigorous walks along the Tiber embankments, swam off the beach at nearby Fregene, and tried (not too fanatically) to eat more sparingly. He threw himself into a spasm of composing. Pagani, with radio in mind, asked him for pieces lasting around three minutes. "But Beethoven wrote. . . ." protested Piazzolla. "Beethoven died deaf and poor. Up to this point, you are neither deaf nor poor," riposted Pagani. The result was a series of short instrumental pieces—"Libertango," "Meditango" (which he called "almost Vivaldian"),[4] "Tristango," "Violentango," "Amelitango" and so on—which found their way on to *Libertango*, Piazzolla's first Italian album. Inventing the titles, he joked to Daniel, was harder than writing the music. In 1980 he described "Libertango" to Walter Acosta of the BBC as "a sort of song to liberty," a celebration of being in a new place with new ideas.[5] It was to enjoy a remarkable life as a popular song, taken up by French singers like Julien Clerc and Guy Marchand and by the Jamaican Grace Jones. Piazzolla sent a cassette of the "Libertango" sequence to his son. One of Daniel's friends heard it and exclaimed, "Son of a bitch! Just look what he's done! It *can't* be!" In the United States, *Playboy* magazine reviewed the *Libertango* album very characteristically: "eight magnificent tangos that tell a girl what's on your mind. . . . We guarantee that before side two of the record is over, she'll be flat on her back."[6]

The "Libertango" pieces—for the most part hard-thrusting, spectacularly rhythmic—sounded different from anything Piazzolla had done before, though largely because of their instrumentation. It is almost as if he were seeking a new sound to appeal to his new European audiences, rather in the way Jazz-Tango had been aimed at the American public, though this time with no compromises. Piazzolla recorded the album in Milan with three ad hoc Italian ensembles (strings, piano, electric guitar, electric bass, marimba, flutes, percussion, and his own bandoneon). His attitudes in the studio sometimes provoked indignant reactions from the musicians he worked with, but they were impressed by his music. One of the violinists told him, "*Astor, questa è musica, e non la merda che facciamo tutti i giorni*" ("Astor, this is music, and not the crap we have to do every day.")[7] He himself came to have a high regard for the percussionist Tullio de Piscopo. "I would like to have Tullio as my drummer forever," he later told an Italian friend, Piergiuseppe Caporale. De Piscopo remembers Piazzolla saying that he was seeking "a new touch for a new tango." He warmly reciprocated Piazzolla's feeling for him.

While Piazzolla was recording in Milan, Amelita suddenly decided to return to Argentina. She wanted to see her son and to get new singing work. Her departure depressed Piazzolla immensely. "I'm not one for living alone anymore," he complained to Daniel. "I'm very confused. . . . If she doesn't come back to Rome I shall have to put an end to this situation. I'm old-fashioned—my woman at my side, or nothing. . . . I don't want any more messes in my life. I want peace. . . . She is the chosen one to be at my side."[8] The chosen one was not so certain as he, despite a bombardment of letters and phone calls.

Outwardly, he put a brave face on things. He told an Argentine reporter that his enthusiasm for Italy was undiminished: "I am at the center of the world," he said.[9] At the end of May 1974 he sought refuge with his old mentor Alberto Ginastera, now living in Geneva. As his widow tells us, the composer had followed his student's progress with a good deal of admiration. Piazzolla spent some happy days in his spacious Geneva apartment, overlooking two of the city's main parks. He found his old teacher very changed, no longer the monastic personality he recalled. He was especially impressed by the affluence in which he now lived. "Incredible," he told Daniel on the phone. "He had a blue cardigan, and the buttons were solid gold." Piazzolla thought that Ginastera's second wife, cellist Aurora Nátola, had both broken his shell and improved his music.

Piazzolla wanted to bring the Quintet to Europe, perhaps to play at the Sorrento and Spoleto festivals. Aldo Pagani was trying hard to arrange international tours. A Mexican tour fell through because the fees ($1,000 per concert) were too low. "I said NEVER," Piazzolla informed Daniel.[10] A Brazilian tour was gradually put together. Meanwhile, his friend Alfredo Radoszynski and his wife arrived in Rome, lodging in a hotel near the Piazza Navona. The 1974 World Cup was then in progress in Germany. On Wednesday, 19 June, Argentina and Italy (old rivals) tied 1–1 in Stuttgart. Piazzolla, who had earlier dined with his friends, went to the Piazza Navona where a crowd was raucously celebrating. He knocked one of the Italian fans off his feet, a deed described to Radoszynski in a not altogether welcome midnight phone call.

Also described were his feelings about Amelita. "Why don't you talk to her?" Piazzolla asked Radoszynski. "I'm going crazy. I can't be on my own." As it happened, his emotional crisis was soon resolved. In July Amelita flew back to Europe, Piazzolla motoring to Paris to meet her. They spent a week or so there, staying in an apartment loaned by a sister of Jacqueline Pons. Piazzolla bought Amelita a Yorkshire terrier, Georgie, who accompanied them in a rather sickly state on the drive back to Rome. Some friends invited them for a week to a castle at Macerata, on the Adriatic. Just as they were preparing to leave, Aldo Pagani phoned from Milan with intriguing news.

Piazzolla-Mulligan

At a chance encounter with saxophonist Gerry Mulligan, who was then spending much of his time in Italy, Pagani had played him "Libertango." As Pagani recalls, Mulligan "without speaking, sits down by the record player, the side finishes, he gets up, turns it over, sits down, doesn't speak, and then says to me: 'Who *is* this? . . . He's phenomenal. . . . Who *is* he?' " Pagani immediately suggested a Mulligan-Piazzolla album. Mulligan jumped at the idea, and, if Amelita remembers rightly, spoke briefly to Piazzolla on the phone. (Tullio de Piscopo also remembers playing Mulligan a Piazzolla cassette, at which he "went crazy.") Piazzolla flew immediately to Milan, met with Pagani and Mulligan, agreed to make the long-playing record—half the music by himself, half by Mulligan—and then hopped back to Rome, from where he and Amelita drove the 160 miles to the Adriatic. "I am still alive," he reported to Daniel. "This Mulligan business will be a big thing for my future. . . . Tomorrow I start to write."[11] He was suddenly very excited.

Piazzolla threw himself with great enthusiasm into the task. He told one of his Roman acquaintances, the photographer Franca Rota, that he needed somewhere quiet to work. She invited him and Amelita to join a party at her house in the Roman Marches. (Franca was very impressed, at the meal table, when Piazzolla crushed open a walnut with his index finger alone). The tranquil surroundings were good for him. He made swift progress with his music for the Mulligan LP, and (another task that summer) some settings of poems by Jorge Luis Borges, a few of whose books he had brought with him to Italy.

The composing stint was soon interrupted. It was time for performing again, which meant the Brazilian tour Pagani had organized—with fees of around $1,500 per concert. During the first half of September 1974, the Quintet (with Amelita) revisited some familiar theaters in Porto Alegre, São Paulo, and Rio de Janeiro, premiering the new Borges settings and a "Retrato de Milton" (an adaptation of a piece from 1969), which Amelita sang in Portuguese in honor of their friend Milton Nascimento. At São Paulo's Teatro Municipal, the audience made her sing "Balada para un loco" three times.[12] An American in the audience at one of these Brazilian concerts would later recall the experience vividly:

> While the other four dark figures fidgeted with their music, their leader, Astor Piazzolla, waited. . . . I could make out creases in his brow which seemed to brand him with a permanent frown. . . . Seconds later, however, he had me and a thousand Brazilians in his hip pocket—in orbit around Jupiter. . . . The quintet descended into a whirlwind of dissonance and percussive effects, then emerged together on a wave of the most tender lyricism imaginable. The sweet-and-sour emotional contour of the music made the concert as exciting as a roller coaster.[13]

The photos of Piazzolla and Amelita printed in the *Jornal do Brasil* show him fit and bronzed, confident and relaxed, and with every evidence of his affection for Amelita. He told a Brazilian reporter that he was now identifying closely with "a baroque style of creation," attributable to the "Roman way of life"[14] he was enjoying.

They were soon back in Italy (September, 1974), Piazzolla in a very upbeat mood. He waxed lyrical to an Argentine reporter about Rome and the pleasure he got from walking the streets, chatting to the tradesmen, looking up at the laundry hanging on the balconies.[15] At some point that autumn, both Nonina and Amelita's mother, Amelia, visited them in Rome. It was Nonina's only visit to Europe. Astor took her on short and, for her, unforgettable excursions to France and Switzerland.[16] Her penchant for long walks amused her son. "Why don't you get a job as a mail carrier?" he asked.

Although Piazzolla was properly filial with Nonina, his first task on returning from Brazil was to finish the music for the Mulligan LP. He reported to all and sundry that he felt "crazier" than ever. Amelita recalls him working with unusual intensity in the Via dei Coronari apartment. When he saw Mulligan's pieces for the album, Piazzolla did not like them, and he decided to write all eight himself. Pagani reminded him of the half-and-half agreement. "Well, tell him the music never arrived," said Piazzolla impatiently. "How can I play this man's music? He doesn't even know how to write." Pagani insisted that at least one of Mulligan's pieces ("Aire de Buenos Aires") be retained.

Piazzolla and Mulligan did the recording in seven sessions (24 September–4 October) at the Mondial Sound studios in Milan. "We seemed like two people possessed," Piazzolla told the Argentine disk jockey Miguel Angel Merellano,[17] a zealous promoter of his music. Possessed they may have been. There were certainly strains and tensions in the studio. "You should have called on Stan Getz; he's the reader," said Mulligan at one point. "Play as you want to," replied Piazzolla. "This can be cleaned up, don't worry." Amelita remembers him asking: "Why didn't they tell me this fellow didn't read?" Mulligan may well have had his difficulties with Piazzolla's music. "In my music there isn't a harmonic scheme that repeats itself every twelve bars," as Piazzolla explained to a magazine soon afterward, "but there *is* perpetual change. And Gerry was a bit blocked by that." Nevertheless, when he heard the tape after the final mixing, Mulligan turned in tears to Piazzolla, telling him "It's twenty years since I've done something different!"[18]

The photographer Franca Rota attended the final recording session and was swept off her feet by the sound of Mulligan's sax—and even more by Mulligan. She declined to dine with the artists that night but later discovered that Mulligan had vainly tried to extract her phone number from Piazzolla and Amelita. Three nights later, she and a sister-in-law went to the Santa Lucia Restaurant for dinner. A merry party led by Piazzolla and Mulligan came in and sat down at an adjoining table. Mulligan positioned himself at the closest possible point to Franca. "We were together for ever after," says Franca Mulligan—as she soon became.

The Piazzolla-Mulligan album, *Summit* (known as *Reunión Cumbre* in Argentina), was one of Piazzolla's—and Mulligan's—most successful. "Gerry used to laugh in disbelief when the royalty statements came each year," recalls Franca. The album aroused some mildly puzzled reactions in Buenos Aires. One critic suggested that it was smothered by Piazzolla's personality, that he had turned Mulligan into "a docile soloist."[19] The comment is fair. Jazz fans tend not to regard the record as among Mulligan's better efforts. "A nice idea that doesn't quite happen," as a standard record guide has it, though the same guide's comment that the music is "drably uninflected" is surely off target.[20] The mixing could certainly have been better, but there are moments on the album when the bandoneon-sax combination is masterly, especially on the tracks "Hace veinte años," "Deus Xango," and "Reunión Cumbre." In "Años de soledad" it approaches the sublime. A French review of the album found it "the most audacious and successful attempt" to fuse jazz with other traditions since Miles Davis's *Sketches of Spain* (1960).[21]

Piazzolla would enjoy Mulligan's company a good deal over the following months. Theatrical designer Eduardo Bergara Leumann, then living in Rome, thought the sight of Piazzolla, Mulligan, and Amelita walking the streets was like "a poem." In October 1974, moving briefly to Paris and summoning his four musicians from Buenos Aires, Piazzolla appeared with Amelita on the popular TV program *Le Grand Echiquier,* and on Monday, 21 October, the Quintet and Mulligan performed at the Olympia. The critics were enthusiastic. "Superb in inspiration, rhythm and fugue . . . very beautiful," wrote one. Another thought that Piazzolla's music had "an infinite sadness, with long riffs where the violence comes in like an echo."[22] Singer Georges Moustaki, also in the Olympia audience, jotted down the lyric for a new song, which Piazzolla immediately wanted to set. Moustaki installed him in his apartment, at the piano and left him working away. When he returned a few hours later, he recalls, "he wasn't there, but already, on the piano, there was the score, and a cassette, and the song was finished." The song, "Le tango du demain," was the first Piazzolla-Moustaki collaboration. Later there would be others.

During these days in Paris, an Argentine reporter took a picture of Piazzolla, the Quintet, Amelita—and the terrier Georgie,[23] who had required constant veterinary attention since July. Also in Paris at the time was Donna Caroll, the singer-wife of Oscar López Ruiz. At dinner with her after the Olympia show, the worst, most sadistic side of Piazzolla's humor suddenly came out. He told her he had learned that her husband was on one of the death-lists of the "Triple A" (AAA, Argentine Anti-Communist Action), the shadowy right-wing death squads then forming in Argentina, with tacit support from the Peronist government. The joke was in appallingly poor taste. López Ruiz, in Buenos Aires, quickly established that there was no truth in the rumor. On hearing this, Donna confronted Piazzolla in his hotel and gave him a severe tongue-lashing.[24]

Back in Italy, Piazzolla and Amelita recorded two new songs, one of them "Una pequeña canción para Matilde," a posthumously published poem by the Nobel Prize-winning Chilean poet Pablo Neruda, which Matilde Urrutia, his widow, had asked Piazzolla to set. (Neruda is said to have told her, "I want it to be Piazzolla," but the story sounds apocryphal; the great poet was not renowned for his knowledge of music). Piazzolla and Mulligan did some promotion for their album; at one session they modeled fur coats while displaying what was obviously going to be *un fantastico LP di Natale*.[25] They also went to Venice to appear in the opening sequence of a documentary on the tango which Rosalía Polizzi was making for Radio Televisione Italiana (RAI). We see them chatting briefly (mostly expressing mutual admiration) and then strolling with Amelita (and Georgie) through the Piazza San Marco. Piazzolla's mood was still very upbeat. "I can't say I'm famous," he told an Argentine reporter interviewing him in the Piazza Navona soon afterward, "but I *am* known. In certain circles . . . the musicians know me. . . . This is a fundamental year for me."[26]

The "fundamental year" was nearly over. At the end of November 1974, Piazzolla and Amelita flew back to Argentina. At a press conference at Ezeiza airport, Piazzolla revealed that he had asked to see the view of Buenos Aires from the flight deck as the plane descended, and that he had wanted to kiss the ground.[27] But this was not to be a long visit. Since their apartment was being rented, Piazzolla and Amelita stayed at the Wilton Palace Hotel on Avenida Callao. Amelita, who had lost her tan in the European autumn, did some sunbathing on the balcony of their room.

Piazzolla's only concert on this trip was at the Teatro Coliseo (3 December), where the Italian crew making RAI's tango documentary (in which Piazzolla and Amelita would feature prominently) annoyed the audience by its onstage intrusions. Piazzolla showcased items from his new European repertory with an ad hoc ensemble (piano, organ, percussion, marimba, flute, electric guitar, and double bass). In the second half, he reverted to playing with the Quintet, with Dante Amicarelli at the piano, standing in for Osvaldo Tarantino at very short notice. The "Libertango" sequence won approval from the critics: "heart-wrenching works," commented *Clarín*. "Sentimental. Strong. Tragic." Piazzolla himself was pleased with the concert, lavishing special praise on Dante Amicarelli—"a genius . . . no, a *real* genius."[28] (His admiration for Amicarelli never waned. Ten years later, at a reception in the Argentine embassy in Ottawa, he strongly recommended him to Mario Benzecry, director of the Orquesta de Cámara Mayo.) After doing a TV spectacular for Channel 13 (20 December 1974), Piazzolla spent the holidays in Mar del Plata with Nonina. While there he called on Aníbal Troilo, who was convalescing after major surgery in a secluded villa near the ocean. "Did you talk about the tango?" journalist Horacio De Dios asked Troilo afterward.

"No, we are friends." He had heard the Piazzolla-Mulligan album. "I didn't like it. I don't understand it," said Pichuco.[29]

The Argentine press found Piazzolla's new European career a matter of more than passing interest. His departure with Amelita for Rome on 9 January 1975 (they spent a few days in Rio de Janeiro *en route*) was well reported. With his Argentine excursion over, Piazzolla found himself busier than ever in Europe—an almost immediate television appearance with singer Georges Moustaki in Paris, and a dash to the Cannes Music Festival to play with Gerry Mulligan. "It was crazy the way they applauded us," he reported from Cannes to Jorge Vimo, an Aerolíneas Argentinas official he had befriended in Rome. "I think this rock-and-roll stuff has reached its limit. Everyone is fed up with the electric crap the English have invaded us with. We are always being invaded by the English. Well, their time is up."[30] From Cannes, Piazzolla went to Saarbrücken to join Amelita. She had gone there on her own (with Georgie in tow) to record some of the songs for *El Pueblo Joven*—a project that disappears from view more or less completely at this point.

The pace quickly became even more frantic. In Paris in mid-March 1975 he recorded "Libertango" and "Undertango" with the popular singer Guy Marchand. Then it was Geneva, for radio and television interviews (and to renew the Volkswagen's license plates). Around this time, too, he recorded a long-playing record with the Italian actress and singer Edmonda Aldini. Piazzolla was in Paris again at the start of April for another appearance on *Le Grand Échiquier,* delighted to find Guy Marchand's version of "Libertango" ("Moi, je suis tango") an instant hit in France. It was reported in July 1975 as selling 30,000 copies a week.[31]

The Brazilian poet Geraldo Carneiro now arrived in Rome for a two-month stay. Piazzolla had first met him two years earlier. "We are thinking of working on something important," he informed Daniel.[32] They wrote around fifteen songs together, but the "something important" was a larger-scale project: an opera about Eva Perón. Piazzolla had evidently been toying with the idea for some time and had even suggested it (back in 1971) to the Intendant of Buenos Aires as worthy of municipal patronage.[33] He was enthusiastic about doing it with Carneiro and went briefly to London at some point to see whether he could interest the BBC. "It's already been done," he was told. He did not know that Tim Rice and Andrew Lloyd-Webber had been working on just such an opera, in pop idiom—the LP of *Evita* was still a year away. He did eventually see the show and quite enjoyed it, although claiming that he would have done "more elaborate, less commercial music."[34]

In April he did more television programs, one of them in Amsterdam, and then went with Amelita and Mulligan to Spain, starting at the Majorca Festival (17–19 April). The 6,000-strong audience rapturously applauded "Años de Soledad" (from the Piazzolla-Mulligan album), but the visit was marred by a particularly fierce altercation with Aldo Pagani. Pagani recalls that Piazzolla arrived late at a rehearsal, after a row with Amelita. Piazzolla later claimed to have hit Pagani fifteen times in the face: "He . . . didn't have the balls to hit back," he told Daniel. "They took me to the bar, and I swallowed a pill and calmed down."[35]

From Majorca they crossed to the mainland for shows in Madrid and Barcelona, where they filled the Teatro Tivoli. Mulligan played jazz during the first half, Piazzolla taking over in the second, with an ad hoc group that included Mulligan's pianist Tom Fay and, at the organ, an old Argentine friend, Waldo de los Ríos. The organist was a former pupil of Ginastera's whose "advanced" arrangements of folk music had made him well known in Argentina. He had settled in Spain in 1960 and was making a very successful career as an arranger. (His album of pop versions of classical pieces reached the British Top Twenty in the spring of 1971, though they fared less well in the United States.) At the end of April, Piazzolla and Mulligan again appeared at the Olympia in Paris. During the opening bars of "Adiós Nonino," the audience rose to its feet. "WOW . . . what a night!" as he put it to Daniel.[36] *Le Figaro* hailed him as the "innovative instrumentalist" reviving the moribund tango in France.[37] *Paris-Match* ran a full-page article about him, suggesting that his music might become "a natural, unforeseen, but apparently irresistible current" in Europe and comparing him to Bartók in classical music and John Coltrane in jazz.[38] An Argentine reporter strolling with him down the Champs-Elysées heard the strains of "Libertango" floating out of a record store. "Yes, there's no doubt," he wrote, "Astor Piazzolla is now a great figure."[39]

Certainly there were signs of growing European recognition. In May 1975 he was awarded the Sagittario d'Oro, an "international arts prize" sponsored by the municipality of Rome, though Eduardo Bergara Leumann recalls that the award was something of an afterthought. The citation referred to his *magnifico e magico "bandonion,"* and his *appassionata eloquenza* and *prodigiosa tecnica trascendentale.*[40] But whatever laurels came his way in Europe, Piazzolla could never quite stop thinking about Argentina. Nostalgia was beginning to gnaw at him—and anxiety. The country's increasingly chaotic and violent politics depressed him. In his letters to Daniel (and in one to Dedé) he excoriated President Isabel Perón and her sinister *éminence grise* José López Rega, the former policeman and astrologer. He was worried about his left-wing daughter Diana, whose husband Osvaldo Villaflor was a political prisoner. "I go on getting dreadful news," he told Daniel. "It's really sad, and it frightens me."[41] He was certain that the armed forces would soon step in, as they did, in March 1976.

Meanwhile he went on writing songs with Geraldo Carneiro and wondering about doing a major Western Hemisphere tour with Mulligan—though not for long. Piazzolla was becoming increasingly irritated by Mulligan's fondness for alcohol. They had at least one big row—about the placement of their names on a theater bill. "I began shouting more than him," Piazzolla informed Daniel, "and I told him that he was the best saxophonist in the world but that as a man he was a bunch of shit like all Americans. I told him to go to hell."[42] Although the two men were never to work again, they were to meet at regular intervals—in Milan, New York, Buenos Aires—and the friendship never really died. Mulligan's admiration for Piazzolla never diminished.[43]

Piazzolla was now thinking seriously of relocating from Rome. He was increasingly disillusioned with the Italian musical scene. He weighed the merits of Barcelona or Paris as places to live, and he still wondered whether he could fulfill his old dream of dividing the year between Argentina and Europe. Before he could act, however, he was suddenly overtaken by crisis. Amelita decided to leave him. The breakup had been building for months. Jorge Vimo, who saw much of the couple in Rome, noticed how "the relationship was worsening. Amelita was getting bored." Eduardo Bergara Leumann remembers at least one huge row, in public. Amelita's situation was close to intolerable. There was nothing much for her to do in Rome—"she reads the paper or goes out walking," Piazzolla reported to Daniel.[44] She did no work with Piazzolla after the Majorca Festival, and his promises that something would turn up sounded less and less credible. He did not like her straying too far from the apartment—"other than going to buy the vegetables and come back," says Amelita. She wanted to resume her career. She wanted to see her son Mariano. She left on 27 May 1975, taking Georgie with her. Piazzolla tried to pretend that nothing was happening and went off to an art exhibition. It was Geraldo Carneiro and his wife who took Amelita to Fiumicino airport. She cried her way down much of the Atlantic.

The news reached Argentina instantly. ASTOR AND AMELITA HAVE SEPARATED! trumpeted *Radiolandia*.[45] Piazzolla, from Rome, confirmed that the separation was "affectionate but final. . . . We've finished it." Amelita declared: "It's a decision we both reached after talking a lot. . . . Astor is the great love of my life, and these seven years we spent together . . . were something very nice."[46] In the Rome apartment, still strewn with photos of the dog Georgie, Piazzolla was seriously depressed. He poured out his woes in letters to Daniel: "Loneliness is god-awful. . . . It's deadly to be here in this city without anybody. . . . I miss Amelita a lot . . .

What a shitty life this is."[47] He once again bombarded Amelita with letters and phone calls, this time in vain. He would never really forgive her for what he saw as her abandonment of him, and on at least one occasion told her so to her face. "I didn't abandon you. We split up," was Amelita's reply. They never worked together again. He fiercely erased the title "Amelitango" on its original score, renaming it "Música de Buenos Aires," and he hardly ever played it in later years.[48] When Eduardo Bergara Leumann referred to Amelita on his television program "La Botica del Ángel" as "Piazzolla's widow," he irately phoned the station and never met Bergara Leumann again. He prohibited any mention of Amelita in the book Diana wrote about him in the 1980s. When French song writer Pierre Philippe praised her recording of "Balada para un loco," he simply said, "You must not think that in this house."

When sorrows come, they come not single spies. Amelita was starting to pack her bags in Rome when, on Sunday, 18 May 1975, in Buenos Aires, Aníbal Troilo was fatally stricken with a cerebral hemorrhage. Aldo Pagani phoned Piazzolla, suggesting a suitable musical tribute. Piazzolla abruptly hung up, but he quickly changed his mind.[49] The resulting *Suite Troileana* condensed his feeling for Pichuco into some of the best of his music in the 1970s. Its movements—"Bandoneón," "Zita," "Whiskey," and "Escolaso" ("Gambling")—evoke the key loves of Pichuco's bohemian life. The music is for the most part fast moving, jaunty, and celebratory, though with some superbly elegiac moments. Asked for his opinion of the Suite, bandoneonist Rodolfo Mederos selected "Bandoneón," with its "magnificent solo," as the best of the movements, but he found "singularly gratifying humor" in "Zita" and a few Bartokian traces in "Whiskey," which he called "perhaps the most intellectual of the themes."[50] Piazzolla was not satisfied with the Italian recording. "It was like mixing mozzarella with barbecue," he said in 1980.[51] He made no effort to re-record the suite, and rarely if ever included it as a suite in his later repertory, though he sometimes played individual movements.

"Just as well I have a lot of work on hand," Piazzolla told Daniel during the final crisis with Amelita, and he described his routine in another letter, this time to Dedé, a few weeks later: "These last 45 days I've been writing all the time, interchanging it with my hobby, the beach. I get up at half past eight, write till noon, and then scram for Fregene, 30 kilometers from Rome."[52] And he *was* busy. Much of his composing effort in the summer of 1975 went into three film scores. The first was for *Il pleut sur Santiago* ("Rain over Santiago"), a Franco-Bulgarian production (directed by Chilean exile Helvio Soto) protesting the destruction of democracy in Chile in September 1973. It includes two of the most instantly appealing of his elegiac tunes, the heart-wrenching "Rain over Santiago," and

"Salvador Allende"—perhaps the finest musical tribute ever written for the martyr-president. The ideological dimension did not greatly concern Piazzolla. He had no compunction about changing the titles of these pieces for later recordings, removing all allusions to the events in Chile.

The second of the 1975 film scores started with a phone call to Piazzolla at the Majorca Festival from actress Jeanne Moreau, who was then making *Lumière*, her first effort as a director. Piazzolla and Pagani went to Paris at the end of April to meet her. On their way to lunch at her apartment in the rue du Cirque, Pagani bought a bunch of roses. Piazzolla insisted it would be more *macho* to arrive without them. When they got there, he snatched the bunch from Pagani and himself presented it to Moreau. He was much impressed by Moreau: "a great actress and a top-class person. Cultured, agreeable, swinging," he informed Daniel.[53]

Moreau was on the point of leaving for the Cannes Film Festival and invited Piazzolla to spend a few days in her country retreat in the hills behind Saint Tropez, but he was too busy. They met again a few weeks later in Paris, without Pagani. They wandered down the Champs-Elysées, went into record stores (Moreau bought him a Jean-Luc Ponty disc), dined at the rue du Cirque, and listened to records half the night. Everyone, he told Natalio Gorin, would expect that he had kissed her. "Nothing like that. First, she is a lady, and second, I am not a sportsman in love."[54] As for the music, Moreau pleaded with him: "Put the bandoneon in, lots of bandoneon . . . that instrument . . . fascinates me."[55] Moreau has intimated to the authors that although she met Piazzolla only two (at most three) times, she was "very touched by his creativity and generosity."[56] She had reason to be. Piazzolla's score for *Lumière* was one of his most striking achievements in film music. Its four movements ("Solitude," "Mort," "Lumière," "L'évasion") are a beautiful combination of delicacy and depth.*

Nadine Trintignant's *Voyage de Noces* was the last of the film commissions of this fertile year. Trintignant phoned Piazzolla in Rome. He flew immediately to Paris, was met by her at Orly, taken to the studios, and given lunch. They watched the film, Piazzolla noting down the sequences, and Trintignant told him: "Now do what you like." Within a few hours he was back in Rome, planning a bandoneon-violin score, for himself and Antonio Agri.[57]

---

*Listeners to the track "Mort" ("Death") on the *Lumière* album are sometimes mystified by the continuous knocking that accompanies the beautifully meditative bandoneon line and may think the record to be defective: the sound is meant to represent a heartbeat.

Into the Electronic Phase

While living in Rome, Piazzolla rubbed shoulders with many in the artistic and cinema worlds—Fellini's scriptwriter Tonino Guerra, for instance, who found Amelita *straordinaria*, or Argentine painters like Carlos Alonso or Antonio Berni. Late in May 1975, the journalist Piergiuseppe Caporale, already a Piazzolla fan, was watching the rising Argentine tennis star Guillermo Vilas play in the Italian Open when he noticed Piazzolla sitting nearby. He requested an interview, and two days later went to "the loft in the Via dei Coronari" with a long-playing record for Piazzolla to autograph. The two men soon started dining together. Caporale's impression is that most of Piazzolla's acquaintances in Rome were Latin Americans, especially Brazilians; there were predictably rumbustious occasions when Vinicius de Moraes came through. He did not find Piazzolla "an easy man" and noticed his "fear of being hurt"—which he put down to the recent break with Amelita, a topic on which Piazzolla was resolutely silent.

Despite his composing frenzy, Piazzolla still hankered after performances with a group of his own. And once again he was in an experimental mood. He began to plan a new ensemble with mostly electronic instruments. His son, Daniel, was to have a role here. He had been learning the synthesizer and taking classes in electronic music, strongly encouraged by Piazzolla. "This ensemble is going to be a terrific spree!" his father told him.[58] Such was the start of Piazzolla's "electronic phase." We should not be too surprised by it. Over the previous decade, avant-garde classical composers and rock musicians, not forgetting the jazz groups interested in what was becoming known as Fusion, had all turned in this direction. Return to Forever, Chick Corea's "electric band," was especially well liked by rock fans—and by Piazzolla. This was a contemporary trend bound to appeal to one of nature's innovators. Pianist Juan Carlos Cirigliano, who would play in the new group, thinks that Piazzolla "wanted to be the Argentine who did all that."

By July he was writing parts for the synthesizer, not finding it easy. With Amelita gone, he was desperate for Daniel to join him. Daniel was very reluctant. His wife Lalla was pregnant, but he yielded to his father's pleas and flew to Rome, with his synthesizer. "Why did you bring this shit with you?" asked his father. He soon warmed to the instrument, and Daniel's company lifted his spirits. They dined nightly at a restaurant in Piazza Navona, watching artists and actors pass by, and went on weekend excursions to the beaches and the mountains. When Antonio Agri arrived in Rome, soon afterward, there was work to be done. Piazzolla spread out the music he was to record on his bed. Agri almost died "of sheer joy." Loading fifteen suitcases into the Volkswagen, they drove to Milan to record the *Suite Troileana* and the three recently composed film scores, as well as playback material for the vocalist Piazzolla had in mind for his new electronic group.[59]

In mid-September 1975, Piazzolla and Daniel dismantled the Rome apartment and flew back to Buenos Aires, along with $15,000-worth of excess baggage. Once there, Piazzolla made a beeline for Amelita. A press photo that month showed them distinctly "sweet on each other"[60] but nothing came of the attempted reconciliation. (Georgie, however, always went crazy with delight when Piazzolla turned up in quest of Amelita at her mother's house.) A few weeks later Piazzolla firmly declared: "If I marry Amelita it will be on one condition: that she never sings again in her life."[61] This *machista* attitude was not a condition Amelita could ever accept. A notary Piazzolla had often used, Natalio Etchegaray, was summoned to the Avenida Libertador apartment to register the division of their belongings. Amelita duly signed the list of Piazzolla's items. "You won't keep it all for me?" he asked Amelita, as Etchegaray remembers it—as if offering everything to Amelita. It was a sign both of his generosity and his indifference to mere material possessions.

His main task in Buenos Aires was to rehearse his new Electronic Octet—"the electrified group," he sometimes called it. Its personnel consisted of old-timers like Agri, Malvicino, and Cirigliano, and newcomers like Santiago Giacobbe (organ), Enrique Roizner (percussion), Adalberto Cevasco (bass), and Daniel Piazzolla (synthesizer). Roizner, included in the group on Malvicino's suggestion, had first met Piazzolla when playing jazz at Michelangelo in 1969–70. Cevasco had once joined Piazzolla in a recording session and was to remember the electronic group with affection, describing it as "a university of music, the best in the world." All the musicians except Agri had jazz backgrounds. Piazzolla allowed far more improvisation in this group than in any other he ever formed, sometimes dispensing with scores altogether and issuing general guidance on the melody with a letter-code. Apart from "Adiós Nonino," the repertory was completely new.

As vocalist, Piazzolla selected the thirty-one-year old José Angel Trelles, whose appearances on television had impressed him. But the voice needed some adaptation. "If he fucks like he sings," Piazzolla jested to Daniel, "he won't give pleasure to any woman. . . . It seems like a Mexican or Chilean voice, or the voice of a good bolero singer."[62] He was rather hard on Trelles at first, telling him at one rehearsal (as Trelles himself recalls): "Sing, you shit, you seem to be cooking sausages with your ass." Trelles, aware that he was the only real "greenhorn" in the group, felt very shattered and insecure.

Duly rehearsed, the Electronic Octet was swept off on a twenty-concert tour of Brazil, starting in São Paulo on 27 September. At a run-through in the large Canecão nightclub in Rio de Janeiro, Trelles mistimed the opening of "Los Pájaros Perdidos," one of Piazzolla's biggest popular hits that year, with words by poet Mario Trejo.

> *Soy sólo un pájaro perdido*
> *que vuelve desde el Más Allá,*
> *a confundirse con un cielo*
> *que nunca más podré recuperar.*

> I am only a lost bird
> Returning from the Beyond,
> mistaking it for a heaven
> I can nevermore regain.

Piazzolla gave him a fierce dressing-down, almost destroying the piano in his fury. Trelles was tempted to abandon the tour there and then—finding his relationship with Piazzolla "very difficult, very tough"—but Piazzolla apologized.

After Brazil, there were appearances in Montevideo and a visit to Asunción, Paraguay, where that country's long-running dictator, General Alfredo Stroessner, was in the audience. The musicians were surprised to find modern equipment readily available in Asunción. As Piazzolla explained a few weeks later, "It's not easy to find a Fender electric piano or a Hammond electric organ, and in Asunción we found both."[63] Then, at last, it was Buenos Aires, for a concert at the Teatro Coliseo (18 October 1975) that proved so successful it was repeated a week later. The press noted Trelles's extreme nervousness onstage, "but when the moment came to sing, he sang. And how!"[64] Yet, although the Coliseo concerts were packed, there was a definite undercurrent of hostility to the experimental octet, especially among Piazzolla's own traditional following. "They got very mad," Adalberto Cevasco remembers; "They were very annoyed. Above all because of the electric bass, the drums. Astor was betraying them." It is not hard to understand their sense of betrayal. With the strings conspicuously absent, the sound of the electronic group *was* strange, often harsher and less nuanced than that of the Quintet or the Nonet, and moving audibly in the direction of rock or Fusion. Piazzolla, however, was never at a loss to justify whatever he was doing at the time. The Octet, he claimed, gave "an answer to a violent world. Everything is violent, and so we play violently."[65]

Piazzolla had plans for the Octet to tour Venezuela and the United States, but they fell through. He took his new group instead to a newly inaugurated *tanguería*, La Ciudad, on Calle Talcahuano, for what was reported as a very large monthly fee.[66] Here Piazzolla played several of the Piazzolla-Ferrer songs and pieces from his new European repertory, interpolating little chats with the audience. He had been advised, he said, to avoid excitement, but he did not care—"I want to die onstage, playing Piazzolla's music."[67]

There were some interesting moments during the run at La Ciudad. Nonina, who did not often hear her son in the flesh, attended one of the shows. At dinner afterward, as Atilio Talín remembers, she asked him about his new arrangement of "Adiós Nonino": "Astor, if Nonino could hear that piece, wouldn't he be surprised? Don't you think it very noisy?" Her son agreed, and next day he rearranged it. On Thursday, 27 November, Aníbal Troilo's widow, Zita, went onstage at La Ciudad and presented Piazzolla with one of her late husband's bandoneons. She described him as the "most talented musician we have," and with obvious emotion Piazzolla replied: "I'm sure that every time I play this bandoneon I shall play it like when we were in Pichuco's house, rehearsing, when Zita prepared us *mate* and gave us bread and salami."[68] When he tried to play the bandoneon, Piazzolla broke it, but he always treasured it thereafter as a relic. A less agreeable moment at La Ciudad was when Piazzolla's old champion of 1953, journalist José Gobello, complimenting him on Trelles's vocal qualities, asked where he had been found. "I didn't find him anywhere," replied Piazzolla dismissively. "They come to ask *me*." Disconcerted by the put-down, Gobello told him he would describe the exchange on his next radio program. "Do what you like," said Piazzolla. "I don't listen to the radio." The two men never met again.

Piazzolla's Argentine profile was once again very high. In December 1975 he had more column-inches devoted to him in the Buenos Aires press than any other artist.[69] At the start of the new year, he moved to Mar del Plata for the summer—to relax, compose, and spend time with Nonina. "But I know that at night my screws come loose," he told a reporter, "so I am going to play at a nightspot."[70] The nightspot was La Botonera, a small theater (no longer standing) on Calle Rivadavia, and he was there for most of January and February. During this run José Angel Trelles finally confronted Piazzolla about the way he had been treating him. "He gave me a kiss and an embrace. And after that it was a filial relationship, marvelous, marvelous."

The usual summer routines quickly set in: strolls with Daniel on the beach to mull over the future of the Electronic Octet, barbecues with Juan Trigueros and Quito González Azcona, games of volleyball. Piazzolla's strenuous volleyball style made González Azcona remonstrate with him: "Look, you've got to perform tonight." "It doesn't matter," his friend would counter. "We've got to *beat* this lot!" Yet there was a sad side to this Mar del Plata stay. Violinist Antonio Agri decided to leave Piazzolla and take a job in the Teatro Colón orchestra. He seems not to have liked the new instrumental format very much, especially the use of percussion. It gave him fewer opportunities to showcase his violin skills. He was replaced by the flutist Arturo "Alemán" Schneider for the Octet's last appearances at La Botonera at the start of March 1976. Schneider found it "difficult, moving, beautiful. I *was* replacing Antonio Agri!" Piazzolla sometimes warned him: "Alemán, improvise, but don't give me jazz, OK?" Piazzolla was seriously annoyed by Agri's departure and sounded off on the subject on the radio and in the press: "What he did is retire," he said, "and that infuriates me. I admit that a mediocrity can retire, but not a genius of the violin like him—and he doesn't even *need* those sad little pesos from the Colón."[71]

"An Electric Piazzolla"
1975–1977

→ Laura

Carnegie Hall ←

→ Piazzolla's Paris

Climax of the Electronic Phase ←

> I'll say this for Astor: he makes the air swing.
> —Arnold Jay Smith in *Down Beat*, 21 October 1976,
> reviewing Piazzolla's Carnegie Hall concert

Laura

In the Argentine spring of 1975, Piazzolla's public statements about his new European phase were very upbeat. "Things have come good for me at last," he declared. It was now "contracts, television, films, records" all the way. He praised the professionalism (and the status) of musicians in Europe. He hoped that 1976 would be a year when he made good money at last.[1] In private he was much less sanguine. Earlier in 1975, feeling down in the dumps in Rome, he confessed to Daniel that he was tiring of travel, that he hoped to make enough money to allow him to return to Argentina. "I hope soon to be with you [at] Kilometer 197," he wrote, "smashing the partridges to smithereens."[2] Kilometer 197, on the Buenos Aires-Mar del Plata road, was a spot where they had gone hunting in earlier days.

There was one thing definitely lacking in Europe. During the summer of 1975, as he told Natalio Gorin, he was usually eating alone in the Rome apartment. He needed "someone who can make me feel happy, who can make me feel a man and young . . . but love is not a sport, or anyway not for me."[3] He wanted (as he told his daughter later, apologizing for his conservatism in these matters) a woman at his side "twenty-four hours of the day."[4] His emotions were still in turmoil during his months back in Argentina. He consoled himself for a while with an eighteen-year-old his children nicknamed "La Chirolita" (Buenos Aires slang for a low-value coin). At La Ciudad, he became besotted with another teenager and had to be restrained by his musicians. "From the rhythm of the life he was leading," Adalberto Cevasco recalls, "it seemed like he was a man of forty." He was not. He was nearly fifty-five.

In the interviews he gave in Argentina, Piazzolla claimed to be an essentially happy man who had overcome his "fear of loneliness." This was pure bravado. When asked what he wanted most of all, his reply was instant: "a partner." His greatest love outside music, he declared, was Dedé—"and, like the tango says . . . you only love once."[5] He and Dedé had exchanged letters over the previous year, and in February 1976 he wrote emotionally to her from Mar del Plata: "There will never be anyone like you. . . . I would give anything to be at your side as I ought to be, but that would be to deceive myself and it would destroy you." He added a postscript: "Don't think so much about the past. Think about the future. The past is dead. The present is alive."[6]

His own "present" came rather dramatically alive again a month later. On Thursday, 11 March 1976, his fifty-fifth birthday, Piazzolla went to the studios of Channel 11 for an interview in its regular *Matinée* program. Daniel went with him, as did Aldo Pagani, then in Buenos Aires. The show's anchorwoman was the pert, attractive Laura Escalada, then in her early forties. Laura had studied singing as a youngster, taking a number of soubrette roles in the theater. In 1953–54 she sang in the chorus in Aníbal Troilo's musical comedy *El patio de la morocha*. At a rehearsal with Pichuco one day, she recalls, "a very annoyed, furious man" came in with some scores under his arm. Troilo calmed him down. One of Laura's companions explained: "That one's a genius; that one's Astor Piazzolla, who does the arrangements." Laura began to take an interest in Piazzolla's music and started buying his records. In November 1969 she was in the crowd at Luna Park, cheering "Balada para un loco," vigorously defending it to a hostile group sitting nearby. By then she was working full time in television, having abandoned the operatic career for which she had trained with a scholarship at the Teatro Colón. On the little screen she sang in musical comedies and commercials, and turned her hand to everything from children's programs to announcing.

The *Matinée* program went on for several hours. During one of its numerous breaks, Laura fell into conversation with Piazzolla. They discovered that they were neighbors on Avenida Libertador and that they both walked their dogs at night. "Why don't we take them out together?" Piazzolla suggested, as Daniel remembers it. Piazzolla was astonished that "a television announcer should know so much about Schumann, Bach, Gershwin. . . . She interested me." He invited her to his show at La Ciudad the next evening. She took some of her studio friends along, and afterward the two of them dined at El Tropezón on Avenida Callao, that most venerable of *porteño* restaurants, now gone forever. "We talked about Brahms while eating *osso buco*," Laura would recollect. "Astor adored Brahms and enjoyed *osso buco* as much as I did. We went on seeing each other every so often, until finally, one night, after a chat that went on for more than six hours, we decided to live together."[7]

Daniel thought that Laura would be as fleeting as "La Chirolita." He was quite mistaken. Only a few weeks after their meeting, on 14 May, Piazzolla and Laura went to a belated birthday party thrown by the celebrated Argentine painter Antonio Berni, and Berni staged a mock wedding for them, complete with marriage register.[8] Piazzolla asked his "bride" to accompany him to Paris when he returned to Europe in June. Laura had her doubts, not least about losing her television job. She consulted a neighbor and good friend, Eva Moccia, who agreed to give Piazzolla the once-over at dinner. She found him "very agreeable," with "so much heart, so much love, so much feeling." She told Laura it would be a "beautiful experience" to be in Europe with "a beautiful person," and, after all, it was not that a great love arrived "bang! in five minutes. Go! Laura, go!" she urged. Laura went.

As they passed through Ezeiza airport, Piazzolla told the press that they were on their honeymoon.[9] From Paris, he wrote Daniel: "Laura . . . is extraordinary and helps me a lot in my craziness, that's to say she saves me from them."[10] As he put it to one reporter: "Laura got rid of all the cobwebs in my head." And to another: "She gave me peace, she helped me to clean myself up."[11] Laura confirms that when she met him, Piazzolla was "in a very bad state in every way—physically, morally, economically." But she did not regret her decision. From Paris she told Eva Moccia that Astor was being "very affectionate" and that she felt "very easy."

Only in April 1988, after Argentina had enacted its first divorce law, were they able to marry legally. But from the first they were a very effective married couple. Like most married couples they had their ups and downs, and there was one big explosion (famous among their friends) when they almost went their separate ways. Laura quickly took charge of Piazzolla's practical arrangements—organizing his clothes, arranging interviews, filtering news to him, calming him down before performances. Says journalist Edmundo Eichelbaum:

Laura put order into everything. She put all his affairs on the rails. He listened to her a lot. And when he had his strongish outbursts, she was able to get him to calm down—that's something I saw myself. I think she tranquillized him. Also, I think, she directed his activity up to a point. He certainly delegated many tiresome things to Laura. She felt that it was her mission to do this.

Other perceptions are similar. "Laura must have been the woman who coddled him most," thinks Quito González Azcona. "She wrapped him in care." Pierre Philippe, staying with them in 1987, found that "she left him the space he wanted. She was Astor's slave. She got out of the way. She wasn't possessive, or maybe she was, I don't know. There was a very great system of protection around him."

Laura was always perfectly open about her role. "I have tried to organize his life," she said in 1983, "so that he can devote himself more freely and joyously to his music." After his death she reiterated this point: "I looked after him a lot, from the moment I met him."[12] Piazzolla recognized her role: "Laura acts as a barrier to save me from arguments," he said in 1980.[13] And there is plenty of evidence that he used her as a shield, as a way of avoiding unpleasant choices. This was highly convenient for him, but it cannot have been at all easy for her. It sometimes led to unfortunate misunderstandings with Piazzolla's musicians, who were not pleased when she accompanied them on tour. Oscar López Ruiz recalls an incident in Paris, during a tour of the early 1980s:

At nine in the morning Laura calls me. "Oscar, Astor wants to talk to you. He says that he expects you downstairs for breakfast at nine thirty, so you can finish arranging everything about the contract, and so on." "Okay, Laura." Well, I go downstairs, my companions are there, and she comes in and sits beside me. We talk of other things, and suddenly she says: "Well, fellows, I'm going to explain the business of the contract." "Just a minute. I have nothing to say to you about the contract. I talk to Astor about contracts." "No, it's that Astor said." "I don't give a damn what Astor says. Go tell Astor that if he wants to talk about the contract, he should come down and talk about it himself." She didn't speak to me for a month.

"We are a closed world of our own," said Laura in 1983. "Laura and I form an indestructible unit," said Piazzolla a year later, "although there are people who don't love us."[14] Second marriages often disrupt relationships established during the new partners' earlier lives. Dedé had been very popular among Piazzolla's friends. Amelita, too, was recognized as *gaucha*, a "good sort." Laura's mettle was different. Many (though certainly not all) members of Piazzolla's inner circle and *barra* came to feel excluded from his life. The *barra* did its best at the outset, even inviting Laura to a dinner at Natalio Gorin's home. Somehow the chemistry was poor. By the start of the 1980s Piazzolla had distanced himself from Natalio Gorin, Quito González Azcona, Juan Trigueros, and Miguel Selinger, though in August 1987, when Selinger's thirteen-year-old son Santiago Astor succumbed to leukemia, Selinger received some touching letters from him. Víctor Oliveros survived the purge, and Gorin eventually recovered his good standing. Some older friends, like Máximo Perrotti, with his happy memories of Parque Chacabuco days, were not so much distanced as self-distanced. Perrotti was still pleased to meet Piazzolla when he was on his own, when "he was a different person." Most of the Mar del Plata relatives saw much less of him now. In his later years, according to third cousin Oscar Cataldi, "he separated himself from the whole family." It has to be remembered here that Piazzolla's commitments increased drastically in the 1980s, when he spent much of his time abroad.

Piazzolla's relationship with his children was badly disrupted. He sometimes had to underline his feelings for Laura in explicit and pointed statements for the benefit of Daniel in particular. From Paris in 1977 he wrote: "Laura is the sweetest and best person I have ever known in my life. She loves me a lot and looks after me as nobody could.... Laura ... has not let me down. I wish everyone was as decent as her!"[15] Daniel was not persuaded. The heartwarming camaraderie he enjoyed with his father in the 1970s gave way to a sad feeling of estrangement. There were seven years in the 1980s when they did not see each other at all. When Piazzolla and Laura bought their house in Punta del Este in 1981, Daniel never went there. The rift sometimes reached the press. ASTOR PIAZZOLLA ACCUSED BY HIS SON!—so ran a headline in March 1984, over a piece in which Daniel declared: "I forgot my father a long time ago."[16] Piazzolla himself told a reporter: "With Daniel ... I have no relationship.... I can't talk to him."[17] One Christmas Eve, Piazzolla phoned his son to offer seasonal greetings. The conversation turned into a monumental row. "You're a shit!" exclaimed Piazzolla. "And you're a *bucketful* of shit!" responded Daniel.[18]

Diana took a much more positive view, at least for a while. She saw rather more of her father than did Daniel, though she, too, never went to Punta del Este. At Christmas 1985 he turned up at her house in the Buenos Aires suburb of Lomas de Zamora, with new bicycles for her children and a basket of candy; when the house was flooded, he helped her buy a downtown apartment. She refused to listen to her brother's diatribes and accused him of fantasizing. For most of the 1980s the relationship of brother and sister was very cool. Later, in the final two years of Piazzolla's life, Diana came to share her brother's viewpoint, and vehemently.

Whatever his children thought, whatever judgments his friends and relatives pronounced, Laura was without doubt the most important person in Piazzolla's life in the years that remained to him. She will be at his side for the remainder of this book.

Carnegie Hall

The show Laura attended at La Ciudad was the first of Piazzolla's second stint there, which ended in April 1976. Laura liked the sound of the Electronic Octet. It appealed to her taste for the "the well-made and the advanced." Not everybody, however, agreed. The dramatist and journalist Roberto Cossa, objecting to the show's sophisticated audiovisual trimmings, sounded a note of warning: "Careful, maestro! the lights of Paris are doing you harm."[19]

Piazzolla next prepared the octet for a brief trip to New York, for an Argentine government-sponsored concert at Carnegie Hall. The New York press advertised the concert (24 May 1976) as "The Ultimate in Music from Buenos Aires," describing Piazzolla's ensemble simply as "his NEW GROUP."[20] The "new group" played twelve pieces, nine by Piazzolla. The final number, "Violentango," brought the audience to its feet. Trelles's version of "Balada para un loco" was also well received, though Piazzolla did nothing to allay Trelles's nerves before the event, telling him, "Sinatra sings here every year, you know." One of the very few reviews of the concert praised his "vocal acrobatics" as "masterpieces."[21] (It was Trelles's last appearance with Piazzolla.) As for the music in general, *Variety* noted that it sometimes "approached the drive of hard rock," but that it soon took on "a predictable sameness that causes attention to lag."[22]

Juan Carlos Cirigliano, who thought that the Carnegie Hall concert confirmed "the weight of the group," was impressed by the attendance of many notable jazz musicians—among them Gerry Mulligan, Paul Desmond, Chick Corea, and flutist Herbie Mann, who presented a long-playing disc to Piazzolla and to his fellow flutist Arturo Schneider. Gratifying as this must have been, Piazzolla himself was not pleased with the concert. The Argentine playwright Kado Kostzer bumped into him the next day in Bloomingdale's, and complimented him: "He said 'no, no. . . .' He meant 'I don't believe you.' " Years later Piazzolla told Gary Burton that he felt the concert "wasn't well organized." It was not. It was neither well publicized nor widely reported. Conductor Ettore Stratta, who was present, remembers that the concert hall was barely half full. It was another ten years before Piazzolla made a real effort to spread his music in North America. While he was in New York, he turned down an offer for a three-month tour with Gerry Mulligan and Stan Getz, in the belief that his opportunities were still greater in Europe. For the time being, they probably were.

The New York trip had its lighter side. A day or two before the concert, Piazzolla and Daniel were given a sumptuous party by their Bertolami cousins in New Jersey, who organized a large family gathering—the "boys," their wives, their now grown-up children. As Daniel recalls:

> We seemed like Don Corleone and his gang, with all those Cadillacs crossing the bridge to New Jersey. We arrived, and there was an enormous table, loaded with cans of beer and a bottle of Chivas Regal whiskey, an entire ham. It was a banquet! A bit later we left this table and went into the dining room, [where there was] a trayful of crabs from Maine . . . , and oysters. I don't know how many people, all eating. It was around eight at night, and we were about ready to die. After eating, everyone sitting down to watch television. A color TV, which for us was a complete novelty.

(Color TV reached Argentina only two years later.) The Bertolamis had offered to ferry the two Piazzollas back to Manhattan the next afternoon. Exhausted by such generous hospitality, the couple caught a bus at 8:30 in the morning. No offense was taken. The "boys" were at the Carnegie Hall concert, as were a few of Piazzolla's childhood friends.

In the summer of 1976, Piazzolla, with Laura now at his side, settled back in Paris, in an apartment at 13 rue Saint Louis en L'Ile. He had as much work on hand as ever. Among other commissions, he was writing the sound track for Alain Delon's movie *Armaguedon*, a rather heavy thriller released early in 1977. His contacts with Delon were minimal—and Delon himself has forgotten about them completely.[23] Piazzolla apparently went to the studios on the outskirts of Paris and chatted amiably with him for about twenty minutes in a caravan he used as dressing room—a "great gentleman," Piazzolla recalled.[24] Daniel Piazzolla, who attended the private viewing of *Armaguedon* early the following year, remembers Delon embracing his father, saying "Many thanks, Astor Piazzolla, for your talent, many thanks."

Piazzolla's performances in the summer and early autumn included television programs in France, Italy, and Belgium (he was now commanding fees of $800–

$1,000 for television work). In September, he appeared as solo bandoneonist accompanied by the RAI orchestra, at the Venice Festival, in a UNESCO-sponsored spectacular in aid of the preservation of the city. Others present at this jamboree were Peter Ustinov, Yehudi Menuhin, Maurizio Pollini, and Paul McCartney and Wings.[25] Piazzolla would never forget the lavishness of McCartney's sound equipment.

He wanted very much to bring the Electronic Octet to Europe for a two-month, forty-concert tour. Impresarios balked at the cost of transporting seven musicians from Buenos Aires, and the fees being proposed ($1,000 per concert) seemed too low to Piazzolla. On his own, meanwhile, he was doing very well. In Europe, he told Daniel, he was definitely in fashion: "Everyone wants to write with me and record. AND I SHALL DO IT, even if it's with Giscard D'Estaing."[26] Valéry Giscard D'Estaing, then president of France, rather enjoyed playing the accordion in public, something not wholly approved of by his fellow countrymen.

Piazzolla's Paris

Paris was now Piazzolla's European base. He would live or stay there many times over the next fourteen years. Ever since his first visit with Dedé, he had loved the city. His records sold better in Paris than in most places. He was also impressed by the favorable treatment he received from SACEM (Société des Auteurs, Compositeurs et Editeurs de la Musique), the French equivalent of SADAIC, which Piazzolla had left in 1975—denouncing it later as "underdeveloped."[27] After seven years in the comparable Italian organization (SIAE), he joined SACEM in January 1982, using the good offices of the publisher Yves Baquet. After a lunch in SACEM's seventh-floor restaurant, Baquet asked him, "Astor, will you sign up or not?" "I'll sign," said Piazzolla. It was a wise decision. SACEM requires a ten-year membership before a member's widow can receive benefits. Piazzolla's death fell six months beyond the limit, though it almost certainly cheated him, Baquet believes, of the organization's Grand Prix, for which he was being proposed the year he died.

Piazzolla never bought property in Paris. Earlier, he could not afford to. Later, he came close at one point to buying an apartment on the rue Saint Martin but decided against it. Until the mid-1980s he and Laura lived in rented apartments; later in that decade they used apartment hotels, a particular favorite being the Roblin, near the Madeleine.[28] The Parisian *quartier* Piazzolla loved above all was the Île Saint Louis. Three of his addresses in the 1970s and 1980s were on the rue Saint Louis en L'Ile (Nos. 13, 56, 30), the little island's "main street." The apartments were small and expensive. Piazzolla was prepared to pay the high rents simply to be able to enjoy the tranquil, residential atmosphere. France's recently deceased president, Georges Pompidou, had also liked that atmosphere, as did the veteran composer Henri Dutilleux, whom Piazzolla often saw shuffling into his doorway with a *baguette* under his arm. As he told pianist Pablo Ziegler, Piazzolla was always powerfully struck by the simplicity of the scene.

Piazzolla and Laura quickly adopted their own private Parisian rituals, never failing to visit the Chapel of the Miraculous Medallion in the rue du Bac and always eating their first meal, on arrival, at L'Escargot on the rue Montorgueil. "We always lived in a very bohemian way," says Laura. Piazzolla certainly explored and enjoyed the restaurants of the world's gastronomic capital and indulged his love of cooking to the fullest. Mario Corcuera Ibáñez, Argentine consul in Paris at the end of the 1970s, remembers "cooking competitions," usually on Saturdays, when Piazzolla and three or four friends gathered to eat a dish prepared by one or another member of the group. "He liked to win," says Corcuera Ibáñez—and he usually did, with a delicious *lapin chasseur*. Dogs, too, always Yorkshire terriers, were very much part of the Île Saint Louis households. The first was a puppy called Windy, who died while Piazzolla was out of town. Laura quickly found a second Windy, not telling Piazzolla for a long time (he did not notice the switch) that her original name had been Mascotte. Windy and later Yorkshire terriers were looked after by Didier Servant, a veterinarian specializing in the breed who practiced at Neuilly-sur-Seine. He and his wife became friendly with the Piazzollas, often receiving invitations to concerts and sometimes to dinner parties. The Piazzollas dined once at Neuilly. Servant was much taken with Piazzolla's "very engaging manner" and "rare qualities."

One of Piazzolla's neighbors on the Île Saint Louis was his new friend, the well-known popular singer Georges Moustaki. "If he had a problem," says Moustaki, "finding a piece of music, renting a car, I was his agent, so to speak, guiding him round Paris." The two men had what Moustaki calls "a sort of permanent gaiety, a permanent relationship which wasn't a professional relationship. We amused ourselves, once, by picking up a tom-tom and playing it as if we were hippies." In 1976 they wrote two more songs together, following up on "Le tango du demain" of 1974. (There would be more in the early 1980s, none of them especially successful.) They went to London that summer to record them. There was a brief *contretemps* with British customs officials over Piazzolla's bandoneon case. Moustaki told them indignantly that his friend was "the greatest bandoneon player in the world." Between recording sessions, Moustaki hunted down spare parts for his motorcycle, parts he could not buy in Paris. His brisk pace from store to store exhausted Piazzolla. "I'm never coming to London with *you* again!" he told Moustaki.

Another French musician Piazzolla got to know very well in Paris a few years later was the young accordionist (and later bandoneonist) Richard Galliano. Piazzolla went backstage at the Olympia one night to compliment him, and he and his wife Giselle soon became very good friends of Piazzolla's, enjoying "some fantastic moments" together. Galliano was later to perform Piazzolla's music with great distinction—not least the music Piazzolla wrote in 1986 for a remarkable modern-style production at the Comédie Française of Shakespeare's *Midsummer Night's Dream* (Songe d'une Nuit d'Eté). When approached by the play's Argentine director, Jorge Lavelli, Piazzolla inquired, "Are you sure—the tango with *Shakespeare?*" He wrote what is perhaps his best theater music, a richly melodic score that contributed, director Lavelli recalls, to the play's "fantastic success" with audiences, though, because of Parisian theater politics, it did not have a long run.

José Pons, who has already appeared in our story, was one of Piazzolla's indispensable Paris friends. Jacqueline Pons often delighted him with her formidable cuisine. Pons sometimes accompanied him to radio and TV studios, acting as interpreter, although Piazzolla's French was now moderately respectable. Pons found him "always very attentive, very merry, an extraordinary friend," never sensing any real nostalgia for Argentina. Piazzolla saw rather less, now, of his old Parisian friend Édouard Pécourt. He still dropped in at the record store from time to time and gave Pécourt his new LPs, but Pécourt never visited any of the Île Saint Louis apartments. He was now, in any case, doing a good deal of traveling, with frequent visits to Spain, England, and (in the early 1980s) the United States. He and his new American wife Jocelyn moved to Oregon, Jocelyn's home state, in 1986.

Argentine artists living in Paris (like the painters Julio Le Parc and Pérez Celis) could always count on seeing something of Piazzolla there, as could Argentine friends passing through—Atilio and Inés Talín, for instance, who accompanied him on some of his European tours. Argentine diplomat Alberto Salem called on him at least once and noted the pleasure Piazzolla got from hearing the bells of nearby Notre Dame. Máximo Perrotti visited from time to time. His wife Solange was French; they were usually in Paris to see an uncle of hers. He remembers numerous excursions, sometimes with pianist Héctor Grané. Perrotti often rented cars on these trips. Whenever he was a passenger, Piazzolla would invariably plead, "Don't go through L'Étoile." Apparently he himself had had one or two small collisions at that spot, which was hair-raising for all normally constituted drivers.

Climax of the Electronic Phase

In August 1976 the Piazzollas, with Atilio and Inés Talín, took a short vacation in Switzerland and northern Italy. It was a chance for Laura to see an old friend, Lydé Mirelmann, then living with her husband Iacob and their children at Clarens, near Montreux, on the beautiful north shore of Lake Geneva. They spent some convivial days together. Iacob Mirelmann drove Piazzolla to Geneva every day for rehearsals of a TV spectacular he was recording. "Europe is treating me very well," Piazzolla told an Argentine reporter who caught up with him in Geneva; he and Laura were living "something very nice."[29] This was Lydé's impression, too. On her frequent trips to Paris she saw a good deal of the couple, often sampling Piazzolla's cooking. She nicknamed their tiny apartment "the house of love and laughter."

Piazzolla could never stay away from performing with a group of his own for long. In October, while Laura stayed in Paris, he returned to Argentina to revive the Electronic Octet. There was a single change of personnel, Luis Alberto "Chachi" Ferreyra replacing Arturo Schneider as flutist. In November he took the Octet to Brazil—Salvador, São Luis, Belem, Manaus, Brasília, Belo Horizonte, Recife, Fortaleza. "An electric Piazzolla has arrived in Rio!" proclaimed *O Jornal do Brasil.*[30] Vinicius de Moraes, who heard him in Rio, rejected all criticism of the "electronic" Piazzolla, insisting there was "no fundamental difference" in his music.[31] At Recife, the musicians (and a large crowd) were held up for several hours by a conference of bishops taking place in the theater. At Fortaleza, next day, as Juan Carlos Cirigliano remembers, Piazzolla declared to reporters: "All bishops are queers. The Pope, too." And here the tour came to a sudden, ignominious end. Its Brazilian agent had been "bicycling" the musicians—Argentine slang for delaying payments. Piazzolla had to dig deep into his own pocket to pay his team. The agent then disappeared altogether.[32] With no money coming in, with almost no further concerts possible, there were angry scenes of recrimination. Piazzolla dissolved the Octet on the spot. Its members vowed never to play with him again, except for one upcoming concert, already booked for 16 December 1976 at the Teatro Gran Rex in Buenos Aires.

Snatching a few days back in Paris, Piazzolla was in Buenos Aires in good time for the Gran Rex show. After a rehearsal late the night before, he went off for a meal with some of his friends, among them his doctor Marcos Asensio and journalist Bernardo Neustadt. Asensio and Piazzolla tried to fool Neustadt into believing that there was a campaign to make "Adiós Nonino" the Argentine national anthem. This particular *cachada*—the kidding with a straight face so typical of Buenos Aires humor—did not succeed. All tickets for the Gran Rex show ("Piazzolla de Buenos Aires") had been sold the day before. Critical reactions were very positive. *Clarín* called it "the musical event of the season"; *La Opinión*, discussing Piazzolla's "annual concert," thought that the pieces played were almost too perfect. These included the extraordinary "500 Motivaciones," in jazz-rock idiom, written in honor of his instrumentalists, and so-called because it had 500 bars. "Piazzolla's tomorrow promises him a classical destiny," the note concluded. "Isn't that the destiny of all avant-gardes?"[33] It was a good intuition about Piazzolla's future.

One thing the press noticed about the Gran Rex concert was the presence (vocally expressed, as we can hear on the recording) of a large number of rock musicians. Piazzolla himself was definitely putting out feelers to the rock world. At a press conference announcing the concert, Natalio Gorin had introduced him to a rock enthusiast colleague, who asked him why he never played "Escolaso"—a theme that ostensibly had a rock atmosphere.[34] Piazzolla included it among the pieces to be played. A day or so earlier he had dropped in at the Café Periscopio to listen to the Cuarteto Alas, a new progressive rock group trying its hand at rock-tango fusion; it had recently expanded from a trio by including a bandoneon in its instrumental line-up. "The music of Buenos Aires today," Piazzolla announced, in one of several favorable public references to rock, "has to have some relation to that 'noise,' that music."[35] This was something about which he would blow hot and cold (mostly cold) for the rest of his life. For the moment he blew hot. Alex Zuker, then a member of the Alas group, thinks that Piazzolla's appearance at the Periscopio must have been "the only time the maestro, surrounded by long hair and noise, ever formed part of a typical rock audience." The maestro graciously invited the group to a performance he gave at Michelangelo. From their bottle-littered table, they applauded him rowdily.

After a quick side trip to Mar del Plata to see Nonina, Piazzolla was back in Paris by the end of December 1976, putting the finishing touches to the music for *Armaguedon** and planning a brand-new (and rather more radical) electronic ensemble. Pierre Fastosmes was busy arranging concerts in France, Italy, and Germany, asking a fee of 9,500 francs (around $1,900) per gig.[36] It was the first time Piazzolla had succeeded in organizing a European tour for one of his ensembles—that old dream, so often frustrated earlier. Daniel was given the job of rounding up the musicians and getting them to France in March, properly attired—"black outfits (shirt and trousers) and on top of that A DARK SUIT for any

---

*In 1977, Piazzolla also wrote music for an Argentine film, David Kohon's *¿Qué es el Otoño?*.

diplomatic receptions."[37] Daniel found it "terribly hard work" to recruit a new team. With the exception of "Chachi" Ferreyra and Daniel himself, all the members of the first electronic group refused even to consider the idea—not surprising after their recent Brazilian experiences. The newcomers roped in were from the younger generation: Osvaldo Caló (electric organ), Ricardo Sanz (bass), Luis Cerávolo (drums), and Tomás "Tommy" Gubitsch (guitar). Gustavo Beytelman, a pianist residing in Paris, was also enrolled. Horacio Malvicino's opinion was that these musicians were too close to "a rock way of playing" for comfort.[38] This was something that probably appealed to Piazzolla in his current mood, with his recent openings to the rock world in Buenos Aires.

Before the musicians flew to Paris, however, Piazzolla had business of his own to finish. In February 1977, he was in Milan to record an album of his own new work as well as the film music from *Armaguedon*. His album, *Persecuta* (also known as *Piazzolla 77*), was certainly one of the best of his European phase. "It's another experiment by the madman Piazzolla," he told his friend Quito González Azcona, "full of fugues, counter-fugues and other irreverences." Among other delights, it includes "Windy," a gentle tribute to his dog (with allusions to the little rattle Windy wore around the house), "Largo tangabile," "Moderato tangabile," and the beautiful "Cité Tango," the best track of all, with its gorgeous, serpentine bandoneon passage.

Milan was not all work. Lydé Mirelmann, with Aída Luz, another of Laura's friends drove there from Switzerland to celebrate Aída's birthday with the Piazzollas. At the hotel where they were all staying, Lydé recalls,

> We waited for Astor to come back from recording. When Astor arrived we had started, well, not to eat, but to drink, of course. He arrived, and we carried on. It was a long evening, very amusing, we enjoyed ourselves a lot, a lot. So much so that afterwards, Aída and I went on laughing in our hotel room, and they knocked on the wall—"what are you laughing about?"—and kept telephoning us all the time.

Back in Paris again, Piazzolla went to Orly airport to meet his new musicians. Édouard Pécourt was with him, mildly disconcerted by "all these youngsters in blue jeans." Piazzolla installed them in a small hotel near the Panthéon, from where some of them occasionally visited the Île Saint Louis apartment—small and very Parisian, as flutist "Chachi" Ferreyra remembers it, with a staircase that creaked. Piazzolla duly introduced his new group to the press: "They are all young, so young!" he said. "I am not so young, but I am not at all tired."[39]

The new electronic group did twenty-two concerts at the Olympia (22 March–10 April), partly at the behest of Georges Moustaki, who had never sung there before and who only agreed to do so if Piazzolla played during the first part of the show. The notices were enthusiastic. The *Quotidien de Paris* thought that Piazzolla and his musicians were the only "strong point of the evening" and praised "the virtuosity, the heart, the rigor of the writing, and the sincerity." *L'Express* acclaimed Piazzolla as "the Boulez of the bandoneon."[40] On Saturday, 26 March, in the early evening, the Octet played for an hour in the Auber station of the Paris Metro (near the Opera). Daniel saw Argentines in the crowd weeping as they heard "Adiós Nonino."

Daniel's recollections of the second Electronic Octet are very upbeat. He is sure that it rejuvenated his father.[41] For electric organist Osvaldo Caló, "it went very fast. It all went very fast." The working atmosphere was excellent to begin with, but Piazzolla's onstage mastery, as "Chachi" Ferreyra remembers, "was not there in other things . . . in labor relations." As time went by there were disagreements, and soon enough a distinct "cooling off" between the musicians and Piazzolla—attributable, thinks Caló, to their different ages and different energies. The agent Pierre Fastosmes was privately appalled—"I was very disappointed, very disappointed. I had expected the normal, habitual style, I was angry and sad; it was a waste of time." Georges Moustaki is fairly certain that the group "didn't work." José Pons recalls it as a "terrible moment" for Piazzolla. "The youngsters didn't behave themselves," he says. "*He* was a difficult man, too, and got annoyed over the slightest thing, so I can't say whether he was right or whether they were. I do know that musically he was always right."

After the Olympia appearances, the group went on a tour of French cities, often playing in the local Maisons de Culture; there were two concerts in Italy and engagements in Switzerland and Belgium. The concerts were all well attended. But in Brussels, at the beginning of May, the whole "electronic" enterprise suddenly collapsed. "The boys," says Ferreyra, "became disenchanted." One of their constant gripes was that they often had to carry their own equipment, something that conflicted with their dreams of instant European stardom, though common enough in Europe itself. A particular complaint on this score drove Piazzolla to fury. He himself loaded the instruments back on to the bus, and the group drove back to Paris amid scenes of violent recrimination like those in Brazil.[42]

Later on, Piazzolla could be brutal when reflecting on his electronic phase: "I failed totally," he told a magazine later, in 1978.[43] It seems likely, however, that he would have liked a longer effort with his two electronic groups, and that he always had a certain nostalgia for the experiment. One of the few cassettes he kept in his car in later years, as Daniel learned, was a recording of the Olympia sessions. Adalberto Cevasco, bass player in the first Electronic Octet, met Piazzolla only once after 1976—in a theater where Cevasco was playing. Piazzolla embraced him. "Do you remember how that group sounded?" he asked. "There was a lot of softness in his eyes," says Cevasco.

The two electronic octets were the closest Piazzolla ever came to attempting a fusion with the rock tradition, the second group being discernibly further down that path than the first. He had once declared himself "a fanatic of the Beatles," and he speculated "that the tango of the future might have " 'something' of the Beatles' rhythm."[44] In 1986, when asked what were his favorite foreign songs, he replied: "Any of Gershwin's, or the Beatles' 'Yesterday.' "[45] But his critics steered him away from going further in the direction of tango-rock fusion. " 'Your group is very good,' " he recalled them saying, " 'But it sounds very much like Liverpool or New York.' They wanted the sound of Buenos Aires. The only person not to realize that it didn't have a Buenos Aires sound was me!"[46] Anyone listening to the "500 Motivaciones" will hardly regret Piazzolla's decision to end his electronic phase. But he continued to be attracted by the best rock groups and sometimes talked of working with them, though he never did. He told a BBC producer in 1989, "Young people who like rock-and-roll also like my music because it is exciting, aggressive, new and romantic."[47]

Up and Down the Atlantic
1977–1981

→► Buenos Aires Again

The Second Quintet ◄◄

→► Paris Again

Piazzolla at Sixty ◄◄

> I began to earn good money only when I was sixty.
> —Astor Piazzolla, talking to Natalio Gorin (1990)

Buenos Aires Again

After the electronic debâcle, Piazzolla and Laura almost immediately drove to Spain in their car, which had acquired the nickname "Gomia."* Piazzolla described the trip to Daniel.

> Paris-Barcelona 1,200 kms. Barcelona to Majorca by boat. We spent a week living like kings. In an old mansion, or rather a castle. . . . We ate like oxen and boozed half the wine in Spain. To be in Majorca with GOMIA was a dream. We saw everything. Schifrin was there—as usual, dead with cold. We became good friends with Bill Conti, the author of the music for *Rocky* [1976]. We got on very well with him and his wife. Also there were other musicians and friends, and TV producers from all over the world. . . . From Majorca to Valencia, another boat. Overland from Valencia to Granada (what a marvel!), and from Granada to somewhere near Torremolinos to

*Buenos Aires back slang (words with the letter order reversed or changed) for "amigo," friend.

spend a week in some apartments [from which you] could touch the sea with your hands. . . . Windy [the dog] crazily rushing up and down. We got as far as Gibraltar: We returned up the whole length of Spain and then went to Switzerland, to change the licence plate on Gomia. . . . I zoomed from Geneva to Paris. We did 6,000 kilometers, all without a hitch.[1]

Piazzolla was now planning a return to Argentina. With the failure of the electronic experiment, he was wondering, not for the first time, where next—and how best—to channel his creativity and musical energy. He needed to tap into his roots once again. "There have been too many years away," he told the press.[2] To his friend Juan Trigueros he expressed a wish to be living in his own apartment again, to eat off his own plates, "and have my real friends eating at home."[3] (He was annoyed to learn that the management of the apartment building wanted to prohibit dogs.) As for his artistic plans, he would obviously need a new ensemble, new musicians for whom he could write and with whom he could record—always one of his permanent needs. To Daniel he fantasized: "The maestro is coming. . . . PIAZZOLLA HAS ARRIVED! DANGER!. . . . What ensemble will he form? MYSTERY!"[4] In the meantime, he put out feelers to Buenos Aires. Could there perhaps be a revival of *María de Buenos Aires* at the Teatro San Martín?[5] This idea was soon abandoned. More promising, the owners of the Auditorio Kraft, a 270-seat hall on Calle Florida, seemed eager to contract him for a long run in 1978.

For the moment his European routines continued. Plans to record with the Greek musician Vangelis in London and Michel Legrand in Paris fell through, but there were further television appearances—in Italy and Spain as well as France. And the autumn found him in the full throes of composing some pieces to mark the upcoming 1978 World Cup, to be played in Argentina. César Luis Menotti, the coach of the Argentine team, visited him at the rue Saint Louis en L'Ile to discuss titles appropriate to soccer and the tournament. He recorded the album (*Mundial 78* or *Piazzolla 78*) in two visits to Milan in December and January. Since the World Cup was soon forgotten, all the soccer related titles—"Mundial 78" ("World Cup 78"), "Penal" ("Penalty"), "Wing," "Corner," and so on—were later changed by Piazzolla, some more than once. "Mundial 78" became "Piazzolla 78" on one album, "Thriller" on another; "Penal" was transformed into "Ritchie"—like Windy, one of Piazzolla's Yorkshire terriers. He claimed to Daniel that it was his best music yet, but when he heard it, the album totally disillusioned him. He later called it one of the "most dreadful" of his records and even suspected sabotage. He swore never to record in Italy again.[6] (In Italian studios, at least, he almost never did.) Not many would place the 1978 album among

Piazzolla's best. It has a run-of-the-mill feel. Surely, we ask, he could be aiming at something higher. Probably, deep down, Piazzolla asked the same question.

In the early weeks of 1978, two young Argentine pianists, Norberto Capelli and Héctor Moreno, then studying in London, paid a brief visit to Paris to consult the French pianists Jacqueline Robin and Geneviève Joy, the wife of composer Henri Dutilleux. They had made arrangements of some of Piazzolla's music and, greatly daring, telephoned him. "Okay, come round tomorrow," he said, in a very friendly tone of voice. He was impressed by Moreno's version of "Verano porteño," which combined the piece's three main themes in the finale. He had not realized, he said, that the three themes could be superimposed on each other. "When we came out," recalls Capelli, "we were crazy about having met him." The pianists later formed a duo and moved to Florence, where they several times renewed their acquaintance with the Piazzollas. Piazzolla talked of writing something for them, but never did.

He and Laura dismantled their Paris household. Tango pianist Atilio Stampone called on them as they were doing so and was cajoled into taking part of their dinner service back to Argentina.[7] On 4 March 1978 they embarked on the cargo-passenger ship S.S. *Río Cuarto*. The captain was friendly. Evidently some of the crew shared the old prejudices. The Piazzollas' large metal trunks were broken into and defaced with gross messages, such as "Madman"—"Ballad for a Madman"—"You are mad." "Look, here I am, returning to Argentina," Piazzolla commented to Laura, "and this is what happens to me!" In Buenos Aires, however, the press was out in force to greet him—to his delight. The interviews began even before he disembarked. To Radio Pacheco he announced that he was abandoning his Electronic Octet and would form a new Quintet. Daniel, waiting at the docks, heard the news with a sense of shock. *Gente* magazine asked Piazzolla his opinion of the current Argentine situation. "I don't know," he said; "I see it as quiet."

It was just the kind of unreflective remark Piazzolla was so expert at making, but unfortunate in the circumstances. Argentina had been under military rule since the overthrow of President Isabel Perón in March 1976, experiencing the "Process of National Reorganization" proclaimed by the generals—"the Process," as the man in the street termed it. In response to the violent insurgency of urban guerrillas, most famously the Montoneros, the military regime had unleashed the most indiscriminate repression in the country's modern history, the so-called *Guerra Sucia* or Dirty War, with its many thousands of casualties. The worst repression was now over, but the word *quiet* was at best ill-chosen, and it was to be held against Piazzolla. So too, to look ahead a bit, was his lunch a year later (4 April 1979) with General Jorge Rafael Videla, the military president. Other artistic notables were there too, including the poet Alberto Girri and Borges's great friend, the novelist Adolfo Bioy Casares. Piazzolla used the occasion to tell General Videla that tango music should be given a more respectable place in Argentine education.[8] In hindsight, he was to present the lunch invitation as an offer he could not refuse: "I have great courage for certain things," he told Natalio Gorin in 1990, "but at that moment I realized that to play a *macho* role wouldn't have done much good."[9]

Some of the statements he made after his return were probably tailored to what the press found it convenient to hear. He was asked, for instance, of his impressions of the "anti-Argentine campaign" in Europe. "It's the lunatic fringe, as always," he said.[10] In fact, notwithstanding such statements (and the notorious lunch), Piazzolla later claimed to have suffered a certain amount of interference from the military regime. At least some of his music was banned from the radio— or so he told a Brazilian journalist in 1986[11]—including the now classic "Preludio para el año 3001." How the words of that vivid song to life and rebirth could possibly have offended anybody, in or out of uniform, is absolutely mystifying. He was definitely prevented from taking his new ensemble to Mexico City in 1978. The Argentine foreign minister summoned him to a private meeting, informed him that the concert where he would appear was organized by subversive left-wing exiles, and told him that if he went he would not be allowed back.[12]

Whatever his fundamental feelings about Argentina (probably never fully worked out), Piazzolla had no wish to uproot himself again. "This time I have come to stay," he told journalist Jorge Göttling on his return from Paris.[13] He and Laura were soon refurbishing the Avenida Libertador apartment as if settling in for a long spell. For decorating the living room ceiling, several 90-kilogram beams (surplus railroad ties) were hauled up the thirteen floors. Part of the terrace was enclosed to accommodate a piano. A reporter visiting Piazzolla noted that the apartment's furnishings were "sober and convenient" and that the photographs on display included the classic "still" from *El día que me quieras*, showing the teenage Astor with Carlos Gardel.[14]

As had been anticipated in Paris, Piazzolla was given an extended contract at the Auditorio Buenos Aires (the renamed Kraft). He therefore needed a new ensemble. Thinking about it in snow-covered Europe in January, he was still not sure what form it would take. A new electronic group? A quintet? A nonet? He told Daniel that he would decide in Buenos Aires, but that his idea was to "return to strings. . . . What most interests them here is a nonet or quintet. . . . We need to think a lot. Electronic things are out and don't interest people any more. They want romanticism, period."¹⁵ In fact, his European fans, his agents, and the record companies all wanted him to return to his most representative form. "Everybody said that Piazzolla was the Quintet," recalls Laura. With an electronic group, "they weren't giving him any more tours, or work—or anything."

Back in Buenos Aires, despite his shipboard statement, Piazzolla consulted various friends, including Oscar López Ruiz, who came down strongly in favor of a revived quintet. Daniel, of course, had been hoping for a new electronic group. He entertained his father and Laura, along with the Talíns, at dinner at his house soon after the homecoming, Piazzolla contributing some wine he had bought in France. "You see, Danny, that I am assembling the Quintet?" he inquired. "It seems a shitty idea," said Daniel. "I always believed that Astor Piazzolla never took a step backwards." The remark did nothing to ease the growing strain between father and son.

But his mind was made up. "This year I'm anti-Edison. . . . I don't want electricity," he said a bit later in Brazil.¹⁶ To his friend Mario Antelo, he put it more simply: "Mario, I want a bit of *sonic peace*." The phrase stuck in Antelo's mind. And to an Argentine magazine Piazzolla commented: "At this stage of my life I can no longer use the word 'experiment.' Those who experiment are those who are not sure what they are doing. I *am*."¹⁷ He was.

The Second Quintet

The Quintet had to be mostly a new group. His old collaborators, the pianists Osvaldo Manzi and Jaime Gosis, were dead; Kicho Díaz was away in Japan; Antonio Agri had a successful group of his own. The new team, however, proved to be remarkably stable, a close-knit group of artists who rapidly acquired a sense of deep comradeship. "At the start we called each other *usted* [the formal 'you']," says violinist Fernando Suárez Paz. " 'How are *usted* doing, Fernando?' 'How are *usted* doing, Astor?' Later on it was: 'How are *tú* [the informal "you"] doing, Fernando?' 'How are *tú* doing, Astor?' And by the end: 'What do you say, you old bastard?' 'What are you up to, you son of a bitch?' "¹⁸

The new group experienced only one permanent change of personnel. Oscar López Ruiz, the first guitarist, pulled out at the end of 1984. Piazzolla turned to Horacio Malvicino, phoning him from Japan to ask him back. Formerly the most bohemian of musicians, Malvicino was now undergoing homeopathic treatment and had to carry at least a dozen or so small flasks around with him. Piazzolla "was terrible," he recalls. "He kept mocking me, he drove me crazy."

The new violinist was Fernando Suárez Paz, then thirty-seven, already a veteran of several tango bands. Piazzolla had not forgotten his fleeting appearances with the Octet. Suárez Paz was doubtful about joining. He had plenty of work and was doing well. His wife Beatriz said to him: "You were always an admirer of Piazzolla, you've always wanted to play with him, so now you've got the chance, go for it!"[19] He never regretted the decision. His dazzling gypsy lightness of touch contrasted formidably with Antonio Agri's incomparable lyricism. Agri, in fact, briefly replaced him early in 1985, after a run-in Suárez Paz had with Laura. Piazzolla probably intended Agri to stay permanently, but in May that year he had a serious automobile accident that put in him a wheelchair for the next two years. An invitation to the Argentine violinist Luis Grinhauz (who played in the Montreal Symphony)[20] came to nothing. Suárez Paz resumed his place, never again to leave it.

Héctor Console, the bass player selected for the Quintet, was slightly older than Suárez Paz. He had played with Horacio Salgán and Atilio Stampone, among others, and had been a Piazzolla fan since the mid-1950s. In the first Quintet, Kicho Díaz had played with an unerring sense of tango rhythm—"a metronome," as Suárez Paz puts it. Console was more fluid, able to achieve astonishingly subtle rhythmic variations, especially in the slower sections of Piazzolla's pieces, something he showed to excellent effect in "Contrabajísimo" (1984), written in his honor. Pablo Ziegler, then in his mid-thirties, was recruited on López Ruiz's recommendation; he was well known as one of the most promising young Argentine jazz pianists. Ziegler had plenty of the "swing" Piazzolla always wanted and adapted his superb talent well to the Quintet. The introduction to "Adiós Nonino" Piazzolla wrote for him contrasts strikingly with Dante Amicarelli's version of a decade earlier: less rhapsodic, more tango oriented.

The second Quintet as a whole, however, sounded somewhat less *tanguero* than the first, closer to chamber music with inflections of cool jazz. According to Piazzolla himself, it represented

> a balanced reduction of the large orchestra. The violin represents the strings; the bandoneon is perhaps the woodwinds; the guitar, piano and double bass take turns in providing the rhythmic part. But it seems to me much more difficult to write for a quintet than for a big orchestra; there are only five instruments, five voices from which *everything* has to be heard. The counterpoint has to be extremely clear, because I don't only work in harmonic blocks. I work contrapuntally, and I always try to learn more so as to enjoy myself more—writing fugues for quintet, always with my sort

of rhythms. The fact that I don't have percussion, too, forces me to evolve; I have to *invent* my percussion with the violin, the bandoneon, the guitar. ... It is not that my music has improvisation, but it *does* have change, it takes flight.... You close your eyes and play. The violinist plays one way one day, another the next day. Sometimes he adds things. The pianist improvises with rallentandos and accelerandos, depending on how he feels. That's what's so nice about it![21]

After three weeks of rehearsals to set up its basic repertory, the Quintet began appearances at the Auditorio Buenos Aires (usually eight shows per week) in May 1978. It did not have the immediate impact Piazzolla wanted. One critic declared that "Astor Piazzolla has found himself again," while noting with relief that the show had "no insufferable singers (and hence no 'Balada para un loco')." *La Prensa*, however, thought that Piazzolla might be falling between two stools, the popular and the classical, and found the shows "an almost cold exhibition of talent and craftsmanship."[22] One of those who heard the Quintet at the Auditorio Buenos Aires was the great racing driver Juan Manuel Fangio. As Atilio Talín recalls, the national hero's taste was too traditional for the music to make much of an impression.

In September, the Quintet interrupted its Buenos Aires run and went to Brazil to open São Paulo's First International Jazz Festival. The trip was organized by Osvaldo Papaleo, a Buenos Aires impresario who offered his services in the belief that Piazzolla's previous overseas tours had been poorly managed. The festival, held in the enormous Anhembi exhibition hall, drew in American jazzmen—Dizzy Gillespie, Milt Jackson, Chick Corea, Keith Jarrett, the blues master B. B. King—as well as the usual bright galaxy of Brazilians. Piazzolla had doubts about taking his group to a jazz festival[23]—indeed, as the Quintet played, a Finnish journalist shouted, "This isn't jazz!"—but the 5,000-member audience could have cared less. The applause was thunderous. The musicians withdrew happily to their dressing room, where they were congratulated by the legendary Benny Carter, whom Piazzolla warmly embraced, and also by the American ambassador.[24] (No Argentine diplomats were on hand, Piazzolla was to remember disapprovingly.) During this visit, Osvaldo Papaleo recalls that the American singer Al Jarreau approached Piazzolla's table in the hotel dining room and sang for him.

There were plans for a visit to Chile later in the year, but it was called off. A territorial dispute between Argentina and Chile had flared up to the point of a serious war-scare during 1978. Happily, the war clouds were blown away by the new Pope, John Paul II, who insisted on mediating. In Argentina itself the Quintet made several incursions into the provinces. It was at Tucumán, in late October, that Piazzolla brought the 1978 season to a close.

What had he achieved? By the end of the Auditorio Buenos Aires run, audiences were beginning to thin out. The Brazilian triumph indicated that appreciation of Piazzolla was still greater abroad than at home. The old hostility was by no means dead in Buenos Aires, although the traditional tango world seemed by now virtually moribund. The old polemics still sometimes surfaced. Looking ahead a bit, we might note here the acrimonious war of words that broke out in September 1979 between Piazzolla and Silvio Soldán, the host of several long running tango programs on TV, whom Piazzolla accused of promoting mediocrity by exalting the "dead" musicians of the past. "By that criterion," retorted Soldán, "you would have to tear down the Teatro Colón, because there they play Bach, Mozart, or Beethoven."[25] Soldán was inclined to believe that Piazzolla's verbal assaults were a publicity stunt. He later invited Piazzolla on to one of his programs, and, he says, Piazzolla "left pleased as punch."

Piazzolla himself was well aware that even now there were limits to his popularity in Argentina. "If I disappear for eight months and then come back," he said, "well, yes, then people are attracted. . . . It seems as if people can't put up with me for 365 days of the year."[26] To journalist Santo Biasatti he once said, "I am two Rexes"—he could fill the Gran Rex for two nights, but not more. The painter Pérez Celis, in Paris a few years later, remembered Piazzolla agonizing over the contrast between his growing international acceptance and the way, in Argentina, "a certain elite preferred to question what he was doing." It was a long haul. But he *was* inching forward. We can only admire his extraordinary persistence.

In November 1978, Laura returned to the stage, singing at the Teatro Presidente Alvear in Oscar Strauss's musical *Three Waltzes*. Piazzolla was reported as very pleased that she was performing again.[27] Early in December he went on a short trip to Paris. There was talk of another film score for Jeanne Moreau. Piazzolla had his doubts about the movie (*L'Adolescente*), "in spite of Jeanne Moreau," as he put it,[28] and nothing materialized. By this point Laura was urging him to take a break. "Either you take vacations or I leave you," she threatened. "In his heart he knew he had to slow down a bit." For the summer of 1978–79 they rented a house ("Ratonia") among the eucalyptus woods of the Rincón del Indio district of Punta del Este. It was the start of an annual routine that quickly led them to become householders in the Uruguayan resort. A reporter tracked Piazzolla down. Sunburned and lightly dressed, he spoke enthusiastically about his extended vacation: "I'm dressed like this all day. I go shopping on my motorbike. I go into the supermarket, and nobody recognizes me. . . . It's beautiful."[29]

Piazzolla spent his fifty-eighth birthday (11 March 1979) with Nonina in Mar del Plata, and then returned to Buenos Aires. He announced plans for a musical comedy, a project that does not seem to have got very far; no doubt to raise a spot of cash, he appeared in an advertisement for Royal Command whiskey—a *nacional* or local whiskey. It quotes him as saying: "The world is moving away from its roots. People are moving away from their origins. Everyone is searching for something."[30] One wonders whether this harmless bromide sold many bottles of whiskey.

The Quintet's second season concentrated heavily on the Argentine provinces. Between April and November 1979 it visited not only the main cities—Córdoba, Mendoza, Rosario, Mar del Plata, Bahía Blanca—but was heard in out-of-the-way places from Resistencia in the Chaco to Comodoro Rivadavia and Ushuaia in the far south. At Ushuaia, Piazzolla broke two of his bandoneons but mended them with plasticine, to the great delight of the audience.[31] The Quintet's appearances in Buenos Aires included a notable sequence of recitals at the Bauen Hotel on Avenida Callao, which went on from July until mid-September. On 14 July the group gave a free concert in the Centro Cultural San Martín, where the full house shouted, "Never leave us, Astor!"[32] On 11 September, at a special function in the Teatro Cómico in Avenida Corrientes, the Quintet shared the bill with Osvaldo Pugliese's orchestra. Piazzolla and Pugliese were interviewed together, expressing mutual admiration and agreeing heartily that musical conditions in Argentina left much to be desired.[33] The 1979 season in the capital ended with three appearances a few days later at the Fantasy cinema in the Belgrano district, whose normal specialty was Disney movies.

Despite his growing confidence with the Quintet, Piazzolla did not neglect other sources of work, still less his growing international dimension. In July he flew to Europe for a couple of weeks to record television appearances in Rome, Naples, and Paris. In Italy he met the popular singer Milva (Maria Ilva Biolcati) and planted a seed that was to blossom magnificently five years later. A star of Italian popular music since the 1960s, she was already something of a Piazzolla fan.[34] At the end of August, he went to Rio de Janeiro to look at a preliminary version of *La Intrusa*, a film by his compatriot Carlos Hugo Christensen, for whom he had agreed to write the music. "Where can we find a piano?" he asked Christensen as they strolled along the Avenida Rio Branco. They found one on the premises of the Fundação Nacional de Arte, and Piazzolla composed some of the film music on the spot.[35]

Finally, in October, Piazzolla and Laura went for a week to New York, where he announced to the Associated Press a commission from the Bolshoi Ballet in Moscow. Earlier that year he had met the Soviet dancers Vladimir Vassiliev and Ekaterina Maximova, then appearing in Argentina. Vassiliev had asked his permission to use "Adiós Nonino" in a film he wished to make of a Somerset Maugham short story. The new Bolshoi commission, said Piazzolla, showed "that we Argentines are not just good at soccer."[36] Vassiliev, for his part, had fallen in love with Argentina and with the tango. "I saw it all as in a dream," he tells us, "with the same pain, anguish, hidden sorrow and wild power of love . . . in the tango as there is in Russian romance and gypsy song." Piazzolla he still salutes, with "the deepest Russian bow," as "the Great Maestro."

Performing and traveling did not slow the pace of Piazzolla's composing. As so often in the past, he was building up a stock of pieces tailored to his latest ensemble. From 1978–79 came "Biyuya" and "Escualo," "Chin Chin," and "Marejadilla," often in the Quintet's repertory thereafter. It is difficult not to feel that he was getting into his stride again as a composer, after the ambiguous efforts of *Mundial 78*. The first piece written after his return to Buenos Aires, "Biyuya," with its driving thrust and intercalated romantic passages for violin and bandoneon, is a masterpiece of tight construction, as is "Escualo," a work of constantly shifting tempos that robbed Suárez Paz of a vacation while he studied the score.

In 1979 Piazzolla wrote yet another film score—for *El Infierno tan Temido* (1980), a psychological drama, with fairly daring nude scenes by Argentine standards, directed by Raúl de la Torre. And in the closing months of the year he was hard at work on a more ambitious project, nothing less than a Concerto for Bandoneon and Orchestra, commissioned by the Banco de la Provincia de Buenos Aires. He gave the press a few anticipatory hints. Like Poulenc's Organ Concerto, he said, it would dispense with wind instruments, since they overshadowed the soloist. It would not, he thought, be "intellectualized" or "problematic."[37]

The Bandoneon Concerto was premiered in the Auditorio de Belgrano on 14– 15 December 1979, with an orchestra conducted by Simón Blech. The reviews were very respectful. *La Nación* gave a good concise description of the new work:

> In the first movement, a marked allegro, we get into . . . a rhythmic pulsation, full of accents and inflections. Rather than the irregular tempos of Bartók or Stravinsky, the passage recalls the Czech, Martinu, with its palpitating percussive richness. The second movement . . . "moderato," is perhaps the most intense and personal. With his bandoneon Piazzolla displays one of his typical themes in a harmonic climate that resembles a chorale.

... The last movement, which could be a "rondo," is where certain techniques (like the repeated use of the güiro or the abuse of the "glissando"
in the harmonies) are more likely to surprise the traditional listeners to
tango bands than to Piazzolla's own youthful public.[38]

A later review of the Concerto's first recording found echoes of Milhaud and
Frank Martin.[39]

Piazzolla was intensely proud of his concerto, which was his first serious effort
since the "Concierto de Nácar" to move his work on to the "symphonic" plane.
Rather significantly, it was quickly followed by a second effort in that vein. For
their 1979–80 summer vacation, he and Laura rented another house in the Rincón
del Indio district of Punta del Este. In January 1980 they attended a concert in
the nineteenth-century Cathedral at Maldonado (Punta del Este's "old city"),
looming over the main square with its inevitable statue of Uruguayan hero General Artigas. It stirred Piazzolla to write something for performance in that setting.
A reporter who saw him that month found him surrounded by manuscript paper
and scores.[40] A Punta del Este friend, Fernando Tesouro, lent him an ancient Karl
Hart (Stuttgart) piano, on whose lid Piazzolla later inscribed his thanks. And on
1 February a local cultural organization, the Centro de Artes y Letras of Punta
del Este, formally commissioned the new work, the Punta del Este Suite for Bandoneon and Chamber Orchestra.

Not everyone thought that Maldonado Cathedral was an appropriate place for
a tango musician to appear, but this is where the Suite was given its first performance, on the evening of Sunday, 2 March 1980. Piazzolla arrived "visibly nervous," according to one report, but he was good-humored. "It's the first time
I've played in a church," he jested. "They offered me the Sistine Chapel once,
but I didn't feel I could." The enthusiastic audience (much of it in tears) insisted
on a repeat of the third movement.[41] A second performance soon followed, at the
Teatro Solís in Montevideo, and the work was premiered in Buenos Aires in April,
with the Camerata Bariloche.[42] The Montevideo performance, on Piazzolla's fifty-
ninth birthday, was overshadowed by news of the death of the bandleader Julio
De Caro in Mar del Plata. Piazzolla paid him a generous tribute in the press.

For most listeners, the Punta del Este Suite is probably more satisfying, more
inspired melodically, than the Bandoneon Concerto. In the middle movement,
which evokes the sound of a harmonium within the luminously hinted framework
of a chorale, Piazzolla is close to his meditative best. "I imagine Bach playing it,"
he said, and he later claimed that it encapsulated church music "from the Middle
Ages to the 19th century ... with a touch of Gregorian chant ... [and] a few

Hindemithian moments."[43] The outer movements also have their charms, especially the final fugue, with its intermittent juxtapositions of bandoneon and woodwinds.

The Bandoneon Concerto and Punta del Este Suite were not, of course, a new departure for Piazzolla. As we have seen, he had never stopped producing "serious" works, works like "Tangazo" and the "Concierto de Nácar." But from now on—far more consciously than ever before—he became a "two-track" Piazzolla, making room for the composition and performance of his new symphonic pieces, complementing his Quintet work with frequent appearances with symphony orchestras and chamber groups. We seriously ask, however, whether the symphonic works reflected Piazzolla's true measure to quite the same extent as the brilliant contemporary chamber music he was creating with his four musicians. For all their intricate craftsmanship, the symphonic works (with the exception of "Tangazo" and the "Concierto de Nácar") lack the dynamic swing of the Quintet. And with the Quintet, he was now ready to take on the world.

Paris Again

For his new scheme of world conquest, Piazzolla once again chose Paris as his main base. In April 1980 he announced that he would be living there for at least the next two years.[44] He and Laura sailed that month to Rotterdam, where he bought a Volkswagen Golf. In Paris, at the end of May, they almost immediately found a fourth-floor apartment at 56 rue Saint Louis en L'Ile. Larger than its predecessor at Number 13, it had a glassed-in balcony, where Piazzolla installed an upright piano.

Two weeks later, Walter Acosta of the BBC Latin American Service traveled from London to interview him for a two-part radio program. This in-depth conversation gives us a marvelous impression of the Astor Piazzolla of the early 1980s. Thanks to his two summers in Punta del Este, he told Acosta,

> I am now in a—shall we say?—tranquillizing period. Very happy, very, very quiet, very peaceful. A strange thing, what made me rest—because I needed it—was . . . the summer of 1979 which I spent in Punta del Este. . . . I composed the complete [Punta del Este] Suite, and these newest works, so in those three months of 1979 and 1980 I was reborn. That long rest—I needed it. My music now is neither nervous, nor stinging, nor aggressive. Quite the contrary. It's of great tenderness, romantic and different. . . . I believe my new work is a new Piazzolla, it's a music that's more

elaborate and more simplified. With respect to the orchestration . . . one is almost arriving at a Mozartian instrumentation. Mozart was simple, that's why he was so beautiful.

His main priority now, he told Acosta, was to bring the Quintet to Europe.[45]

First, however, he had to rejoin it in Mexico, in early June, a week or so after the BBC interview, to take part in Mexico City's first-ever Tango Festival. Osvaldo Pugliese's band was also playing at the Sala Ollín Yolitzli, the festival's venue. The bass player Humberto Pinheiro, someone Piazzolla had often seen at La Noche in 1963, organized an all-day barbecue for the two ensembles, inviting other Argentine musicians living, as Pinheiro was, in Mexico. Among those Piazzolla saw, with delight, was Alberto Fontán Luna, his old vocalist from the 1946 band.

And with even greater delight, no doubt, he was able to spend some time with his daughter. For several years now, Diana had been living with her second husband, Osvaldo Villaflor, in exile in Mexico, where she worked as a journalist. She had been disgusted by her father's lunch with General Videla. "I no longer have a father," she told the newspaper *El Sol de México*, a news story that reduced Piazzolla to tears—as did a letter from her he received at the São Paulo jazz festival.[46] Diana now met Laura—"a really nice person," she thought—for the first time. She and Piazzolla stayed a night at Diana's house, going to the market and preparing dinner for the family. Laura bought clothes for the children. Piazzolla pleaded for his daughter's understanding over the notorious lunch: "Look, I went and had lunch with the soldiers because I was scared. Period." The bad time between them was over.

Diana had been commissioned by the Mexican edition of *Playboy* to write a profile of her famous father. Piazzolla read it and liked it. "Would you feel like writing my life?" he asked her. He had often told her that he wanted a biography only after he was dead. Diana suggested a novelized version of his earlier life. Her father agreed, and let Diana interview him (with tape recorder) over the twenty days he and Laura were at the Hotel del Prado. "Put down anything you like," he said, "but not my relationship with Amelita and with that 'Mandrágora.' "

Back in Paris after Mexico, and more than ever determined to give his work a European base, Piazzolla started a collaboration with the French song writer Pierre Philippe. Philippe was working with the rising young singer Jean Guidoni but was dissatisfied with the music for his lyrics. "But what did you want?" asked Guidoni's agent. "I want Astor Piazzolla," said Philippe. To his astonishment, the agent telephoned Piazzolla instantly, and Philippe went straight to the rue Saint Louis en L'Ile. They were to work intermittently together for the next few years:

a handful of songs for Guidoni, and a spectacle, *Crime passionnel.* This was a ninety-minute rock extravaganza with Guidoni singing, Piazzolla playing his squeezebox, and the whole thing amplified unbearably. Philippe felt fairly close to Piazzolla during these years but did not always find him congenial. He recalls a dinner with him when a waiter, noticing Piazzolla, put on a tape of his music, a gracious enough gesture. Piazzolla simply told the waiter to make sure the proper fee was paid to SACEM. This did not strike Philippe as gracious. Perhaps it was simply that Argentine and French humor did not mesh well on this occasion.

The return to Paris marked an important change in Piazzolla's annual routine. A large part of the rest of his life was to be dominated by the demands of international touring—at first in Europe, but later in Japan and North America as well. Piazzolla and his Quintet were soon to harvest applause in hundreds of cities, large and small, in a score of countries. In Argentina his growing European popularity meant something approaching genuine respectability for the former *enfant terrible*, despite continuing resistance to his music, a little of which is amazingly still there today. But for the first few years it was still a hard slog. Real acclaim came to Piazzolla only very late in life, with almost no time left to enjoy it. Héctor Console puts the early foreign tours in context:

> At the outset it was hard, hard. I can only imagine what it must have been like for the first Quintet.... He did the driving, tested the sound systems; we did everything ourselves. We always arrived in places tired out. They were long journeys, the kind you'd nowadays do by plane. A whole tour of France, town by town, by car. It was tremendous. But he enjoyed it so ... with his "Let's see what happens, let's see what happens." We had four or five years like this. Then came Milva. Then came Gary Burton.

Laura describes the first European tours as "tough, self-sacrificing," poorly remunerated, much of the travel done in "a ramshackle little car." On tour, the Quintet's hectic routine soon settled into a regular pattern. Piazzolla usually started the day sipping *mate* in one of his musicians' hotel rooms. If the schedule permitted, he nearly always had an afternoon siesta. "When he got up he was already plugged in, was already at the concert," says Console. There were few rehearsals except, sometimes, to see whether the sound equipment was adequate. There were occasional arguments, usually about plane timetables or hotels— "Foolishnesses, things that had no real importance." The Quintet was a peripatetic "little platoon," together all the time—"traveling or playing, or checking the sound, or lunching or dining, or quarrelling or drinking *mate*," as Fernando Suárez Paz puts it. For Piazzolla, Suárez Paz believes, the Quintet was a vital need: "It lifted his spirits; it gave him the desire to go on living." Whatever the tensions, the little eruptions, the fits of temper, it was a happy platoon, and usually a distinctly merry one.

At the end of September 1980, Piazzolla met his little platoon at Orly airport, accompanied by the agent Pierre Fastosmes. The musicians took to Fastosmes immediately—"a marvelous person," says Console. For his part, Fastosmes found the Argentines "formidable musicians, great artists." He attended all their concerts, which always gave him "goose bumps," and learned Spanish from eating with them. At the end of the tour he told them that he had never worked with more professional artists, that it had been a "real pleasure" for him.[47] This first European tour opened at Douai on 1 October 1980, and covered Belgium and Germany (where one of Piazzolla's more passionate followings grew up) as well as France. There was a side trip to Sava in Yugoslavia to entertain the Twenty-First General Conference of UNESCO (20 October). The tour, however, could hardly avoid being affected by the fallout from the Argentine situation. The revolutionary left had been defeated in the Dirty War, but it could still express its views abroad. Both in Brussels and Paris there were hostile demonstrations where the Quintet played. In Brussels, the local Montonero group insisted on meeting Piazzolla at his hotel, demanding that he repudiate the military regime. The argument was heated. Oscar López Ruiz lent moral support to his beleaguered friend.[48]

One of the Quintet's early engagements (5 October) was at the Olympia in Paris. They were back in Paris three weeks later for two concerts (23–24 October) at the Théâtre des Champs-Elysées—the scene, as Piazzolla did not fail to point out, of the notorious premiere of Stravinsky's *Rite of Spring*. Here there were bomb threats. The placards of the demonstrating Montoneros—with their leader, Mario Firmenich, on hand—denounced Piazzolla as a puppet of the dictatorship. Piazzolla refused to issue a statement, telling his musicians that if he did, he would never be able to go back to Argentina.[49] The French musician Olivier Manoury, then learning the bandoneon, was eager to meet Piazzolla, but the demonstration blocked his way backstage.

The music played in these Paris concerts is a good sample of the Quintet's repertory as it moved into the wider world: older pieces (the "Cuatro Estaciones Porteñas," the "Concierto para Quinteto," "Tristezas de un Doble A," and the inevitable "Adiós Nonino") along with works newly composed for the Quintet

("Biyuya," "Escualo"). Reviews of the concerts bordered on the ecstatic. Claude Fléouter, in *Le Monde*, suggested that Piazzolla was achieving "sublimated popular music" and waxed lyrical about the Quintet's high quality. *Le Figaro*, in similar vein, found the music "superb" and the musicians "remarkable"—"Piazzolla quite simply raises the tango to the rank of an authentic musical art."[50]

Among Piazzolla's last European engagements that autumn, after the rest of his little platoon had flown back to Argentina, was a performance of the Punta del Este Suite with the Camerata Bariloche at the Beethovenhalle in Bonn. Pianist Mónica Cosachov, then playing with the Camerata, remembers it as "a marvelous experience which we shared so happily, so excitedly." To one of the German critics present, it seemed almost as if the chamber group was energized by Piazzolla's bandoneon.[51] The Bonn concert was further evidence of his wish to promote the new symphonic repertory. So too was his three-week visit to Argentina in November–December 1980, when he performed both the Bandoneon Concerto and Punta del Este Suite at two notable concerts (29–30 November). The concerts were at the Estadio Obras Sanitarias in Buenos Aires, with the Orquesta Sinfónica Nacional under Simón Blech. René Aure, who arranged the televising of the concerts, remembers Piazzolla's nervousness about playing in so large a stadium, but the audiences greeted him deliriously.

Piazzolla used these concerts to premiere a new symphonic work, his Three Tangos for Bandoneon and Orchestra. One critic hailed the third movement as "an impressive exhibition of imagination and rhythmic power," similar to Stravinsky's Symphony in Three Movements, and thought that the work as a whole was evidence of "the mature and dexterous language [Piazzolla] has achieved in this, his latest stage."[52] Some tango enthusiasts, by contrast, saw the opening of the second movement as a plagiarism of Sebastián Piana's "Milonga triste" (1936), a piece Piazzolla had once arranged for the first Quintet. Journalist José Gobello played a tape of the concerts to Piana, who immediately spotted the similarity. In print, Gobello tactfully described it as more in the nature of a "reminiscence."[53] According to Gobello, Horacio Ferrer passed on the allegation of plagiarism to Piazzolla, who was seriously downcast.

While in Buenos Aires, Piazzolla gave a number of interviews, one of them at the Avenida Libertador apartment. Cacho Tirao was also there, examining the score of some recently written guitar pieces. Their composer was in expansive mood, underlining his pleasure at being back in Buenos Aires and, turning slightly sharper, fierce about the shortcomings of younger Argentine musicians—"To the conservatory, boys!" he exhorted. Reverting to his lighter vein, he recounted the story of a certain Dr. Constantini from Rosario, who had presented a bandoneon to the Pope. *"Ah, questo è lo che suona Piazzolla!"* ("Ah, that's what Piazzolla plays!"), the Pontiff had exclaimed.[54]

A day or two later, Piazzolla went to Mar del Plata, to be guest of honor at a show where Eladia Blázquez and Raúl Lavié were singing his songs and to premiere the Bandoneon Concerto on his native turf with the municipal orchestra at the Teatro Auditorium (7 December). During the intermission, he announced his intention of composing a bandoneon-piano concerto, which he hoped would be played with the distinguished *marplatense* concert pianist Manuel Antonio Rego. It was never written. There is a Punta del Este Suite, but no Mar del Plata Concerto. The Mar del Plata municipality and orchestra could not afford (or simply preferred not to pay) the $10,000 which Piazzolla named as his fee.

He was soon back on the Île Saint Louis. Before Christmas 1980, he again performed the Punta del Este Suite with the Camerata Bariloche at the Salle Gaveau. He also attended a guitar recital at UNESCO (17 December), when Roberto Aussel played three of the guitar pieces Cacho Tirao had been inspecting at Avenida Libertador 4854—"Campero," Tristón," and "Compadre," which later became part of his "Five Pieces for Guitar" (1984). Piazzolla told Laura that he wanted a white Christmas, so they drove to Berchtesgaden in the Salzburg Alps, where the dog Windy cavorted crazily in the snowdrifts, in the shadow of Hitler's old lair. After the holidays Piazzolla dashed to Rome to record a television program with Milva.

Also traveling to Paris that December was Horacio Ferrer. "Get ready to start work on January 2!" his old friend ordered him.[55] This was to be his last collaboration with Piazzolla; it made much less of an impact than their earlier work together. During the four or five months Ferrer stayed in Paris, they wrote more than a score of new songs, with the singers Jairo and Rubén Juárez specifically in mind. They saw a good deal of each other once again, Ferrer often dropping in for supper at the apartment. On his way home from the Île Saint Louis one night, with the tune of their song "Será que estoy llorando" ringing in his ears, Ferrer rubbed the snow from the roof of a parked car, took out pen and paper, and began writing the lyric. He was impressed by the intensity with which Piazzolla worked, often from nine in the morning to seven at night—"he never left the piano!"

Jairo was also impressed. He was then living in France but had got to know Piazzolla three years earlier, having appeared with him on one of the first color TV programs to be seen in Argentina, in the company of an entirely mute Diego Maradona. "When you went in the door of the apartment," he recalls, "you saw Astor's back; he was vigorously playing the piano on the balcony. Terrific!" Rubén

Juárez, then thirty, whom Ferrer had persuaded to make the trip to Paris, had not met Piazzolla before. He was to be introduced at the apartment, and they would take some food. Not hamburgers, insisted Ferrer: "The Maestro doesn't eat hamburgers." Juárez, who shared Piazzolla's love of joking, decided to risk it, took some hamburgers—and, he recalls, "with me, he laughed." Juárez threw himself heart and soul into his work with Piazzolla, though sometimes pleading with him not to write too many high notes. He hoped very much to make an album of the new Piazzolla-Ferrer repertory, but Piazzolla's terms were too steep for the record company.

Piazzolla at Sixty

On Wednesday, 11 March 1981, Piazzolla turned sixty. He celebrated with a dinner at 56 rue Saint Louis en L'Ile, inviting Jairo and Juárez, Ferrer and his wife Mariela, and José and Jacqueline Pons. "A few people, but good people," Piazzolla said, dictating into a Sony recorder he had just bought as a present for Laura. "You will be hearing this within ten days, when Laura goes to Buenos Aires. You will hear the *master's voice*, as they say in English." The tape was to go to some of his Buenos Aires friends—Víctor Oliveros, Kico Salvo, Mario Antelo, and "the powerful" Atilio Talín.

He has started the day, he tells his friends, by going out to buy a newspaper with Windy. He plays a new bandoneon piece, "Pedro y Pedro"—a tribute to two of his bandoneonist predecessors, Pedro Maffia and Pedro Laurenz. He recounts various pieces of news: the upcoming recording of some television music, the songs he is writing with Ferrer, and, most important of all, Laura's recent purchase of a house for them at Punta del Este, a house he himself will not see until November. "My little dog Windy is looking at me," he dictates. "She must be thinking I'm crazy, talking to myself. . . . I'm recording, Windy, that's all I'm doing." A bit later he reports phone calls from Buenos Aires—Oliveros, Salvo, Talín—and expresses pleasure. Laura enters the room. "Just as well I'm not playing the bandoneon, or she would be criticizing me. . . . That's Laura's voice, not one of Windy's barks."

The machine goes on again during dinner and captures a high-spirited jumble of laughter and jokes. Piazzolla identifies his guests one by one, describing José Pons as "a very proper man, terribly Argentine, terribly French." Everyone sings "Happy Birthday" and Windy adds her sharp bark. Horacio Ferrer, allowed "two minutes" by his host, speculates that thirty or forty years later, someone might say, "How I would like to have been there! And we *are* here." They drink champagne. Piazzolla plays his bandoneon, Jairo and Rubén Juárez sing. . . . The recorder clicks off.[56]

The new house in Punta del Este was one of the subjects Piazzolla raised three months later, in the last really substantial letter he was ever to write to his son. "I'm moving all my things to Punta del Este," he told Daniel, "and I'm delighted that I shan't have to see certain faces again. . . . I am really fed up with people and with certain 'friends.' "[57] However we interpret this, it seems certain that Piazzolla was clearing the decks, eager to establish a new routine, one that would give him "space" for his final bid for international acclaim.

The new sexagenarian was busier than most people half his age. Two weeks after the birthday party he flew to Venezuela for a performance of the Punta del Este Suite with the Caracas Chamber Orchestra (2 April). Doubling back to Paris, he recrossed the Atlantic for a concert at the Twelfth Inter-American Musical Festival, held at the Kennedy Center in Washington (10 May). Guillermo Scarabino, a noted Argentine conductor who often included "Tangazo" in his repertory, directed the orchestra. The Bandoneon Concerto "scored the big pop hit of the evening," according to the *Washington Post*, whose critic panned the concerto but noted Piazzolla's body language: "more involved than anything in memory."[58] Scarabino remembers the concert as a great success. A month later Piazzolla wrote to him: "The happiness of playing for the Americans and you is still following me round. . . . I have received the cassette tape. . . . I congratulate you, it sounds just how I like it."[59]

His calendar was crowded well into the autumn of 1981. On 25 June, he appeared on *Le Grand Echiquier* TV program again, with the Lyons Symphony Orchestra, a tribute to the French conductor Serge Baudo. Piazzolla's new orchestral arrangement of "Adiós Nonino," another contribution to the symphonic repertory, was premiered and favorably received by critics.[60] In August he went to Greece, invited there by a new friend, Manos Hadjidhakis—with Mikis Theodorakis the best-known Greek musician of the time. Earlier that summer he had been introduced to Hadjidhakis by Georges Moustaki on the Île Saint Louis. Piazzolla had not quite caught his name. Over dinner he started a long discussion of his own music, asking Moustaki to play some of his records. "He was a bit, just a bit egocentric that day," recalls Moustaki. Not long afterward Piazzolla saw the movie *Topkapi* (with music by Hadjidhakis) on television. (He was an avid TV watcher in Paris.) He phoned Moustaki, asking him if the writer of the sound track was "the gentleman we dined with. He's marvelous. Why didn't you tell me about him?" "Because you didn't let anyone get a word in edgeways," replied Moustaki. Piazzolla and Hadjidhakis—"a sweet man, very affectionate, and very respectul of Astor's talent," as Laura remembers him—would meet again on several occasions. He could never, however, get his tongue round the name of Piazzolla's most famous piece, always referring to it as "Adiós, Los Niños" ("Farewell, Children").

The highlight of the Greek visit in August 1981 was a performance at Heraklion, in Crete, in the ancient Cathedral of St. Mark. Here Piazzolla gave a delightful impromptu lecture (in English) on the history of the tango, cleverly illustrating a sequence of tango styles with bandoneon solos. Susana Rinaldi, the most celebrated female tango singer of her generation, was also on hand. At the end of the talk, Piazzolla thanked Hadjidhakis: "Thanks to you . . . we are able to show our art in Greece. . . . I'll come back to Greece again." (He did, in July 1990.)

September 1981 found him further east, on his first and only visit to Israel. This visit, too, arose out of a meeting earlier that summer, this time with Rubén Kanalenstein, a Uruguayan philosopher living in Israel, who was researching an article on Piazzolla for an Israeli paper. Kanalenstein had greatly relished the conversations, also much admiring Piazzolla's relationship with Laura. Piazzolla expressed strong interest in visiting Israel. Kanalenstein had contacts who made it possible. The concerts (13–14 September) were sold out a month beforehand. Piazzolla appeared with the Israel Symphony Orchestra (under Ariel Levanon) in Tel Aviv's 3,000-seat Mann Auditorium; he played the Bandoneon Concerto, the Three Tangos, and the orchestral version of "Adiós Nonino." He gave a press conference at the Sheraton Hotel, telling reporters that he was now solidly based in Europe again: "I come and go. . . . I go to Buenos Aires every eighteen months or two years."[61] He also gave a few private bandoneon recitals and spent a nostalgic evening with Enrique Barenboim, the former renowned Buenos Aires piano teacher and father of the celebrated pianist and conductor Daniel.[62] Rubén Kanalenstein showed him around the Old City in Jerusalem. "He was so astonished, so admiring of everything," Kanalenstein recalls, "and he felt so many vibrations."

The year's travels were by no means over. He jetted across the Atlantic again, this time to New York, to take part in a Columbus Day gala in Madison Square Garden. Laura saw him off at the airport. The airliner was moving away from the gate—Piazzolla told the story to his friend Albino Gómez in New York—when he suddenly realized that he had packed the wrong scores for the show. He made a scene, was allowed to speak to the captain, and after a good deal of fuss was let off the plane. The right music duly found, he managed to book a place on a later flight. This time, as he settled back in his first class seat, he found himself next to an elderly lady who seemed oddly familiar. It was Greta Garbo, one of the screen idols of his youth. Piazzolla agonized all across the Atlantic. Should he speak to her? He was too shy. And, as always, Garbo wanted to be alone.

The Madison Square Garden gala (Sunday, 11 October 1981) was an impressive splash. Designed to launch the new Spanish-language UNIVISIÓN TV network in the United States, it was transmitted by satellite to twenty Spanish-speaking countries. It was Piazzolla's largest-ever audience, but he was overwhelmingly eclipsed that afternoon by Spanish pop singer Camilo Sesto and Venezuelan soap star (and general Latin American heartthrob) José Luis "Puma" Rodríguez.[63] Diana Piazzolla was asked by the Mexican TELEVISA network (a co-sponsor of UNIVISIÓN) to cover the gala. She flew to New York with her husband and spent three happy days with her father. In his dressing room, she had the thrill of meeting "Puma" himself. She presented her father to Jacobo Zabludowsky, a prominent TELEVISA executive and TV personality, who was also in New York. Piazzolla could not resist the joke, obvious to him, if to nobody else: when Zabludowsky greeted him, as his daughter squirmed, he riposted, "I zalute-ovsky you, too."

Arriving at Ezeiza airport from Paris at the end of October, Piazzolla was grilled by reporters in the usual way. The version of "Libertango" sung by Jamaican singer Grace Jones ("I'll Never See His Face Again") was now in all the world's record stores. "The arrangement isn't mine," he commented. "It's horrible, but I shall make money with it." (Although the record was a runaway success, he seems not to have made much money with it.) He had seen Grace Jones on stage and had been gratified when her frenetic audience demanded an encore of "Libertango."[64]

Now, at long last, he could take a look at his new house. Almost before he had time to get his new bearings, however, he heard that Carlos Hugo Christensen's film *La Intrusa* (with *his* music) had been banned in Argentina. With the help of his friend Fernando Tesouro (who still has Piazzolla's scrawled draft), he got a statement into the press, denouncing the censors. Why, he asked, did they not censor instead "the ninety per cent of television programs that are mediocre and immoral?"[65] Rather characteristically, Jorge Luis Borges, on one of whose stories the movie was based, issued a statement backing the censors.

In December 1981 Piazzolla briefly crossed to Argentina to play with the Quintet at Mar del Plata's Teatro Auditorium (6 December). Nonina listened from a box. Later that month there were two concerts (20–21 December) at the Teatro

Gran Rex in Buenos Aires. "The audience left as if it had just been at a beautiful party," reported *La Nación*.[66] Then it was back across the muddy estuary to Punta del Este for Christmas. Piazzolla was absolutely delighted with his new house. "And nobody knows where it is," he informed a reporter. "We've told the police not to show anyone the way there."[67]

ſharks and Concertos
1981–1985

++ Punta del Este

Cultural Diplomacy—and an Accolade ++

++ Piazzolla-Milva

A Carlos Gardel Opera? ++

> It was a bit like putting the lid on all that stuff about not being a
> prophet in your own country.
> —Astor Piazzolla, on being made an Illustrious Citizen of Buenos Aires
> (*Clarín*, 3 April 1986)

Punta del Este

"Punta," as its people call it for short, is a pleasant spot. Its leafy residential districts, buried in extensive woods of pine, eucalyptus, and mimosa, fan out behind the little point where the River Plate meets the Atlantic Ocean. It had grown spectacularly in the 1970s, with numerous high-rise apartment blocks appearing along the shore, and it was increasingly a favorite vacation spot for well-to-do Argentines, as well as Uruguayans. The summertime Argentine colony was a large one. Piazzolla's house, the Chalet El Casco, on its 3,315 square meter double-lot,* was located in the Barrio del Golf, five or six blocks from the Atlantic beach and a block or two from the fourteenth hole of Punta del Este's oldest golf course, at the Cantegril Country Club. Piazzolla borrowed heavily to buy the house. Its seller, Gustavo Magariños, at that time the Uruguayan ambassador in Belgium, stipulated a recital from Piazzolla as part of the agreement. The debt was paid off by the end of the 1980s.

*It has since been enlarged and renamed "Al Sur."

Piazzolla spent almost all his remaining summers at "Punta." Uruguay became his legal domicile. His affection for the resort was "indescribable," says his *puntaesteño* friend Fernando Tesouro. It was something Piazzolla himself often underscored in interviews. One reason he liked Punta del Este was that it reminded him of the tranquil Mar del Plata of his youth, before it was overwhelmed by "the frenzy of theaters and nightlife, and the restaurants with long lines outside," as he told a reporter in 1986.[1] Its profusion of trees recalled his Manetti grandparents' *quinta*. As Laura tells us, he also appreciated the courteous atmosphere, the way in which the locals greeted him with a happy *"Don Piazzolla, ¿cómo le va?"* ("Don Piazzolla, how *are* you?").

When the Piazzollas were away, the house was looked after by its two servants, Ana Corbo and Federico Fernández. Piazzolla often telephoned them from abroad. If telegrams in French arrived, they phoned him in Paris and spelled out the words, letter by letter. "As a boss, there aren't words to describe him," says Federico. "He was more than a boss, he was a friend," says Ana. Piazzolla was generous to them, buying them a color TV, a refrigerator, a new kitchen, and a car, whose tank he sometimes replenished for their trips to Minas, the inland town from which they had come. He was generous to others, too. The workmen who built him a new garage were rewarded with a barbecue.

"It did him a lot of good to disconnect himself from everything," says Laura. Piazzolla's summer routine was simple. He became very fond of cycling again, taking lengthy morning rides through the tree-lined streets. Laura sometimes met him at his halfway point, and he would merrily ride circles around her. They did a certain amount of moviegoing. If Piazzolla composed, it was during the day—never at night—with his stints at the piano interspersed with turns around the big garden. He was proud of his garden; guests were always taken on an obligatory tour of inspection. He listened to a good deal of music on the large hi-fi in the living room, much of it classical (Beethoven, Bartók, Rubinstein recordings), and, as in Paris, he remained an avid TV watcher—never missing a news bulletin, says Laura. He had no particular liking for the beach, though sometimes he walked there. He was fonder of rambling in the deep woods behind the house, often with Federico. Kico Salvo, also present on such forays, noticed Piazzolla's skill with a slingshot—hitting insects, birds, or fallen fruit with unerring aim. Salvo also marveled at his friend's accuracy at throwing stones and his adeptness at bouncing stones on water—a talent observed forty years earlier by his fellow *marplatense* Roberto Pansera.

There were always several dogs at the Chalet El Casco. Piazzolla loved chasing them round the garden. They were given Christmas presents every year—a whole chicken each. Two of the dogs, Sonny and Zum, stayed at Punta del Este all year round. (Zum was part Dobermann and once dragged Piazzolla twenty yards along the beach before he let go of the leash.) Ritchie, a terrier, was too delicate to travel to Paris and was eventually given to the Buenos Aires jeweler Ricardo Saúl and his wife Marta. They had become friendly with the Piazzollas at the end of the 1970s and later bought an apartment in Punta del Este. Windy, who has appeared in our story already, sometimes went to Paris and sometimes stayed with the Saúls or Laura's friend Lydé Mirelmann in Buenos Aires; it was there in June 1986 that she was summoned to the canine valhalla, an event that provoked an emotional effusion from Piazzolla in a letter to Daniel:

> I am going through a bloody difficult moment (Laura and I are). Our little Windy has died, and I never thought I was going to suffer so. . . . She was almost 10. She gave me a lot of happiness and luck. It's what happens when one of these creatures loves you. It's really a god-awful blow and it will take me a bit to get over this sorrow. If you are kind enough I ask you to call Laura when she reaches Buenos Aires; she is there between 22 and 30 June. Call her (do it for me) and tell her you have heard what happened to Windy. . . . It's not an order. If you want to, fine, if not, we shall remain friends. Tell Diana to finish the book soon, as there is interest in it here.[2]

Windy was replaced by Flora, another Yorkshire terrier. Piazzolla nicknamed her "Mumuki," a name he also gave to Laura—and to a composition of 1986.

Though Piazzolla sometimes patronized local restaurants (like the Lutèce, not far from the house), much of his entertaining was done at home. On days when there were dinner parties, he would busy himself happily working in the kitchen and selecting the wines. He did not often play his bandoneon at these parties. If a musician friend was present, somebody might play the piano. Lydé Mirelmann remembers Piazzolla and Eladia Blázquez improvising piano-bandoneon duets. House guests sometimes played cards, but Piazzolla himself much preferred Scrabble. He always won the fierce arguments that habitually accompany that game. Eladia Blázquez recalls that on these occasions, whenever she implored him, "Let me have my revenge," he invariably refused, making sure that he quit while well ahead.

Many of those who visited the Chalet El Casco were from Buenos Aires: Atilio and Inés Talín, José Bragato, lawyer Víctor Sasson. Víctor Oliveros went three times, Donna Caroll (but not her husband, Oscar López Ruiz) at least once. When television personality (and summertime resident of Punta del Este) "Pipo" Mancera was widowed in the mid-1980s, he was invited to eat with the Piazzollas several times each week. The talented singer and composer Eladia Blázquez and her friend Cristina Justo, who often spent their summers in Punta del Este, were frequent guests at the Chalet. Piazzolla had become friendly with Blázquez in the mid-1970s and his admiration for her work was very strong. He even allowed her to add words to "Adiós Nonino"—something on which he had previously maintained a strict taboo. Very nervous, she played him a cassette of her version: "he listened to it, and began to open his eyes," she remembers, "and I noticed a slight moistness in his eyes . . . and he was giving my words the OK."

> *Adiós Nonino . . .*
> *qué largo sin vos será el camino . . .*
> *y mi adiós . . . a tu amor,*
> *tu tabaco y tu vino . . .*

> Farewell, Nonino . . .
> how long the road will be without you . . .
> and my farewell . . . to your love,
> your tobacco and your wine . . .

Piazzolla did not form a wide circle of new *puntaesteño* friends. He saw little of Carlos Páez Vilaró, for instance, though they sometimes encountered each other when shopping—"ours is a supermarket friendship," jested the affable painter. He saw more of the notary and local politician Fernando Tesouro, who handled many of his transactions, including the purchase of the house and the incorporation of a company ("Libertango Limitada") Piazzolla formed in 1983 after joining SACEM in France. They were by no means strangers. Tesouro, also a tango singer with television appearances and recordings to his credit, had first met Piazzolla in his 676 days. He accompanied the Quintet on a couple of its Brazilian tours in the 1980s. In some ways he acted as one of Piazzolla's "filters"—less effective, he believes, than the "implacable" Laura. Piazzolla sometimes did his press or television interviews at Tesouro's friendly house on Avenida Buenos Aires.

Casual visitors were not encouraged at the Chalet El Casco, but there were always exceptions. In the early summer of 1988, a teenage musician, Marcelo Nisinman who was then learning the bandoneon, delivered a fan letter to the house. Laura phoned Nisinman the next day, asking him to visit. Piazzolla chatted with the youngster for two hours about the greatness of Bach and pianist Glenn Gould, about the need for musicians to *study*. Nisinman wanted to study composition. Piazzolla undertook to find him a good teacher and did so in Buenos Aires a couple of months later. Something of a friendship grew up between Piazzolla and the Nisinman family, whose house in the Caballito district of Buenos Aires he sometimes visited over the next year or two.

Although Piazzolla had now turned his back on Buenos Aires, he still needed a base there. In 1981 he sold Avenida Libertador 4854–13A to his agent, Atilio Talín, and bought a fifth-floor apartment a few blocks away, at 4408. This was less a home than a way station, as Daniel (who almost never went there) describes it. Piazzolla continued to visit Mar del Plata, while Nonina was still alive, as often as he could. Later on, he still spent occasional weekends there, sometimes with Laura, sometimes with someone from the old *barra*—Víctor Oliveros, perhaps, or Kico Salvo, who had an apartment in the resort.

What "Punta" gave Piazzolla, above all, was the chance to fish for shark. During his first summer there, he went to the waterfront and sought out Dante Rinaldi, who ran fishing trips for visitors. Dante, the son of a former mayor of Punta del Este, had plied his trade for twenty years, and was thoroughly experienced. He was fully booked up when Piazzolla first approached him and at first could only take him out with another client. Piazzolla did not like this and eventually paid Dante to take him fishing alone. His total haul with Dante was between 200 and 300 sharks. He had not often fished for shark from a boat before. Dante taught him how to entice the sharks on to the fishing lines and how to play the lines. He was an excellent pupil—one of the very best, Dante later declared.[3] They normally went out for six or seven hours, three times a week, making for the waters around the Isla de Lobos, five miles offshore, where sharks of all kinds were drawn by a large sea lion colony. Piazzolla often laid up to four lines. The captured sharks were filleted for consumption by the Chalet El Casco dogs, and their jawbones festooned the garden.

Dante's client quickly became his friend. He was quite able to cope with the physical demands of the sport. "Astor was never tired. Never," Dante remembers. "Afterward . . . he *was* a bit lame." Dante was aware that people sometimes thought Piazzolla unfriendly, but he himself always found him "a calm fellow, a joker, yes, but calm." Piazzolla undoubtedly used Dante as a confidant. "I have money to live on," he once told him, "and I want to come here to Punta del Este for good, to compose here." This was purest wishful thinking. "I am in love with Laura," he said, more than once. "Laura is my love." Whenever there were tensions in the household, Dante was certainly aware of them. Piazzolla was generous to him: he bought him sonar equipment and new reels from Japan. He did, however, have a minor cross to bear on his fishing trips. Dante's burly assistant, Kito Albornoz, could never get his name right, always calling him "Castor" Piazzolla. One of Albornoz's jobs was to drench Castor with bucketfuls of water, to cool him down in the fierce summertime heat.

They usually set out in the morning, in one of Dante's two boats—the *Dante A. F.* (the "A. F." stood for his son Alfredo Francisco) or the *Renata* (its name when bought; Dante, like any true sailor, knew better than to change it). Piazzolla often asked Dante to brew some *mate*—"How he loved taking *mate!*"—and more often than not, a shark would turn up as he did so. Though highly respectful of Dante's expertise, Piazzolla sometimes affected superior insight. On a very rare winter visit to Punta del Este, he asked Dante to take him out, telling him he had discovered that sharks liked cold water. Dante knew this to be untrue. They caught a very large conger eel that day, but no sharks.

Shark fishing seems to have answered a deep existential need for Piazzolla. "All the rages I have inside me—I take my revenge on a shark," he told a reporter in 1983, adding that he sometimes swam from the boat, even though Dante told him this was crazy.[4] "Astor, how *can* you do it?" Eladia Blázquez asked him one morning, when menacing storm clouds were gathering over the Atlantic. "I'd die of fright." "No, no, for this one shouldn't be afraid," replied Piazzolla. He even claimed to derive musical inspiration from his trips: "Sometimes I think out a complete work," he told Diana. "Until I feel a shark is near."[5]

Laura sometimes went with him and fished for bass. When she did not, she dropped him off at the waterfront, leaving him happily singing an Italian nonsense-song of his own invention. When she collected him at the end of the day, their ritual was to pick up a newspaper from a kiosk on Avenida Gorlero (Punta del Este's main street) before going home. Piazzolla's friends were sometimes invited along. Some, Víctor Sasson among them, always refused. Eladia Blázquez only went on shorter trips. Fernando Tesouro, no great enthusiast, went a few times, never failing to observe his friend's euphoria on catching a shark. Pablo Ziegler, whenever he went, found himself involved in hours of conversation—plans, worries, "record companies, producers, agents." José Bragato contented himself with catching smaller fish but was impressed by Piazzolla's stamina: "He had the soul of a sailor; while I was vomiting, he was eating." (Piazzolla was always delighted when his friends were seasick.) On one occasion, Bragato remembers, Piazzolla landed a variety of shark with two sexual members. He struck it on the head with a stick, exclaiming, "Look, I only have one, and it's no use to me, and this fellow has two!"[6]

One of Piazzolla's most regular companions on his forays to the Isla de Lobos was Daniel Rabinovich; he was a member of Les Luthiers, an Argentine group combining music and humor in its shows, and very popular all over Latin America. Rabinovich had vacationed at Punta del Este since boyhood. He had first heard Piazzolla at 676, and first met him across a dinner table in São Paulo in 1975. He was already a keen fisherman, but shark fishing was new to him and Piazzolla duly instructed him. On their expeditions there were long conversations, "or rather monologues by Astor," says Rabinovich, who relished the experience. They talked about "the tango, about singers, travel episodes, moments onstage ... about Debussy and Ravel." Rabinovich was twenty years younger than Piazzolla and larger all round, but he sensed that Piazzolla "had triple my strength."

Kico Salvo once asked Piazzolla why the sharks had to die. "These creatures are bad," said Piazzolla, "so I have no remorse in killing them. They're bad." The subject was, however, one on which he could be defensive. Nicholas Tozer, then of the *Buenos Aires Herald*, recalls a summer afternoon in the late 1980s. He heard a commotion at the reception desk and found Piazzolla protesting vehemently about a recently published article on the evils of shark fishing. "He delivered me such a philippic," Tozer remembers. Piazzolla's fury was only abated when a young *Herald* employee approached him and said: "Maestro, can I ask you for an autograph?"

Cultural Diplomacy—and an Accolade

Among Piazzolla's tasks during his first summer at the Chalet El Casco was the composition of "Le Grand Tango," a ten-minute piece for cello and piano, dedicated to Mstislav Rostropovich, to whom he sent the score. Rostropovich had not heard of Piazzolla at the time and did not look seriously at the music for several years.[7] Written in ternary form, the work bears all Piazzolla's hallmarks: tight construction, melodic inspiration, rhythmic complexity, all apparent from the fierce cello scrapes at the beginning. Its largely tender mood, notably on display in the cello's snaking melodic line in the reflective middle section, becomes more profoundly complex in its emotional range toward the end. With its intricate juxtapositions of driving rhythms and heart-rending tags of tune, it is just about the most exciting music Piazzolla ever wrote, a masterpiece. Piazzolla was eager for Rostropovich to play it, but the chance did not come for eight years. Rostropovich, having looked at the music, and "astounded by the great talent of Astor," decided he would include it in a concert. He made some changes in the cello part and wanted Piazzolla to hear them before he played the piece. Accordingly, in April 1990, he rehearsed it with Argentine pianist Susana Mendelievich in a room at the Teatro Colón, and Piazzolla gently coached the maestro in tango style—"Yes, tan-go, tan-go, tan-go." The two men took an instant liking to one another.[8] It was, says Mendelievich, "as if Rostropovich had played tangos all his life." More recently, cellist Yo-Yo Ma has described "Le Grand Tango" as one of his "favorite pieces of music," praising its "inextricable rhythmic sense . . . total freedom, passion, ecstasy."

But Piazzolla also needed his rest. In December, a few days before going to Buenos Aires for the Gran Rex concerts, he suffered a partial loss of vision, almost certainly from a transitory cerebrovascular ischemia. Although he recovered his full sight almost immediately, the episode was a sobering one, reminding him that he could not take his health for granted. He did very little for the remainder of the summer. In early April 1982, he and Laura made a brief trip to Paraguay, where they underwent a civil marriage ceremony, something they had already done in Paris.

April 1982 was an especially dramatic month. It brought Argentina's first foreign war in over a century. Piazzolla, like many of his compatriots, was initially enthusiastic about his country's repossession of the Falkland (Malvinas) Islands. He donated one of his bandoneons to the war effort in the course of a television marathon.[9] A day after the seizure of the islands, an Argentine force of 500 overwhelmed a handful of British Marines on faraway South Georgia. Inspired by this gallant feat of arms, Piazzolla dedicated a newly written piece to the victorious Argentine commander, Captain Alfredo Astiz, and his men. Piazzolla was blissfully unaware that Astiz had taken on some peculiarly odious roles during the Process and Dirty War. His friend and doctor Marcos Asensio, hearing of the dedication, refused to go out to dinner with him in protest. Piazzolla struck the piece from his repertory, but he did not throw it away; he used it in the music he later wrote for the movie *L'Exil de Gardel*.[10]

The Quintet was now about to leave on another European tour. Piazzolla wanted to give his musicians a rehearsal in some public venue—a practice he would make standard for the rest of the 1980s. With entertainment at a low ebb because of the war, the Teatro Regina was available. Atilio Talín suggested to Piazzolla that he invite tango singer Roberto "El Polaco" Goyeneche to appear with him. Piazzolla feverishly wrote some new pieces for the old and sadly diminished tango veteran to sing, and enlisted Horacio Ferrer and Eladia Blázquez in the effort. Goyeneche probably never even looked at the material he was sent. He arrived at the first rehearsal in a visibly nervous state. Piazzolla took in the situation at a glance, and then, in a gesture of great sensitivity, went up to the singer. "Polaco, don't worry. . . . What do *you* want to do? Your own stuff? Whatever you want, 'La Balada...' " The repertory chosen was an entirely traditional one; however, when singing the Discépolo classic "Cambalache" (1935), Goyeneche slipped in an improvised allusion to British prime minister Margaret Thatcher, then being picturesquely vilified in the Argentine press. The audience loved it.

Atilio Talín remembers the Regina shows as "the success of the season." They certainly emptied Caño 14, Buenos Aires's most famous *tanguería*, it even had to close down entirely one evening, as Jorge Göttling recalls. (It closed down for good soon afterward.) Kico Salvo, for his part, could never forget the sight of Goyeneche in the cold dressing room, in shirt sleeves, drinking glass after glass of the cheap whiskey he favored. But Goyeneche's confidence grew during the two weeks at the Regina. "You know what worries me, Roberto?" asked Piazzolla after the final show. "If you and I die, there'll be no real tango people left."[11]

The European Community was supporting Britain in the South Atlantic war, while Brazil, in line with its traditional foreign policy, remained resolutely on the sidelines. As a piece of "cultural diplomacy," the Argentine foreign ministry (where Piazzolla's old friend Mario Corcuera Ibáñez now worked as director of cultural affairs) invited the Quintet to undertake concerts in Italy, Portugal, and Brazil. Since the Quintet was about to leave for Europe anyway, with shows arranged in Germany, France, and Spain, Piazzolla accepted the proposal.

The war was over by the time the musicians reached Rome for the start of the cultural-diplomatic offensive, which is chronicled with exceptional vividness and humor in Oscar López Ruiz's memoir.[12] The campaign began badly. The musicians were lodged in a low-grade hotel near the Piazza di Spagna. The Argentine cultural attaché arrived late to meet them. Piazzolla gave her a severe tongue-lashing. At the concert in the Teatro Sixtina, the Argentine ambassador asked Piazzolla if there was anything he needed. "Yes," he replied, "a cultural attaché."

After its appearance at Milan's Teatro Lirico, where the audience was thin but enthusiastic,[13] Aldo Pagani enticed the Quintet into a well-paid gig at Santa Margherita near Portofino. Here Pablo Ziegler found that the piano was woefully inadequate. Pagani resorted to some hands-on management. "Come with me," he ordered Ziegler and López Ruiz; "we are going to get a piano!" and the three of them disappeared. Piazzolla grew more and more worried. Suddenly Ziegler reappeared, riding a noisy motorcycle into the hall with a trailer holding a baby grand—a surreal prelude to a successful concert.

In Portugal, the next stage of the journey, the Argentine cultural attaché gave the musicians proper attention, putting them in a first-class hotel and taking them sightseeing in Lisbon and Estoril. But here there was another setback: Piazzolla severely injured one of his fingers on a rusty nail in his bathroom. At a dinner that night, the Argentine ambassador said he supposed that Piazzolla would want to return immediately to Argentina, given his incapacitating injury. "No way!" declared Piazzolla. "Tomorrow we shall play, and we will play better than ever." He had not visited Lisbon before and was told not to expect a large crowd. An audience of 5,000 held him to five encores.

The final cultural-diplomatic target was Brazil. When the Quintet's plane reached Rio de Janeiro on 3 July, the entire Brazilian population was glued to television, watching the Brazil-Argentina game in the 1982 World Cup, then unfolding in Spain (where the Quintet had played a week or two earlier). By the time the connecting flight reached Brasilia, Brazil had won. The embassy official who met the Quintet decided to take them to the hotel in a car without diplomatic markings, lest Brazilian euphoria be turned against the visiting Argentines. The concert at the Teatro Nacional the next day, however, passed off without incident, and the Quintet flew on to São Paulo, arriving on the day of the Brazil-Italy match (5 July). This time Brazil lost, in a particularly exciting game. "Viva Italia!" shouted Piazzolla, over and over again, from the window of his hotel room. "I rarely saw him amusing himself so much," says López Ruiz. He was almost voiceless at the following day's concert. So ended his contribution to Argentine cultural diplomacy. He never ceased, however, to be a more effective ambassador than most diplomats. "My musicians and I understand very well," he said soon afterward, "the commitment we have to go out into the world and say 'We are Argentines.' "[14]

The rest of 1982 had an altogether more conventional pattern, Piazzolla dividing his time between the Quintet and his symphonic work. In July he was in Mendoza (en route to Chile, to attend some concerts that included his music) to perform the Bandoneon Concerto with the Córdoba University Symphony under Maestro Scarabino, to wild acclaim.[15] One other appearance of these middle months of 1982 deserves to be singled out. On Tuesday, 17 August, in Córdoba, a crowd of teenagers, who had the right under recent provincial legislation of free entry to the gallery of the San Martín theater, were unable to get in, as the gallery seats were already taken. Piazzolla saw to it that they were given empty seats in other parts of the theater,[16] a gesture that was loudly applauded.

At the start of October, Piazzolla was in Puerto Rico, performing the Bandoneon Concerto with the local orchestra, conducted yet again by Scarabino.[17] Soon afterward there was another sweep through Brazil, and then something of a landmark: the Quintet's first visit to Japan for a few concerts in Tokyo, though on this occasion they did not visit the Japanese provinces. At the end of November, Piazzolla made his first and only trip to Cuba—for the tenth festival of the Nueva Trova musical movement, with Alberto Cortez as vocalist.[18] From Havana he sent an ecstatic postcard to Diana in Mexico: "We had a FABULOUS success. ... They ALL love us a lot." Che Guevara's father, he told her, had been to hear them.[19] Atilio Talín, who was with Piazzolla on this trip, recalls that his real reactions to Cuba were a good deal less euphoric and that he was not at all impressed by his reception from the Cuban authorities. A Cuban reporter, gratified by Piazzolla's description of his music as "revolutionary," asked him: "Do you express in your music what you cannot say openly in Argentina?" To prevent a provocative answer from Piazzolla, Talín jumped in and cut off the questioning.

In early December, Piazzolla was back in Buenos Aires, where he summoned the press to meet a young German film director, Peter Keglevic, for whose film *Bella Donna* he had agreed to write the music. The two of them showed a video of extracts from the film.[20] Piazzolla wrote the music over the next two weeks at the Chalet El Casco, where he quickly settled back into his summer routine, though he could not entirely avoid being hunted down by reporters. One of them found him on a motorcycle in a leafy street, wearing a cap and Bermuda shorts, and looking well tanned.[21]

In mid-December 1982 he made a quick trip to Mar del Plata to see his mother, who was now seriously ailing. He and the Quintet also performed in front of the Obelisk on the Avenida 9 de Julio, one of Buenos Aires's supreme urban symbols, a recital recorded by both Swiss and French television.[22] This was a brief interruption in the Punta del Este summer. A much more serious one, though not unexpected, occurred soon afterward. On the last day of 1982, Nonina died.

She was eighty-five. After Nonino's death she had opened a kiosk selling toys and stationery. In 1973 she had sold the Calle Alberti property, buying a small apartment at Calle Avellaneda 3013. One of her friends, Juan Mastropasqua, tells us that she was "in no way aware that she had a genius as her son" until her later years, when "she began to be, not exactly a personality ... but being Piazzolla's mother was something that carried weight." "The only thing I reproach him for," she said in 1972, "is that he still hasn't devoted a tango to me."[23] He never did. There is no "Adiós Nonina." Well into her eighties, Nonina had continued her habitual long walks. Her spirits always rose remarkably when Astor came to visit her—usually twice a month when he was within reach. In her final year her mind began to wander. "Have they let you out of prison?" she once asked her sister Argentina—who gamely replied, "Yes, a little while back." In her last months, her Bertolami nieces took her in, her nephew Egnio displaying particular solicitude. Egnio's wife Nelly, who often stayed up late to chat with her, found herself admiring Nonina's merry character and prodigious memory.

Argentina's husband, good-hearted "Uncle Ercolino," took a major hand in the funeral arrangements. Daniel Piazzolla had arrived with his wife, Lalla, and their two children to spend New Year's Eve with his in-laws at Batán, a small town near Mar del Plata. He had often paid his grandmother a visit on New Year's Day. This year he had to go to her funeral. Uncle Ercolino was in floods of tears. Piazzolla and Laura flew in from Punta del Este to attend the interment (2 January 1983) in the Piazzolla family vault. They then flew straight back to Punta del Este,[24] the briefness of their visit arousing unfavorable comment from some of the relatives. Piazzolla was, however, deeply touched by the care his cousins had given his mother. To Egnio he wrote: "I shall never forget your love for Nonina and the care she received. . . . If I had had a brother, I would have liked him to be you."[25]

On 11 March 1983, his sixty-second birthday, Piazzolla played his Bandoneon Concerto at the opening concert of the Fourth International Guitar Festival at Liège, Belgium, with the Liège Philharmonic Orchestra under a young Argentine conductor, Alicia Farace. A year earlier, with the Antwerp Philharmonic, she had conducted the European premiere of "Tangazo." She paid Piazzolla a visit in his room at the Brussels Hilton to discuss the concert, and she persuaded him to play his tango "Decarísimo," which put a knot in her throat. She remembers the performance itself as being like a "fairytale."

> Throughout the concert I really had to guess at what he wanted. It was a challenge. He was truly inspired, his sound was rich, of an incredible beauty, with sublime touches. We exchanged conspiratorial glances which I still remember vividly. I think it was there that I learned what the word "share" could mean. To share a stage with *him*!

There had earlier been a guitar recital by Cacho Tirao. It was the first time he had worked alongside Piazzolla since 1971, and he was impressed and gratified to see that he was now "a musician famous throughout Europe."

Meanwhile, a spectacular triumph awaited him at home: a concert at the Teatro Colón (11 June 1983). René Aure, who helped organize the event, recalls that the management of the Colón took some persuading. But the significance of the concert was certainly not lost on Argentines. One magazine compared it to the accolades heaped on Johann Strauss the Younger in Vienna a century earlier. It may have been, as *La Nación* put it, an "atypical night" at the Colón, but it was unquestionably "Piazzolla's apotheosis," the final triumph of his "great contemporary chamber music." An ad hoc nonet joined forces with the Colón orchestra, under Pedro Ignacio Calderón, to play in the first half the "Concierto de Nácar," and in the second, the Bandoneon Concerto and the orchestral arrangement of "Adiós Nonino." The last brought the house down: "it seemed as if the Colón was going to collapse," as one report has it. Piazzolla won a ten-minute standing ovation and had to take five bows. The future ballet star Maximiliano Guerra, then aged sixteen, and present in the theater, was overwhelmed. Had it been a movie, he thought, "they would have shown light coming down from heaven." Afterward a large crowd acclaimed Piazzolla in the street—"autographs, congratulations, applause."[26]

Piazzolla's next venue was more intimate. In July the Quintet played at La Capilla, formerly a Syrian-Orthodox chapel, in Calle Suipacha. "If you install a salamander and baptize it Pantaleón," Piazzolla told Lino Patalano, the impresario who refurbished La Capilla, "I'll do the winter season for you." Patalano complied with the request. A reporter asked Piazzolla how, after his 3,500-person audience at the Colón, he liked playing to a mere 200 people. "It's enough that people respect me," he said. "There is nothing nicer than a stage, a music stand, musicians."[27] At one of these shows Piazzolla paid a graceful compliment to his old collaborator Roberto Di Filippo, who had come to hear him: "a great bandoneonist, technically the best I've known in my life." They had never lost touch. Di Filippo and his wife Ofelia often attended Piazzolla's birthday dinners at the Félix Restaurant. After one of them, Piazzolla proposed that he and Roberto form a bandoneon duo for a two-month tour. Di Filippo declined: "No, you'd keep giving me the score only half an hour beforehand."

Once again it was time for the international touring season—first Brazil, then Europe again. The Brazilian tour—Rio, São Paulo, Santos, Belo Horizonte, Vitoria, Porto Alegre, and elsewhere—got off to a bad start. Through some oversight, the impresario had failed to secure the proper visas, and the musicians were almost stopped from taking the stage. Fortunately, a Piazzolla fan in the Brazilian government was able to arrange a meeting with the relevant authorities: after what Piazzolla described as "two thousand cups of coffee," they found a way to let the tour go on.[28]

The European tour—Germany, Austria, Italy, France—took place against the backdrop of the imminent elections in Argentina. These were the first democratic elections in ten years, a contest between the Radical Party candidate, Raúl Alfonsín, and his respectable Peronist adversary, Italo Luder. Everybody expected

Luder to win. On the flight up the Atlantic, Piazzolla announced pontifically that Alfonsín would win 52 percent of the vote, a piece of instant political science greeted with instant scorn. Piazzolla insisted: 52 percent *exactly*. The prediction was forgotten over the next few weeks as the Quintet did the rounds of theaters like Vienna's Konzerthaus, the Palazzo dei Congressi in Lugano, and the Théâtre Musical de Paris-Châtelet. The Châtelet concert was held on 30 October 1983—election day in Argentina. Early next morning, Oscar López Ruiz and Pablo Ziegler, who were sharing a room, were waked by Piazzolla, who threw himself on Ziegler's bed, and shouted: "Alfonsín won with 52 percent of the votes! Wake up, you idiots, Alfonsín has *won*!"[29] Back in Argentina, on 11 December, the Quintet was one of the groups that played at the inauguration gala at the Teatro Colón. It was, Piazzolla said, "something I had never done before: play for the president of my country."[30]

Piazzolla-Milva

Early in 1984 the Quintet appeared at the Teatro Roxy in Mar del Plata. Mar del Plata, Piazzolla told reporters, was a sadder place for him now "because Nonina is no longer here."[31] There was, however, a joy awaiting him there. His daughter Diana had now returned from her eight-year Mexican exile; she traveled to Mar del Plata to greet him. A reporter found the two of them together and observed Piazzolla in a benignly tolerant mood. "Everyone does what they want," he pointed out. "She asked me once: 'Papa, would you ever stop playing the bandoneon?'" That, of course, was unthinkable, so he told her that in her position, he too "wouldn't stop being a Peronist."[32]

Not long after this touching reunion, he flew to Rome to record the music he had written for Marco Bellocchio's film *Enrico IV* (released later in 1984), a screen adaptation of Luigi Pirandello's classic play. Bellocchio was pleased with the music, believing that Piazzolla found "a very strong point of contact" with the character of the deluded King Henry IV.[33] The highlight of the score is undoubtedly "Oblivion," with its almost unbearably nostalgic tune—one of Piazzolla's true gems, though one that is perilously close to schmaltz.

After the recording stint, Piazzolla went to Monte Carlo for a concert, attended by Prince Rainier, and then did a TV appearance with Milva. This was appropriate, for 1984 and 1985 were to be the years of their extraordinary collaboration, a collaboration that gave a definite and perhaps the decisive boost to Piazzolla's European fortunes. As it developed 1984 was really the key year in his international takeoff. Milva's reputation among European artists was at its peak. Her brilliant repertory covered Bertold Brecht, Luciano Berio, and Mikis Theodorakis as well as spirituals and protest songs. She and Piazzolla had a high respect for one another. Piazzolla described her in good Argentine fashion as a *fuera de serie* and as "an incredible human being."[34] "No Argentine," he declared, "sings the 'Balada para un loco' better than . . . Milva"[35] (was this perhaps a sideswipe at Amelita?). For her part Milva remembers Piazzolla as *molto serio*, as having given her a "musical richness that will remain with me all my life." She invited Piazzolla and the Quintet to join forces with her in March 1984 on a tour of Germany, Switzerland, Austria, and Holland. In Germany alone there were about thirty shows, Piazzolla calculating that audiences totaled 200,000 people.[36] The musicians could not resist ribbing Piazzolla about Milva's presence. He was once again running a typical old-fashioned tango band with vocalist in tow, they told him. The joke amused him at first, but he soon wearied of it.[37]

The pace after the first tour with Milva was absolutely grueling. Between March and the end of November 1984, Piazzolla did more than 150 concerts, which was to be roughly his average for the rest of the decade. The musicians (minus Console, who stayed in Europe) had a two-week break in Argentina, and then started another European tour—Italy, Germany, Holland, Belgium, Austria, and Switzerland. In July the Quintet made its first incursion into Canada, for the Montreal International Jazz Festival and for two concerts at a festival in Quebec City. From that time on, jazz festivals became regular dates in the Quintet's annual calendar. At the Spectrum in Montreal, the audience of 15,000 tittered when it first caught sight of Piazzolla's bandoneon, but it was swiftly dazzled. A critic for *Le Soleil de Québec* reported that he had never heard a more enthusiastic ovation at the Quebec festival. Charles Dutoit, the rising conductor of the Montreal Symphony, asked Piazzolla to write a Concerto for Quintet and Orchestra. Piazzolla promised he would, though he never did.[38]

Over the next few weeks, the Quintet swept through Mexico and Central America (a dozen or so concerts), with Raúl Lavié as vocalist. This was Lavié's only regular appearance with Piazzolla. On his forty-seventh birthday (22 August), Lavié found himself singing with Piazzolla in a stadium in Mexico City—the concert hastily transferred from the florid Palacio de Bellas Artes, which had proved too small to meet the demand for seats. Lavié was with the Quintet again in November for a ten-day, fifteen-concert tour of Japan—Tokyo, Osaka, Nagoya. Like most of the musicians, he has somewhat blurred recollections of Japan, where neither the schedule nor the language barrier allowed much off-duty tourism, though the concerts were a success. It was on this particular Japanese trip that Oscar López Ruiz decided to quit. Alluding to his various run-ins with Laura, he told Piazzolla: "You have the right to be with whoever takes your fancy, but the logical thing is for me to go." And go he did, at the end of the tour.

Piazzolla's division of time between the Quintet and his symphonic work became more evident than ever during these months. He himself was constantly darting to and fro. Back briefly in Buenos Aires in June, he played his Bandoneon Concerto with the National Symphony Orchestra under Juan Carlos Zorzi (13 June), then almost immediately flew to Chile, to hear a performance of his "Serie de tangos sinfónicos."[39] After the Canadian visit, he took a short break in Punta del Este, largely to write film music for Lautaro Murúa's *Cuarteles de invierno* (released in September 1984) and to put the finishing touches to his new "Tango Suite" for two guitars. This was intended for the talented Brazilian brothers Sergio and Odair Assad. He had met them the previous October in José Pons's apartment in Paris, when they nervously played him their arrangement of "Escolaso" from the Suite Troileana. A reviewer of the Assads' recording of the "Tango Suite" [1985] described the work as "extraordinarily individual and expressive music" from "a Szymanowski of the Pampas."[40] The Assads themselves regard the suite as "a landmark in the history of guitar duos."

After his Uruguayan break, Piazzolla was soon crisscrossing the map again. Back in Italy, before the Mexican trip, he took part in a "Piazzolla Week" at Nervi—another performance of the Bandoneon Concerto, the La Scala ballet dancing to his music. It was a distinct sign of the European recognition that was now coming his way. But the absolute highlight of this busy year was his series of appearances with Milva at the Théâtre Bouffes du Nord in Paris in September. Micheline Rozan, Peter Brook's partner at the theater, had heard Milva and Piazzolla in Germany and had told Milva: "I want Milva and Piazzolla together."[41] Filippo Crivelli, the Italian *metteur-en-scène* of the show, found working with Piazzolla an absolute delight. He was impressed by his "simplicity, accessibility, *humility*." Piazzolla's only request was for something on which he could rest the leg on which he played his bandoneon. An austere cube of black wood was duly made. He took it on many later tours.

Micheline Rozan knew her business. The shows were the talk of the autumn season in Paris. *L'Express* compared Piazzolla to "one of those nice big dogs that always seem happy to see you again," and Milva to "a red-brown panther." *Le Figaro* described Milva as "the creature of some forbidden dream" and thought the show a good lesson for "unconditional disco admirers"—two hours with rhythm without percussion.[42] There was minimal amplification. "Piazzolla is very strict on that point," Milva told an Italian reporter.[43] The Bouffes du Nord stint had its comic moments. Milva liked moving around from one gig to another and hated having to appear in the same place night after night. She took out her frustration on the musicians. Fernando Suárez Paz retaliated by teasing her about her Spanish: "Ah, Milva, tonight you're singing 'Los Pájaros Podridos?' ("The Rotten Birds") "What? 'Isn't it 'Perdidos'? ("Lost Birds")" "No. 'Podridos.' " Piazzolla was not very amused.

Among his final engagements in 1984 was an appearance in Toulouse, where the municipality had organized a lavish tango festival, with a galaxy of Argentine musicians on hand: bandoneonist Osvaldo Piro, singer Susana Rinaldi, the Paris-based Cuarteto Cedrón, and Osvaldo Pugliese's band. Here, at the Théâtre du Capitole on 29 November, Piazzolla played with the Toulouse Chamber Orchestra, receiving "persistent and warm applause." They repeated the concert a few days later at Albi. While in Toulouse, Piazzolla announced that after a "long rest" in Punta del Este, he would be returning to his Paris base. As he explained:

> Paris is rather like the navel of the universe, artistically and geographically. I could play every day for Argentines, but that base is too distant to be coming and going all the time on marathon journeys. Here you can give a concert in one capital city and do another the next day in another capital, without great effort. This moving around gives me new experiences, and it allows me the indispensable artistic enrichment to go on advancing.[44]

In January 1985 Piazzolla had a small operation on his right hand, from which all sense of touch had suddenly gone. Technically, he was suffering from carpal tunnel syndrome. He was treated by Dr. Ignacio Uriburu in Buenos Aires. The doctor's receptionist asked his occupation. His name did not register with her. His modest answer—"musician"—greatly impressed Dr. Uriburu. Piazzolla told Uriburu that he was due to play in Vienna in two weeks' time. Uriburu doubted whether the hand would be back to normal in under a month. It was, however, and in due course Uriburu received a telegram: CONCERT A SUCCESS. HAND A MARVEL. Piazzolla saw Dr. Uriburu again a few months later and had a second small operation, this time on an elbow.

He celebrated his sixty-fourth birthday in Paris—he and Laura were now at 30, rue de Saint Louis en l'Ile. A day or two later he went to Liège, to the Fifth International Guitar Festival, to premiere (15 March) his newly written, sixteen-minute Concerto for Bandoneon, Guitar and Strings. Cacho Tirao was the guitarist; the orchestra was the Liège Philharmonic under Cuban musician Leo Brouwer, whom Piazzolla much admired. The work was performed a second time soon afterward at the Church of St. Étienne du Mont in Paris, with Roberto Aussel as guitarist.[45] At the South American premiere, in Montevideo in December, the guitarist was the Uruguayan Baltasar Benítez, with whom Piazzolla gave a number of recitals around that time. Many listeners find this the most satisfying of Piazzolla's concertos. The balance between the two leading instruments is well maintained throughout; the melodic material is first-rate. According to Pablo Ziegler, it was partly inspired by the music of William Walton. Its composition was rapid: Cacho Tirao had nervously telephoned Piazzolla at Punta del Este in January to ask how it was progressing, and he received the score within a week. Another new work premiered at Liège was "L'Histoire du Tango," a set of four guitar-flute pieces, surely one of Piazzolla's most entrancing "serious" compositions. Each piece evokes a setting and a period in tango history: a bordello (1900), a café (1920), a nightclub (1940), a concert hall of the near future (1990). The work became very popular among the world's flute-guitar duos over the next few years.

Early in April, Piazzolla joined forces with Milva for another swing through Italy. This was Antonio Agri's tour as part of the second Quintet. "You've been able to . . . harvest something of what you sowed," Piazzolla told him. The "enthusiastic applause" reported at the Bologna concert on 12 April[46] was, as usual, echoed up and down the peninsula. Héctor Console noticed, however, that the Quintet usually got *more* applause than Milva.

Piazzolla was naturally eager to reproduce his European triumphs with Milva in Buenos Aires. There had been much curiosity about her there after the intriguing reports of the Bouffes du Nord shows. On 6 June she and Piazzolla appeared in a lavish spectacle at the Teatro Ópera. The press duly noted Milva's bare feet on stage, her "feline movements and black lamé dress." Her reception, though warm, was not absolutely overwhelming. "In the Piazzolla+Milva equation," commented *Clarín*, "Piazzolla goes on mattering more to us."[47]

A Carlos Gardel Opera?

The Quintet's second European tour of 1985 took in a new territory. On the European mainland Piazzolla's name was by now almost a household word. Across the water in England he was hardly known at all. London, in so many ways the world's musical capital since World War II, was shamefully ignorant of tango music of any kind. The Quintet made its London debut at the end of June, at the filled-to-capacity Almeida Theatre, Islington. "Electrifying music . . . the audience roared their approval," reported *The Guardian*. "It was like going to inspect an interesting hillock," wrote a critic ignorant of Piazzolla, "and uncovering an erupting volcano."[48]

While in London, Piazzolla was the guest at a round table broadcast by the BBC Latin American Service. Author Simon Collier was one of those who took part. At one point that afternoon, Piazzolla took Collier to one side and asked him for a favor. His great ambition, he explained, was to write an opera (in tango idiom) based on the life of Carlos Gardel. He very much wanted a libretto in English, and if possible from Tim Rice, the co-author (with Andrew Lloyd-Webber) of *Evita*. Would Collier act as a go-between? Collier agreed. (By coincidence he and Rice had been schoolmates many years earlier.) Rice told Collier that he felt honored by the suggestion but was unable to help, as he was then working on *Chess*, a new musical of his own. The opportunity slipped by.

The "Gardel opera" was to loom large over the remaining years of Piazzolla's active life. He probably first talked about it in Paris in 1984 with journalist Edmundo Eichelbaum. They had known each other for many years. (Eichelbaum's wife had been a school friend of Dedé's.) He certainly mentioned the idea to Plácido Domingo, with whom the Quintet appeared on *Le Grand Échiquier* TV program in 1984, at Domingo's invitation. As Piazzolla recalled, the tenor showed instant interest in the lead role. "Man, if I don't do it," he said, "nobody will do it."[49] Over the next few years the two men occasionally met and exchanged a few words at concerts. Domingo still regrets "not having had the luck of working with him more, and getting to know him better."

Piazzolla entrusted the libretto to his friend the songwriter Pierre Philippe, who in due course produced the draft for a four- or five-hour opera. Philippe's impression is that Piazzolla "wanted to do something very adventurous. . . . There was to be an evocation of Carlos Gardel in the cinema, an evocation of New York in 1930," and so on. Philippe quickly became a great admirer of Gardel. In 1987 he paid a Christmas visit to Punta del Este, hoping to work on the opera, though nothing much got done. In Buenos Aires, Piazzolla's agent Atilio Talín showed him Gardel's house and a few turn-of-the-century tenements of the kind where Gardel had grown up.

The next phase of this project was a commission from the Philadelphia-based American Music Theater Festival. Its artistic director, Eric Salzman, had spent time in Buenos Aires some years earlier and had studied with Alberto Ginastera. He knew the tango world and liked Piazzolla's music. He went to see Piazzolla in New York and found him delightful to deal with—"courtly, old world, charming," speaking an instantly recognizable "New York Italian" English. Salzman was much less pleased with Philippe's libretto, which he found "absolutely unstageable." He gave it to the Cuban-born American dramatist Eduardo Machado to rework in English. Piazzolla did not altogether like the results. Although there were further attempts at reworking and several phone calls from Salzman to Piazzolla (some to Punta del Este), the Philadelphia scheme ran aground. Piazzolla continued to pin his hopes on Philippe's libretto.

Piazzolla wound up his 1985 European season with a performance of the Punta del Este Suite and the Bandoneon and Guitar Concerto with Roberto Aussel and the Toulouse Chamber Orchestra at the Châtelet theater in Paris.[50] A day or two later he flew home to Argentina, where, on 2 December, he received the title of Illustrious Citizen of Buenos Aires in a ceremony at the Centro Cultural General San Martín.[51] Some of his admirers had been working behind the scenes to get him the honor—one of them being Alfredo Radoszynski, who made one of the speeches at the ceremony. Piazzolla was delighted with the award. Like his impressive accolade at the Colón, it showed him that he had at last "arrived" at home, as well as abroad. He was at last a prophet in his own country.

Abroad, meanwhile, his star was rising very fast indeed. That same month he was given the Académie Française du Disque's prize for the best foreign record of 1985. Made by the Quintet in Belgium on its second European tour, it was his music for Fernando Solanas's movie *Tangos: L'exil de Gardel*. The film, a fresco of interwoven stories of Argentine exiles in Paris, was one of the bigger successes of the sadly ephemeral New Argentine Cinema of the 1980s, part of the vigorous cultural stirrings that accompanied Argentina's return to a stable democratic way of life under President Alfonsín. Piazzolla and Laura had seen the movie several times in Paris "to spy out the reactions of the French." They discovered that the most fervent reactions were when Gardel's image appeared on the screen, something that made Piazzolla himself mildly tearful.[52]

Le Figaro called the music "magic." *Variety* praised the "pulsating, energetic . . . score."[53] It had already been given prizes at the Venice and Biarritz festivals, and at the New Cinema Festival in Havana. Now, in the Uruguayan summer month of February 1986, there came word that the score had won a César, the French equivalent of an Oscar. Piazzolla was out near the Isla de Lobos with Dante and Daniel Rabinovich. Laura radioed him the news.*

---

*Piazzolla worked just once more with Solanas, writing the music for his movie *Sur* (1988), another film dealing with the torment of Argentina's still only-too-recent past. *Variety*'s review (18 May 1988) highlighted the music as "the soul and motor of the film, with Astor Piazzolla and his quintet performing superb choral duties and Roberto Goyeneche crooning with soulful abandon." *Sur* was Piazzolla's last serious film music. He also wrote (but did not record) two pieces for Solanas's film *El viaje* (1992).

Globetrotter with Bandoneon
1985–1988

→← Piazzolla-Burton

Piazzolla and *Tango Argentino* →←

→← "That Second Homeland . . ."

From Opera Revival to Operation →←

> When the rain started, umbrellas went up, but only a few spectators de-
> parted, and their places were quickly occupied. . . .There was something
> mesmerizing about these five men in somber black trousers and shirts.
> Mr. Piazzolla stands front and center, one foot propped on a large
> box. . . .The bandoneon has a rich, organ-like, mournful sound, but it
> can be aggressive and lyrical in turn. . . .The fans . . . went decidedly wild.
> —*Wall Street Journal*, 23 September 1987,
> reviewing Piazzolla's Central Park concert

Piazzolla-Burton

In the early 1980s, Piazzolla attended a concert in Paris given by the celebrated
jazz duo of Gary Burton and Chick Corea. He went backstage and greeted Burton:
"Hello. Do you remember me?" "Oh, absolutely," replied Burton, as he recalls.
"I've been listening to your records . . . all these years. . . ." "Would you be interested in doing some project together?" asked Piazzolla. "I would love to," said
Burton. In 1985, out of the blue, Piazzolla phoned Burton from Paris and told
him that he was "ready to start on something." Burton pleaded with him to wait
until "some of the technical and mechanical things" had been discussed. A frequent visitor to Buenos Aires, he was there again at the end of Piazzolla's 1985–
86 summer. Piazzolla turned up at the club where he was playing, at about two
in the morning. As Burton remembers,

He was very . . . keyed up and excited, and energetic. . . . He'd already written all the music. He said: "When I flew home, I was all excited. I could
just hear the music, I just went ahead, I couldn't stop, I just had to do it."
He had written all the music. The whole concert. . . . And he seemed so—
almost demonic, demon-like in his talking about it. . . . And my bass player
. . . said: "You're really gonna do this? This guy kinda scared you a little
bit?"

They would meet again a few weeks later. Meanwhile, the Quintet held its
"public" rehearsals for 1986 at Sham's, a fashionable club in the leafy suburb of
Belgrano. It was then swept off on a three-week tour of Brazil (16 April–3 May),
where its "purely instrumental show" was hailed by one magazine as "modern
and experimental . . . an intelligible and moving exhibition."[1] While there, Piazzolla recorded music for a new monthly TV show, *Chico & Caetano*, hosted by
Chico Buarque and Caetano Veloso. Chico Buarque had never gotten around to
working on the music Piazzolla had sent him through journalist Eric Nepomuceno
back in 1974, and the atmosphere between them was at first rather frosty. Antonio
Carlos Jobim, the great Brazilian musician, who was on hand, dispelled it with a
timely intervention. "Astor, the same thing happens to me," he told him.[2] Piazzolla announced to the Brazilian press that he was hoping to write a "tango
Mass"—though he thought the Argentine church might object. "In Argentina the
clergy rules more than the government does," he commented.[3] The Church and
the tango have never really gotten along.

Next came the Quintet's first incursion into the United States, Piazzolla's first
time there with an ensemble in ten years. His visit attracted far more coverage in
the New York press than in 1976, and his three concerts at the Public Theater at
the end of May were very well received. "Piazzolla knows his Bartók, Stravinsky
and Gershwin, [and] treats his quintet as a miniature orchestra," noted *New York
Times* critic Jon Pareles.[4] He could still make a big impression on those hearing
him for the first time. Jazz critic Peter Watrous, also at the Public Theater,
remembered

this barrel-chested little guy leading a group that looked like it was suffering
a collective hangover. . . . Modern tango, I figured, who needs it? Then the
music started, and it was brilliant and I was wrong. Baroque in their detail,
Piazzolla's compositions turned out to be enormously varied, full of everything from stop-time figures and bass vamps to pizzicatos, slurs, counterpoint and fugues, the textures borrowed from Stravinsky, Basie, Berg,

Ellington and other modernists. . . . Rarely has music so controlled sounded so liberated.[5]

A real thrill for Piazzolla in New York was his meeting, after years of long distance admiration with the legendary jazzman Gil Evans, who declared the Public Theater concerts to be the best he had heard in twenty years. The two men did not have much time to get acquainted, but on his long American visit the following year, Piazzolla would hear Evans at the Sweet Basil, the Greenwich Village club where Evans played every Monday during the last four years of his life. In March 1988, Evans died, in Mexico.

While in New York, the Quintet also recorded its first American album, *Tango: Zero Hour*, with producer Kip Hanrahan for his American Clavé label. Piazzolla was certainly very pleased with the outcome of this first collaboration with Hanrahan, whose imaginative style greatly appealed to him. Their work together over the next three years was intense. "No matter how many fights about anything we had," says Hanrahan, "and no matter how many times we swore we'd never talk to each other again, there was always a 4:00 A.M. phone call in a couple of weeks from Astor, as if nothing had happened." *Tango: Zero Hour* won very positive reviews over the next year or so. "Piazzolla and his quintet . . ." commented *Keyboard* magazine, "wrap the tango in ribbons of intricate polyphony without smothering its fiery spirit." *Down Beat* praised the quintet's "razor-sharp rhythms and taut ensemble interaction . . . [its] alternately delicate and diabolical sounds."[6]

Gary Burton now came to New York for rehearsals of the new Piazzolla-Burton pieces. It was still not quite clear to him how his vibraphone meshed in, and he was mildly frustrated. Laura, however, noticed that Burton had a good effect on Piazzolla: "He called him 'the seminarist,' because he said that talking or being with Gary gave him peace, that when he got nervous Gary said, 'Easy, Astor, easy. . . . Don't worry,' and calmed him down." A few weeks later, Burton joined Piazzolla in Italy, at the start of the first of the Quintet's European tours of 1986. He expected a reasonable stint of rehearsals. "Things were starting to get organized . . . ," he recalls, "and suddenly [Piazzolla] said: 'Well, it's enough for today, let's go eat.' Same thing happened next day. . . . I was amazed that we got through all the music without getting lost or having a problem. But we did." At a jazz festival in Milan on 2 July, Burton sat in the audience, listening carefully to music described by a local critic with a magnificent chain of adjectives: *tenebroso ed ironico, sfuggente, equivoco, perverso ed insieme struggente, nostalgico, amaro e tenero, do-*

loroso e allegro, inquieto e sereno (dark and ironic, receding, equivocal, perverse and at the same time all-consuming, nostalgic, bitter and tender, sorrowful and joyous, restless and serene).[7] Two days later, at Ravenna, Burton (*elegantissimo,* according to one reporter) played with the Quintet for the first time.[8]

These few months were a frenzied whirl for the Quintet—Canada, Europe, Japan, Europe again, Chile (in November). At the Montreal Jazz Festival, at the end of June, the musicians literally jumped for joy while playing, having just heard that Argentina had won the 1986 World Cup, thanks largely to the tactical skill of Diego Maradona. (This was the World Cup when Maradona's hand—"the hand of God," he called it—played its questionable role in scoring the goals that knocked England out of the tournament.) "I *love* Maradona," declared Piazzolla.[9] Several other jazz festivals were visited that summer, in Ravenna, Nice, Pescara, Montreux. Piazzolla by this stage was constantly rubbing shoulders with great jazz musicians he admired: Miles Davis, Lionel Hampton, Pat Metheny, Michel Petrucciani, and Jim Hall. In Rome, in mid-July, a newspaper vividly sketched "the great Piazzolla" guiding "a handful of romantic heroes, all rigidly clothed in black, almost a symbol of mourning for lost happiness."[10] A few days earlier he fulfilled an old ambition—an ambition that had been growing on him in recent years—and visited Trani, the town of his ancestors. He went to the town hall, made inquiries, and located his grandfather's house. "Everything very nice, and *full* of Piazzollas," he scrawled on a postcard to Daniel.[11]

In August 1986 the Quintet and Gary Burton leaped across the globe to Japan. Burton was amazed at the way Japanese students of the bandoneon, by the score, "would arrive at the airport[s] to meet Astor . . . with their little flags and things." Piazzolla explained to him, "Yeah, it's been going on for a while in Japan." At one of the more important concerts, at the Sapporo jazz festival, distinguished jazz-rock guitarist Al Di Meola had his first "very warm meeting" with Piazzolla. Bumping into Gary Burton in an elevator, Al Di Meola asked him: "What's he like? I am really interested in Piazzolla." Burton's reply—"It's the hardest music I've ever played in my life"—stuck in Di Meola's mind. Soon after the Japanese tour, Piazzolla sent him the score of his "Tango Suite," suggesting it might be suitable for him.

One of the more spectacular dates for the Quintet that summer was an appearance with Milva in the ancient Roman Arena at Verona (3 September 1986)—a lavishly staged tribute to Maria Callas nine years after her death. In a telephone chat with his friend Mario Antelo, then traveling in Europe, Piazzolla told him of the jamboree: "Look, Laura isn't going to come with me. Why don't you come?

The theater's a bit on the old side, but I'll get you good seats." Antelo was present to witness his friend's triumph, as well as the elephants accompanying selections from *Aida*. When the Quintet started playing "Libertango," as violinist Fernando Suárez Paz recalls, a troupe dressed in incongruous Spanish garb appeared on-stage, dancing in a way that bore no resemblance to the tango. Piazzolla was furious, and was about to leave in protest. His musicians' laughter calmed him down.

In retrospect, for Piazzolla, the indisputable highlight of his world-spanning 1986 travels was the Montreux International Jazz Festival in July. It became some kind of reference point for him. The Montreux program was ecumenical; it included rock musicians like Eric Clapton and Brazilian stars like Gilberto Gil. For Piazzolla, Gary Burton, and the Quintet, it was the triumph of the year. The musicians found it daunting enough to be playing immediately after Miles Davis. They were listened to in a dead silence lasting ten minutes. "We didn't know whether the silence was due to total failure or to complete triumph," says Horacio Malvicino. "After those ten horrible minutes, people started to stand up. Some applauded, some shouted, many were in tears."[12] It was the fourth time Burton had played with the Quintet, and the first on which he felt his vibraphone really meshing in.

The six pieces Piazzolla wrote for his collaboration with Burton (presented on their splendid 1987 album as "Suite for Vibraphone and New Tango Quintet") are all sensitively tailored to Burton's instrument. It is most prominently show-cased in "Vibraphonissimo," but it is always intimately integrated with the music, more so than had been true of Gerry Mulligan's sax in 1974. With Mulligan, Piazzolla was clearly moving in the direction of jazz. With Burton, he succeeded in pulling a great jazz musician into the sound-world of the tango, to which he himself was increasingly reverting. "Vibraphonissimo" is altogether more *tanguero* than any of the pieces on *Summit*. Similarly, the rhythmic vigor of the piece titled "Laura's Dream," its percussive effects, and the soaring violin of Suárez Paz all combine in an expression of drama and melancholy in a completely Piazzollean idiom.

Back in Buenos Aires in early November, en route to Punta del Este, Piazzolla played a cassette of the Montreux concert to a reporter. The "Little Italy" piece, he explained, was "full of childhood reminiscences, from when I lived in New York. . . . Now the vibraphone is coming in. . . . Listen how Suárez Paz makes his entry. . . . Now we just take it away . . . , now Gary comes in again. . . ."[13] Piazzolla and Burton would never collaborate again with the intensity of 1986, though over the next two years they sometimes joined forces. Burton always hoped that Piazzolla would take their "concert" to Argentina, but Piazzolla proved reluctant. Burton later sensed that Piazzolla was becoming very excited about the Gardel opera, "that he wanted this big opera thing to be his final success." Burton would play "Laura's Dream" many times in his own concerts in the future and to record it again more than once; he is in no doubt that Piazzolla is one of the most important musicians he has known: "There is a certain quality about very major independent musicians," he says, "a certain kind of charisma." Piazzolla had it.

Piazzolla, for his part, was convinced that his months with Burton were somehow deeply significant. "With Gary I began a new phase," he told Diana soon afterward. "I discovered a Piazzolla that even I didn't know."[14] Horacio Malvicino's reflections confirm this. At the time, he noticed how, in rehearsal, the musicians detected "something different" in Piazzolla's bandoneon playing, something "very modern, a new sonority. . . . A new Astor has been born, and who can say what will happen tomorrow?"[15] "Tomorrow" did not turn out to be as long as any of Piazzolla's admirers would have wished. Yet he certainly now felt more confident than ever in his own tango-based musical language while remaining permeable to new influences. He felt able to assimilate new trends, to work with musicians from other traditions, especially jazz. His own compositions and performances hinted at new directions. *He was still able to renew his art.*

The César of 1986 and the collaborations with Milva and Burton all demonstrate Piazzolla's increasing international prominence. In the later 1980s he won the greatest following among the world's music lovers he was to enjoy in his own lifetime. As pianist Pablo Ziegler puts it, "It was the boom, the big boom, of Astor in the world," adding that he, like all Piazzolla's musicians, "spent the boom years on an airplane."[16] Piazzolla was now deluged with requests for new works—from chamber groups, guitarists, cellists, pianists. "I'm like a supermarket of music," he joked.[17] While he was pleased by such requests, there was no possible way he could satisfy them all. Meanwhile, his performing schedule grew steadily more hectic. The tours, as Laura says, "became more intense, more demanding." For the musicians, the tours became altogether more comfortable. "Very nice tours," Héctor Console remembers, "not ones where you had to load up the car. By then they came to collect us. By then the concerts began to pay well."

The musicians noticed interesting variations in their different national audiences. In Japan, as tango singer Raúl Lavié points out, Piazzolla had to overcome a strong local affection for traditional tango music. Héctor Console feels that Japanese audiences "enjoyed our stuff but the halls were never full, as they were in Holland and other places." The Dutch sometimes seemed to him like Italians "for the row they set up." Spanish audiences, by contrast, never really took to Piazzolla, who was certainly puzzled by this. There may be some truth in Laura's speculation that it had something to do with the country's recovery after the long cultural freeze of the Franco era and its resolute turn toward the European Community. When asked which country he liked the best, Piazzolla usually replied: "The one that likes *me* best." That country could well have been Brazil, where he had perhaps the most passionate of all his followings. "If there was a public that really adored Piazzolla, it was the Brazilians," says Carlos Páez Vilaró.

The intense touring rhythm of 1986 set the pattern for the rest of the decade. Tours tended to last for just under one month, with seventeen or eighteen concerts. "Then there was a ten-day rest," Console tells us. "The pressure went down, and then, after ten or fifteen days it started up again. After ten or twelve concerts it began to rise. After seventeen concerts it became intolerable. There was a lot of tension." Piazzolla's habitual insistence on punctuality seems to have grown greater. He hated it when one of his musicians arrived late at an airport. But airports were sometimes also the scene of comedy. At Munich, on one famous occasion, Customs officials took Fernando Suárez Paz off and stripped him to his underwear. In a gesture of protest Suárez Paz then removed his underwear and started playing his violin. "When he heard the violin, Astor found the door, saw the scene, and almost died laughing."[18]

Even on these later tours, despite the pressures, the old clowning instincts often surfaced. They still remained rather schoolboyish—chairs being suddenly withdrawn, for instance. In San Francisco in 1988 Piazzolla turned up in the dressing room with a stained package, which he handed to Pablo Ziegler. "Take it," he said. "I was passing by a Chinese restaurant, and there was a duck hanging there, and I remembered how much you like duck." Later that year, touring with Milva in Japan, Piazzolla bought himself a red wig to imitate her hair and wore it at the final concert in Tokyo. His English tour manager, Sarah Vardigans, has wondered ever since quite what the Japanese audience made of this.

Piazzolla and Tango Argentino

Piazzolla's favorable reception in New York in May 1986 reinforced his determination to spread his music in the United States. His ambition was further strengthened by the astonishing American triumphs of *Tango Argentino*, the music and dance show that was all the rage in New York in 1985, a show that featured five of his own pieces. It is not widely known that Piazzolla himself came fairly close to being its musical director and main star. Claudio Segovia, co-producer with the late Héctor Orezzoli of *Tango Argentino*, had first conceived the idea of the show in the early 1970s, with Aníbal Troilo in mind. During 1976, while living in Paris, he consumed numerous ice creams with Piazzolla and Laura—it was the hottest European summer of the decade—and came to visualize Piazzolla opening the show, bathed in a single spotlight. Piazzolla suggested a bandoneon duo with Leopoldo Federico as perhaps more dramatic. Segovia thought this "a very generous gesture," as did Federico when told about it.

They went on talking about the possible show for several years, Segovia once even flying to Punta del Este to continue the discussion. Piazzolla, however, insisted on a firm contract, and Segovia could not yet offer one. In mid-1983 he very reluctantly eliminated Piazzolla from his plans and went ahead without him. *Tango Argentino* was an overwhelming success when staged for six days in Paris that autumn. It returned to Paris in 1984, at the time of the Piazzolla-Milva show at the Bouffes du Nord. Piazzolla both bewildered and saddened Segovia with some gratuitously derogatory statements to the press, describing the show as "a caricature from the past" and heaping scorn on singer Roberto Goyeneche and pianist Horacio Salgán, both at that point in the cast.[19] His remarks were doubly bewildering, since earlier that year he had coincided with part of the *Tango Argentino* cast on an Italian television program "and at the end," as Segovia recalls, "to our astonishment Piazzolla appeared, greeting the dancers, which surprised us a lot." He did not see the show itself until its third Paris run in 1989, at the Théâtre Mogador, when, to much applause, he was photographed onstage with the cast.

Tango Argentino's extraordinary success in the United States did not escape Piazzolla. The show certainly revived American interest in the tango. Tango classes in New York suddenly became "a growth market," according to the *Village Voice*.[20] Piazzolla surely sensed that the time was ripe for further incursions into "that second homeland of mine I have still to conquer," as he said to Diana.[21]

That did not mean neglecting Europe. In March 1987 he played his Bandoneon and Guitar Concerto and the Punta del Este Suite in Milan, with the CARME (Italian Chamber Music Association) orchestra. He had been invited by guitarist Marco De Santi, whose version of his "Five Pieces for Guitar" had so delighted Piazzolla three years earlier that he made a point of meeting De Santi when next in Milan. They had gotten along well. De Santi found Piazzolla "an incredible, fantastic man, full of enthusiasm for everything." Playing with him now, De Santi was astonished by his absolute control of the audience. Piazzolla gave him some advice: "Whatever happens, you always smile." The first violin in the CARME orchestra, Anahí Carfi, an Argentine who had long resided in Italy (she had been first violin in the La Scala orchestra since 1970) had always thought of Piazzolla as essentially a classical musician and was thrilled to be working with him. He told her of his wish "to start a new stage of his artistic activity," working with chamber groups far from stadiums and large halls with elaborate sound systems.[22] It was an idea that grew on him over the next few years.

In the meantime, it was back to the hurly-burly of touring. Toward the end of March the Quintet started a sweep through Italy, with a quick side trip to Amsterdam, that lasted until the end of April. At Trani, on 29 March, they played in the 900-year old cathedral where Pantaleo Piazzolla and Rosa Centofanti had been married 107 years earlier. Milva was once again on hand for much of this tour. "For me," she declared, "this music is an absolutely undeniable love."[23] ATER (Agenzia Teatrale Italiana), the Italian agency that had organized Piazzolla's Italian forays for several years, asked one of its employees, Sarah Vardigans, an Englishwoman, to act as tour manager for the Quintet. She had never heard of Piazzolla but was soon captivated by the music, by the Quintet, and by the man himself—"great, fabulous, one of the funniest men I've ever met." She hugely enjoyed being with these "crazy" musicians who were "always teasing each other" and were so protective of Piazzolla, always making sure he had company at dinner. She was also amused at how Piazzolla and Milva, both renowned as "difficult" characters, set up a running competition to see who could behave better.

"That Second Homeland . . ."

During the middle months of 1987, Piazzolla and Laura made New York their base. They rented an apartment on the north side of East 27th Street, between Lexington and Third. It had mice; Laura spent three days cleaning it before it was habitable. Piazzolla was obviously pleased to be living once again in the city of his boyhood. Kip Hanrahan remembers that he "kept mentioning how much of a New Yorker and an American he felt all his life, and how important it was to make his music heard in the States." How *did* the New York of the 1980s strike him? Laura was later to describe his life as "a love-triangle: Buenos Aires, New York, Paris."[24] Piazzolla once told Víctor Oliveros that New York was the place he would most like to have been born in and to die in. He was well aware, as he told a reporter in 1986, that New York was "*everything*, the place where everything explodes . . . [with] the best music, the best cinema, the best theater." By the same token, he missed the village atmosphere of the Île Saint Louis. He added that he was sometimes slightly scared by his sense of comfort in Paris, and that he might some day succumb to the lure of New York's dynamism.[25] To the veterinarian Didier Servant, he once expressed regret that New York had supplanted Paris as "the world's great cultural center."

In the weeks before the Quintet's arrival for its second American incursion, he was working hard on *Tango Apasionado*, a musical drama based on two short stories by Jorge Luis Borges ("La intrusa" and "Hombre de la esquina rosada," for both of which Piazzolla had already written music). The adaptation was by Graciela Daniele and Jim Hall. It was to be choreographed by Daniele, whose previous experience had mostly been with Broadway musicals. She had left Argentina in 1957 with only two records in her luggage—one of Mozart, one of Piazzolla. She had been put in touch with Piazzolla by Max Ferrá, artistic director of INTAR, a small organization promoting Latin arts, which was to sponsor the show. Piazzolla and Laura visited her in her apartment.

> Suddenly I realized. Good God! The Maestro was writing music for *me*! It was the most extraordinary collaboration I have ever experienced. . . . There were about three songs in the work, and I said to him, "We need music like . . ." And he said, "Don't explain the scene, just give me a word that will inspire me: passion, jealousy . . ." And I said, "something like Kurt Weill." He came back with a Kurt Weill-type tango. It was no good. I had to call him. "Astor, I think, I've given you the wrong instructions, it's not Kurt Weill." He cut me short: "If the piece is no use, I'll bring you a different one tomorrow." At ten the next morning he brought me it.

Piazzolla took a hand in auditioning members of the cast. For musical director, he selected Pablo Zinger, a Uruguayan who had lived in New York for ten years and who worked for the Spanish Repertory Theater—by coincidence very close to the Piazzollas' apartment. Piazzolla phoned Zinger out of the blue. "This is Astor Piazzolla." Zinger, a great fan, refused to believe it, and replied with a jocular "And I'm Christopher Columbus!" Over the next few weeks, he saw much of Piazzolla. He had heard that he could be "difficult" but found him "polite, open, content with himself, a man happy in his own skin." *Tango Apasionado* opened at the Westbeth Theater Center early in October 1987 and won a certain critical acclaim. "A music-theater-dance piece of breathtaking intensity," said the *New York Times*, though the *Village Voice* described it as a "gorgeous mistake."[26] Unfortunately, the Borges estate objected to the use of the short stories, and the show was closed.

In August 1987, the Quintet arrived for its North American tour, which took in points as far apart as Miami and Minneapolis, Portland (Maine) and Denver, Albuquerque and Montreal. Among its more memorable American dates that month were appearances at the Santa Fe Chamber Music Festival, combined with two "discussion rehearsals" with the local youth orchestra. The Denver and Santa Fe concerts were later broadcast on National Public Radio.[27] American cellist Carter Brey, who knew little or nothing of Piazzolla, went to one of the Santa Fe concerts in the Saint Francis Theater. By his own account he was "skeptical and bored" when the Quintet appeared onstage.

> Here were five middle-aged men, all dressed in black, solemn and funereal, their potbellies overflowing their belts. It was a sight that could have elicited an easy laugh, but there was something about their leader that commanded instant attention. Astor had a quality that would have served him well had he been a policeman or a gangster instead of a musician: you felt compelled to stop smirking and watch him warily. And when he wrung the first phrase of Adiós Nonino from his bandoneon, I sat up and listened as if I were hearing music for the first time.

Brey invited Piazzolla to his own concert the following night. Afterward Piazzolla asked for his address so that a copy of "Le Grand Tango" could be sent to him. When it arrived, Brey recalls, "I realized that I had a masterpiece in my hands." He would give the first American performances of the work on a tour not long afterward.

On 18–19 August 1987, the Quintet played at S.O.B.s (Sounds of Brazil) restaurant in Greenwich Village, a nightspot noted for its promotion of Latin American music. Gerry and Franca Mulligan went, and Franca remembers that Piazzolla was "terrific, on top form." That same night the Cuban saxophonist Paquito D'Rivera introduced himself uninhibitedly to Piazzolla: "I'm Paquito D'Rivera, but what I've just heard—*fucking hell*, what stuff!"[28] It was, he tells us, "as if I had known him all my life." After the Quintet's appearances (25–26 August) at Nightstage in Cambridge, Massachusetts, journalist Fernando González speculated in the *Boston Globe* that Piazzolla was on the point of being "discovered in the United States."[29]

In late August the Quintet stood down, while Piazzolla recorded what would later become another Kip Hanrahan album, *The Rough Dancer and the Cyclical Night*—the music from *Tango Apasionado*. He and Hanrahan talked of making a live recording of the show, "but we both knew," says Hanrahan, who was surely right, "that the music would be more interesting as raw material for an Astor record." The recording was done at Radio City by an ad hoc group consisting of Piazzolla himself, Pablo Zinger (piano), Andy Gonzalez (bass), and Rodolfo Alchourron (electric guitar). After the first takes, Hanrahan and Piazzolla spent a day or two in the studio, "fooling around with alternative endings, replacing the previous larger band parts with second and third bandoneon overdubs." Paquito D'Rivera and Fernando Suárez Paz (summoned, he recalls, to replace a violinist unable to reproduce the tango style)[30] recorded their parts a few days later. D'Rivera's sax, which Piazzolla particularly wanted, covered parts that were sung in the show itself. The last part to be recorded was Pablo Zinger's delicate piano solo of the track "Leijia's Game." To Zinger's delight, Piazzolla and Laura turned up at the studio to listen.

Kip Hanrahan was to recall a particular moment during this stint. He and Suárez Paz were in the studio trying to "run down some rough edges," when Piazzolla burst in. "What the hell do you two think you are doing . . . [If] you try to 'correct' anything I'll shoot you . . . ! Turn it into chamber music and you'll be *eating dinner* with Borges tonight!"[31] (Borges had died in June 1986.) Hanrahan also recounts that during these days his wife Nancy took Piazzolla to a New Jersey radio station for an interview. A listener phoned in, more or less in tears, and said that his long dead father would be proud to hear him talking to Piazzolla. Another listener was abusive, declaring that "the fascists" in Argentina should have killed him for being the assassin of the tango. "We had heard about that kind of reaction before," says Hanrahan, "but we always thought it was part of the myth."

On Sunday, 6 September 1987, Piazzolla and the Quintet performed before an audience of 4,000 people in Central Park. The afternoon was rainy (the concert was almost called off), but this in no way lessened the enthusiasm of the audience, which broke into applause as Pablo Ziegler began his piano introduction to "Adiós Nonino." Reviews (including the one used as this chapter's epigraph) were eulogistic. "We didn't play well," violinist Suárez Paz remembers. If true, it went unnoticed by the crowd. The Argentine pianist and conductor Carlos Franzetti had often heard Piazzolla before, but he felt that the "concert was particularly inspired." Gil Evans told him a few days later that it had been "one of the most incredible concerts of my life."[32]

A few days later Piazzolla was at Princeton University to record his Bandoneon Concerto with the St. Luke's Orchestra, conducted by his old friend, pianist and composer Lalo Schifrin. Schifrin found his compatriot in very good form. There was one other musical collaboration Piazzolla began during this time in New York, one that came to much less than any serious music lover would have wanted. Robert Hurwitz, who produced the records of the Kronos Quartet, took Piazzolla to one of its concerts. The Quartet's meticulous musicianship, and its repertory on the cutting edge of contemporary music were bound to attract him. He went backstage to compliment the musicians. "I asked him if I could call him in a few days," David Harrington, founder of the Kronos Quartet, remembers. "I *did* call him in a few days. By then he had finished 'Four for Tango,' and he said: 'Shall I send it to you?' " (The Quartet still plays the five-minute piece from photocopies of the original score.) The Kronos musicians decided to include it on their next album, *Winter Was Hard*, recorded mostly in November 1987. Enthusiastic over the experience, they asked Piazzolla for a "large quartet piece." He agreed to write one.

From Opera Revival to Operation

Their long stay in New York over, Piazzolla and Laura returned to Paris in September 1987, installing themselves at the Hôtel Roblin—the days of rented apartments were now past. Piazzolla learned that his old friends Máximo and Solange Perrotti were in town. He left a comic note for them at their hotel.

> Dear Sir: I am 19 years old, I play the bandoneon, and I have a tango, just one, but what a tango! It is called "Prepárense" and if you dare to publish it we could make a lot of dough. . . . What do you think? I am next door in the Hotel Roblin. . . . Room 51. (signed) *Astor Canaro*

The Piazzollas and the Perrottis went off to dine, with the pianist Héctor Grané, at La Tour de Saint Germain, ending the evening at Les Trottoirs de Buenos Aires, Paris's principal tango stronghold since its opening in 1981.[33] It was there, around this time, that the *chamamé* accordionist Raúl Barboza had his second meeting (after twenty years) with Piazzolla. Barboza's wife Olga had recently written to numerous musicians to mobilize some favorable publicity for her husband. Piazzolla was the only one to answer. "Raúl isn't commercial," he wrote. "He is a fighter, and deserves my esteem." The Barbozas treasured the remark. As luck would have it, Barboza and his guitarist were rehearsing "Adiós Nonino" when Piazzolla arrived at the nightspot. Piazzolla was gracious. In the interval he chatted with the accordionist, and he stayed for the second half of the show. As he left he said: "Well, *negro*, there it is. Now it's your turn. It's tough, but carry on."

The Quintet's autumn 1987 tour brought unmistakable signs of the adulation

Piazzolla was now winning in Europe. On his first-ever visit to Stockholm in early October, he was wildly applauded by an audience of 1,200 in the Berwaldhallen, the concert hall of Swedish radio. It was a "dazzling evening," according to the local press, one in which he "conquered another country and added it to his tango empire."[34] He dined after the concert with his old friend Albino Gómez, then Argentina's ambassador in Sweden, at a fashionable Stockholm restaurant. "It was hard to have a good conversation," recalls Gómez, "because the fellows from the [Argentine] colony kept coming up to greet him, to ask for autographs."[35] At his Milan concert, a month later, he was besieged in his dressing room by "all those who wanted to shake his hand, extract an autograph from him, get him to sign a record."[36] Such scenes were now becoming commonplace on all his tours.

His main task that autumn, however, was a revival of *María de Buenos Aires* in France. He would not play in it himself, his role being taken by the Paris-based bandoneonist Juan José Mosalini. He obviously hoped for a big success—forty or fifty performances, at least. For the benefit of *Le Monde*, he defined the work as "un opéra populaire, comme Porgy and Bess."[37] The *operita* had been substantially revised and was now in fact a genuine opera rather than something more resembling an oratorio. In its new form it had seven singers rather than two, musical rearrangements by the pianist Jorge Zulueta, and a full operatic staging from the producer, Jacobo Romano. The Argentine mezzo-soprano Margarita Zimmermann took the role of María, and despite her normal classical repertory, took it with enthusiasm, claiming that María had "the scale of the great heroines."[38]

The revived *operita* was performed first (20 November 1987) at Tourcoing. Film, opera and theater director Sergio Renán, heading there on the train from Paris, was amused to discover that many of his fellow passengers were obviously Argentines. There were later performances at Montpellier and (in January 1988) at Douai, but not the long run for which Piazzolla hoped. The influential British magazine *Opera* gave the production its approval, but French critics panned it. *Le Monde*, while hailing Piazzolla as "the Karajan of the bandoneon," thought that Mosalini's bandoneon-playing was the sole redeeming feature. *Le Figaro* found the enterprise emasculated by its fear of "picturesqueness" and longed for Milva in the part of María.[39] (Milva *was* originally to have alternated with Zimmermann, but the deal fell through.) Pierre Philippe agreed with the press. He remembers that, for whatever reason, Piazzolla became angry with Horacio Ferrer, who had flown to France for the revival: "Horacio went to dinner on his own in Lille. I went and dined with Astor. He was happy that I, like him, found that *María de Buenos Aires* was a disaster."

Piazzolla himself beat a hasty retreat to Argentina. At the start of December

1987 he twice played the Bandoneon Concerto with the Camerata Bariloche at Luna Park and again at the Chateau Carreras stadium in Córdoba; all three concerts were for charity. At Luna Park he was presented with a diploma naming him honorary president of the Argentine Bandoneonists Association. There was another real pleasure for him in Buenos Aires. Diana's long-awaited book about him was to be published, and he happily attended its launch at the Cinzano Club on 30 November. Diana had worked on it in Mexico and finished it back in Argentina. Its first three quarters are a charmingly novelized reconstruction of Piazzolla's life up till 1955, based heavily on tapes Diana had recorded in Mexico in 1980. The remainder contains an impressive set of statements from Piazzolla himself, from his musicians, from Dedé, and from Laura—but not, as Diana had promised, from Amelita. Diana had shown the manuscript of *Astor* to her father. It so engrossed him that he missed an appointment with his cardiologist. He loved the book, and later he often gave copies of it as presents to his friends. At the launch, Diana, feeling slightly ill, sipped water, while the guests around her drank champagne. One of them was the violinist Simón Bajour, who, since leaving Piazzolla in 1961, had worked in Cuba and studied under David Oistrakh in the Soviet Union. Piazzolla inscribed his copy: "Simón, I wish you were still playing the violin with me!" Dedé was also there. It was the last time she saw Astor.

During the Uruguayan summer of 1987–88 Piazzolla was hard at work on some new music for the Quintet, notably the three "Camorras"—"I," "II," and "III"— for his next Kip Hanrahan album. After *Tango: Zero Hour*, Hanrahan and Horacio Malvicino had challenged him to write "something even more complex and beautiful." He was also thinking (or anyway thinking ahead) about the Gardel opera. With Pierre Philippe staying at the Chalet El Casco at the end of 1987, Piazzolla phoned the caricaturist Hermenegildo Sábat, suggesting that he might design the scenery. Sábat was noncommittal; he was later very annoyed when in Montevideo soon afterward, to see an interview in the newspaper, *El Día*, in which Piazzolla seemed to be taking his participation for granted. When he was finally able to talk to Piazzolla at the Chalet El Casco, he was handed Philippe's plan for the opera. He found it "delirious . . . totally absurd." Sergio Renán, who also talked with Piazzolla about the opera at Punta del Este, got the impression that "deep down" he was not "very sure of being able to do it well."

In writing for other people's stage projects, however, he had definitely not lost his touch. Among his composing tasks in 1988 was music for the play *Famille d'Artistes*, by Alfredo Arias and Kado Kostzer, to be produced in Paris. Kostzer went to the Avenida Libertador apartment to deliver a script to Piazzolla, explaining that one of the play's characters, a municipal lawyer, was lame. As he was escorted to the door, Kostzer was mortified to realize that Piazzolla walked with a slight limp. He was relieved when the phone rang next day: "Well, I read your work. . . . Yes, I was delighted by it. Such tenderness. Especially the lawyer character, a marvelous character." Both Kostzer and Arias talked to Piazzolla about the music—Arias, and the actress Marilú Marini, at the Hôtel Roblin in Paris. There Piazzolla nominated Richard Galliano as the play's musical director. This was Piazzolla's last work for the theater; the score is a charming sequence of rather simple pieces, songs, choruses, bandoneon tunes. The play itself was staged in Paris in March 1989 to great acclaim. The legendary *grande dame* of the Argentine theater, Iris Marga, took one of the main roles, making her debut in a French-language part at the age of eighty-eight.

Toward the end of the Uruguayan summer, in March 1988, Piazzolla was interviewed by the magazine *Acción*. Across in Argentina, the briefly prominent fascist Colonel Aldo Rico had recently led a pathetic military rebellion against President Alfonsín. He was, like Piazzolla, born under the sign of Pisces: "And I said to my wife, 'That's why he needs to be on top!'" joked Piazzolla. He was still very interested, he said, in capturing a strong American audience, but less interested now in a long stay in the United States. As so often in his remarks to the press in the 1980s, he could not resist denouncing the state of Argentine musical culture, contrasting it unfavorably with that of Brazil.[40]

In one respect, however, he was in a conciliatory mood. On Monday 11 April, back in Buenos Aires before leaving on his 1988 travels, Piazzolla went to the headquarters of the Argentine Performers Association on Calle Viamonte for a meeting with a large group of tango musicians, a veritable constellation of the greatest alive. Among them were Osvaldo Pugliese, Horacio Salgán, Atilio Stampone, Alfredo De Angelis, Héctor Stamponi, José Basso, Roberto Rufino, Eladia Blázquez, Jorge Vidal, and Ernesto Baffa. He had worked with some; he had played tricks on others; with Vidal, of course, he had once come to blows. The old quarrels were at last to be forgotten in a grand reconciliation scene, discreetly arranged by Atilio Talín and Leopoldo Federico. Horacio Salgán wondered whether Piazzolla might use the occasion to make provocative comments about him. He did not. He spoke gracefully and well:

Today I realize the stupidity of quarreling between ourselves for so long. . . . How *couldn't* I be a man of the tango, when I can still remember playing with "El Gordo" at the Tibidabo ... [and] when I ... heard the things Horacio Salgán did, I thought to myself: "Am I *ever* going to be able to do something like that!"[41]

Horacio Salgán was touched. Leopoldo Federico found the meeting deeply moving: "He embraced Jorge Vidal, Alfredo De Angelis. . . . It was a sensational meeting." It was an emotional day all around. A few hours earlier, Piazzolla had married Laura under Argentine law. They celebrated that evening with a dinner at—where else?—the Félix Restaurant in Avellaneda.

It was time to go out on the road again, or at any rate up through the skies. This year's North American tour (April–May 1988) was another huge continental sweep—taking in major cities like Atlanta, San Francisco, Seattle (Piazzolla's old friend Édouard Pécourt drove up from his new home in Oregon to hear him), and Vancouver.[42] At San Francisco's Great American Music Hall, there was such demand for seats that during the performances the management opened the doors so that those left outside could hear the music. Brian Auerbach, reviewing the performance, noted that "Piazzolla's passion is transmitted to his fellow musicians like no other since Ellington. His power to make the listener feel like an intimate is unparalleled. . . . This is the most creative drum-less group I've heard. . . . When he finally left the stage ... it felt as if time had stopped."[43] A large crowd applauded him afterward in the street.

San Francisco is the headquarters of the Kronos Quartet. David Harrington, who attended the concert, which he found "fantastic," invited Piazzolla to the Quartet's rehearsal next day. Piazzolla, Suárez Paz, and Console all went, and, as Harrington recalls, "there was this enormous energy all of a sudden in the room." Suárez Paz remembers the occasion as almost a class or seminar on tango music. For Harrington, the Argentines were "marvelously supportive of us. They respected our efforts and enlarged our perspectives, all within an hour." Kronos, however, was still waiting for its "large quartet piece" from Piazzolla.

At the start of May 1988, in New York again, Piazzolla worked with Kip Hanrahan on his new album, *La Camorra*, the pieces written during the Punta del Este summer and premiered at the Quintet's pre-tour public rehearsals (once again at Sham's in Belgrano). These recordings were his last with the Quintet. He told Natalio Gorin two years later that he regarded them as his best ever. Listening to these dense, beautiful tracks, marvelously recorded, it is hard to avoid the feeling that they embody a lifetime's musical development. Do they also reveal a forward thrust, toward a new and original synthesis? The contrasts between the three "Camorras" are in themselves remarkable. "Camorra I" is a thoroughgoing evocation of the tango music of the 1940s. With its pure tango cadences, its superb swing, its strong bandoneon coloring, it takes us back to the "danceable" tango with which Piazzolla had broken. (It is also persuasive evidence for the many who believe that Piazzolla was becoming more, rather than less, *tanguero* in his later years.) "Camorra II" is a more personal Piazzollean statement, with characteristic dissonances and shifting rhythms. "Camorra III" is again a showcase for the Quintet as a whole; it includes an extraordinarily lyrical violin part for Suárez Paz and superb piano passages for Pablo Ziegler.

On Saturday, 7 May, Piazzolla joined forces with Lalo Schifrin at a concert in New York's Beacon Theater—another performance of the Bandoneon Concerto, which the *New York Times* critic thought "diaphanously lovely."[44] Next day the Quintet was in the ballroom of the Charles Hotel in Cambridge, Massachusetts, where Gary Burton joined it for two pieces—"working very hard to catch up," according to the *Boston Globe*'s critic, Michael Ullman. Pablo Ziegler, Ullman thought, sounded "like a Latin Bill Evans," and given Evans's influence among jazz musicians of his generation, this was no small compliment. (Ullman knew Piazzolla's music, and had once amusingly described it as "Webern trying to make sense of Carmen Miranda.")[45] A day later the musicians were in the Hall of the Americas at the Organization of American States in Washington, where people were packed six or a dozen deep around the sides of the hall.[46] America's adulation of Piazzolla was beginning to rival Europe's. He had suddenly acquired what the *New York Times* called "a flavor-of-the-month fashionability."[47]

To what extent was this true? Piazzolla himself was mildly frustrated, as Sarah Vardigans remembers, by the difficulty of making headway in the United States. He was well aware of the great American habit of embracing ephemeral crazes and then forgetting about them; he had said as much in Brazil in April 1986, when commenting on the success of *Tango Argentino*.[48] Such a comment, however, underestimated the "space" available in the amazingly diverse and lively American culture for high-quality music of the kind Piazzolla could offer. The appearance of *Tango: Zero Hour*, the Princeton recording of the Bandoneon Concerto, and now *La Camorra* certainly reinforced his American reputation. Reviews of these albums over the next year or so were uniformly favorable, and sometimes ecstatic.

For many of those who applauded him in North America, he had not been a familiar figure, but there was something in his music—perhaps because of its links with jazz—to which they could relate without difficulty. *Rolling Stone* magazine, overjoyed by the Pangaea label's 1988 reissue of *Tango: Zero Hour*, declared that "Piazzolla's music contains nearly everything worthwhile life has to offer."[49]

As Karl Loder was to write three years later, in *Esquire*, Piazzolla, "the one-man Pink Floyd of the *nuevo tango* . . . is totally, passionately *out there*. . . . But what really makes the stuff *sing* . . . is its trippiness. Piazzolla creates exotic tango dreamscapes in which anyone who ever navigated the brooding seas of 1960s psychedelia will feel right at home."[50]

Piazzolla never saw this comment. Another comment, which he could possibly have seen, appeared in the December 1988 issue of *Playboy*. Reviewing some of his recent recordings, Robert Christgau, a leading writer on rock, observed that Piazzolla's music, with its "characteristic dissonances and mood swings," was nothing less than "historic pop transformed into contemporary chamber music." Christgau described Piazzolla as "a belated cult hero in the U.S." His cult status has strengthened notably in the years since. He will never be as famous in the short term as Madonna or Garth Brooks. He would not have minded. "I wouldn't know what to do if the majority liked my music," he said in 1986. "I prefer it that the nonthinking public never becomes interested in my music."[51] And today? It is easy enough to find Piazzolla's albums in any large American record store, some of it in the World or International sections, some of it in the Jazz sections, some of it—increasingly, most of it—in the Classical department. In 1997, five years after his death, *Billboard* magazine called him—no small tribute—"the hottest composer around."[52]

In June 1988 the Quintet, with Milva once again on hand, toured Japan: four concerts in Tokyo, and eight in other cities, including Nagoya, Kyoto, and Osaka. At the start of July it went to Turkey—Piazzolla's only visit there—for a performance at the Istanbul Music Festival. Once again Sarah Vardigans acted as tour manager. While they were in Japan, Piazzolla asked her if she would become his personal manager outside South America. She made it clear that she could not be responsible for promotion as such, but, impressed by the passionate following he attracted wherever he went, she readily agreed.

When Piazzolla arrived at Istanbul airport on 4 July, he was greeted by a long-standing admirer, Hayri Erenli, who was thrilled to meet his idol in the flesh. He drove Piazzolla to his hotel and was with him over the three days he spent in Istanbul. The concert (5 July) at the Atatürk Cultural Centre—the largest enclosed hall in Turkey at the time—was sold out. The Turkish press gave it excellent coverage. At the concert, Piazzolla paid tribute to Turkish bandoneonist Orhan Avsar. The two men had never met, but Avsar (who died in 1974) had done much to promote Piazzolla's music in Turkey. On the following day Hayri Erenli took Piazzolla and some of the musicians on a boat trip along the Bosphorus, pausing for lunch at a seafood restaurant. The photographs he took that day show the party in very merry mood. The heat in Istanbul was ferocious, and Piazzolla, Erenli recalls, was very careful not to expose himself to the sun.

To Erenli, Piazzolla seemed to exude good health. But there was a price to be paid for his hectic globetrotting. Nature had given him a first drastic warning in 1973; there had been another warning in 1981, and an episode a year or so later that put him in the Sanatorio Cantegril in Punta del Este for a few days and brought his doctor, Marcos Asensio, across from Buenos Aires. In Rome in 1986, Horacio Malvicino, who had once studied medicine, took his blood pressure and was appalled. "This fellow is going to explode," he said to himself, but he could not persuade Piazzolla to call off his concerts. Over the next year or two, Malvicino noticed, he became reluctant to go on walks through the streets whenever the Quintet was in Paris. Laura confirms that his right leg, and especially the ankle, were troubling him more and more and that walking became an ordeal. The doctor and musician Eduardo Lagos, whom Piazzolla sometimes consulted about prescriptions, thought that he was turning a blind eye to his health problems. Neurologist Dr. Ramón Leiguarda saw him regularly during the middle and late 1980s and detected an auricular fibrillation, but recalls him as "sparing in his medical controls . . . not someone who looked after himself."

In hindsight, at least to the press, Piazzolla blamed his worsening health on the strain of the revival of *María de Buenos Aires* in 1987. Afterward, "I had some very intense chest pains," he recalled, "and I thought it was bronchitis."[53] It was not bronchitis. Back in Buenos Aires, Laura, frightened by how tired he was becoming, eventually put her foot down. She made him consult the heart surgeon, Dr. Dardo Fernández Aramburu, who told him: "Mr. Piazzolla, you must have an operation, we must operate on your heart, and *soon*." The Quintet was just back from its trips to Japan and Turkey. Another European tour was scheduled for a few weeks later. In the meantime the musicians were recording music Piazzolla had written for an animated film, *Piso Cero*. It was never finished. Piazzolla was tense and irritable. There were terrible arguments in the studio. Piazzolla suddenly announced: "I am going to have to dissolve the Quintet because I have to have heart surgery."[54] The father of Piazzolla's young bandoneonist friend Marcelo Nisinman, who had undergone similar surgery, assured him that it was nothing, that he would feel much better afterward. Despite his own imminent hospitalization, Piazzolla made a point of visiting his old friend Roberto Di Filippo, who had just returned home after a serious operation.[55]

His quadruple bypass surgery was performed on 10 August 1988, with Dr. Fernández Aramburu completing the operation in about three and a half hours.

Coming out of the anaesthetic, Piazzolla had hallucinations, and next morning, in a very agitated state, he gave a male nurse a black eye. "Don't you know what's going on?" he asked Dr. Fernández Aramburu. "They've kidnapped me. They kidnapped me last night. Today I'm in prison, they've got me here, they won't let me play, and on top of everything they're going to take my car away. I don't *want* to give my car to them!" There were no further complications. Three weeks later he was given a clean bill of health.

Piazzolla felt very low after the operation. Diana found her father "depressed, sad, sad." Laura told her that he was weeping a lot. His first excursion was to the jewelry store on Avenida Quintana owned by his friend Ricardo Saúl. By October he was well enough to be able to think about traveling. Dr. Fernández Aramburu gave his permission, and he and Laura went for a short vacation to Europe (France, Germany, Italy), touring in a rented automobile. "He had to put up with me doing the driving," Laura recalls, "and I was pleased as punch, because I could show him that I drove well." Back in Punta del Este for the summer, Piazzolla's one big regret was that the doctors had placed shark fishing off limits. There would be no brave excursions through the swell to the Isla de Lobos. He had to content himself with easier fishing off the nearer-lying Isla de Gorriti. Daniel Rabinovich, who went with him on some of these less dramatic trips, remembers that "he didn't like it much."

Sextet and Tragic Coda
1988–1992

→ The Sextet

Intimations of Immortality—and Mortality ←

→ Tragic Coda

In 2020? In 3000 Too? ←

> Piazzolla was miles ahead of us all.
> —Composer Giya Kancheli talking to violinist Gidon Kremer (1997)

The Sextet

Early in 1989 Piazzolla wrote to his Turkish admirer Hayri Erenli, who had sent him some tea and a teapot. "I did not write before," he told him, "because my health was not O.K. Now I feel wonderful. I feel strong as a Turk."[1] When Sara Braceras went to the Chalet El Casco to interview him for *La Nación* in February, she found him relaxed and sunburned, with the dog Flora constantly nearby. He told her that 1989 would be a year "with a lot of movement. I shall be constantly on tour."[2] He was already forming a new group for a whole string of international appearances—more than 100 in all. Many of them had already been booked for the Quintet. The schedule was rearranged to lessen the strain on Piazzolla, though it hardly lessened the strain on his new personal manager Sarah Vardigans.

The new group was a sextet: two bandoneons, cello, guitar, double bass, piano. Piazzolla evidently wanted to try something new, but his decision to eliminate the violin (rather than create a septet) was one he came to regret. The team was a mixture of old Piazzolla hands—Héctor Console, José Bragato, and Horacio Malvicino (for whom the Sextet "was not a good experience")—and newcomers. For the second bandoneon, Piazzolla selected Julio Oscar Pane, an excellent young instrumentalist. Pane left the Sextet, for personal reasons, after its first tour. His replacement, Daniel Binelli, was a veteran of Osvaldo Pugliese's band. For his pianist, Piazzolla invited Gerardo Gandini, one of Argentina's most talented composers, a former pupil of Ginastera, and a virtuoso pianist as brilliant at improvising Irving Berlin songs as writing his own classical works. Gandini's playing gave the Sextet "a very novel color," says Binelli, with Piazzolla constantly challenging the pianist to surpass himself—" 'Now play a solo in the Bartók style.' " Gandini himself recalls Piazzolla telling him, "Gandini, put a bit of Scriabin into it!" and commenting on his "Messiaen-type cascade of notes" in performances of "Buenos Aires Hora Cero," a standard piece in the Sextet's repertory.[3]

In retrospect Piazzolla clearly saw the Sextet as a mistake. One problem was the second bandoneon, included to reduce the strain on him. But he played as vigorously as ever. Perhaps remembering his easy partnership with Leopoldo Federico in the Octet, he found that Binelli did not adapt well to his style—or so he told Natalio Gorin.[4] There were times, says cellist José Bragato, when the two of them achieved "a real display of bandoneon technique."[5] Piazzolla seems to have set up a kind of rivalry with Binelli, as if to underline Piazzolla's leadership and prove the superiority of his own bandoneon playing. Binelli himself was to look back on the collaboration as very special but also "very tough. Too much so. Very intense."[6]

The inclusion of a cello instead of the traditional violin gave the Sextet a darker sound than the Quintet, especially audible in the new pieces Piazzolla wrote for the group—"Luna," "Sex-tet," "Preludio y fuga." There is not much lightness of spirit in these pieces, not even very much playfulness, despite their skillful construction. Gerardo Gandini found the "somber tone" attractive. Binelli suggests, plausibly enough, that it represented "what was happening to Astor; it was the music of his bypass operation." Malvicino found the Sextet's coloring "terrific" in certain pieces, but adds that "to listen to a whole concert in that vein wasn't very entertaining."[7] Nevertheless the Sextet had some brilliant moments. Gandini's verdict on his seven months with Piazzolla is well worth including here: "When Piazzolla was in good form, it was like playing with Charlie Parker. It was fantastic."

On 15 March 1989 Piazzolla moved across to Buenos Aires and began a month of rehearsals with his new ensemble, borrowing the house of his new friends the Nisinmans, which had a good piano. The young Marcelo Nisinman asked if he could record some sessions. "Okay," said Piazzolla, "but I don't want to know where the microphone or the recorder is." Nisinman noticed an almost electric atmosphere as the rehearsals proceeded: "six crazies, going at high speed," he says, with Piazzolla especially respectful toward Gandini.

Piazzolla introduced the Sextet and part of its new repertory to the press and the public at the Club Italiano in mid-April. In the audience, Leopoldo Federico whispered to Armando Rolón, "He continues to be the best of all of us." Piazzolla told reporters that he was partially returning to the sound of De Caro's orchestra of the 1930s and that his challenge was to constantly surpass himself.[8] This was dangerous bravado. Dr. Fernández Aramburu wondered whether it was too soon for him to be thinking of touring again, but Piazzolla brushed aside all such doubts: "I feel terrific," he told the heart surgeon. "I'm working at full tilt."

The duly rehearsed Sextet now left on a whirlwind tour of North America (21 April–25 May), appearing in a score of cities at fees of between $7,000 and $10,000 per concert. Hearing the group at the Lincoln Center's crowded Alice Tully Hall on 24 April, *New York Times* critic John Rockwell found the music "very striking," even though "its effects were often somber."[9] While in New York, Piazzolla gave an update to the press on his plans for the Gardel opera. The idea of an American production had by now faded away. Piazzolla claimed there had been misunderstandings: the American Music Theater Festival wanted a chamber opera, while he himself wanted something like "*Aida* or *Madame Butterfly* . . . so the work is now being proposed for the Paris Opera."[10]

After the concert at Eugene, Oregon (12 May), Édouard Pécourt and his wife Jocelyn joined Piazzolla, Laura, and the musicians for dinner. Pécourt found his friend "very tired, above all in his appearance. He nonetheless still had energy, and it didn't seem that he wanted to abandon his feverish activity. But physically, one saw a face all used up by fatigue." Pécourt was not to see him again. In Los Angeles, a day before the first concert (16 May), Piazzolla received an astonishing phone call at his Santa Monica hotel. "Astor, do you remember me?" It was the George Greeley whose death had been announced over the phone from Hollywood in 1958. Piazzolla's spine tingled. Greeley attended the concert and afterward saw Piazzolla in the dressing room. He could offer no explanation whatever for the telephone messages that had so dashed Piazzolla's hopes.[11] The matter remains a complete mystery. Another acquaintance from the past visited him at his hotel— Jorge Calandrelli, with whom he had so often rubbed shoulders at 676, now a successful composer and arranger in the United States. "Jorge, you should write tangos," Piazzolla told him.

Piazzolla had not performed in Los Angeles before. Don Heckman, who interviewed him for the *Los Angeles Times*, explained to his readers that in Argentine music he was "what Duke Ellington and Louis Armstrong were to jazz." The concerts were in Royce Hall on the campus of the University of California, Los Angeles. His admirers turned out in force and gave him a raucous reception. Writing up the concerts, the distinguished jazz expert Leonard Feather observed that the acclaim Piazzolla was now winning in the United States was "an oddity that defies classification; this group is no more pop or jazz or soul than it is rock or fusion or R&B"—yet the music's "inherent quality," he suggested, demanded attention in a "world dominated by semiliterates who equate energy with talent."[12]

Before leaving the United States at the end of May, Piazzolla made a quick dash to the Spoleto USA Festival in Charleston, South Carolina, to watch a production[13] of his second collaboration, mostly conducted by mail, with choreographer Graciela Daniele. This was *Dangerous Games*. Its first part was a recycling of some of *Tango Apasionado*, with all traces of Borges removed; the second was a version of the Orpheus myth with allusions to the recent Argentine military regime. Its musical direction was entrusted to guitarist and conductor Rodolfo Alchourron, who was then living in New York. Eric Salzman, of the American Music Theater Festival, helped form the consortium backing the show, and it was staged with success on both the East and West Coasts. According to Daniele, Piazzolla was pleased by the production. (Eric Salzman is not so sure.) Later that year (October 1989), in an apparently "hyped-up" form, it flopped completely on Broadway and closed immediately. It was panned by the critics, who accused Daniele of displaying sex and violence under the guise of criticizing sexism and militarism.

After the United States, the Sextet, with Binelli now taking Pane's place as second bandoneonist, went to Chile. It was booked for a single concert at Santiago's Teatro Oriente (Tuesday 6 June) and a TV appearance. In press interviews, Piazzolla again talked of the Gardel opera—his "dream." It was his last time in the noble little country whose fish and wine he so enjoyed. He was obviously pleased by his "marvelous reception by the Chileans," and he praised Chile's remarkable recent progress under the "iron hand" of General Pinochet.[14]

In Buenos Aires again, the Sextet made its official debut at the Teatro Ópera (Friday 9 June), to which Atilio Talín had invited Argentina's Peronist president-elect, Carlos Menem. Rather predictably, Piazzolla had been displeased by Menem's triumph. During the election campaign, he had supported the Radical party candidate, Eduardo Angeloz, to the extent of sending a message to be read at his final rally. His statements about Menem were fierce. His friend Ricardo Saúl was with him in the dining room of the Colonia-Buenos Aires ferry when he suddenly said, very loudly, "If that man is the winner . . . I shall leave the country," a position he reiterated to the press and to Bernardo Neustadt on TV. Menem countered this bombardment very astutely, saying that Piazzolla was one of Argentina's glories. Argentina needed him; he should stay.

The president-elect and his wife, Zulema (whose stormy estrangement from her husband captured so many headlines later on), arrived at the theater with an impressive retinue; Atilio Talín had to find ninety extra seats at short notice. They were warmly applauded. "Thank you, Mr. Menem, for being here," said Piazzolla from the stage. "You have asked me to stay . . . and I *shall* stay."[15] Menem stood up and gestured exultantly. Author María Susana Azzi, who was there, remembers the audience going wild. During the intermission, the Menems, Piazzollas, and Talíns all drank champagne together in the dressing room. "I want you to know I have never been a Peronist," said Piazzolla. "What's that got to do with it?" asked Menem, oozing his notorious charm. "I have been a *piazzollista* all my life." The ice was broken. President Menem remembers the evening as "marvelous." Piazzolla remained well disposed toward him, hoping, as he told Rostropovich in April 1990, that he might perform "the miracle" of restoring Argentina's battered fortunes.[16]

On 17 June 1989 the Sextet played at the Teatro Solís, in Montevideo, before going on to Europe for the first of two planned tours. This would be a strenuous seven weeks of crisscrossing the map in the way the Quintet had so often done: Holland, Britain, a transatlantic side trip to Montreal (2 July), Sweden (for the Stockholm Jazz Festival), Germany, Italy (with Milva once again on hand), and finally Switzerland. At Amsterdam's Royal Carré Theater (26 June), the Sextet appeared with Osvaldo Pugliese's band. The two groups played separately but joined forces for performances of "La Yumba" (Pugliese's classic tango) and "Adiós Nonino." Gandini, in a piano section linking the two tangos, had finished his improvisation on "La Yumba" and was starting on "Adiós Nonino" when he unexpectedly reverted to playing a snatch or two from "La Yumba"—a musical joke that puzzled Pugliese's musicians and the audience. (Pugliese himself was bemused, as he told tango expert "Vasco" Izurieta soon afterward.) Piazzolla smiled broadly. The audience burst out laughing.

In Glasgow for his first British appearance since 1985, Piazzolla announced jestingly: "This is our first time in Scotland, but we know all about you. Especially . . . your whiskey." One reviewer of the concert was close to ecstatic: "Call me over the top. Call me what you will, but file this man under 'indispensable.' "[17] Moving south of the border to London, the Sextet played at the Wembley Conference Centre (30 June). At a late night party at the Argentine embassy after the concert, Piazzolla was greeted by Teddy Peiró, an Argentine bandoneonist long resident in England. Peiró fell to his knees, bowed his head, and refused to shake hands. "You must know that I *hate* you!" he told Piazzolla, explaining that he was now only the second-best bandoneonist in Britain. "Don't worry," Piazzolla smilingly replied. "I am leaving tomorrow." Peiró was impressed by Piazzolla's stamina. A drooping Daniel Binelli turned to him at one point and said: "If they don't throw him out, Astor will go on until it's time to go to the airport."[18]

At the Stockholm Jazz Festival the Sextet's audience applauded "almost to the point of delirium," Ambassador Albino Gómez remembers. Once again, Piazzolla was in excellent form at a party, this time under the light of the midnight sun— old records played, merry reminiscences and stories, peals of laughter. Gómez and his friends recorded a lengthy interview with him in which he stressed the importance of his plans for the Gardel opera. He was still hoping for a Paris production. "It's going to be the biggest leap forward of my life," he declared.[19]

There was an unexpected addition to this frenzied European schedule. On Monday, 10 July, the musicians flew from Berlin to London and went from there to Bristol, to record a forty-five-minute recital for BBC-TV's Channel 2 (broadcast in June 1990) before flying next day to Italy. Tony Staveacre, the producer, had traveled to Berlin the previous week to persuade Piazzolla to make the detour. When the Sextet played—in the setting of an "elaborate bandstand . . . with fancy railings, hanging baskets and fairy lights"—they "held an audience and studio crew spellbound," says Staveacre, who regards this encounter with Piazzolla as one of the most memorable in a long broadcasting career.[20]

Despite his outward show of animation, Piazzolla was clearly strained by the tour. Sarah Vardigans, who accompanied the Sextet on three of the four 1989 tours, thought him much less ebullient now. On the longer bus journeys, he behaved "just like a little kid, a spoiled kid." There was much less jokiness among the musicians. In Italy, Milva found him "hard and bad-tempered."[21] Gerardo Gandini sensed that Piazzolla "was progressively tiring." Yet there were still the lighter moments, when the old Piazzolla flashed out. In Glasgow, for instance, he arranged for the musicians to go to a tailor's, ostensibly to try on some shirts; when they arrived, they were fitted out with kilts and merrily photographed. "Afterwards we went off to play, very contented," recalls Daniel Binelli.

Back in Buenos Aires after the first European tour, Piazzolla invited his old friend Ambassador Mario Corcuera Ibáñez to a small dinner party. "Do you know what we're celebrating?" he asked him. "We're celebrating a year of life." Introducing Corcuera Ibáñez to three of his fellow guests, he explained: "These are my companions from the intensive therapy unit." It was the anniversary of his bypass operation. He did not forget to send a suitable letter to Dr. Fernández Aramburu. "I have been working hard and well," he told him. "Perhaps I have gone over the limit a bit, but I am beginning to take better care of myself. Thanks to you, I am a new man—the man of thirty years ago."

It was soon time to be off again. This time it was a swing through Brazil (20 August–8 September 1989), where one critic who heard the Sextet praised Piazzolla's *inesgotável criatividade* ("inexhaustible creativity") and sensed that he was making "a leap into the future" with themes reflecting characters from Greek tragedy "who travel inexorably towards death." Piazzolla's old friend, the Brazilian journalist Eric Nepomuceno found him "still the old lion onstage." The ever-appreciative Brazilian audiences, however, thought some of the new music mildly puzzling.[22] Héctor Console remembers a moment on this tour when he told Piazzolla: "We're going to do the Quintet again. I don't *like* the Sextet." Piazzolla gave what Console interpreted as a nod of assent.

At the end of the Brazilian tour, both Console and Bragato quit the Sextet in unhappy circumstances. Console's mother had died during the tour. Having known this was likely, he had nonetheless yielded to Piazzolla's insistence that he go to Brazil, and he bitterly regretted that he had consented. He had no further wish to work with Piazzolla. Bragato wanted to take his wife Gina on the second European tour to show her Italy but was told he could not. Bragato suspected Laura's influence. His friendship with Piazzolla came to a very acrimonious end. Piazzolla certainly took the departure of Console and Bragato very hard, "much harder than anyone could imagine," says Laura. The two new members of the Sextet—bass player Angel Ridolfi and cellist Carlos Nozzi—were both experienced classical musicians, though neither was a stranger to the tango genre. Whatever their merits as musicians, Piazzolla did not conceal his unhappiness over the change in his team. With Ridolfi, recalls Gandini, his relationship was "tempestuous." During a concert in Cologne, Piazzolla stopped halfway through a piece and told him: "You are *ruining* my music!"[23] Poor Ridolfi sometimes found himself breakfasting at a separate table in the hotels where the Sextet stayed.

Gandini recruited Nozzi by telephone from São Paulo. He was watering his backyard at the time, and he asked that Piazzolla call in person to confirm the invitation. Piazzolla did, adding some practical instructions: "Bring everything in black, all your clothes in black, Nozzi—even the underpants." There were a few days of rehearsals at Gandini's house, and the reconstructed team then flew to Paris to play the first concert of the second European tour. It was at a Giorgio Armani fashion parade at the Musée Rodin, with Milva on hand, on 18 September 1989. Over the next six weeks, the Sextet crisscrossed the map once more—France,

Belgium, Germany, Switzerland. In Paris again, the Sextet played at the Auditorium Porte Sainte Eustache (6 October). One of those attending was Françoise Thanas, a translator and theater expert who had met Piazzolla on several occasions over recent years. She thought he looked tired and drawn, but to the veterinarian Didier Servant, also present, he seemed as vigorous as ever—like "a man carried away by a river in furious flood." Carlos Nozzi, whose observations (as a newcomer) were perhaps especially perceptive, certainly found him to be tiring in the later stages of the tour, although most of the time he was a "firecracker, hyperactive. He never stopped." But Piazzolla *was* clearly longing for the tour to end. "I want to go home," he would say. "I want to get up in the morning and eat what *I* like, not what the hotel likes."

The applause for the Sextet was greater than ever. During the first part of the concert at Zurich's Tonhalle (18 October), Piazzolla played the Bandoneon Concerto with an orchestra, the Sextet taking over for the second half. "And now we must show them how to play the tango!" he told his musicians. Emerging from the theater afterward, Carlos Nozzi was flattered by the way people on the sidewalks applauded *him* simply for being part of the Sextet. Four nights later the group was at the celebrated and raucous Fabrik nightspot in Hamburg's Altona district, in a smoke-filled atmosphere of clinking glasses and chatter. The musicians played to a youthful audience more accustomed to the sounds of rock. "After the first piece," Nozzi recounts, "there fell a silence such as I had never heard before." Piazzolla made a short speech in English, telling the audience that Germany had produced many great composers and that therefore he felt honored to be playing in Hamburg. The audience loved it.

During the last week of October, the musicians based themselves at the Hotel Eden in Cologne, commuting from there to a recording studio at Neunkirchen, twenty-five miles out in the countryside. In this rustic setting they started work on a new album for Vera Brandes's Intuition label. Brandes had released Kip Hanrahan's albums in Europe, and by agreement with Hanrahan, she was now assuming responsibility for the production of Piazzolla's records, with Hanrahan remaining artistic director. She had first met Piazzolla three years earlier in New York, finding him "a very dignified man, very self-assured, charming, warm, strong, confident." She remembers that before driving to Neunkirchen for one of the sessions, Piazzolla asked her to go into the nearby Cathedral with him, to pray for "a good outcome for the recording." Their prayers were not answered. No more than four tracks were recorded. Piazzolla grew very dissatisfied with the bass playing; there was a huge row, and the project was abandoned. A few weeks later in New York, Kip Hanrahan suggested to Piazzolla that it should be revived, but it was not. He found Piazzolla more "impatient and intense" than he had been before, "frightened that he wouldn't finish the work he needed to do, the music he needed to write."

After the abortive stint at Neunkirchen, Piazzolla went to Paris and the musicians to Chiasso, the southernmost town in Switzerland. He joined them there for the last three concerts of the tour. At some point over the next day or two, Piazzolla took Gandini and Malvicino to the side, separately, and told them he was going to disband the Sextet. He was exhausted by this kind of touring; his future lay with chamber groups and symphony orchestras. Both Gandini and Malvicino were crestfallen. Malvicino tried to dissuade him: "Look, Astor, to get rid of a group with this terrific quality and play with a symphony orchestra is the same as getting rid of a marvelous girl and fucking an inflatable doll."[24] The last of the Swiss concerts was played at the Victoria Hall in Geneva (5 November). Piazzolla announced his decision to the audience. Gandini inserted a musical quotation into his improvisation during "Mumuki." "What was that you just played?" Piazzolla asked him during the intermission. "Today, at the last concert, you play that garbage?" He had not recognized the bars from Beethoven's "Les Adieux" Sonata.[25]

A very downhearted party returned by train to Paris. A bus was waiting to take the musicians to the hotel where they would spend the night before flying home. Piazzolla was staying on in Europe for a few more weeks. Carlos Nozzi found the scene "very sad." Malvicino, who had played with Piazzolla on and off for nearly thirty-five years, felt it more sharply. "With total simplicity," he recounts, "he sat down in the front seat of the bus—it's a movie style finale—and we went first to his residence, and he got out, and, very slowly, said 'chau,' and walked away. And there it all finished. It was something tremendous. I never wanted to see him again."[26]

Later that month Piazzolla flew to New York to perform his "Five Tango Sensations" with the Kronos Quartet at Lincoln Center (25 November). The work was a distillation of "Sette Sequenze," pieces for bandoneon and strings he had written in 1983 and recorded that year in Munich with a quartet from the Graunke Orchestra. The Kronos musicians were still waiting for their "large quartet piece." This was a substitute. They had rehearsed the work with him in September in Munich, at the time of the Sextet's concert at the Deutsches Museum. Now they recorded it with him, a three-hour session in a small studio in Manhattan. It was Piazzolla's last time in a recording studio. "Basically, we sat down, got the sound, and played," says David Harrington. "We've never done a recording quicker, and probably never will again." The Kronos musicians sensed what Harrington memorably defines as "a centered sternness" in Piazzolla: "He just pulled the sound out of Kronos."

On 11 December 1989, briefly back in Europe, he joined forces with the Orchestra della Svizzera Italiana at the Kursaal in Lugano for another performance of the Bandoneon Concerto. So ended a remarkable year, in some ways his *annus mirabilis*. It was time once again for the solace of the Uruguayan summer.

Intimations of Immortality—and Mortality

He wanted, and needed, to slow down. He was tired of the incessant routines of travel, the sheer hassle of frequent appearances in four continents. He looked forward, or so he said, to spending more time with his grandchildren. His interest in them so far had not been especially marked, though he approved of his grandson Daniel Astor's wish to become a drummer. At one of their rare meetings he handed the boy a supermarket bag containing about $1,400 in miscellaneous bills so that he could buy a drum kit.[27]

A fortune-teller had once told him that he would live to be eighty-three. "I only hope that there doesn't come a day," he said in 1979, "when I can't go on writing and playing."[28] He told Diana that he would like to end up like the grand old veterans Arthur Rubinstein or Pablo Casals, "to live in a house by the sea, to have a grand piano, a bicycle, my dogs, to go shark fishing, to compose without stopping, to have my glass of whiskey at seven in the evening. . . ."[29] In the summer of 1989–90, Piazzolla once again fished off the Isla de Lobos with Dante Rinaldi. Was this a gesture of confidence or defiance? Dante advised him to stop touring and to rest and relax in Punta del Este. "Yes, but if I stop playing. . . ." said Piazzolla, and they chugged out on the *Renata* in the old way, Dante saying to himself that "a man ought to put a limit to the cycle of his life." His *puntaesteño* friend Fernando Tesouro thought that Piazzolla was perhaps drinking more whiskey than usual. The Argentine ballet dancer Maximiliano Guerra visited Punta del Este that summer, to perform a solo he had devised for Piazzolla's "Contrabajísimo." Piazzolla went to one of his rehearsals. He told Guerra that he had thought of him when writing "La Camorra"—and left him a few sheets of paper sketching a possible ballet.

In February, Sara Braceras once again interviewed him for *La Nación*. He told her he was now determined to organize "a new life," playing with orchestras and chamber groups, with no fixed ensemble of his own, and no more than 100 concerts per year. As for the Gardel opera, journalist Edmundo Eichelbaum in Paris was translating Pierre Philippe's libretto into Spanish. The opera, he told

her, would now be produced at Seville in 1992, as part of the Columbus quin-
centennial festivities; Plácido Domingo would definitely be in the title role. He
outlined his calendar for 1990: first the United States, and then his Paris "headquarters" for tours of Europe and Japan.[30]

A lengthier interrogation awaited him at the beginning of March 1990. Piazzolla had consented to tape some extensive reminiscences for journalist Natalio
Gorin. They were published in 1991 under the title *A manera de memorias* (By
Way of a Memoir). Gorin found his friend in reflective, even somber mood—
"kind of exhausted, very quiet," no longer "the fellow with the easy joke." The
interviews were a chance for Piazzolla to reflect on a life that was ominously close
to the threescore years and ten mentioned in Psalm 90 as the normal human
span.

> I have an expectation: that my work will be listened to in 2020. And in
> 3000 too. At times I am sure of it, because the music I make is different.
> . . . I am going to have a place in history, like Gardel. . . . My music can
> please or not, but no one will deny the way it's made: it's well orchestrated,
> it's new, it's of this century, and it has the smell of the tango, which is what
> makes it attractive the world over.[31]

Before he left Punta del Este, Piazzolla went to a farewell party at the Tesouros'
house on Avenida Buenos Aires. The photographs taken that evening show him
sad-eyed and looking older than his years. He celebrated his sixty-ninth birthday
in Buenos Aires. Both Víctor Oliveros and Ricardo Saúl, veterans of earlier, more
bohemian, birthday parties, were struck by the formality of the dinner: tuxedos
were required. Someone else who saw Piazzolla around then was Sarah Vardigans,
then vacationing in Buenos Aires. Her role as personal manager was being transferred to Ingrid Widgren-Fisher, an Argentine married to an Englishman and
living in France. Vardigans thought that Piazzolla "seemed fine." Piazzolla himself
was not so sure. A few days before he set off on his travels again, he invited Oscar
López Ruiz and his wife Donna to join him at the Café Mozart. There, Mónica
Cosachov and Tomás Tichauer were to play their highly successful piano-viola
version of "Le Grand Tango." This was the work Piazzolla had dedicated to
Rostropovich and which Rostropovich rehearsed in Buenos Aires that same
month, in a room at the Teatro Colón. López Ruiz had not seen Piazzolla for a
while, and complimented him on his appearance. "Thanks," said Piazzolla "but
I think maybe the little tubes are worn out." López Ruiz, in the old way, told
him to stop fooling. "May God hear you!" exclaimed Piazzolla.[32]

Tragic Coda

The Piazzollas flew first to New York. One of those who visited Piazzolla there, at the Gramercy Park Hotel, was the Italian producer and conductor Ettore Stratta, who had met him on many occasions in both Europe and South America. He wanted to discuss a possible album—Piazzolla plus symphony orchestra. Would London or Buenos Aires be the better place for recording? "It doesn't matter," Piazzolla told him, "because I work everywhere." Stratta made his record of "symphonic tangos," but without Piazzolla.

Piazzolla had already mapped out his European strategy for 1990. He would play mostly with chamber groups, principally string quartets drawn from the chamber orchestras of Mantua and Salzburg. In mid-May he teamed up with the Mantua Chamber Orchestra, under Bruno Pizzamiglio, at Mantua's Teatro Bibiena for a performance of the Bandoneon and Bandoneon-Guitar concertos. This concert was repeated at Vicenza a few days later with the Pedrollo Orchestra. Marco de Santi, the guitarist for these concerts, relished his renewed contacts with Piazzolla. They talked of "various projects, of doing something in Germany, of the possibility of making a record." It was not to be.

On 21 May 1990 Piazzolla began a short tour with four musicians from the Mantua chamber orchestra: his collaborator of 1987, Anahí Carfi (first violin), Pierantonio Cazzulani (second violin), Stefano Pancotti (viola), and Marco Scano (cello). Their opening appearances, at the Teatro Smeraldo in Milan and the Teatro America in Bologna (24 May) reflected the pattern of subsequent concerts: a string quartet by Alberto Ginastera and Piazzolla's "Four for Tango" in the first half, with Piazzolla playing his "Five Tango Sensations" with the quartet in the second half. The work lasts barely twenty minutes. At the Milan concert, the audience demanded an encore. Piazzolla played two short pieces. This failed to satisfy the audience. When the lights came on, there were shouts of disapproval.[33] (At one or two later concerts the police had to be called.) Gerry Mulligan was present at the Teatro Smeraldo, and greeted Piazzolla with a cry of "When are we going to do another record?" The encounter was witnessed by Aldo Pagani, Piazzolla's old Italian agent, who offered him a new contract with an immediate up-front payment of $100,000. Piazzolla refused, telling him that he preferred the "complete freedom" he now enjoyed.

There were a few further concerts in Italy, including dates at Perugia and Udine. The Mantua musicians quickly overcame their initial shyness of Piazzolla and found him agreeable to work with. "For all of us it was a marvelous experience," says Anahí Carfi. She noticed, however, that he was tiring easily. Laura confided to her that "Astor was not well, that the doctors had advised him to rest, to stop playing." He himself was determined to carry on. "As long as I'm alive, I shall play," he told Carfi. He was open with her about his current ambitions. He told her he wanted to raise his music "to the classical level," so the public that enjoyed Beethoven, Schubert, and Mozart could also "feel Piazzolla." On the human level, Carfi found the minitour very pleasant. Piazzolla woke her, breakfasted with her, and gave her paternal advice about drinking and smoking. Musically, things were much less satisfactory. The Italian audiences who remembered Piazzolla's Quintet were frustrated and unhappy. "The public that came to experience Piazzolla," says Carfi, "wasn't the public that . . . [came] to experience Ginastera. . . . *And it didn't work, it absolutely didn't.*"

In mid-June 1990 Piazzolla and the Mantua group flew to Finland to play at a festival at Ikaalinen (15–16 June). Given the long entrenched importance of the tango in Finnish culture, it was hardly surprising that the press showed great interest in the visit. For the first time in his life Piazzolla listened to a Finnish tango band, afterward describing it as "very European, not Argentine." He remarked, not at all originally, on the scenery: "One well understands the music of Sibelius." Every musician going to Finland says the same. This was the last time Piazzolla played to audiences in a country that had never heard him in the flesh before. They were disappointed. One critic found the concerts "a disconcerting experience," while another, more hostile, roundly declared the music to be "nonsense you can't make head or tail of."[34] Piazzolla was, in fact, feeling very ill in Finland. He consulted doctors at Ikaalinen. They advised him to stop performing.

From Finland, the Piazzollas went on a short sightseeing trip to Leningrad, though Piazzolla was too tired to go on to Moscow as they had planned. A tour of Portugal with the Mantua musicians fell through. There were a few more concerts, in Switzerland and Holland, this time with the Salzburg musicians. On 24 June, Piazzolla linked up with the Kronos Quartet at a festival in Ulezen, Germany. They had what David Harrington remembers as "a great rehearsal," in which Kronos added "Adiós Nonino" to its repertory. "He felt like another member of Kronos," says Harrington. "He never once made us feel less than he was, and we just loved that. He just willed the best out of all of us." It was the day of the Argentina-Brazil game in the 1990 World Cup, then unfolding in Italy. "If Argentina wins," announced Piazzolla, "I'll take everybody to dinner." Argentina won (1–0), but he forgot. When Harrington went to the hotel dining room, Piazzolla and Laura were enjoying a quiet candlelit dinner.

The start of July found the Piazzollas in Athens. In the shadow of the Acropolis, in the ancient Herodes Atticus theater, Piazzolla performed (3 July) with a local orchestra conducted by his good friend Manos Hadjidhakis: "Three Tangos for

Bandoneon and Orchestra," the Bandoneon Concerto, and the inevitable "Adiós Nonino." It was the last concert he ever gave. Hadjidhakis organized a suitably festive dinner party, attended mostly by Greek intellectuals, says Laura—"really fascinating people." The Piazzollas then flew back to Paris, to their rented sixth-floor apartment in the Résidence Orion-Les Halles, 4 rue des Innocents, where they overlooked the round-the-clock scenes of animation in the little Square des Innocents below.

Laura had had enough. She was unhappy about the organization of the tours, unhappy about the standard of the hotels and theaters chosen. She had liked Sarah Vardigans as manager but did not care for her successor, Ingrid Widgren-Fisher, or her English husband. "I saw that for Astor the tour was very traumatic," Laura recounts. "It was very tough, and he was suffering a lot, and I said to him: 'I am going to cut it short, this tour.' " She was true to her word. All further concerts were canceled. Laura suggested to Astor that he needed "a sort of spiritual cure," and the two of them drove to Italy to visit Padre Pio's church at San Giovanni Rotondo. Piazzolla had long been a devotee of the Franciscan priest, on whose hands stigmata were said to have appeared at Mass. He was very moved by the visit. On their return to Paris, Laura went off on a two-day pilgrimage to Lourdes, bringing back a phial of holy water for him.

To celebrate Laura's birthday on 24 July, they dined with their good Parisian friends Richard and Giselle Galliano at Graziano's in Montmartre. As Laura tells it, Piazzolla and Giselle both had slightly too much champagne. Galliano told Piazzolla that the restaurant had once belonged to the popular singer Dalida, long since dead. "She's not coming? She's not going to sing?" asked Piazzolla. The talk turned to music—the greatness of jazz pianist Bill Evans, the Gardel opera. In the car, on the way home, Piazzolla suddenly remarked: "I'm closing the door of my stomach, I've done too much, I need to rest." Over the next few days there were meetings with Pierre Philippe and Edmundo Eichelbaum about the Gardel libretto. At one point Piazzolla telephoned Plácido Domingo. The musician Olivier Manoury, who had recently mended one of Piazzolla's bandoneons, saw him in a record store. He asked him if the repairs had been satisfactory. "Yes," said Piazzolla, and then left abruptly. One of those he spoke to by phone on the evening of Friday 3 August was Kip Hanrahan, with whom he joked about "the boredom of touring with classical musicians." Next day, he and Laura honored their old Parisian custom of visiting the Chapel of the Miraculous Medallion in the rue du Bac.

But clearly all was not well. Atilio Talín remembers frequent phone calls,

Piazzolla checking whether he had the right blood pressure pills or not. Acquaintances in Europe sensed that something was amiss. In Milan, Angela Pagani thought that his eyes looked strange, and he surprised her by giving her a begonia plant—never his habit before. Natalio Gorin, in Milan to cover the Holland-Germany game in the World Cup, phoned Piazzolla and was disturbed by his "weakened voice."[35] On 25 July, Piazzolla phoned Diana to wish her a happy forty-seventh birthday. She asked him how he was. "Only so-so." He had always been so upbeat before. Now it was: "No, I couldn't write anything at Punta del Este. It's odd." Then a final flash of optimism: "Everything's going to change."

As always, he had plans. He was thinking of future concerts—concerts with a revived Quintet, at the Teatro Colón (to play with Mario Benzecry's Orquesta de Cámara Mayo), with the Mantua group in Buenos Aires. He needed to write a chamber piece Rostropovich had commissioned. When they met in April, Piazzolla asked if he could add a bandoneon to the planned cello-piano-guitar-percussion lineup. "If you yourself play it, certainly," replied "Slava."[36] He had entrusted a new arrangement of "Adiós Nonino" to violinist José Carli. He had told the Assad brothers, at the Café de la Paix only recently, of his wish to write more for them. Robert Hurwitz, from New York, who was with them, remembers Piazzolla telling them, "Just continue to work at the high level you do; don't be discouraged." The comment seemed valedictory. Record producer Vera Brandes drove from Cologne to Paris to meet him for a discussion of future projects, including the Gardel opera—and has wondered ever since whether her hasty car drive embodied an intuition.

There was more film work in the wind—for a major, star-studded picture, as publisher Yves Baquet remembers. Piazzolla was hoping, too, for further collaborations with jazz musicians—Chick Corea or Michel Petrucciani, perhaps, but definitely with Al Di Meola. "When I finish my opera," he had told him in Amsterdam a few weeks earlier, "this is the next project." He had several unfulfilled nonmusical ambitions. He had never visited Disneyland, and he wanted to. He was hoping to buy a new house in Punta del Este, on the little "point" itself. But the main task now was the opera. Visiting the singer Jairo's house at Triel-sur-Seine for dinner earlier that summer, he claimed to have it mapped out in his head. Everything else had to be set aside, including the "big quartet piece" for the Kronos Quartet. Piazzolla phoned David Harrington and arranged for the advance he had received from Kronos to be wired back. As for the opera itself, he had done little more than sketch out one or two themes—one portraying Gardel's adored mother, Doña Berta. It was time to grapple with the music. There had been too many delays. Piazzolla had a sudden impulse to complete the work in the United States. "That way we can be near Plácido," he told Laura. "Pierre Philippe can come too." A few days in Buenos Aires—the plane tickets were already bought for 11 August—and then it would be back to that "second homeland" for the music to crown his career.

It was not to be.

On the morning of Sunday, 5 August 1990, he was getting ready to go to Mass at Notre Dame with Laura. Just out of the shower, he suddenly fell to the bathroom floor, stricken by a cerebral hemorrhage, completely paralyzed on his right side. It was the fate he had feared worst of all. We have Daniel's word for it that he often said: "If, some day, I'm completely paralyzed, kill me." He was rushed to intensive care at the Hôpital Ambroise-Paré in Boulogne-Billancourt, on the southwestern outskirts of Paris.

Jairo, who was recording in Provence, flew back to Paris and went to the hospital. He took Piazzolla's hand and sang to him. José and Jacqueline Pons visited every day. Aldo Pagani remembers traveling to Paris to offer help. Laura's sister Circe flew in from New York. Richard Galliano abandoned the master classes he was giving in the provinces and returned with Giselle to be with Laura. Piazzolla remained in a deep coma. A doctor who saw the brain scans told José Pons that it would be best for him to die immediately. One of the surgeons asked Yves Baquet to use his influence with Laura, to prevent her from moving Piazzolla from Paris. But Laura, strongly supported by Diana and Daniel, was determined that her stricken husband should die in Argentina.

It was the height of the vacation season. Airliners were full. On 11 August, President Menem, after a phone call from Atilio Talín, authorized Aerolíneas Argentinas to rearrange the seating in a southward-bound 747 so that Piazzolla could come home. Richard Galliano will never forget "the image of that plane taking off." During the flight (AR 171), Laura sat quietly in the first class section, enduring her own nightmare, sometimes going aft to see her husband. The other passengers "behaved very well, very respectfully," as head purser Fernando Fondevila remembers. The plane reached Ezeiza airport at 12:55 P.M. on Tuesday, 14 August. Waiting for it in the VIP lounge were Daniel, Diana, and Atilio Talín. An ambulance took Piazzolla to the intensive care unit at the Sanatorio Mater Dei in the Palermo Chico district. Late next evening President Menem briefly visited the clinic, afterward declaring, "I have faith that Astor will pull through."[37] And indeed, on the evening of 21 August, he emerged from his coma and recovered some kind of consciousness, though not his power to speak. For the family, there was suddenly hope. Daniel told the press that his father was "conscious in every sense" and that his recovery was "almost a miracle. Right now my father is listening to a work by Bach. I have my old man for a bit longer."[38]

"A bit longer" was longer than anyone could have wanted. Piazzolla's nearest and dearest lived through twenty-three agonizing, terrible months. Those who were less near and dear picked up what news they could. Gary Burton remembers intermittent phone calls: " 'Astor's gone home,' 'He is better,' 'He is worse again.' This went on for a long time." Al Di Meola—who later said that his times with Piazzolla were "like being with Bach"[39]—expressed his feelings in music, in his "Last Tango for Astor," recorded in October 1990.

In Room 419 at the Mater Dei, they played him music and showed him the television. He tried to scrawl messages, sometimes just about decipherable, on pieces of paper. "How alone," one such message read. So Diana told her mother. In mid-October he was taken to the Avenida Libertador apartment. He spent a few days there in a wheelchair, mostly watching TV.[40] It was too much for Laura, especially on the weekend, when his nurses were off duty. "No, kids, I'm going crazy," she told Diana and Daniel. By the end of the month he was installed at ALPI (Asociación para la Lucha contra la Parálisis Infantil) in Palermo. Originally a pioneering center for polio victims, it now treated a wide variety of neurological disorders. Though its doctors were excellent, its buildings were austere. "Really depressing, that place," says Diana. It depressed Laura, too.

"He is a man with a lot of will to live," Laura told the press.[41] He had his own way of showing it. "He was ill-humored," recalls Mariano César Azzi, one of the ALPI physical therapists. "He was on a very bad wavelength." His condition, however, seemed to be improving. Toward the end of November he could eat again—mashed potatoes, flans—and showed signs of pleasure when he heard the meal trolley approaching. But early in December 1990 pneumonia set in and he was taken to another hospital, the Sanatorio Otamendi y Miroli. He recovered, and returned to ALPI, but an intestinal hemorrhage in mid-January 1991 sent him to yet another hospital, the Santísima Trinidad in Palermo. At the end of January he was moved to Lesit, a private clinic in the Caballito district. On 11 March, Laura and her friend Eva Moccia took him a cake for his seventieth birthday, but he did not really notice it. In May there was a recurrence of pneumonia, and he was taken to intensive care at the Santísima Trinidad, returning the following month to Lesit. Over the next year, Piazzolla went back and forth between Lesit and the Santísima Trinidad at least ten times, as the doctors tried to handle his growing respiratory difficulties and other serious problems. Extreme Unction was administered more than once.[42]

Not all of Piazzolla's friends were allowed to see him during this time. Others were dissuaded from visiting—two of the Mar del Plata cousins and Dante Rinaldi among them. There were many who simply preferred not to see him. Atilio Talín was an assiduous visitor. President Menem looked in several times, insisting that no publicity be given to his visits. Oscar López Ruiz took his wife Donna, who spoke to Piazzolla in English, thinking he might respond to the language of his boyhood; he caressed her face with his "good" left hand. Young Marcelo Nisinman took his bandoneon and played to him. Piazzolla's former agent Roberto Capuano, on several visits, thought that he was trying to communicate something. Marta Saúl had the feeling that "he had a certain perception, sometimes anyway." To Víctor Sasson it seemed "as if he understood and didn't understand." Antonio Agri got the impression "that he knew me—but we all said the same."

How much *did* he know? Neurologist Dr. Ramón C. Leiguarda describes him as "absolutely aphasic; he lost *language*, in other words the capacity to understand or read written material . . . he could not see the right-hand half of his field of vision." Dr. Leiguarda also points out that musical capacity is located in the nondominant hemisphere—in Piazzolla's case, the left hemisphere—so that he possessed at least some ability to write music, and he certainly tried to, encouraged by Laura. Occasionally, says Dr. Leiguarda, he could hum snatches of melody. During the "better" periods of his final ordeal, he was able to signal moods and sometimes more precise information. When Daniel, on the point of leaving one day, absentmindedly left his keys on the side table, Piazzolla pointed to them.[43] When Daniel Astor, now nineteen, tapped out rhythms on his grandfather's legs or on his side table, Piazzolla joined in.

The main burden of visiting fell on Laura and the children. Diana and Daniel saw more of him now than they had since their childhood. (For both Laura and Diana there was a double burden: Laura's mother died in December 1990, and Diana's husband was very sick.) Piazzolla appreciated his children's devotion: "When we entered the room, his face lit up," says Diana. "When we left, he became sad." Laura's arrivals and departures produced the same effect, as Natalio Gorin noticed. Laura usually went in the mornings, the children in the afternoons. The bad feeling between them meant that they did not care for their visits to overlap. Diana had come to share her brother's very negative opinions of Laura, and there were no olive branches proffered during Piazzolla's final tragedy.

They played him Bach, Stravinsky, and his own music through headphones. Later, he did not wish to listen to his own music at all. Sometimes he seemed to like hearing whole operas, sometimes Buenos Aires's newly operating F.M. Tango radio station; but more often, as time passed, his eyes simply settled on the TV screen. Daniel often wondered what he actually saw on the little screen. Diana occasionally took in a harmonica. What memories did it bring? Daniel once showed him a little image of the Virgin of the Miraculous Medallion, but Piazzolla made what Daniel could only interpret as a reproachful gesture, as if to say that the Virgin had let him down. Laura, for her part, strove valiantly to brighten up the rooms where her stricken husband lay. Her friends Eva Moccia, Lydé Mirel-mann and Marta Saúl—as well as Eladia Blázquez and Cristina Justo—all rallied around generously.

In the end, there was nothing that could be done for him. Laura still hoped that "perhaps he would be left a little bit more time." In March 1992, many Argentine radio stations marked his seventy-first birthday by playing his records. Piazzolla was gradually sinking. His weight fell to seventy-four pounds—"more like Mahatma Gandhi than Astor Piazzolla," says Daniel. He retained whatever consciousness he had until the end. When the Israeli embassy in Buenos Aires was blown up by Middle Eastern terrorists (17 March), with the loss of twenty-nine lives, Daniel was certain he saw horror in his father's face as he watched the TV reports.[44]

In May, the doctors talked of a possible tracheotomy, but the family said no. On Wednesday, 1 July, after what turned out to be his final transfer from Lesit to the Santísima Trinidad, he was operated on for peritonitis. Two days later, Daniel and Diana were visiting him when Laura entered. They did not greet her. Daniel bent to kiss his father, and Piazzolla pushed him away, as if reproving him for impoliteness to his wife. The end came next day, Saturday, 4 July—a day when "The Star-Spangled Banner," the tune that had always thrilled him, was blaring out across the land of his distant boyhood. Summoned to the Santísima Trinidad from work, Daniel again tried to kiss his father. Again the face was averted. Piazzolla fixed his eyes on the TV and kept them there. The final struggle began. It was time for both Extreme Unction and the civilized aid to departure—in Daniel's words, "morphine, morphine, morphine, morphine . . . until he died." Laura and Eva Moccia had been there almost all day. Late that evening Daniel's wife, Lalla (and young Daniel Astor), arrived at the hospital with coffee and sandwiches. Diana and Daniel left the room to take a much-needed break. Daniel went to a lounge two or three floors down. He heard footsteps on the stairs. It was his sister. "Papa just died." He had died at 11:15 P.M., holding Laura's hand. It was she who closed his eyes.

His body was taken to the Concejo Deliberante, the seat of Buenos Aires's city council. For once, Laura and the children were agreed: the coffin was closed.

There, on the Sunday, friends and admirers came to pay their respects: the Minister of Culture; musicians such as Horacio Malvicino, Pablo Ziegler, Hugo Baralis; bandleaders such as Osvaldo Pugliese; film directors such as Francisco Solanas; friends such as Víctor Sasson; and many, many others. Dedé was there; Amelita too. Horacio Ferrer arrived early, as did playwright Kado Kostzer, accompanied by the great actress Iris Marga. President Menem sent a wreath of chrysanthemums, and on the Monday morning he appeared in person. He told the press: "All great men are controversial; even Jesus Christ was controversial."[45]

The funeral procession—about twenty cars—set out from the Concejo Deliberante at 10:45 A.M., taking about an hour to reach the Jardín de Paz, a private cemetery at Pilar in the northern suburbs. After a short service in the chapel, the coffin was taken to its resting place as Piazzolla's music—"Contrabajísimo"—sounded from the cemetery's loudspeakers. There were the short farewell speeches customary in the Latin world. As the coffin was lowered into the ground, Diana, gripping Daniel's arm, thanked her father "for having loved us so much."[46]

Even in death, Piazzolla could not quite escape controversy. Some members of the family had assumed that his body would be taken to lie alongside Nonino and Nonina in Mar del Plata, and they were indignant when it was not. This, apparently, was not Piazzolla's final wish. "He had asked me very specially," says Laura, "not to take him to Mar del Plata. He had asked me that very specially."

In 2020? In 3000 Too?

The tributes around the world were generous. News of Piazzolla's death was the main story on Italian radio on 5 July (along with the worsening Yugoslavian situation and a rumor that Hitler's grave had been found). *Corriere della Sera* called him *Il grande compositore argentino*. In the United States, National Public Radio carried a tribute on its morning news program, and the *New York Times* hailed him as the "Modern Master of Tango Music." The two leading newspapers in Paris summarized his life under the headlines "La noblesse de tango," and "la dignité du tango." A Brazilian magazine declared that he had given tango music "the nobility of the great tragedies," and one in Mexico City placed him "among the greatest creators of this half-century." A British obituary noted sadly that "English critics ignored him . . . [but] Piazzolla's tangos . . . will live as long as music is appreciated for its ability to convey the human emotions."[47] There were hundreds of similar tributes in scores of countries around the world.

Having brought this story to its close, what do we need to say about Piazzolla's achievement? In a life of constant change, of constant struggle, he transformed a tradition of popular music into something authentically his own. His tangos never ceased to breathe a Buenos Aires atmosphere, but in painting his own big village, he painted the world; and in so doing, as the great Brazilian Hermeto Pascoal has said, he "succeeded in universalizing Argentine music." Does that make him Argentina's Gershwin or Ellington? He belongs, certainly, in the same pantheon, the pantheon of the twentieth century's leading musical masters. As Plácido Domingo puts it, he was "one of the great ones, great ones of today's music."

Piazzolla's awareness in the 1980s that his music was in demand by all sorts of musicians was strikingly confirmed in the years after his death. His music has been and is being performed and abundantly recorded by an extraordinary number of different artists, and with a wide variety of different instruments. Some of these efforts stand out. Over and above the superb Piazzolla albums produced by Al Di Meola (1996) and Gary Burton (1998)—"timeless, magnificent music," one reviewer said of the latter[48]—Piazzolla's works occupied half the tracks on a record made in 1995 by Daniel Barenboim ("a really extraordinary experience," he tells us) with bassist Héctor Console and bandoneonist Rodolfo Mederos. Among chamber ensembles performing Piazzolla's music, we might note the G-String Quartet in Germany, with its remarkable album of 1996, and the Quinteto Suárez Paz, with its excellent *Milonga del Angel* CD. Violinist Gidon Kremer's Piazzolla album (recorded in 1995–96) had a six-figure sale. Kremer did a second in 1996–97, assisted by Milva and the Assad brothers, and in 1998 he produced a sparkling new version of *María de Buenos Aires*, not to mention another Piazzolla CD in 1999. In November 1996, Mstislav Rostropovich, in St. Petersburg, finally recorded "Le Grand Tango." Another virtuoso cellist, Yo-Yo Ma, recorded a Piazzolla album the following year, with Antonio Agri, Horacio Malvicino, Héctor Console, Gerardo Gandini, and again, the Assads. Reviewing yet another notable CD of 1997 (Emanuel Ax and Pablo Ziegler in piano duo), *New York Times* critic Jon Pareles observed that Piazzolla's music was "becoming an international staple."[49]

The performances and the tributes go on and on. It is not our job to chronicle them. Nor do we need to search for explanations of the continued interest in Piazzolla, an interest that is manifestly spreading. His music can speak for itself, and it will continue to do so, certainly in the year 2020, and maybe in 3000 too (to use the dates he himself threw out on that summer day in Punta del Este)—if the human race gets that far.

This note concentrates mostly on Piazzolla's own recordings, in historical sequence. Most have appeared on compact disc at one time or another. We make no attempt to list all the many compilations of his music that have subsequently been issued. There is a good deal of duplication here, and record labels sometimes shamelessly mix recordings from different periods and ensembles without explanation. Far too many compilations, inexcusably, have no liner notes at all. Recordings of Piazzolla's music by other artists have also proliferated; here we have included only a few. For updated discographic information, we recommend the reader with access to the Internet to visit the admirably comprehensive Web site maintained by César A. Luongo (**http://www.piazzolla.org/works/astorcd.html**), to whom we are grateful for some of the information here. A country of release is shown below for each album (after the *label* and the *number*). This does not mean that the CD has not been released elsewhere (or by more than one label), still less that distribution is restricted to the country indicated. We can give no guarantee that all these albums are easily obtainable, though many of them are.

1944–1960

Some of Piazzolla's recordings with Francisco Fiorentino are on *Francisco Fiorentino con Orquesta dirigida por Astor Piazzolla* (EMI/Pampa 8 35746–2: Argentina) and on an identically titled shorter album (El Bandoneón EB-CD-7: Spain). The 1946 band may be heard on *Astor Piazzolla y su Orquesta Típica, "El Desbande"* (El Bandoneón EB-CD-2: Spain); *Astor Piazzolla y su Orquesta Típica, "Se Armó"* (El Bandoneón EB-CD-31: Spain); *De mi bandoneón* (EMI 8 32311–2: Argentina), an anthology. The Suite for Oboe and Strings ("Opus 9") is among the works on *¡Tango! Music by Piazzolla, Bragato, Arizaga* (Dorian DOR-90201: USA). *Astor Piazzolla-Paris 1955. Ses premiers enregistrements* (Sono Punch; Éditions Univ-erselles EU 1045: France) is a collection of Piazzolla's 1955 Paris recordings, some of which are also on the compilation *Astor Piazzolla et Compagnie* (Vogue VG 671 670086: France). *Astor Piazzolla. Octeto Buenos Aires* (Diapason DP 10276: Argentina) is a reissue of the Octeto Buenos Aires's one full-length LP, and Piazzolla's work with the string orchestra of 1955–57 (including the LP *Tango en HI-FI*) appears on the compilation *A. Piazzolla* (Music Hall 10.003–2: Argentina). The Jazz-Tango recordings from the New York years have been dragged from their well-deserved obscurity on *Take Me Dancing! The Latin Rhythms of Astor Piazola* [sic] *and His Quintet* (P-Vine/Blues Interactions PCD-2877: Japan) and *Astor Piazzolla & His Orchestra. Evening in Buenos Aires* (P-Vine/Blues Interactions PC-2885: Japan).

1960–67

For the first Quintet's rehearsal at Dr. Eduardo Lagos's house, hear *Ensayos* (Jazz & Fusion JF 9503: Argentina). *Piazzolla interpreta a Piazzolla* (RCA/BMG ECD 1030: Argentina) and *¿Piazzolla o No? Bailable y Apiazolado* (RCA/BMG ECD 50612: Argentina) are the "avant-garde" and "danceable" albums from 1961. (The first has precious bonus tracks of the Piazzolla-Troilo bandoneon duo of 1970). There are many compilations of the Quintet's subsequent recordings and those of the "new octet" of 1963: *Tiempo Nuevo* (Columbia/Sony Music 2–470061: Argentina); the two-CD set *Todo Piazzolla* (Columbia/Sony Music 2–484601: Argentina); *Leyendas* (Columbia/Sony Music 2–478708: Argentina); *Los Más Grandes Éxitos* (Columbia/Sony Music 2–470163: Argentina); *La Historia de un Idolo, Vol. I* (Columbia/Sony Music 2–461659: Argentina); *La Historia de un Idolo, Vol. II* (Columbia/Sony Music 2–461660: Argentina); CDs 1–3 of the excellent six-CD set *Todo Piazzolla en la Casa Epic* (Sony Music ESCA 6710–6715: Japan), with Roberto Yanés's recordings with Piazzolla on CD 6. (CDs 1 and 3 include the settings by Piazzolla of two poems by his daughter, Diana.) The "new octet" album of 1963 has been reissued as *Tango contemporáneo. Astor Piazzolla y su Nuevo Octeto* (Columbia/Sony Music 2–484746: Argentina). The sound track for the movie *5° Año Nacional* is on *Astor Piazzolla y su Quinteto-Osvaldo Berlingieri y su Orquesta* (Music Hall MH 10.041–2: USA). *Introducción al Ángel, Vol. I* (Melopea CDMSE 5041: Argentina) contains radio recordings from 1963. The Philharmonic Hall LP was reissued as *Concierto en el Philharmonic Hall de New York* (Polydor POCP1248: Japan), and the "Borges" LP as *Astor Piazzolla y su Orquesta. Canta Edmundo Rivero, "El Tango," textos de Jorge Luis Borges* (Polydor 829866–2: Argentina); both of these seem to be rarities. For Piazzolla's supposed re-creation of tango history, hear *La Historia del Tango, Vol. I, La Guardia Vieja* (Polydor 314 511 638–2: USA) and *La Historia del Tango, Vol. II, La Época Romántica* (Polydor 314 511 639–2: USA).

1967–74

The original double album of *María de Buenos Aires* is now a two-CD set: *María de Buenos Aires* (Alfa AFCD-14/15: Spain). *María de Buenos Aires* (Dynamic CDS185/1–2: Italy) is an Italian reconstruction (without Piazzolla) of the 1968 version. Piazzolla's suite from the *operita* and his music for Páez Vilaró's film *Une Pulsation* can be heard on *Pulsación* (Alfa AFCD-1: Spain). The Piazzolla-Ferrer-Baltar collaboration is preserved on several albums: *Amelita Baltar interpreta a Piazzolla-Ferrer* (Columbia/Sony 2–478783: Argentina); *Piazzolla-Baltar-Ferrer 1970–1972–1976* (BMG ECD 1031: Argentina); CDs 4–5 of *Todo Piazzolla en la Casa Epic* (see above). The Quintet's later albums of this period may be heard on *Astor Piazzolla. Concierto para Quinteto* (BMG/RCA 74321 23172–2: Argentina), which includes the four-bandoneon recording from 1971 and part of the music for the movie *Con alma y vida* (1970); *Adiós Nonino* (Trova JWDC-5002: Spain); *Piazzolla en el Regina* (RCA/BMG 74321 21373–2: Argentina), recorded live at the Teatro Regina in March 1970, plus the two pieces written after the row over *Last Tango in Paris. Astor Piazzolla. Muerte del Angel* (Milan 73138 35841–2: Argentina) is live from a concert at the Teatro Odeón in June 1973, displays Osvaldo Tarantino's piano playing beautifully, and is interesting when heard alongside the *second* Quintet's early recordings. The Nonet's two classic 1972 LPs are combined on *Astor Piazzolla y su Conjunto 9. Música Popular Contemporánea de la Ciudad de Buenos Aires* (BMG/RCA

ECD 1071: Argentina). Hear also *Tristezas de un Doble A* (Personality PRS 23192 : Italy), the concert at the Istituto Italo-Latinoamericano in Rome; *A. Piazzolla y su Noneto* (Saludos Amigos CD 62050: Italy); *Onda Nueve* (West Wind/Latina 2213: Germany). A good Canadian anthology covering these rich years (excellent liner notes by Pierre Monette) is *Astor Piazzolla. Tangamente* (Just a Memory JAM 9107/9–2: Canada).

1974–78
The 1974 *Libertango* LP has often been reissued—for example, *Libertango* (Tropical Music 68.904: Germany). All Piazzolla's work with Italian groups (including his film music) is collected on a nine-CD set (three boxes), *Carosello Italiano 1974–1984* (Carosello 300 532–2, 300 533–2, and 300 534–2: Italy). The 1977 and 1978 Milan albums may be heard on *Persecuta* (Kardum KAR 976: France) and *Chador* (Kardum 975: France). Reissues of *Summit*, the Piazzolla-Mulligan LP, include *Reunión Cumbre. Astor Piazzolla-Gerry Mulligan* (Trova CD 5055: Argentina), which has the tracks in their proper order; not all reissues do. The "Suite Troileana" is combined with the music for the movie *Lumière* on *Suite Troileana* (Trova 50.408: Argentina). Beware of *Lumière* (Tropical Music 68.942: Germany), which unforgivably omits the opening bandoneon solo in the "Suite Troileana." Other sound tracks from the mid-1970s are *Rain over Santiago* (ans Records ans 12015–2: USA) and *Armaguedon* (ans Records ans 12012–2: USA); some titles from the first of these appeared under new names on *Piazzolla-Agri* (Trova CD 5019: Argentina). Piazzolla's "electronic" phase is more patchily represented: hear *Desde Argentina. Astor Piazzolla y su Nuevo Conjunto* (Music of the World CD 12520: ?Italy). José Angel Trelles's singing can be appreciated on *Astor Piazzolla con José Angel Trelles* (Personality PRS 23199: Italy) and *Oblivion. Piazzolla & José Angel Trelles* (Atoll ATO 8624: France). The 1977 Paris Olympia recordings of the second Electronic Octet have not so far been reissued. Once again there is a good Canadian three-CD anthology covering the "European" phase (and the start of the next phase): *Piazzollissimo. Astor Piazzolla 1974–1983* (Just a Memory JAM 9103/5–2: Canada).

1978–88
Many of the recordings of the second Quintet were live, since Piazzolla largely avoided studios at this period: *Concierto para Quinteto* (Alfa AF CD-5: Spain), from one of the Gran Rex concerts in December 1981, excellent; *Live in Lugano 1983* (Ermitage ERM 124: Italy); the two-CD set *Libertango* (Milan 73138 35843–2: Argentina), from a 1984 Mar del Plata concert; *The Vienna Concert* (Messidor CD 15922–2: Germany) and *Tristezas de un Doble A* (Messidor 15970–2: Germany), recorded in Vienna in 1983 and 1986, respectively (the latter was the first Piazzolla album actually to appear as a compact disc); *The Central Park Concert* (Chesky Records JD 107: USA) from 1987. There are many compilations, such as *Milonga del Ángel* (Saludos Amigos CD 62036: Italy); *Il Bandoneon di Astor Piazzolla* (Replay RMCD 4123: Italy); *Astor Piazzolla. Messidor's Finest Volume Two* (Messidor MSDR 15843: Germany); *Escualo* (SUM Records SD 242.003: Argentina). The Teatro Regina appearance (May 1982) with Goyeneche is preserved on *Astor Piazzolla-Roberto Goyeneche* (BMG/RCA 74321 18920–2: Argentina), as is the Bouffes du Nord show (1984), *Milva and Astor Piazzolla Live at the Bouffes du Nord* (Dischi Ricordi DMRL 6332: Italy; also Metronome 825 125–2: Germany).

The Piazzolla-Burton collaboration can be savored on *The New Tango* (Atlantic Jazz 7 81823–2: USA). The revived and revamped *María de Buenos Aires* appears (without Piazzolla) on *María de Buenos Aires. Opera Tango.* (BMG/Milan 73138 35602–2: USA). Sound tracks from the movies of this period are *Musiques de film* (Milan CD 280: France), with music for *L'Exil de Gardel* and *Enrico IV*; *El Infierno tan Temido* (ans Records ans 12011–2: USA); *A Intrusa* (ans Records ans 12013–2: USA); *Sur* (Milan 73138 35619–2: USA). Piazzolla's three memorable albums with Kip Hanrahan—*Tango: Zero Hour, The Rough Dancer and the Cyclical Night*, and *La Camorra*—are collected in a three-CD set, *Astor Piazzolla. The Late Masterpieces* (American Clavé AMCL 1022: USA). The first was reissued on the Pangaea label (PAND 42138: USA) and again more recently on Nonesuch, which has also reissued *La Camorra* (79516–2: USA)—both with liner notes by Fernando Gonzalez. Piazzolla's symphonic work is less well represented. His only known recording of the Punta del Este Suite (Caracas, April 1981) appears on *Astor Piazzolla. Libertango* (Saludos Amigos CD 62037: Italy). Its quality is very rough. The Bandoneon and Bandoneon-Guitar Concertos have fared better: *Concierto para Bandoneón. Tres Tangos* (Elektra Nonesuch 79174–2: USA), and *Concierto para Bandoneón y Guitarra. Historia del Tango* (Music Hall MH 10.020–2: USA). The Bandoneon Concerto (and "Concierto de Nácar") can also be heard on *Concierto de Nácar* (Milan 73138 35842: Argentina), a recording of the spectacular 1983 Teatro Colón concert.

1988–90

The Sextet's recordings were mostly live: at the Club Italiano in Buenos Aires, *Tres minutos con la realidad* (Milan 73138 35844: Argentina); in Amsterdam, on CD 1 of the two-CD set *Astor Piazzolla & Osvaldo Pugliese. Juntos* (Lucho 7704–2: Netherlands), reissued as *Luna* (EMI 7243 8 35595: ?England); in Bristol, *Astor Piazzolla Live at the BBC 1989* (Intuition 3226–2: Germany), liner notes by Tony Staveacre; at its penultimate appearance (4 November 1989), *The Lausanne Concert* (BMG/Milan 73138 35649–2: USA). *57 Minutos con la Realidad* (Intuition INT 3079–2: USA) combines some of the Bristol tracks with four from the truncated sessions at Neunkirchen in October 1989. Piazzolla's November 1989 recording with the Kronos Quartet can be heard on *Five Tango Sensations* (Elektra Nonesuch 9 79254–2: USA), and his last-ever concert (Athens, July 1990) on *Astor Piazzolla. Bandoneón Sinfónico* (Milan Latino 74321 34268–2: France).

Piazzolla by Others

The albums mentioned at the end of chapter 15 are *Gary Burton–Astor Piazzolla Reunion* (Concord Jazz CCD-4793–2: USA); *Di Meola plays Piazzolla* (Bluemoon 2–92744: USA); *Mi Buenos Aires Querido. Barenboim-Mederos-Console* (Teldec 0630–13474–2: USA); *Gidon Kremer. Hommage à Piazzolla* (Nonesuch 79407–2: USA) and *Gidon Kremer. Astor Piazzolla. El Tango* (Nonesuch 79462–2: USA); *Yo-Yo Ma. Soul of the Tango* (Sony Classical SK 63122: USA) a Grammy winner in 1999; *Los Tangueros. Emanuel Ax-Pablo Ziegler* (Sony Classical SK 62728: USA); *Rostropovich. The Russian Years* (EMI Classics 7243 5 72016 2 9: England), a thirteen-CD set with "Le Grand Tango" on CD 13; *G-String Quartet Plays Astor Piazzolla* (Koch Schwann 3–6423–2: Austria). *Astor Piazzolla—Quinteto Suárez Paz* (Milan Sur 74321 49136–2: France). From scores of other records released, and without denying merit to any of them, we confine ourselves to recommending our favorite small handful: the Kronos Quartet's *Winter Was Hard* (Elektra Nonesuch 9–79181–2: USA), with Piazzolla's "Four for Tango" on track 7; *Sergio and Odair Assad. Latin American Music for Two Guitars* (Nonesuch 9 79116–2: USA), which includes his "Tango Suite"; *Astor Piazzolla. Ballet Tango. Richard Galliano* (Milan Sur 873032: France), in which Galliano plays the work dedicated to him by Piazzolla; the Ensemble Paris Tango's *Songe d'une Nuit d'Été* (Milan 873091: France), his music for Shakespeare's *Midsummer Night's Dream* (Richard Galliano on bandoneon); *Le Grand Tango. Piazzolla. Cirigliano* by the Musica Camerata Montréal (CBC Records MVCD 1079: Canada); *Piazzolla Classics* (Milan 73138 35640–2: USA), for performances of "Tangazo" and the "Three Tangos" by the Buenos Aires Symphony under Pedro Ignacio Calderón; *Music of Latin America* (Helicon HE 1025: USA), with Carter Brey and Christopher Riley playing "Le Grand Tango" on track 7; *Música de las Américas* (Mayo Ed. Fonograf DDDCooo1: Argentina), for the Orquesta de Cámara Mayo's version of "Las Cuatro Estaciones Porteñas"; Gidon Kremer's *Tango Ballet* (Teldec 3984–22661–2: Germany) and his sparkling new version (1998) of *María de Buenos Aires* (Teldec 3984–20632–2: Germany); the remarkable Phil Woods, *Astor & Elis* (Chesky JD 146: USA) and last but assuredly not least, the superb *Piazzolla x Piazzolla* (Milan Sur CDA 0681: Argentina) by Daniel Piazzolla's Octet.

GLOSSARY OF

SOUTH AMERICAN TERMS

candombe   Dance rhythm of African origin, still popular in certain carnivals in South America. Two features of the dance (its so-called *cortes*, pauses, and *quebradas*, improvised movements) were incorporated into the tango.

Candomblé   One of the three most important Afro-Brazilian cults (Yoruba-derived).

chacarera   Argentine popular dance in 3/4 or 6/8 time (depending on the region), and the music and words belonging to it.

chamamé   Dance and musical genre (generally lively and upbeat) common in Paraguay and the north east of Argentina.

confitería   Establishment where confectionery is sold, often also serving as a tea shop, café, or bar.

Guardia Vieja   ("Old Guard") The formative phase of tango music, from the 1890s to the early 1920s.

güiro (or guero)   Instrument in Latin American dance music made from a notched gourd and scraped with a stick.

habanera   Cuban dance in 2/2 time with dotted rhythm; one of the main influences on the birth of the tango.

lunfardo   Vocabulary (largely Italian-derived) used originally in low-life and semi-delinquent circles in late nineteenth- and early twentieth-century Buenos Aires, and which later had a fundamental influence on colloquial Buenos Aires Spanish and on tango lyrics.

malambo   Tap dance popular in Argentina, Uruguay, and Chile, danced exclusively by men.

marplatense   Inhabitant of Mar del Plata.

mate   A Paraguayan tea very popular in Argentina and Uruguay and to a lesser extent in Chile.

milonga   An improvised rural song-form that around 1860 added dance steps (strongly influenced by the habanera and the mazurka), and which mutated into the tango around 1880. (The word is also a synonym for dance-gathering, cabaret, or cabaret-girl.)

orquesta típica   Standard term since 1911 for a tango band or orchestra.

pai do santo   Priest or elder of the Afro-Brazilian Candomblé cult.

pasodoble   (lit. "double step") Spanish dance in quick 2/4 time.

porteño   Inhabitant of the city of Buenos Aires.

puntaesteño   Inhabitant of Punta del Este, Uruguay.

quinta   Small farm.

ranchera   An Argentine popular dance and song, adapted from the mazurka.

tanguero   (1) *Adjective*: pertaining to the tango. (2) *Noun*: a person from the particular culture of the tango's adherents and fans, with its distinctive ways of feeling and behaving.

zamba   Argentine scarf dance in 6/8 time, and associated song, *not* to be confused with the more famous Brazilian samba.

NOTES

References are given for quotations and information taken from sources *other than* authors' interviews. Interview material is only referenced when it is not obvious from the context that it is being used. Lists of interviews used in each chapter may be found under the chapter headings below. Unless otherwise indicated, all books, newspapers, and magazines cited were published in Buenos Aires. For details of books or articles (referred to by author's name) see Sources 3, p. 307

Abbreviations Used in Notes
General
AP Astor Piazzolla APBR "Reportaje a Astor Piazzolla en el Brasil"* APHC "Piazzolla Hora Cero"* APMR Rostropovich-Mendelievich rehearsal* AP60 "Astor Piazzolla. Sesenta Pirulos"* DaP Daniel Piazzolla DiP Diana Piazzolla DPA Diana Piazzolla, *Astor* (1987) DW Dedé Wolff **Info.** information from **Int.** interview HFAP Horacio Ferrer, "Mi vida con Astor Piazzolla"* LEP Laura Escalada Piazzolla MAAP *La Maga*, Piazzolla issue (1996)* MSA María Susana Azzi NGM Natalio Gorin, *Astor Piazzolla. A manera de memorias* (1991) NPR National Public Radio USA. OLR Oscar López Ruiz, *Piazzolla loco loco loco* (1994) SPE Alberto Speratti, *Con Piazzolla* (1969) VOC Víctor Oliveros collection

Newspapers and Magazines
AF *Ambito Financiero* AN *Antena* BG *Boston Globe* CA *La Capital* (Mar del Plata) CC *El Cronista Comercial* CL *Clarín* CLR *Clarín Revista* CN *Confirmado* CR *Crónica* CS *Corriere della Sera* (Milan) CV *Convicción* DE *Democracia* DP *Diario Popular* EX *L'Express* (Paris) FI *Le Figaro* (Paris) GE *Gente* GL *O Globo* (Rio de Janeiro) GU *Guión* JB *Jornal do Brasil* (Rio de Janeiro) MA *Marcha* (Montevideo) ME *El Mercurio* (Santiago, Chile) MO *Le Monde* (Paris) MU *El Mundo* NA *La Nación* NG *Noticias Gráficas* NO *Noticias* NYT *New York Times* OP *La Opinión* PA *El País* (Montevideo) PD *Página 12* PR *La Prensa* RA *Radiolandia* RA2 *Radiolandia 2000* RE *La Repubblica* (Rome) RZ *La Razón* SD *Siete Días* SDI *Siete Días Ilustrados* SE *La Semana* SI *Satiricón Interviú* SO *Somos* TA *Tiempo Argentino* TC *Teleclic* TVG *TV Guía* UH *Última Hora* VA *Variety* (New York) VE *Veja* Rio de Janeiro. VI *Visión* WP *Washington Post* (Washington, D.C.)

*For details, see Sources 2, pp. 306–7.

Chapter 1
*Interviews
and Statements*
Dedé Wolff, Enriqueta Bertolami, George Bertolami, Kip Hanrahan, Joseph Hurley, Martín Piazzolla, Argentina Manetti de Provenzano, Ana María Tiribelli.

1. SD 4 November 1972.
2. Info. (birth certificate.) Omar Bertolami.
3. Info. (wedding certificate) Omar Bertolami.
4. SD 4 November 1972.
5. DPA 31.
6. W. H. Auden, "Letter to Lord Byron."
7. NGM 22.
8. SPE 28–29.
9. AP in SE 21 July 1983.
10. SD 4 November 1972.
11. SPE 23–24.
12. GE 9 August 1973.
13. SPE 31.
14. *Ercilla* (Santiago) 12 January 1966.
15. DPA 49.
16. CL 8 May 1976.
17. NGM 22.
18. CL 8 May 1976; Watrous 15.
19. RZ 26 November 1967; press clipping 1969 (VOC).
20. GE 21 August 1969.
21. DPA 72; info. Gabriel Clausi.
22. GE 21 August 1969.
23. NGM 118; SE 21 July 1983.
24. DPA 74; SE 21 July 1983.

25. SPE 39–41.
26. AP in BG 23 August 1987.
27. DPA 80–82.
28. DPA 83–84; *La Información* (New York) 29 December 1932; *La Prensa* (New York) 27 and 29 December 1932, 8 April 1933.
29. RA 10 November 1978.
30. SE 21 July 1983.
31. NPR int. 30 October 1987.
32. DPA 87; AP int. with Tony Staveacre, July 1989.
33. Press clipping (Édouard Pécourt collection).
34. APHC.
35. Terig Tucci in NO 1 August 1947.
36. DPA 85.
37. *Ercilla* (Santiago) 12 January 1966.
38. APHC.
39. SE 21 July 1983.
40. APHC.
41. SPE 46.
42. Growel 49; APHC; CL 14 December 1978.
43. "Carta de Piazzolla a Gardel," CL 14 December 1978.
44. SPE 47.

Chapter 2
*Interviews and
Statements*
Dedé Wolff, Diana Piazzolla, Simón Bajour, Hugo Baralis, Enriqueta Bertolami, Pedro Blumetti, Gabriel "Chula" Clausi, Eu-

genio Carlos Corsi, Roberto O. Cova, Jorge Göttling, Marcelo Moro, Reynaldo Nichele, Martín Piazzolla, Elva Botto de Sasiain, Víctor Sasson, Héctor Stamponi, Poupée Wolff.

1. GE 9 August 1973.
2. Roberto O. Cova int.; Eugenio Carlos Corsi int.
3. SD 4 November 1972.
4. BG 23 August 1987.
5. DPA 102–03, with photo.
6. CL 8 May 1976.
7. SPE 51.
8. DPA 104; Elva Botto de Sasiain int.; SPE 50; SE 21 July 1983.
9. DPA 104; NGM 32.
10. CA 23 February 1939.
11. DPA 106; NGM 32.
12. SE 21 July 1983.
13. BG 23 August 1987.
14. Elva Botto de Sasiain int.
15. DPA 111.
16. SPE 51; Gabriel Clausi is sure the recordings were made, but there is no trace of a commercial release.
17. Info. Gabriel Clausi.
18. NGM 33.
19. DPA 115.
20. Héctor Stamponi int.
21. APHC.
22. NGM 101.
23. NGM 45.
24. *Sintonía* 3 January 1940, with photo.
25. SPE 53; NGM 46.
26. DPA 119.

27. NGM 101; SE 21 July 1983.
28. AP to DW 20 February 1941 and 9 February 1942. All letters from AP to DW courtesy of DW.
29. RZ 22 April 1964.
30. Rivero 84.
31. TA 18 January 1986.
32. DPA 126–27.
33. DPA 126–27.
34. NGM 57.
35. DPA 142.
36. DPA 176–77.
37. APHC.
38. Giuseppetti 1.
39. CL 9 July 1992.
40. CL 3 July 1975.
41. DPA 147; *Queréme así, piantao, piantao*: film by Eliseo Alvarez, 1997.
42. SE 21 July 1983.
43. Perrotti 189.
44. MAAP 6.

Chapter 3
Interviews and Statements
Dedé Wolff, Diana Piazzolla, Daniel Piazzolla, Yves Baquet, Hugo Baralis, Enriqueta Bertolami, Nelly Sorrentino de Bertolami, Pedro Blumetti, Roberto Capuano, José Carli, Homero Cárpena, Gabriel "Chula" Clausi, Angel Díaz, Ofelia Di Filippo, Leopoldo Federico, Angel Fiasché, Alberto Fontán Luna, Atilio Fruttero, Héctor Grané, Horacio Mártire, Roberto Pansera, Édouard Pécourt, Rafael Pereyra, Máximo Perrotti, Enrique Roizner, Armando Rolón, Francisco "Kico" Salvo, Martial Solal.

1. Baralis: MAAP 10 and int.
2. MU 2 September 1944.
3. AP to DW 6 and 10 August 1945.
4. DPA 175.
5. Atilio Stampone: MAAP 11.
6. DPA 151; Ofelia Di Filippo int.
7. NGM 50.
8. NO 1 August 1947.
9. DPA 149.
10. SPE 68.
11. DPA 151, 182.
12. DPA 153.
13. DPA 149.
14. SPE 67.
15. PA 24 January 1982; SE 2 February 1984.
16. MU 18 and 25 June 1949.
17. MU 17 September 1949.
18. Federico: MAAP 12.
19. BG 23 August 1987.
20. APHC.
21. SE 21 July 1983.
22. DaP int. with Tony Staveacre, 31 January 1997.
23. Info. DW.
24. DPA 182.
25. Castro Volpe; AP to DW November 1952.
26. Juan José Lertora, letter to editor, CL 22 August 1992.
27. Enriqueta Bertolami int.; info. DW.
28. Rivero 106.
29. E.g., APBR.

30. Roberto Capuano int.
31. *Jazz Magazine* (Paris) January 1985.
32. APHC.
33. AP to DW, 7 February 1948.
34. DPA 154.
35. SPE 69–70; DPA 158.
36. Gobello 238–40.
37. AP to Vicente and Asunta Piazzolla and DaP and DiP 22 February 1955.
38. AP to DiP and DaP 16 November 1954.
39. NGM 57.
40. E.g., *France-Soir* (Paris) 17 July 1976; NPR int. 18 April 1988.
41. CV 14 November 1979; Rosenstiel 355.
42. SPE 72–73; CV 14 November 1979; NPR int. 3 June 1988.
43. DPA 215.
44. AP to José Gobello 5 January 1955; "Cartas autógrafas."
45. BG 23 August 1987; *Brigite* December 1980.
46. MA 15 June 1973; ME 12 July 1992; CV 14 November 1979.
47. Rome, 7 March 1955: Bibliothèque Nationale, Paris: Lettres Autographes, Fonds Nouveau.
48. RZ 22 April 1962.
49. APHC.
50. Lalo Schifrin: MAAP 33.
51. SPE 74.
52. "Cartas autógrafas."
53. Zalko (1998) 280; *Cantando* 14 January 1958.

54. 13 April 1955.
55. CL 9 July 1992; SPE 74.
56. AP to Vicente and Asunta Piazzolla and DiP and DaP 7 and 22 February 1955.
57. HFAP.
58. AP to Nadia Boulanger, 9 May 1955: Bibliothèque Nationale, Paris: Lettres Autographes, Fonds Nouveau.

Chapter 4
Interviews
and Statements
Dedé Wolff, Diana Piazzolla, Daniel Piazzolla, Rodolfo Alchourron, Bernardo Altman, Yves Baquet, George Bertolami, José Bragato, Angel Cárdenas, Juan Carlos Copes, Oscar Del Priore, Leopoldo Federico, Cecilio Madanes, Horacio Malvicino, César "Pipe" Márquez, Horacio Mártire, Eduardo Matrajt, Rodolfo Mederos, María Nieves, Roberto Pansera, Walter Provenzano, Armando Rolón, Alberto Salem, Jorge Sobral, Fernando Suárez Paz.

1. DPA 175–76; SPE 74–75.
2. APBR.
3. DPA 179.
4. Horacio Malvicino: MAAP 13 and int.; DPA 178–79.

5. *De Frente* 10 October 1955.
6. Malvicino: MAAP 13.
7. Malvicino: MAAP 13; Di Palma 14.
8. DPA 185; NPR int. 18 April 1988.
9. Pujol 191–94.
10. OLR 27.
11. NO 25 August 1955.
12. NGM 61.
13. APHC.
14. DPA 186.
15. SPE 129–30.
16. Leopoldo Federico: MAAP 12.
17. *Queréme así, piantao, piantao*: film by Eliseo Álvarez, 1997.
18. Canaro 519–23.
19. APHC.
20. "La música en el cine," *La Revista de Mar del Plata* (Mar del Plata) May 1958.
21. DPA 186; NPR int. 18 April 1988.
22. APHC; DPA 185–86.
23. *Cantando* 5 December 1957.
24. DE 3 February 1958.
25. AP to DW 6 February 1958.
26. AP to DW, 9 February 1958 (misdated January).
27. AP to DW 9 February 1958.
28. NGM 62.
29. AP to DW 19 February 1958.
30. AP to DW 4 April 1958.
31. AP to DW 11 April 1958.
32. AP to DW 28 April

and 2 May 1958.
33. PR 29 April 1958.
34. AP to DW 5, 23 and 25 March 1958.
35. AP to DW 19 April 1958.
36. AP to DW 19 March and 2 April 1958.
37. AP to DW 13 March and 3 April 1958.
38. DPA 186.
39. 23 March 1959.
40. RZ 22 April 1962.
41. DPA 191.
42. NGM 95–96; Gómez (1995) 287–88, and int.
43. DPA 187.
44. CL 14 June 1959.
45. See Roberts, chpts. 4–6.
46. NG 20 April 1961.
47. CL 14 June 1959.
48. GE 25 May 1972; *Expreso Imaginario* January 1977.
49. AP to DW 8, 11, and 12 January 1959.
50. AP to Yves Baquet 26 January 1959. Courtesy of M. Baquet.
51. *Billboard* (New York) 14 June 1986.
52. Juan Carlos Copes: MAAP 18, and int.
53. AP to DW 24 and 26 September and 5 October 1959.
54. AP to DW 8 October 1959.
55. DW to Emilio Wolff 28 April 1960.
56. SPE 78.
57. SO 15 July 1983; info. (death certificate) Omar Bertolami.

58. Juan Carlos Copes: MAAP 18 and int.
59. Info. DW.
60. DPA 187; info. DW and Poupée Wolff.
61. APHC.
62. NGM 70.
63. DW to Emilio and Lola Wolff 21 March 1960.
64. *Información*, 12 July 1960; RA 12 August 1960; *Cantando*, 2 August 1960.
65. RZ 11 July 1960; RA 12 August 1960; NO 24 November 1960.
66. RA 12 August 1960; DE 12 July 1960.

Chapter 5
Interviews
and Statements

Dedé Wolff, Diana Piazzolla, Daniel Piazzolla, Rodolfo Alchourron, Mario Antelo, Dr. Marcos M. Asensio, Simón Bajour, Hugo Baralis, Jorge Barone, Enriqueta Bertolami, Nelly Sorrentino de Bertolami, José Bragato, Gary Burton, Jorge Calandrelli, Roberto Capuano, José Carli, Oscar Castro-Neves, Juan Carlos Cirigliano, Félix Della Paolera, Héctor De Rosas, Oscar Del Priore, Edmundo Eichelbaum, León Jacobson, Eduardo Lagos, Oscar López Ruiz, Nicolás "Pipo" Mancera, Egle Martin, Horacio Mártire, Liebe Mártire, Eduardo Matrajt, Rodolfo Mederos, Sergio Mihanovich, Ben Molar, Édouard Pécourt, Máximo Perrotti, Alberto Salem, Víctor Sasson, Miguel Selinger, Jorge Sobral, Martial Solal, Atilio Stampone, Jorge Strada, Atilio Talín, Corradino Tenaglia, Nelly Vázquez, Roberto Yanés, Poupée Wolff.

1. CL 12 August 1984.
2. Azzi (1991) 28.
3. RZ 19 April 1962.
4. OLR 93.
5. CL 19 April 1961; MU 1 December 1961.
6. NG 20 April 1961; GE 14 December 1967.
7. NG 23 January 1961; CL 21 March and 14 April 1961.
8. RZ 22 October 1961.
9. Newspaper clipping 1962 (VOC).
10. NGM 69.
11. NGM 69.
12. OLR 32.
13. Gorin (1998) 199.
14. NGM 161.
15. DE 3 December 1961.
16. OLR 69–71.
17. CL 19 April 1962.
18. OLR 132–35; DPA 208.
19. Oscar Del Priore int.
20. RZ 9 August 1964.
21. NA undated clipping 1983; PR 10 August 1963; RZ 10 August 1963; NA 9 September 1963.
22. CL 27 December 1962 and 29 July 1964.
23. NGM 124.
24. OLR 35–38, 41–42, 49–50, 81–83.
25. Héctor De Rosas: MAAP 24.
26. MA 22 September 1961.
27. OLR 84–85.
28. OLR 42–43; NGM 124.
29. NYT 27 May 1965.
30. OLR 75–78.
31. SPE 85.
32. OLR 118–20.
33. NA 7 August 1965.
34. Vázquez 254.
35. Teitelboim 201.
36. Eduardo Bergara Leumann int.; Barone 65.
37. *Tanguera* 1963 VOC.
38. RZ 22 April 1962, 9 August 1964.
39. *Ercilla* (Santiago) 12 January 1966.
40. *Flash* 14 February 1984.
41. Dr. Marcos M. Asensio int.
42. *Tiempo Cotidiano* (Córdoba) 20 May 1979.
43. GE 23 February 1967.
44. DaP: MAAP 35.
45. GE 27 January 1974.
46. OLR 230–32.
47. NA 24 February 1967.
48. Press clipping 1969 (VOC).
49. APBR.
50. *Historia del tango* XVI, 3082.
51. MU 7 December 1961.
52. SG 8 May 1970.
53. *Sección Aurea* March 1995.
54. NA 26 February 1971.
55. MU 13 March 1966.
56. PR 7 August 1967.
57. Neustadt 106.
58. Press clipping October 1967 (VOC).

59. CL 29 October 1967;
PR 1 December 1967;
Gaceta de la Tarde La
Plata. 23 December
1967.
60. CN 18 January 1968.

Chapter 6
Interviews
and Statements
Dedé Wolff, Daniel Pia-
zzolla, Diana Piazzolla,
Laura Escalada Piazzolla,
Rodolfo Alchourron, Oscar
Araiz, Amelita Baltar,
Santo Biasatti, Oscar
Castro-Neves, Juan Carlos
Cirigliano, José "Pepe"
Corriale, Héctor De Rosas,
Alicia Farace, Horacio Fe-
rrer, Jorge "Fino" Figue-
redo, Albino Gómez, Gus-
tavo Kerestezachi, Eduardo
Lagos, Carlos Alberto "Po-
cho" Lapouble, Raúl Lavié,
José Domingo Ledda, Egle
Martin, Carlos Páez Vilaró,
Néstor Panik, Lino Pata-
lano, Alfredo Radoszynski,
Hermenegildo Sábat, Ar-
turo Schneider, Miguel
Selinger, Oscar Emilio
"Cacho" Tirao.

1. HFAP.
2. Joâo Carlos Pecci, *Vinicius sem ponto final*
(Sâo Paulo, 1994) 367.
3. CN 18 January 1968.
4. *La Tribuna* Rosario. 5
April 1968.
5. GE 23 May 1968.
6. Courtesy Egle Martin.
7. Amelita Baltar in *El*

Tribuno (Salta) 28 July
1968.
8. Neustadt 119–20.
9. Reviews from: NA 10
May 1968; PR 10 May
1968; *Primera Plana* 14
May 1968.
10. GE 25 July 1968.
11. Pepe Corriale int.
12. APBR.
13. Alfredo Radoszynski
int.
14. VI 5 July 1968.
15. DPA 197.
16. SPE 113.
17. LEP int.
18. SPE 117; GE 26 Decem-
ber 1968.
19. HFAP.
20. Páez Vilaró 199–202.
21. Pujol 202.
22. Páez Vilaró 203.
23. Gorin (1998) 200.
24. Azzi (1995) 158.
25. Ferrer (1977) 225.
26. HFAP.
27. CL 16 November 1969.
28. NGM 151.
29. *Análisis* 25 November/1
December 1969.
30. CL 13 November 1969.
31. *La Nueva Provincia*
(Bahía Blanca) 25
March 1970.
32. APHC.
33. SDI 22 June 1970.
34. ME 12 July 1992.
35. NGM 161–62.
36. Longoni and Vechiarelli
139–41.
37. SE 21 July 1983.
38. AN 27 January 1970.
39. *Anahí* 13 February 1970.
40. SG 8 May 1970.
41. AP to DW 10 February
1970.

42. AN 5 May 1970.
43. Press clipping 1969
(VOC).
44. *Para Ti* 23 December
1968; Baltar: MAAP 25.
45. GE 23 April 1970.
46. SG 9 January 1970; AN
13 January 1970.
47. Growel 50; CL 13 Au-
gust 1970.
48. PR 26 December 1970.
49. CR 5 September 1970.
50. CR 11 September 1970.
51. NA 1 November 1970.
52. AN 9 February 1971.

Chapter 7
Interviews
and Statements
Daniel Piazzolla, Laura Es-
calada Piazzolla, Antonio
Agri, Mario Antelo, Ame-
lita Baltar, Hugo Baralis,
Tomás Barna, Oscar Ca-
taldi, Oscar Del Priore,
Federico Erhart del Campo,
Pierre Fastosmes, Georges
Moustaki, Eric Nepomu-
ceno, Carlos Páez Vilaró,
Aldo Pagani, Hermeto Pas-
coal, Édouard Pécourt, José
Pons, Alejandro Szteren-
feld.

1. Press clipping 1971
(VOC).
2. HFAP; CR 28 February
1971.
3. RA 25 February 1972;
see also SD 27 March/2
April 1972.
4. OP 10 June 1971.
5. *La Gaceta* 16 April 1971.
6. Info. RAI.
7. RZ 26 August 1971.

8. CN 12 October 1971.
9. RZ 29 October 1971;
   NA 10 November 1971.
10. José Bragato: MAAP 32.
11. LEP int.
12. NGM 70.
13. Gorin (1998) 202.
14. *El Meridiano* (Caracas) 6 February 1972.
15. CR 10 February 1972; RA 25 February 1972; CL 7 February 1972.
16. RA 25 February 1972; GE 25 May 1972.
17. GE 23 March 1972.
18. DaP int.
19. OLR 158–63.
20. Corriale: MAAP 32.
21. JB 29 April 1972; *O Día* (Rio de Janeiro) 8 May 1972.
22. OLR 121–22; GE 25 May 1972.
23. *Folha de São Paulo* 4 May 1972; OLR 122–23; GE 25 May 1972.
24. OLR 124–25.
25. *Jornal da Tarde* (São Paulo) 4 May 1972; OLR 126–27.
26. Gorin (1998) 188–89.
27. NA 11 June 1998.
28. CL 22 August 1972, 1 April 1973, 16 April 1973.
29. OP 26 August 1972.
30. OP 24 October 1972; SD 15 October 1972; RA 20 October 1972; SDI 9 October 1972.
31. CR 5 October 1972.
32. CL 15 October 1972.
33. OP 24 October 1972.
34. Humphrey Carpenter, *Benjamin Britten: A Bi-*ography (New York 1993) 160–61.
35. CR 8 April 1973.
36. *Última Hora* (Montevideo) 14 June 1973; MA 15 June 1973; *El Eco-nomista* 5 October 1973.
37. CC 23 August 1973.
38. CC 28 July 1973.
39. GL 25 August 1973; GE 27 January 1974.
40. GE 9 August 1973.
41. GE 9 August 1973.
42. SI clipping 1976 (VOC).
43. DPA 199.
44. GE 17 January 1974.
45. GE 27 January 1974.
46. GE 12 June 1975.
47. RA 22 March 1974.

Chapter 8
Interviews
and Statements
Dedé Wolff, Daniel Piazzolla, Diana Piazzolla, Laura Escalada Piazzolla, Antonio Agri, Mario Antelo, Dr. Marcos M. Asensio, Eladia Blázquez, Gary Burton, Vera Brandes, Emmanuel Chamboredon, Ana Corbo and Federico Fernández, Mario Corcuera Ibáñez, Saúl Cosentino, Edmundo Eichelbaum, Félix and Irma Estrada, Horacio Ferrer, Amílcar "Quito" González Azcona, Natalio Gorin, Gustavo Kerestazachi, Mónica Cosachov, León Jacobson, Marta Lambertini, Raúl Lavié, Oscar López Ruiz, Horacio Mártire, Juan B. P. Mastro-pasqua, Gianni Mesticheli, Lydé Mirelmann, Bernardo Neustadt, Víctor Oliveros, Aldo Pagani, Jesús Hipólito "El Tuco" Paz, Máximo Perrotti, Enrique Roizner, Armando Rolón, Hermenegildo Sábat, Francisco "Kico" Salvo, Marta Saúl, Ricardo Saúl, Atilio Talín, Juan Trigueros, Pablo Ziegler.

1. SE 21 July 1983.
2. Gorin (1998) 204.
3. Perrotti 190.
4. OLR 203.
5. Atilio Stampone: MAAP 11.
6. Watrous 15.
7. *Flash* 12 April 1988.
8. SPE 90.
9. CC 26 April 1976.
10. SPE 90.
11. AN 10 February 1970.
12. *Así en Crónica* 21 December 1980.
13. AP in MAAP 4.
14. VE 30 April 1986.
15. NGM 164–65.
16. OLR 251.
17. RZ 9 August 1964.
18. Atilio Talín: MAAP 33.
19. Ana Corbo-Federico Fernández int.
20. SO 15 July 1983.
21. SO 15 July 1983; SPE 131; SE 21 July 1983.
22. SPE 130.
23. HFAP.
24. OLR 244.
25. OLR 114–16.
26. GU 3 November 1967.
27. *Los Grandes del Tango*, December 1990, 33.

28. Héctor De Rosas: MAAP 24.
29. SPE 121–22.
30. CN 12 October 1971.
31. DPA 222.
32. Víctor Oliveros: MAAP 26.

Chapter 9
Interviews and Statements

Dedé Wolff, Daniel Piazzolla, Diana Piazzolla, Laura Escalada Piazzolla, Rodolfo Alchourron, Hugo Baralis, Raúl Barboza, Vera Brandes, Gary Burton, Héctor Console, Pepe Corriale, Oscar Del Priore, Edmundo Eichelbaum, Pierre Fastosmes, Gerardo Gandini, Amilcar "Quito" González Azcona, Maximiliano Guerra, León Jacobson, Mónica Cosachov, Francisco Kröpfl, Marta Lambertini, Carlos Alberto "Pocho" Lapouble, Oscar López Ruiz, Yo-Yo Ma, Horacio Malvicino, Egle Martin, President Carlos S. Menem, Gianni Mesticheli, Carlos Nozzi, Héctor Olivera, Aldo Pagani, Ricardo Romualdi and Fabio Fabiani, Lalo Schifrin, Atilio Stampone, Atilio Talín, Oscar Emilio "Cacho" Tirao, Dr. Ignacio J. F. Uriburu, Pablo Ziegler.

1. ME 12 July 1992.
2. Perrotti 191.

3. Neustadt 119.
4. SD 22 December 1982.
5. DPA 218–19.
6. SO 15 July 1983.
7. NA 12 July 1992.
8. SPE 99–100.
9. NGM 37.
10. OLR 215–17.
11. CL 12 August 1984.
12. OLR 19.
13. RZ 9 August 1964.
14. Info. LEP.
15. ME 12 July 1992.
16. CL 12 August 1984.
17. GE 25 August 1966.
18. *Jazz Hot* (Paris) April 1975.
19. *Billboard* (New York) 14 June 1986; Watrous 16.
20. NGM 141–43.
21. *Los Angeles Times* 16 May 1989.
22. WP 3 May 1981.
23. *Chicago Tribune* 20 June 1988; *Uusi Suomi* (Finland) 14 June 1990, translation courtesy Ambassador Hugo Urtubey.
24. *Club de Tango* May-June 1995.
25. *Keyboard* (Cupertino, Calif.) October 1987.
26. This beautiful description is by Paul Badde, trans. Eugene Seidel. Liner-notes, *Astor Piazzolla y su Quinteto Tango Nuevo. Tristezas de un Doble A*, Messidor CD 15970–2.
27. DPA 149–50.
28. *Down Beat* 21 October 1976.

29. Dr. Ignacio J. F. Uriburu int.
30. GE 12 June 1975.
31. CL 20 June 1982.
32. AP to DaP, 13 June 1974.
33. Carlos Nozzi int.
34. OLR 210.
35. OLR 221–22.
36. *Jazz Hot* (Paris) April 1975; see also APHC.
37. MO 1 December 1987.
38. SPE 106.
39. *Los Angeles Times* 16 May 1989. The *Oxford English Dictionary* describes "to rotten" as a "very rare" verb.
40. SPE 96–98.
41. NGM 83; SD 7 November 1975.
42. *El Diario* (Paraná) 30 December 1968; SE 29 December 1983; *La Maga*, July 1996; SO 15 July 1983.
43. NGM 79.
44. Kuri 93–107.
45. CN 31 December 1969/ 6 January 1970.
46. Ferrer (1996) 147–67.

Chapter 10
Interviews and Statements

Daniel Piazzolla, Antonio Agri, Amelita Baltar, Mario Benzecry, Eduardo Bergara Leumann, Piergiuseppe Caporale, Adalberto Cevasco, Juan Carlos Cirigliano, Natalio Etchegaray, Aurora Nátola Ginastera, José Gobello, Amílcar "Quito" González Azcona,

Tonino Guerra, Frank Luther, Horacio Malvicino, Franca Mulligan, Aldo Pagani, Angela Pagani, Pierre Philippe, Tullio de Piscopo, Alfredo Radoszynski, Enrique Roizner, Atilio Talín, José Angel Trelles, Juan Trigueros, Jorge Vimo.

1. OLR 167.
2. *Audio* March 1974.
3. AP to DaP 31 March 1974. All letters from AP to DaP courtesy of DaP.
4. SD 23 September 1974.
5. APHC.
6. *Playboy* March 1976.
7. NGM 38.
8. AP to DaP 11, 13, and 28 May 1974.
9. AN 21 May 1974.
10. AP to DaP 11 May 1974.
11. AP to DaP 8 August 1974.
12. JB 3 September 1974; CR 18 September 1974.
13. Hodel 6.
14. JB 3 September 1974.
15. SD, 23 September 1974.
16. RA 14 July 1978; photo in GE 5 December 1974.
17. Sleeve notes, LP Trova DA-5000.
18. *Jazz Hot* (Paris) April 1975.
19. OP 19 August 1975.
20. Cook and Morton 947–48.
21. *Jazz Hot* (Paris) April 1975.
22. FI 26 October 1974;

MO 23 October 1974.
23. SDI 4 November 1974.
24. OLR 244–46.
25. Italian press clipping (VOC).
26. GE 5 December 1974.
27. RA 6 December 1974.
28. CL 7 December 1974; AN 10 December 1974.
29. *Historia del tango*, XVI, 3097.
30. AP to Jorge Vimo 11 February 1975.
31. CL 3 July 1975.
32. AP to DaP 31 March 1975.
33. *Jazz Magazine* January 1985.
34. Giron 8.
35. AP to DaP 2 May 1975.
36. AP to DaP 2 May 1975.
37. FI 30 April 1975.
38. 26 April 1975.
39. RA 16 May 1975.
40. Carlo Corpolongo to AP 19 May 1975 (VOC).
41. AP to DaP 1 June 1975.
42. AP to DaP 2 May 1975.
43. Frank Luther int.
44. AP to DaP 19 May 1975.
45. RA 6 June 1975.
46. GE 12 June 1975.
47. AP to DaP 1, 12, and 24 June 1975.
48. Info. DaP.
49. Gorin (1998) 177–78.
50. AN 9 November 1976.
51. APHC.
52. AP to DaP 19 May 1975; AP to DW 9 July 1975.
53. AP to DaP, 2 May and 12 June 1975.

54. AP to Gorin 7 August 1975: NGM 89.
55. CC 20 September 1975.
56. Armelle Oberlin (secretary to Jeanne Moreau) to MSA 29 September 1997 (fax).
57. NGM 92.
58. AP to DaP 12 June 1975.
59. DaP: MAAP 34.
60. RA 19 September 1975.
61. AN 28 November 1975.
62. AP to DaP 26 June 1975.
63. *Actualidad* clipping 1975 (VOC).
64. AN 28 October 1975.
65. CA 2 February 1976.
66. SD 21 November 1975.
67. *La Capital* (Santa Rosa) 29 November 1975.
68. *Historia del tango*, XVI, 2981–82.
69. AN 13 January 1976.
70. UH 21 December 1975.
71. CC 26 April 1976.

Chapter 11
Interviews and Statements
Laura Escalada Piazzolla, Diana Piazzolla, Daniel Piazzolla, Dr Marcos M. Asensio, Yves Baquet, Gary Burton, Osvaldo Caló, Oscar Cataldi, Pérez Celis, Adalberto Cevasco, Mario Corcuera Ibáñez, Juan Carlos Cirigliano, Edmundo Eichelbaum, Luis Alberto "Chachi" Ferreyra, Richard Galliano, Amílcar "Quito" González Azcona, Natalio Gorin, Kado

Kostzer, Jorge Lavelli, Julio Le Parc, Oscar López Ruiz, Lydé Mirelmann, Eva Moccia, Georges Moustaki, Víctor Oliveros, Édouard Pécourt, Máximo Perrotti, Pierre Philippe, José Pons, Marta Saúl, Arturo Schneider, Miguel Selinger, Didier Servant, Ettore Stratta, Atilio Talín, José Angel Trelles, Juan Trigueros, Pablo Ziegler, Alex Zuker.

1. CC 20 September 1975; UH 21 September 1975; CL 25 September 1975.
2. AP to DaP 25 February 1975.
3. AP to Gorin 21 July 1975: NGM 111.
4. DPA 206.
5. RA 19 March 1976; SI clipping, early 1976 (VOC). The tango "Sólo se quiere una vez" ("You only love once") by Claudio Frollo and Carlos V. G. Flores was recorded by Carlos Gardel in March 1930.
6. AP to DW 7 February 1975.
7. DPA 206–07.
8. Info. Pepe Wolf.
9. GE 17 June 1976.
10. AP to DaP (undated) 1976.
11. RA 17 December 1976; GE 13 January 1977.
12. SE 21 July 1983; TC 13 July 1992.

13. *Vosotras* 18 December 1980.
14. SE 21 July 1983; CL 12 August 1984.
15. AP to DaP, 6 July and 7 August 1977.
16. DP 25 March 1984.
17. TA 3 February 1985.
18. DaP: MAAP 35.
19. CC 15 March 1976.
20. NYT 23 May 1976.
21. *Down Beat* 21 October 1976.
22. VA 2 June 1976.
23. Annik Kerlirzin (secretary to Alain Delon) to MSA 18 May 1998 (fax).
24. NGM 91.
25. CL 26 September 1976.
26. AP to DaP (undated) summer 1976. 27. TA 28 January 1984.
28. Info. José Pons and LEP.
29. RA 10 September 1976.
30. JB 12 November 1976.
31. *Panorama* February 1977.
32. DaP: MAAP 35.
33. CL 16 December 1976; OP 18 December 1976.
34. Gorin (1998) 181.
35. *Vosotras* 30 December 1976.
36. Fastosmes publicity leaflet (VOC).
37. AP to DaP 30 December 1976 and 18 January 1977.
38. Horacio Malvicino: MAAP 36.
39. *Le Matin de Paris* 19 March 1977.
40. *Quotidien de Paris* 25

March 1977; EX 28 March/4 April 1977.
41. DPA 205–6.
42. DaP: MAAP 35.
43. CLR 29 October 1978.
44. *Cooperativa Latinoamericana* October 1969.
45. RZ 8 April 1986.
46. *La Gaceta* (Tucumán) 25 July 1978.
47. Staveacre 27.

Chapter 12
Interviews and Statements

Laura Escalada Piazzolla, Daniel Piazzolla, Diana Piazzolla, Antonio Agri, Mario Antelo, René Aure, Daniel Barenboim, Santo Biasatti, Norberto Capelli, Pérez Celis, Héctor Console, Pierre Fastosmes, Horacio Ferrer, Alberto Fontán Luna, José Gobello, Albino Gómez, Jairo (Mario Rubén González), Rubén Juárez, Rubén Kanalenstein, Mónica Cosachov, Oscar López Ruiz, Horacio Malvicino, Olivier Manoury, Osvaldo Papaleo, Pierre Philippe, Umberto Pinheiro, Manuel Antonio Rego, Guillermo Scarabino, Silvio Soldán, Fernando Suárez Paz, Atilio Talín, Fernando Tesouro, Vladimir Vassiliev, Pablo Ziegler.

1. AP to DaP 17 June 1977.
2. SD 27 October 1977.
3. AP to Juan Trigueros 7 August 1977.

4. AP to DaP 5 September 1977.
5. AP to DaP 13 October 1977.
6. APHC.
7. Atilio Stampone: MAAP 11.
8. *El Andino* (Mendoza) 3 April 1979; *El Territorio* (Resistencia) 7 April 1979; SE 19 September 1979.
9. NGM 164.
10. *Para Ti* 3 July 1978.
11. VE 30 April 1986.
12. OLR 233–37.
13. NA 30 March 1978.
14. CLR 30 July 1978.
15. AP to DaP 19 January 1978 (misdated 1977).
16. APBR.
17. *Periscopio* September 1978.
18. CL 12 July 1992.
19. Fernando Suárez Paz: MAAP 38.
20. NA 24 June 1998.
21. NA 18 December 1981.
22. OP 14 May 1978; PR 20 May 1978.
23. APBR.
24. *Ultima Hora* (São Paulo) 13 September 1978; OLR 128–29; CL 16 September 1978.
25. *Así en Crónica* 30 September 1979.
26. SE 19 September 1979.
27. RA 20 October 1978.
28. APBR.
29. AN 13 February 1979.
30. GE 22 March and 5 April 1978.
31. SE 20 June 1979.
32. CV 18 July 1979.
33. SE 19 September 1979.

34. DPA 212.
35. Note by Alexia Aguirre de Lima in César A. Luongo, "Piazzolla Film Compilation": http://www.piazzolla.org/works/astfilm.html.
36. CL 12 July 1979; NA 14 October 1979.
37. CL 13 December 1979.
38. NA 16 December 1979.
39. *Down Beat* September 1988.
40. GE 31 January 1980.
41. GE 6 March 1980; NA 13 March 1980.
42. CN 15 March 1980; *T. V.Guía*, 16 April 1980.
43. GE 6 March 1980; *Brigite* (December 1980).
44. CL 10 April 1980.
45. APHC.
46. Osvaldo Papaleo int.
47. OLR 222–23.
48. OLR 241–43.
49. Fernando Suárez Paz: MAAP 38.
50. MO 25 October 1980; FI 27 October 1980.
51. *Bonner Rundschau* (Bonn) 19/20 November 1980; *General Anzeiger* (Bonn) 20 November 1980.
52. NA 2 December 1980.
53. *Precisiones*, undated.
54. CL 1 December 1980.
55. CR 11 June 1981.
56. AP60.
57. AP to DaP 25 June 1981.
58. WP 11 May 1981.
59. AP to Scarabino 15 June 1981.

60. *T. V. Semanal* 18 July 1981.
61. CL 16 September 1981.
62. Daniel Barenboim int.
63. NYT 11 and 13 October 1981.
64. RZ 24 November 1981.
65. CL 22 November 1981.
66. NA 23 December 1981.
67. *Revista 10* 15 December 1981.

Chapter 13

Interviews and Statements

Laura Escalada Piazzolla, Daniel Piazzolla, Dr. Marcos M. Asensio, Sergio and Odair Assad, René Aure, Nelly Sorrentino de Bertolami, Eladia Blázquez, José Bragato, Ana Corbo and Federico Fernández, Mario Corcuera Ibáñez, Filippo Crivelli, Ofelia Di Filippo, Plácido Domingo, Edmundo Eichelbaum, Alicia Farace, Jorge Göttling, Maximiliano Guerra, Raúl Lavié, Oscar López Ruiz, Yo-Yo Ma, Nicolás "Pipo" Mancera, Juan B. P. Mastropasqua, Susana Mendelievich, Milva, Lydé Mirelmann, Marcelo Nisinman, Víctor Oliveros, Carlos Páez Vilaró, Roberto Pansera, Pierre Philippe, Argentina Manetti de Provenzano, Daniel Rabinovich, Alfredo Radoszynski, Dante A. Rinaldi, Francisco "Kico" Salvo, Eric Salzman, Fernando Tesouro, Oscar Emilio "Cacho"

Tirao, Nicholas Tozer, Marta Saúl, Atilio Talín, Dr. Ignacio J. F. Uriburu, Pablo Ziegler.

1. SD 4 December 1986.
2. AP to DaP 22 June 1986.
3. PD 18 January 1992.
4. SO 15 July 1983.
5. DPA 221.
6. José Bragato: MAAP 33.
7. Mstislav Rostropovich to Simon Collier, 16 January 1999.
8. APMR; Rostropovich to Collier, 16 January 1999.
9. Burns 87.
10. NGM 163.
11. Longoni and Vechiarelli 198.
12. OLR 164–88, on which these paragraphs are based.
13. CS 24 July 1982.
14. TA 2 January 1983.
15. *Los Andes* (Mendoza) 19 July 1982.
16. RZ 23 August 1982.
17. Report in *The San Juan Star-Portfolio* 10 October 1982.
18. CR 26 December 1982.
19. 24 November 1982.
20. CL 5 December 1982.
21. TA 2 January 1983.
22. RA2 17 December 1982.
23. SD 4 November 1972.
24. *El Atlántico* (Mar del Plata) 2 January 1983.
25. AP to Egnio Bertolami 4 January 1983.
26. Reports in CV 14 June 1983; NA 13 June 1983;

CV 14 June 1983; CR 12 June 1983; *Revista 10* 15 June 1983.
27. SO 15 July 1983.
28. OLR 129–30.
29. OLR 246–49.
30. SE 29 December 1983.
31. TA 28 January 1984.
32. SE 2 February 1984.
33. Gorin (1995) 207.
34. DPA 213.
35. RZ 29 April 1985.
36. CL 13 April 1984.
37. Fernando Suárez Paz int.
38. CL 12 August 1984; DP 11 July 1984; CL 15 July 1984.
39. CL 15 June 1984; ME 16 June 1984.
40. *Ovation* (New York) June 1986.
41. Gorin (1995) 201.
42. EX 21–27 September 1984; FI 9 and 22 September 1984.
43. CS 6 April 1985.
44. CL 1 and 2 December 1984.
45. CL 28 March 1985.
46. RE 14/15 April 1985.
47. NA 8 June 1985; CL 8 June 1985.
48. *Guardian News Service* July 1992; John Gavall, "Ginastera and Piazzolla. Part 2," *Classical Guitar* (London) December 1985.
49. NA 20 September 1987.
50. RZ 27 November 1985.
51. NA 1–3 December 1985.
52. CL 3 April 1986; TA 18 January 1986.
53. FI 6 November 1985; VA 4 September 1985.

Chapter 14
Interviews and Statements

Laura Escalada Piazzolla, Diana Piazzolla, Dedé Wolff, Rodolfo Alchourron, Mario Antelo, Alfredo Arias, Dr. Marcos M. Asensio, Simón Bajour, Rául Barboza, Carter Brey, Gary Burton, Pérez Celis, Héctor Console, Graciela Daniele, Ofelia Di Filippo, Al Di Meola, Paquito D'Rivera, Hayri Erenli, Leopoldo Federico, Dr. Dardo Fernández Aramburu, Kip Hanrahan, David Harrington, Robert Hurwitz, Kado Kostzer, Dr. Eduardo Lagos, Raúl Lavié, Dr. Ramón C. Leiguarda, Horacio Malvicino, Marilú Marini, Franca Mulligan, Eric Nepomuceno, Marcelo Nisinman, Víctor Oliveros, Carlos Páez Vilaró, Pierre Philippe, Daniel Rabinovich, Sergio Renán, Hermenegildo Sábat, Horacio Salgán, Eric Salzman, Marco de Santi, Ricardo Saúl, Lalo Schifrin, Claudio Segovia, Didier Servant, Fernando Suárez Paz, Atilio Talín, Sarah Vardigans, Pablo Ziegler, Pablo Zinger.

1. VE 24 April 1986.
2. Eric Nepomuceno int.
3. VE 30 April 1986.
4. NYT 25 May 1986.
5. Watrous 15.
6. *Keyboard* October 1987;

Down Beat September 1988.

7. CS 4 July 1986.
8. RE July 1986.
9. RZ 7 August 1986.
10. RE 23 July 1986.
11. 15 July 1986.
12. DPA 208–09.
13. CL 9 November 1986.
14. DPA 208.
15. DPA 209–10.
16. Azzi (1991) 156.
17. ME 12 July 1992.
18. CL 12 July 1992.
19. *Libération* (Paris) 14 September 1984.
20. 10 June 1986.
21. DPA 223.
22. Anahí Carfi in Gorin (1995) 217.
23. CS 1 April 1987.
24. TC 13 July 1992.
25. SD 19 June 1986.
26. NYT 10 November 1987; *Village Voice* (New York) 10–17 November 1987.
27. Info. Sheldon M. Rich.
28. D'Rivera: MAAP 28.
29. BG 23 August 1987.
30. Fernando Suárez Paz: MAAP 38.
31. Liner notes, *Astor Piazzolla. The Late Masterpieces,* American Clavé, AMCL 1022.
32. Steve Sacks, liner notes, *Astor Piazzolla. The Central Park Concert,* Chesky Records JD 107.
33. Perrotti 193.
34. *Svenska Dagbladet* (Stockholm) 9 October 1987.

35. Gómez (1996) 55–56.
36. CS 7 November 1987.
37. MO 1 December 1987.
38. CL 20 September 1987.
39. *Opera* February 1988; MO 1 December 1987; FI 23 November 1987.
40. *Acción* March 1988.
41. MAAP 37.
42. Info. Peter Prestfelder.
43. *Ear,* No. 6 (1988).
44. NYT 6 May 1988.
45. BG 10 May 1988.
46. WP 11 May 1988.
47. NYT 12 May 1988.
48. VE 30 April 1986.
49. 1 December 1988.
50. *Esquire* May 1991.
51. *Billboard* 14 June 1986.
52. *Billboard* 6 September 1997.
53. *Flash* 18 October 1988.
54. Suárez Paz: MAAP 38.
55. Ofelia Di Filippo int. Roberto Di Filippo died in February 1991.

Chapter 15
Interviews and Statements

Laura Escalada Piazzolla, Diana Piazzolla, Daniel Piazzolla, Dedé Wolff, Antonio Agri, Mariano César Azzi, Yves Baquet, Daniel Barenboim, Mario Benzecry, Enriqueta Bertolami, Daniel Binelli, José Bragato, Vera Brandes, Gary Burton, Jorge Calandrelli, Roberto Capuano, Anahí Carfi, José Carli, Héctor Console, Mario Corcuera Ibáñez, Al Di Meola, Plá-

cido Domingo, Dr. Dardo Fernández Aramburu, Fernando Fondevila, Richard Galliano, Gerardo Gandini, Natalio Gorin, Maximiliano Guerra, Kip Hanrahan, David Harrington, Robert Hurwitz, Israel Oscar "Vasco" Izurieta, Jairo (Mario Rubén González), Dr. Ramón C. Leiguarda, Oscar López Ruiz, Horacio Malvicino, Olivier Manoury, President Carlos S. Menem, Lydé Mirelmann, Eva Moccia, Eric Nepomuceno, Marcelo Nisinman, Carlos Nozzi, Víctor Oliveros, Aldo Pagani, Julio Oscar Pane, Hermeto Pascoal, Édouard Pécourt, José Pons, Dante A. Rinaldi, Armando Rolón, Marco de Santi, Víctor Sasson, Marta Saúl, Ricardo Saúl, Didier Servant, Ettore Stratta, Atilio Talín, Fernando Tesouro, Françoise Thanas, Sarah Vardigans.

Epigraph: Mark Swed, interview with Gidon Kremer, *Schwann Opus* Vol. 8, No. 4 (Fall 1997) 15–16A.

1. AP to Hayri Erenli, February/March 1989.
2. NA 28 February 1989.
3. AF 30 July 1997; MAAP 40.
4. NGM 166.
5. José Bragato: MAAP 41.
6. Azzi (1991) 66.
7. MAAP 40–41.
8. CL 19 April 1989.

9. NYT 27 April 1989.
10. NA 24 April 1989.
11. NGM 63.
12. *Los Angeles Times* 16 and 18 May 1989.
13. Info. Spoleto Festival USA.
14. ME 5 and 6 June 1989; NA 9 June 1989.
15. NA 11 June 1989.
16. APMR.
17. *Folk Roots* (London) September 1989.
18. *Chasqui* (London) July-September 1992; Teddy Peiró to MSA 5 November 1995.
19. Gómez (1996) 321.
20. Staveacre 26–27; info. Tony Staveacre.
21. Gorin (1995) 202.
22. VE 23 August 1989 and 15 July 1992.
23. Vera Brandes int.
24. Gerardo Gandini: MAAP 40.

25. Gerardo Gandini: MAAP 40 and int.
26. Malvicino: MAAP 41 and int.
27. DaP and Daniel Astor Piazzolla int. with Tony Staveacre, 31 January 1997.
28. CLR 28 October 1979.
29. DPA 224.
30. NA 18 February 1990.
31. NGM 15.
32. OLR 182–83.
33. CS 24 May 1990.
34. *Satakunnan Kansa*, 16 and 17 June 1990; Aulis Alatalo, unidentified Finnish newspaper. Translations from Finnish newspapers courtesy of Ambassador Hugo Urtubey.
35. Gorin (1998) 207.
36. CL 20 July 1994.
37. NA 15 August 1990; CL 16 August 1990.

38. NA 23 August 1990.
39. Moerer 115.
40. NA 18 and 27 October 1990.
41. NA 14 November 1990.
42. Sequence of hospitals: info. DW.
43. DaP int. with Tony Staveacre, 31 January 1997.
44. DaP int. with Tony Staveacre, 31 January 1997.
45. CL 7 July 1992.
46. CL 7 July 1992.
47. Tributes: Info. RAI; CS 6 July 1992; NYT 6 July 1992; FI 6 July 1992; MO 7 July 1992; VE 15 July 1992; *Plural* (Mexico City) October 1992; *Classical Guitar* (London) August 1992.
48. *Nashville (Tennessee) Scene* 18 June 1998.
49. NYT 16 January 1997.

SOURCES

1. Interviews and Statements

By country (or country of residence) of those interviewed or those supplying statements. Interviews by María Susana Azzi unless marked MSA-SC (joint interviews) or SC (interviews by Simon Collier). Interviewing took place between April 1995 and July 1998.

Argentina Antonio Agri; Rodolfo Alchourron; Dante Amicarelli; Mario Antelo; Oscar Araiz; Alfredo Arias; Dr. Marcos M. Asensio; René Aure; Mariano César Azzi; Ernesto Baffa; Simón Bajour; Amelita Baltar; Jorge Barone; Tomás Barna; Santo Biasatti; Mario Benzecry; Eduardo Bergara Leumann; Enriqueta Bertolami; Nelly Sorrentino de Bertolami; Daniel Binelli; Eladia Blázquez; Pedro A. Blumetti; José Bragato; Maestro Pedro Ignacio Calderón; Roberto Capuano; Angel Cárdenas; José "Pepe" Carli; Homero Cárpena; Oscar Cataldi; Adalberto Cevasco; Gabriel Clausi; Juan Carlos Copes; Héctor Console; Mario Corcuera Ibáñez; José "Pepe" Corriale; Eugenio Carlos Corsi; Mónica Cosachov; Saúl Cosentino; Cristóbal Cotton Cook; Roberto O. Cova; Angel Díaz; Héctor De Rosas; Oscar Del Priore; Félix Della Paolera; Ofelia Di Filippo; Horacio De Dios; Federico Erhart del Campo; Félix and Irma Estrada (Félix Restaurant); Natalio Etchegaray; Leopoldo Federico; Dr. Dardo Fernández Aramburu; Aldo Ferrer; Horacio Ferrer (first interview, Paris, MSA-SC); Luis Alberto "Chachi" Ferreyra; Angel Fiasché; Jorge "Fino" Figueredo; Fernando Fondevila; Atilio A. Fruttero; María de la Fuente; Gerardo Gandini; José Gobello; Amílcar "Quito" González Azcona; Natalio Gorin; Jorge Göttling; Maximiliano Guerra; Israel Oscar "Vasco" Izurieta; León Jacobson; Jairo (Mario Rubén González); Rubén Juárez; Rubén Kanalenstein; Francisco Kröpfl; Eduardo Lagos; Marta Lambertini; Carlos Alberto "Pocho" Lapouble; Jorge Lavelli; Raúl Lavié; José Domingo Ledda; Dr. Ramón C. Leiguarda; Julio Le Parc; Oscar López Ruiz; Mario Frieiro Pombo; Aída Luz; Cecilio Madanes; Horacio Malvicino; Nicolás "Pipo" Mancera; Néstor Marconi; César "Pipe" Márquez; Egle Martin; Horacio Mártire and Emilia Rosa Teresa "Liebe" Wolff Mártire; Juan B. P. Mastropasqua; Eduardo E. Matrajt; Rodolfo Mederos; Susana Mendelievich; Carlos S. Menem (President of the Argentine Republic); Hilda Fischer de Merellano; Gianni Mestichelli; Anamaría Micheli; Sergio Mihanovich; Lydé De Luca de Mirelmann (Lydé Lysant); Negra Manetti de Misino; Eva Moccia; Ben Molar; Marcelo Moro; Bernardo Neustadt; Reynaldo Nichele; María Nieves; Marcelo Nisinman; Carlos Nozzi; Héctor Olivera; Víctor Oliveros; Julio Oscar Pane; Roberto Pansera; Osvaldo Papaleo; Lino Patalano; Jesús Hipólito "El Tuco" Paz; Rafael Pereyra; Máximo Perrotti; Daniel Piazzolla (one of several interviews, MSA-SC); Diana Piazzolla (MSA-SC); Laura Escalada Piazzolla; Martín "Pepito" Piazzolla; Humberto Pinheiro; Argentina Manetti de Provenzano; Walter Provenzano; Alfredo Radoszynski; Manuel Antonio Rego; Sergio Renán; Osvaldo A. Robles; Juan Miguel "Toto" Rodríguez; Armando Rolón; Ricardo Romualdi and Fabio Fabiani; Hermenegildo Sábat; Alberto Salem; Horacio Salgán; Francisco "Kico" Salvo; Elva Botto de Sasiain; Víctor Sasson; Marta Saúl; Ricardo Saúl;

Maestro Guillermo Scarabino; Arturo Schneider; Claudio Segovia; Miguel Selinger; Jorge Sobral; Silvio Soldán; Atilio Stampone; Héctor "Chupita" Stamponi; Ana María Stekelman; Fernando Suárez Paz; Alejandro Szterenfeld; Atilio Talín (one of several interviews, MSA-SC); Corradino Tenaglia; Oscar Emilio "Cacho" Tirao; Ana María Tiribelli; Nicholas Tozer; José Angel Trelles; Juan Trigueros; Dr Ignacio J. F. Uriburu; Nelly Vázquez; Jorge de la Vega; Jorge Vimo; Dedé Wolff (first of several interviews, MSA-SC); Sofia Dolores "Poupée" Wolff; Roberto Yanés; Pablo Ziegler.

United States   Bernardo Altman; Sergio and Odair Assad; Leandro J. "Gato" Barbieri; Daniel Barenboim; George Bertolami; Carter Brey; Gary Burton; Jorge Calandrelli; Oscar Castro-Neves; Pérez Celis; Graciela Daniele; Al Di Meola; Plácido Domingo; Paquito D'Rivera; Max Ferrá; Kip Hanrahan (SC); David Harrington, Kronos Quartet (SC); Joseph Hurley (SC); Robert Hurwitz; Frank Luther; Yo-Yo Ma; Franca Mulligan; Édouard Pécourt (SC); Peter Pretsfelder; Eric Salzman (SC); Lalo Schifrin; Ettore Stratta; Sarah Vardigans (SC); Pablo Zinger (SC); Alex Zuker.

France   Yves Baquet (MSA-SC); Raúl Barboza (MSA-SC); Osvaldo Caló; Emmanuel Chamboredon; Filippo Crivelli; Edmundo Eichelbaum; Pierre Fastosmes; Richard Galliano; Héctor Abel Grané; Gustavo Kerestezachi; Kado Kostzer (MSA-SC); Olivier Manoury (SC); Marilú Marini; Georges Moustaki (MSA-SC); Pierre Philippe; José Pons; Didier Servant; Martial Solal (MSA-SC); Françoise Thanas (MSA-SC).

Italy   Norberto Capelli; Anahí Carfi; Tonino Guerra; Milva (Maria Ilva Biolcati); Aldo Pagani; Angela Pagani; Néstor Panik; Marcello Pirras; Tullio De Piscopo; Marco de Santi.

Uruguay   Ana Corbo and Federico Fernández; Carlos Páez Vilaró (MSA-SC); Dante A. Rinaldi; Fernando Tesouro (MSA-SC).

Belgium   Alicia Farace.

Switzerland   Aurora Nátola Ginastera.

Russian Federation   Vladimir Vassiliev (Director, Bolshoi Theater)

Brazil   Eric Nepomuceno; Hermeto Pascoal.

Germany   Vera Brandes; Sonia Alejandra López (SC).

England   Teddy Peiró.

Mexico   Alberto Fontán Luna.

Turkey   Hayri Erenli (SC).

2. *Miscellaneous Sources*

Astor Piazzolla–Mstislav Rostropovich–Susana Mendelievich: Rehearsal of "Le Grand Tango," April 1990 (**APMR**). Tape. Courtesy of Juan Carlos F. Martinelli: Centro Astor Piazzolla, Buenos Aires.

"Astor Piazzolla. Sesenta Pirulos" (**AP60**), recorded in Paris by Piazzolla on his sixtieth birthday, 11 March 1981. Tape. Courtesy of Jorge Strada, Director, Biblioteca Publica de música "Astor Piazzolla," Mar del Plata.

Horacio Ferrer: "Mi vida con Astor Piazzolla" (**HFAP**). Reminiscence specially written for the authors.

Interviews with Piazzolla on National Public Radio, USA, 30 October 1987, 19 April 1988, 3 June 1988. Tape (**NPR**). Courtesy of Carlos Groppa, Los Angeles.

La Maga, No.20, Buenos Aires, May 1996 (**MAAP**). Special Piazzolla issue.

"Piazzolla Hora Cero: Reportaje a Astor Piazzolla, 1980" **(APHC)**. Interview by Walter Acosta, BBC Latin American (Spanish) Service, 11 July 1980. Tape. Courtesy of Jorge Strada, Director, Bibliotica Publica de Música "Astor Piazzolla," Mar del Plata.

"Reportaje a Astor Piazzolla en el Brasil, 1978" **(APBR)**. Tape of Brazilian radio interview, September 1978. Courtesy of Jorge Strada, Director, Biblioteca Pública de Música "Astor Piazzolla," Mar del Plata.

3. Books and Articles

Astarita, Gaspar J. *Piazzolla del 46.* Buenos Aires, 1996.

Azzi, María Susana. *Antropología del tango. Los protagonistas.* Buenos Aires, 1991.

————. "The Golden Age." In Simon Collier, Artemis Cooper, María Susana Azzi, and Richard Martin, *¡Tango! The Dance, the Song, the Story.* London and New York, 1995.

Bach, Caleb. "A New-Age Score for the Tango." *The Americas,* 43:5/6 (1991), 14–21.

Barone, Orlando, comp. *Diálogos Jorge Luis Borges-Ernesto Sábato.* Buenos Aires, 1996.

Borges, Jorge Luis. *Para las seis cuerdas.* Buenos Aires, 1996.

Burns, Jimmy. *The Land That Lost Its Heroes.* London, 1987.

Cacopardo, Fernando A., ed., *Mar del Plata. Ciudad e historia.* Madrid–Buenos Aires, 1997.

Cancionero Eladia Blázquez. Buenos Aires, 1982.

Cancionero Horacio Ferrer. Buenos Aires, 1980.

Canaro, Francisco. *Mis bodas de oro con el tango.* Buenos Aires, 1957.

"Cartas autógrafas de Astor Piazzolla." Academia Porteña del Lunfardo, *Comunicación Académica,* No. 1, 380, 30 June 1996.

Castro Volpe, José. "Con Aníbal Troilo triunfa en Brasil el tango moderno." *Historia del tango,* 16, 2995–96.

Collier, Simon. *The Life, Music and Times of Carlos Gardel.* Pittsburgh, 1986.

————. "A round table with Piazzolla." *La Voz del Tango.* Encino, CA, July–August 1997.

Cook, Richard, and Brian Morton, eds. *Penguin Guide to Jazz on CD, LP and Cassette.* London, 1994.

Di Palma, Mark. "Nuevo Tango Guitarist Horacio Malvicino." *Guitar Review,* Summer 1989.

Fernández Schenone, Jorge. *Los antiguos veraneos en Mar del Plata.* Mar del Plata, 1996.

Ferrer, Horacio. *El tango, su historia y evolución.* Buenos Aires, 1960.

————. *El libro del tango,* 2nd ed. Buenos Aires, 1977.

————. *El siglo de oro del tango.* Buenos Aires, 1996.

García Brunelli, Omar. "La obra de Astor Piazzolla y su relación con el tango como especie de música popular urbana." *Revista del Instituto de Investigación Musicológica Carlos Vega,* No. 12, Buenos Aires, 1992.

Giron, Luís Antônio. "Entrevista: Astor Piazzolla. O tango é dos jovens." *Veja.* Rio de Janeiro, 30 April 1986.

Giuseppetti, Angel. "Orquestaciones de Aníbal Troilo." Academia Porteña del Lunfardo. *Comunicación Académica,* No. 1, 411, August 1997.

Gobello, José. *Crónica general del tango.* Buenos Aires, 1998.

Gómez, Albino. *Diario de un joven católico.* Buenos Aires, 1995.

————. *Lejano Buenos Aires.* Buenos Aires, 1996.

————. *Vivencias tangueras de un porteño viajero.* Buenos Aires, 1998.

Gorin, Natalio, comp., *Astor Piazzolla. A manera de memorias.* Buenos Aires, 1991. [**NGM**]
———. *Astor Piazzolla.* Rome, 1995.
———. *Astor Piazzolla. A manera de memorias,* 2nd ed. Buenos Aires, 1998.
Los Grandes del Tango, Año 1, No. 8, December 1990. [Special issue, "Astor Piazzolla"]
Los Grandes del Tango, Año 2, No. 85, November 1992. [Special issue, "Amelita Baltar"]
Gray, Marianne. *La Moreau. A Biography of Jeanne Moreau.* London, 1995.
Growel, María. "Latest Tango in Buenos Aires." *Americas,* Washington, D.C., January 1978.
La historia del tango, Vol. 16. Buenos Aires, 1980.
Hodel, Brian. "Astor Piazzolla." *Guitar Review,* No. 64, Winter 1986.
Klinkowitz, Jerome. *Listen. Gerry Mulligan. An Aural Narrative in Jazz.* New York, 1991.
Kuri, Carlos. *Piazzolla. La música límite.* Buenos Aires, 1992.
Lefcovich, S. Nicolás. *Estudio de la discografía de Fiorentino.* Buenos Aires, 1988.
———. *Estudio de la discografía de Aníbal Troilo.* Buenos Aires, 1990.
Legido, Juan Carlos. *La orilla Oriental del tango.* Montevideo, 1994.
Longoni, Matías, and Daniel Vechiarelli. *El Polaco. La vida de Roberto Goyeneche.* Buenos Aires, 1996.
López Ruiz, Oscar. *Piazzolla, loco loco loco.* Buenos Aires, 1994. [**OLR**]
Manrupe, Raúl, and Portela, María Alejandra. *Un diccionario de films argentinos.* Buenos Aires, 1995.
Moerer, Keith. "Astor Piazzolla's Tango!" *Stereophile,* September 1997.
Neustadt, Bernardo. *No me dejen solo.* Buenos Aires, 1995.
Páez Vilaró, Carlos. *Cuando se pone el sol.* Punta del Este, 1995.
Perrotti, Máximo. *Síncopa y contratiempo. Memorias de una editorial musical.* Buenos Aires, 1993.
Piazzolla, Diana. *Astor.* Buenos Aires, 1987. [**DPA**]
Pujol, Sergio. *Jazz al sur. La música negra en la Argentina.* Buenos Aires, 1992.
Rivero, Edmundo. *Una luz de almacén.* Buenos Aires, 1982.
Roberts, John Storm. *The Latin Tinge.* New York, 1979.
Rosensteil, Léonie. *Nadia Boulanger. A Life in Music.* New York, 1982.
Rubinstein, Arthur. *My Many Years.* New York, 1980.
Saito, Mitsumasa. *Astor Piazzolla. El Luchador del Tango.* Tokyo, 1998. [In Japanese, with an excellent discography]
Sierra, Luis Adolfo. *Historia de la orquesta típica. Evolución instrumental del tango.* Buenos Aires, 1966.
Sopeña, Germán, ed. *Testimonios de nuestra época. Del socialismo al liberalismo.* Buenos Aires, 1991.
Speratti, Alberto. *Con Piazzolla.* Buenos Aires, 1969. [**SPE**]
Staveacre, Tony. "Tango Take Two." *The Listener,* London, 21 June 1990.
Teitelboim, Volodia. *Los dos Borges: Vida, sueños, enigmas.* Buenos Aires, 1996.
Vázquez, María Esther. *Borges. Esplendor y derrota.* Buenos Aires, 1996.
Watrous, Peter. "Astor Piazzolla." *Musician,* No. 103, May 1987.
Zalko, Nardo. "Un entretien inédit avec Astor Piazzolla." *Tango. Bulletin de l'Académie du Tango de France,* No. 3, Paris, 1997.
———. *Un siècle de tango. Paris-Buenos Aires.* Paris, 1998.

INDEX

Abbreviations used in Index:

AP = Astor Piazzolla **1946b** = 1946 band **Oct** = Octet (1955–57) **StrO** = string orchestra (1957) **JT** = Jazz-Tango quintet (New York) **Qu1** = first Quintet (1960–74) **63oct** = "Contemporary Octet" (1963) **68sxt** = ad hoc sextet (1968–69) **Non** = Nonet, also known as Conjunto 9 (1971) **1EO** = first Electronic Octet (1975–76) **2EO** = second Electronic Octet (1977) **Qu2** = second Quintet (1978–88) **Sxt** = Sextet (1989)

Individuals listed are or were of Argentine nationality unless noted otherwise.